D1084054

THE LIFE AND LYRICS OF
RICHARD ROLLE

AS GATHERED FROM CONTEMPORARY
MANUSCRIPTS

RICHARD ROLLE

(From Cotton MS. Faustina, B. VI. Pt. ii. fol. 8b)

The Life of Richard Rolle

Together with an Edition of his

English Lyrics

(Now for the first time published)

By

Frances M. M. Comper

WITH EIGHT ILLUSTRATIONS

BARNES & NOBLE, Inc.
New York
METHUEN & CO. Ltd
London

First published, 1928
by J. M. Dent and Sons Ltd.

This edition, reprinted, 1969
by Barnes & Noble, Inc.
by special permission

To the Memory of
GEORGE CONGREVE, S.S.J.E.

FOREWORD

THE lyrics of Richard Rolle are the expression of his life, and therefore I have not hesitated to couple them with the life. He was a great mystic because he was a great lover, and these lyrics are his love-songs. As far as we know he was the first English mystic who has told us of his mystical experiences, not only in verse but in prose. He began by writing in Latin which was then considered the correct medium by which to express any serious thought, but before long he breaks free from convention, and in order to reach those he wishes to help, among whom were many women, he not only translates the works of others into English, but ventures to write himself in the vernacular, and composes commentaries upon the Psalms and Canticles, besides writing many tracts and epistles. In this he was a pioneer, leading the way which others were so quickly to follow: notably Walter Hilton and Dame Julian of Norwich, whose names have somewhat wrongly eclipsed Richard's, since they were his disciples, Hilton more especially owing much to Richard, by whom he was greatly influenced.

Until lately Richard has been strangely neglected by his fellow-Englishmen. No doubt this is partly because it has not been easy to have access to his writings, they being for the most part still unprinted; and many of the manuscripts are difficult to decipher and to translate except by the scholar. The present writer makes no claim to being such, yet it is not possible to spend several years transcribing manuscripts, copied by various scribes, of the works of one man, without gaining some very definite impression of his character.

When history altogether fails then we must reconstruct
by aid of intelligent conjecture and imagination, which in
this case has been strengthened by long hours spent in
the quiet rooms of cathedral and university libraries, or
wandering across the Yorkshire wolds which, though now
for the most part cultivated, cannot lose their contours nor
their streams and rivers. The distant view across the
Vale of Pickering and York must be almost as Richard
saw it centuries ago. Though swept by the wind and often
bathed in mist, yet on a sunny day the chalk pits glisten,
and the white roads wind like a ribbon up and down the
dip of the hills, the effect being not unlike a sea petrified
during a heavy swell. But the great abbeys and priories
have for the most part entirely disappeared. In many cases
the stones have been scattered and are found built into
the walls of some cottage, or used upon a farm. Of the
nunnery of Yedingham, within a mile or two of Thornton-
le-Dale, where Richard was born, all that can be seen is
a strip of boundary wall, and that was probably only re-
built with the stones from the convent. At Hampole,
where Richard died and where he had some official connection with the Cistercian Priory, being styled confessor
to the nuns there, no traces are found, beyond the grassy
mounds which cover the foundations of the convent, and
a few stones, some built into the school-house and others
in the garden of a private house; nor do we know the site
even of his shrine which attracted such numbers of pilgrims,
nor where his bones lie buried.

But his writings, although so long neglected, remain,
and they must be the data whereon to build his life. Yet
even here we are confronted with a grave difficulty, for
those who have written of Richard and still are writing,
hand him down to fame as the author of *The Prick of
Conscience*, a long, turgid and pedantic poem no more like
to the known works of Richard than is the *Novum Organum*
to *As You Like It*. Let those who have weighted Richard's

name with the *Prick*, conscientiously read from beginning
to end that document of nearly ten thousand lines in
verse, and then let them scan these short, unpretentious
lyrics and judge for themselves.

When Richard lived England had hardly ceased to be
bilingual. The great religious houses which were so plentifully scattered over Yorkshire bore Norman names, and
the greater part of their monks had come from France
and even farther afield. Yet in Richard we have a typical
Englishman and, we might add, a typical Yorkshireman.
Neither Yorkshire nor its people have ever lost their characteristics. There is a certain sturdiness of outlook, an
independence and common sense, which we find stamped
on all that Richard writes, that still refreshes us in Yorkshire even now, when we get off the beaten track.

Except for his early years spent at Oxford, he seems
never to have left the three Ridings. Although a wanderer
he was a hermit, and although a hermit a wanderer. If
he had been born in Italy, probably he would have become
a friar and followed Francis, to whom some have likened
him. There are truly many points in common between the
hermit who trod the wolds of Yorkshire, and the friar who
toiled up the steep slope to the Carceri, and the still steeper
slopes of the Penna; yet it is a relation of contrast rather
than of likeness. What comparison can there be between the
son of a Yorkshire peasant and of an Umbrian merchant-
prince of the fourteenth century; between the shy sensitiveness of Richard and the unselfconscious abandonment
of Francis? It is partly because Richard is so typically
English that he makes so strong an appeal to us. He would
have had to meet a colder blast than the winds which sweep
across the wold if he had gone forth naked, as Francis,
to espouse poverty. The *Fioretti* could never have blossomed
in the soil of these northern moors; they would have wilted
and withered.

Yet there is the supernatural likeness which all great

saints bear to one another, since they are lovers of the same Beloved; and to Richard as to Francis was added the gift of song, by means of which they gave expression to their love, though here again we are struck by a contrast rather than a likeness. Richard's lyrics are personal and individual; he pours out his heart by himself as he "sings his prayers with notes." Francis sings in company, and his fellow-wayfarers catch up the song and join with him in the refrain. There are no refrains in the songs of Richard save what he hears the angels sing as he sits in the chapel at night before supper.

Not long ago I watched the tapestry-makers at Beauvais. The pattern is placed behind the worker, and he must trust to the reflection in the mirror which lies below his frame; all that he can actually see is the reverse side of his work, which appears as a confusion of knots and broken threads, as his needle plies in and out with first one colour and then another. In the same way have I tried to weave from the broken threads of evidence, and from the assorted colours of his own words, a true and consistent portrait of Richard, the saint and hermit. And as the maker of tapestry can only see what he has made when, his work finished, he cuts it from the frame; so in like manner it is my hope that from this book may emerge a true picture of one who for nearly six centuries has been strangely neglected by his fellow-countrymen.

I personally think of him as being simple in manner, yet reserved and shy, so that to a stranger he might appear almost brusque; but full of kindness and sympathy and ever ready to help another. He is sensitive to any mis-judgments, and these are apt to make him withdraw himself from his fellows or acquaintances who are on the outlook to pick his character to pieces.

Often he gives excuse to his detractors, for, like all men of genius, he is careless of convention. The thought of the opinion of others has no part in shaping his course

or determining what he may say or write, although afterwards he may suffer much mental anguish from their
adverse judgments. As with all true mystics, he must give
out that which he has received of God, and he recks not
whether his reputation suffers in this giving so long as he
can help a soul to rise. Nor can he forbear to speak out
against the abuses in the Church and among the ministers
of God. Such evils rouse him to passionate protest, and
coming from a layman, as he then was, they provoke
great anger among the ecclesiastical authorities. Thus he
withdraws more and more into himself, and confines himself
to helping those who like him live in seclusion, and begins
to write for nuns and anchoresses.

Though he has trodden far in the way of penance there
is no trace of hallucinations brought on by excessive fasting
or unbalanced austerity, and he shows his common sense
in the wise advice he gives to others. The body must be
not overdriven or else the soul will suffer. His mind is ever
alert and his ear receptive to the supernatural; thus he
partakes of the waywardness of the poet and the mystic.
It is impossible to foresee what he will do. He leaves
Oxford suddenly when nineteen, and before his course of
study is completed; and returning home at the call of
some inward voice, he flees as suddenly from his father's
house—to which apparently he never returns—to wander
forth, disguised in his sister's clothes, as a hermit with no
means of livelihood, to find God unhindered in "wilderness,"
or solitude.

For the most part he appears to have lived within touch
of other men; yet his life is truly that of a solitary, although
never lived in loneliness. For day nor night he is never
parted from his Beloved, for whom he sings his songs as
doth the nightingale. He dies suddenly, struck down by the
plague. Those of his spiritual children who remain draw
up an Office to commemorate his feast "after he shall
be canonized," but either they die themselves, or have

not sufficient influence among the comparatively few remaining clergy, after the plague has ceased its ravages, to carry through the necessary formalities, although the list of attested miracles was enough for the canonisation of many saints.

Therefore, neither in life nor in death does Richard seem to have had his deserts, yet he least of all would have heeded any neglect. Enough reward is it for a saint if he has rescued a soul from sin, or quickened the love of God in a few hearts. If the songs of love he sang can still wake an echo of divine love in the hearts of those who read them here, no time nor labour spent upon this book can have been wasted.

No one can be more keenly aware of its inadequacy than is the writer. The chapters on Oxford may by many be considered superfluous, yet let it be remembered that if Oxford can mean so much to her sons to-day, much more must the Oxford of the fourteenth century have meant to those poor students who first forgathered within her walls; when men whose names even yet shed lustre upon this ancient university were disputing in her halls and preaching in her churches. The memories of such men as Roger Bacon and Grosseteste were still green, and the numbers of churches and monastic houses were sufficient to have given great impetus to Richard's imaginations and desires. Ockham was then expounding his theories and lighting that spark which was enkindled in the hearts of many who listened, and which laid the foundation of mysticism; and Richard may well have sat among his disciples, in company with Burleigh and Bradwardine, who were then students of Merton. It is impossible that such influences should not have shaped the character of a lad as susceptible as Richard was, and that during the most impressionable years of his life. This is my apology for these chapters if one is needed.

I should like here to thank Miss Wardale, Ph.D., M.A.,

for her help over difficult readings in the MSS. of the
lyrics, and more especially for the interest in these early
writers she awoke in me when I had the privilege of having
her for my tutor. I also owe my especial gratitude to
Mr. Ernest Rhys, to whose kindly interest and encourage-
ment this work is due; to Mr. Falconer Madan, late Bodleian
Librarian, who has never failed in coming to my aid both
now and in past years: and to all who by their advice and
sympathy have helped me through what has been a difficult
task; especially I wish to thank the Rev. L. W. Grensted,
the Rev. T. H. Passmore and Professor Clement Webb.
Not least do I owe a most sincere debt of gratitude to Miss
E. Miller and my brother for reading the proofs, more
especially as the whole burden was left to them, since I
was prevented by illness from doing so myself.

CONTENTS

PART ONE—THE LIFE

CONTENTS

Yorkshire from early times was sought out as a solitude for hermits—The islands of Coquet and Farne—SS. Cuthbert, Henry, Bartholomew — Richard's attraction towards the solitary life and praise of it—He accepts the squire's offer of a cell on his estate and begins there his life as a hermit—The life of voluntary suffering and penance has been in all ages the means to attain union with God—Richard treads the *via purgativa*—His advice to others concerning fasting, watching and hardships, and his own practice—Tempted of the devil and by the powers of evil—They attack him through others by calumny and detraction—This time of conversion "wherein he was truly turned to God" lasted for three years until the "opening of the heavenly door."

Richard's attraction for us—Simplicity of holiness—Definition of mystical contemplation—Symbolic projection and self-identification with the object translated into terms of mysticism—Divine union possible only by means of self-negation—Richard's description of his experiences difficult to fit into any recognised scheme—He is akin to the Doctors of the early Church — Modern writers on mysticism — Mgr. Farges' account of mystical contemplation and how far Richard's experiences correspond to the threefold way of Purgation, Illumination and Union—He likens this union to Heat, Song and Sweetness—The Holy Spirit is our guide, and inspires our souls with this holy wisdom, which is mystical contemplation.

Richard describes this Divine Union to which he has attained as High Love of God—It is a generating love; born of suffering whose pivot is the will of God—It is experienced as heat and light—His similarity to the later Spanish mystics —Both describe love as fire and flame—Examples given—The imagery of music especially characteristic of Richard—His definition of Heat and Song and Sweetness, and how great rest is necessary to enjoy them—The three degrees of Love: Insuperable, Inseparable and Singular, as given in *The Mending*, in *The Form* and in *The Commandment of Love*—The heavenly melody or song, which belongs more especially to the last degree—Love is Diffusive, Unitive and Transformative—Comparison with Mgr. Farges—Seven experiments by which we can tell if we have attained to Singular love—Richard answers the questions: What is love? Where is love? How shall we love God stalwartly, devoutly and sweetly?—His rhapsodies of love and his similes—Perfect love includes our neighbour—This heat and song and sweetness can never cease —Death is the gate to joy: therefore he longs for death, which shall be for him "as heavenly music."

Difficulty of ascertaining the sources which Richard drew upon until we have further knowledge—Some however are

PART TWO—THE LYRICS

APPENDICES

LIST OF ILLUSTRATIONS

This portrait of Rolle is taken from a Cotton MS. (Faust. B. VI. ii.) in the British Museum of a northern poem called *The Desert of Religion*. The authorship of this poem is unknown, although it has usually been ascribed to Walter Hilton. It describes the trees which grow in the wilderness, or desert, of religion. These symbolical trees are drawn on the first side of each page; the reverse side is divided into two columns, the one containing the poem itself, while on the other some saint of the desert is depicted.

On the first side of the page containing this picture of Richard the Hermit there is a rude drawing of a tree, with six leaves on either side, representing the twelve abuses that grow among religions. They are as follows:

A prelate negligent :	A discipil inobediente.
A ʒongman idill :	Ane alde mane obstinate.
A mownke cowrtioure :	A mounke pletoure.
Ane habite preciouse :	Mete daintinouse.
New tithandes in clostere :	Strivynge in þe chapitour.
Dissolucioun in þe qwere :	Irreverence aboute þe auter.

In the picture the hermit is represented seated on the grass in a white habit, with the sacred monogram in gold on his breast, and holding a book in his left hand. On either side is a stiffly drawn tree. Above, resting on clouds, are three angels bearing a scroll with the words: *Sanctus, sanctus, sanctus; Dominus Deus Sabaoth; pleni sunt celi et terra gloria tua.* Round the illustration the following verse is written:

" A solitari here : hermite life i lede,
    For ihesu loue so dere : all flescli lufe i flede;
    þat gastli comforthe clere : þat in my breste brede,
    Might me a thowsande ʒcere : in heuenly strengthe hauc
        stedd

There is no evidence that this picture is a genuine portrait. It recalls some early portraits of St. Francis. The hair is light in colour, and cut evenly round the head, and the beard divided into two small points. The saint's face is not emaciated, but of a clear complexion with a touch of red upon the cheeks. Only the lower portion of the picture is seen in our illustration, so that we can have the figure of the hermit on a larger scale.

A bag for alms can be seen suspended from the Bocardo Tower, which those imprisoned there for debt let down to the passers-by with the cry: "Pity the poor Bocardo birds."

(i.) *University College.* This is the earliest picture I can find of University College. It was drawn in the reign of Queen Elizabeth by Neele, *c.* 1566, and shows the buildings covering the site now occupied by the existing western quadrangle. The pavement of the High, having been raised by frequent reparations, became higher than that of the college, as can be seen in the engraving, where some of the windows come nearly to the ground, and others are half sunk beneath it, so that persons entering the college had several steps to descend.

(ii.) *East view of East Gate.* This is from a sketch by J. B. Malchair, engraved by J. Skelton. Wood thus describes it:

"The East Gate, which was the chiefest Gate, had sometime two round towers on each side to defend it, as also a pair of gates thwarted with a chain, in the time of Edward III., and before; which I understand were usually, with other gates, kept shut in the night season; as also a chain crossing the way leading from the gate to Holywell, to secure the suburbs, being then in the tumultuous times of the Barons' wars. The towers above mentioned, with smaller ones which existed in other parts of the city wall, though of use in times of war, yet afterwards they became as much, if not more so, to the Mayor and Commonalty in times of peace; for they demised them to poor people, who made them their habitations, and to inhabitants living near the wall . . . yet by this means they were much decayed."

"In the Ashmolean Museum is preserved an old rental book, dated from 1453 to 1479, in which an ornamental letter O is the initial. In this letter is comprised a small view of the Abbey Church, which appears at that time to have had a spire. In this particular it is probably correct; in others so small a sketch cannot be relied upon as presenting a correct view of the Abbey buildings." — From a note on this plate in *Oxonia antiqua restaurata* (London, 1843).

The same verse as in the Faustina MS. (with the omission of one line) is written across the side of the illustration. The hermit's robe is of vivid green; and he wears a black cap with a white band edging it.

PART I

THE LIFE

PART I—THE LIFE

CHAPTER I

OXFORD IN THE DAYS OF RICHARD ROLLE

"When he was of adult age Master Thomas Neville, at one time Archdeacon of Durham, honourably maintained him in the University of Oxford, where he made great progress in study."—LESSON I.

Sources for the Life of Richard Rolle—Born at Thornton-le-Dale, *c.* 1300—Sent to Oxford to study by the help of Thomas Neville—William of Durham's foundation of the *Aula Universitatis*—Beginnings of the University—Importance of the Jews—Description of the city in the fourteenth century—The earliest colleges—Its walls and gates—Its sixteen churches—Its markets and crowded streets —Poverty of the scholars—Constant fighting among the students —Dirt and squalor—Outbreaks of pestilence and provision against them—How Richard fared amidst it all.

THE exact date of Richard Rolle's birth is uncertain, although it is generally accepted that he died in 1349. There is certainly no mention of him after that date, and early in that year the Black Death raged in Yorkshire with unusual violence for several months. It was the worst outbreak in the north of which we have records. In the city of York three-fourths of the inhabitants died, and out of ninety parish priests in the East Riding only thirty were left. It is thought that Richard was one of the many victims and it was most probably owing to the depletion of the monasteries by this terrible devastation that his name never appeared among the roll of canonised saints. But the nuns of Hampole to whom he ministered in his later life had prepared, or possibly themselves written, the nine Lessons for the Offices of Matins and also the hymns, versicles, antiphons, etc., for Matins and Lauds, which are known as the *Officium*. This Office was included in the *York Breviary* [1] with this note:

The Office of Saint Richard, hermit, after he shall be canonized by the Church, because in the meantime it is not

---

[1] Surtees Soc., vol ii., app. v. (1882).

allowed to sing the canonical hours for him in public, nor to solemnize his feast. Nevertheless having evidence of the extreme sanctity of his life, we may venerate him and in our private devotions seek his intercessions, and commend ourselves to his prayers.

It is good to know that Newman included the name of *Blessed Richard of Hampole* in his list of English saints, although unfortunately it was one of the lives which were never written.

These nine Lessons are generally known as the *Vite*. Nine more were added which contain an account of the miracles worked at Richard's shrine, and were to be read during the octave of the feast. These are referred to as the *Miracula*. The *Vite*, being the main source of his life, are of great importance. There are only three known MSS. of the *Officium*, and all are imperfect. One is at Lincoln in the Cathedral Library, another in the British Museum, and a third in the Bodleian Library at Oxford. The latter is the most complete and the only one containing the *Miracula*. Two of these are dated: the second (6 December, 1381) and the sixth (15 August, 1383). These dates at least prove that thirty years after Richard's death his memory was more than a mere tradition.

Moreover it is noticeable that in his writings there are no references to his old age, although many to his youth. The largest number of autobiographical passages are found in the *Melum contemplativorum ardentium in amore Dei*—to give the full title, which is generally shortened to the *Melum*. There he constantly speaks of himself as a youth, *juvenculus, puer* and *pusillus*, and in the same book he refers to the intrigue which the wife of Edward II. carried on with Mortimer in 1325–6. From this we infer that he was born quite at the beginning of the century; most critics suggest 1300, though it may have been a few years earlier.

The *Legenda* [1] give us quaint and picturesque incidents

---

[1] They are given in full in my translation from the Office in the *York Breviary* (vol. ii., app. v.) printed by the Surtees Society, which Messrs. Methuen have allowed me to include here from my modernised edition of *The Fire of Love and Mending of Life*, as translated by Misyn from the original Latin of Richard Rolle. Dr. Woolley has collated the three MSS. in his *Officium and Miracula of Richard Rolle of Hampole* (S.P.C.K., 1919).

in his life, but fail us entirely in his later years, and leave gaps to be filled in. Several of the antiphons, versicles and responses, and the hymns in the Office throw sidelights on his character and on the estimation in which he was held. We find also many autobiographical allusions in his earlier Latin treatises, notably in the *Melum*; the *Liber de amore Dei contra amatores mundi*; his tract *Judica me Deus*; and the most important passages of all are those given us in the *Incendium Amoris*, which was translated into English about fifty years after Rolle's death by Richard Misyn as *The Fyer of Lufe*.

We are told in the *Vite* that "the hermit Richard" was born at Thornton, near Pickering. There are many Thorntons in Yorkshire, but Thornton-le-Dale is the traditional place of his birth. It is in the North Riding though only ten miles distant from the Derwent, which has always been the boundary at that part between the North and East Riding. It is still famed as one of the prettiest villages of the Riding. In Richard's days the old Norman church stood on the slope of a hill on the same site as the present much-restored building, which is reached by steps and has a flagged causeway running along the south side which fronts the road. At the foot of the slope the beck, known as Thornton Beck, tears along, but beyond the narrow bridge [1] the road has been widened out for the convenience of motor traffic. One has to shut one's eyes to these modern eyesores which would have filled Richard with alarm, and imagine oneself back in the narrow winding lanes, just wide enough for a cart to pass, and soft and yielding under the horses' feet. The ancient ball-headed cross, tall and slender, still stands on the green, though the stocks below are a modern reproduction. Under a row of cottages which go by the name of the Poorhouse, there is a round-topped tunnel which leads into a cell said to be the old prison, and called by the villagers the Black Hole. Mr. Gordon Home, writing in 1904, says it was in use fifty years ago.[2]

A little path runs along the beck, which remains quite unaltered from the time of Richard, and climbing

---

[1] This is seen in the illustration facing p. 58.
[2] *The Evolution of an English Town*, by Gordon Home (Dent & Sons, 1905), p. 279.

up behind the village one has a charming view of Thornton lying amid a cluster of trees. It has, as Mr. Home says,

almost an idyllic aspect, its time-worn roofs of purple thatch and mellowed tiles nestling among the masses of tall trees that grow with much luxuriance in this sheltered spot at the foot of the hills. The village is musical with the pleasant sound of the waters of the beck that flows from Dalby Warren, and ripples along the margins of the roadways, necessitating a special foot-bridge for many of the cottages.

This neighbourhood is crowded with names which occur in the *Vite*. Yedingham Priory, for a nun of which priory he wrote the epistle known as the *Ego Dormio*, is close to the bank of the Derwent, just within the North Riding; the village lying on the other side of the bridge in the East Riding. We crossed this bridge coming to Thornton but there were no remains of the priory to be seen. Pickering lies about four or five miles east of Thornton and its beautiful church must have often been visited by Richard; but few traces are left of the Norman church at Thornton in which he was probably baptised. There were both vicars and rectors of Thornton in the thirteenth and fourteenth centuries, and a list of them has been placed in the porch. Between the years 1282 and 1304 the vicar was Thomas de Amcotes, and the rector from 1267 to 1323 was Robertus de Overleye *vel* Everley. Both names appear to be Norman.

I was told at Thornton-le-Dale that the tradition that Richard Rolle was born there is strong among the oldest inhabitants of the village, but the name Rolle is not now to be found there. We know that his father was called William, and that he was a "dear friend of John de Dalton"; for the latter "loved his [Richard's] father . . . with warm affection." [1] John de Dalton constantly occurs in the records of those days, and the name Dalton is still well known in the Ridings.

In all probability Richard's parents were poor, for though they sent their son to be educated, possibly at some neighbouring abbey, or school attached to a monastery, they were glad to avail themselves of Master Thomas de

[1] See Lesson III., p. 303.

Neville's help in providing maintenance for him at the University of Oxford.[1]

In the register of the Archdeacons of Durham the date against Neville's name is 1334; Richard must have left Oxford long before then, hence *olim* must refer to some later time. Neville himself could not have long left the university, for the course of study to become even a Master of Arts took then quite seven years. One reason why he was anxious to help William Rolle to send his son there may have been that his interest in Oxford was still fresh. One of the archdeacons preceding him was William, generally known as William of Durham, and the founder of University College. William had been driven from the schools of Paris with many others in the troubled year of 1229. He was first rector of Wearmouth, then archdeacon, and afterwards bishop-elect of Rouen, at which city he died in 1249.[2] He left 310 marks to the University for the support of ten or twelve poor masters, all of whom were to study divinity, and one at least to be in priest's orders; a preference being given to men from the diocese of Durham.

William of Durham's name has come down to posterity as the first Englishman to leave money to the University for the purpose of maintaining scholars, but it was many years before his bequest yielded sufficient income to do more than support four poor masters who already acted as regents in the schools of art. As far back as 1253 a house had been bought near the church of St. Mary the Virgin, where the new buildings of Brasenose now stand. In 1280 a committee was appointed to inquire into the state of the

---

[1] See Lesson I., p. 301. I give the original of the passage in the Lection since it is ambiguous and needs some explanation:

"Cumque adulcioris etatis fieret magister thomas de Neuile olim archidiaconus dunolmensis ipsum honeste exhibuit in uniuersitate Oxonie ubi ualde proficiens in studio, pocius desiderauit plenius et profundius imbui thologicis sacre scripture doctrinis, quam phisicis aut secularis sciencie disciplinis."

[2] For this chapter see *The History of the University of Oxford from the earliest times to the year* 1530, by H. C. Maxwell Lyte (Macmillan, 1886), pp. 70–82 sqq. Also compare Mr. Falconer Madan's clear and concise *Oxford outside the Guide-books* (Blackwell, 1923), to which book I am much indebted; *The Mirror of Oxford*, by Rev. C. B. Dawson (Sands, 1912); *Oxford* (in "Historic Towns" series), by C. W. Boase (Longmans, 1903).

fund and to draw up a scheme for future government. This was in reality the foundation charter of the present University College. They appointed certain scholars who were to be provided with rooms in this house which was henceforth called *Aula Universitatis*, or the Hall of the University. The members of the foundation were generally known as "scholars of University Hall," although properly speaking they were the "scholars of the Hall of William of Durham."

When the revenue increased more scholars were received, and clerks "of good character" were admitted to lodge and board there at their own expense. By the help of new benefactors a library was established in the Hall, from which books might be borrowed; and disputations were held there on certain days. Latin was prescribed as the language for ordinary conversation, and the practice of reading aloud at meals was enforced. The scholars were subjected to a severer discipline than the other members of the Hall, and it was enjoined that they must "live honourably as clerks in a manner befitting saints, not fighting, not using scurrilous or low words, not reciting, singing, or willingly hearing, songs or tales of an amatory or indecent character, not taunting or provoking one another to anger, and not shouting so as to disturb the studies or repose of the industrious."

By these statutes of 1292 it was expressly laid down that natives of the neighbourhood of Durham should be preferred to other candidates of equal merit. Probably this ordinance had a great bearing upon Richard's life, for parts of the North Riding were in those days under the ecclesiastical jurisdiction of Durham, and so by this proviso a point could be stretched in his favour. The Neville and the Percy families were practically the owners of all that district of Yorkshire, which would make it the more likely that Thomas de Neville should have been friendly with Richard's parents and taken an interest in the boy—who was only five years younger than himself —using his influence to obtain his admission among the scholars of the *Aula Universitatis*. If this was so, Richard would have lived in the earliest Hall, not in the larger buildings on the southern side of the High, to which the Hall was afterwards removed about the year 1343.

It must have been an ordeal for a child coming straight

from the freedom of his home to find himself under strict
supervision, having to express his wants in a strange
tongue, and adapt himself to city life. If, as is surmised,
he did become a scholar on the foundation of William of
Durham, a further rule in the statutes of 1292 may have
been one of the causes which led to his hasty exit from
Oxford when he was nineteen, for in that Hall every scholar
was obliged to become an "opponent" in the schools
within seven years of his first attendance at lectures. It is
unlikely that Richard was under thirteen, more probably
he was fourteen, when he came to Oxford, and judging
from what we know later of his character we can well
imagine his dread of such a test, as well as his dislike, which
we shall touch upon again, of disputations and theological
arguments.

It is interesting to try to reconstruct the Oxford of the
first half of the fourteenth century. In its corporate capacity
the University was then possessed of no property; nor must
we forget that a university degree was originally merely
the gaining of a diploma in order to exercise the right to
teach. The term Bachelor was used for the student who
had ceased to be a pupil but had not yet become a teacher,
or a master; and the masters who were actually engaged
in teaching were called *Regentes*, or Regent Masters, to
distinguish them from those masters who had retired from
the work of a teacher, these being named *Non-Regentes*
or Non-Regents.

The Faculty of Arts used at that time to assemble in the
church of St. Mildred, which has now entirely vanished.
Degrees were granted, and other secular business was
transacted in the church of St. Mary the Virgin. Lectures
were given wherever a sufficiently large building could
be found, sometimes in a church, or in a hall if large enough;
and later in the cloisters, the schools and churches of the
monastic houses and friaries. For the sake of economy
the students, when they could, lodged together in hostels
or inns (both the French and English words were in use),
entries and halls. It was probably the Jews who first built
stone houses in Oxford, as they did at Lincoln and other
places, and many of these hostels and halls were hired
from them, as such names as Moysey, Lombard and
Jacob Hall testify. The earliest houses bought with the

bequest of William of Durham were most likely built by them.

The Jews were banished from England in 1290, and had been driven from the city of Oxford some twenty years or more before Richard entered her walls. Their expulsion was carried out with an atrocity which remains as a black blot upon the pages of her history. Before then they had occupied quite a large portion of the town, known as the Great and Little Jewry. It covered the ground from the corner of the High at Carfax, to the present great gate of Christ Church. In those days the Jews were the only possessors of capital, and both abbots and barons relied upon loans from them for the building of their abbeys and castles. For this reason their power was very considerable, and though constant disputes arose between the Jews and the ecclesiastical authorities, leading often to grave disturbance, little redress could be obtained, and the bitter feelings evoked by these broils led in the end to their expulsion. Yet Oxford was indebted to the Jews for more than loans of money and stone houses, since it was in the Hebrew books belonging to the Rabbis that Roger Bacon studied science; and the medical school, which seems to have been established as early as the twelfth century, may have been Jewish in origin.

When Richard first came to Oxford there must still have been traces left of the Jewries, although both had been ruthlessly pillaged. The Jews' cemetery occupied the site of the present Botanical Gardens, having been removed from the opposite side of the High, where afterwards Magdalen Tower was built upon the site.

The "Little Hall of the University," as Wood names it, was close to St. Mary's, which church served as the chapel for the scholars in the Hall, so that Richard would have heard mass there, and have listened to many a sermon and lecture within its walls. Of the old church only the tower and the spire (now restored) remain. In those days it was a long, low building, in style transitional between Norman and Early English, but later, in Edward II.'s reign, a Congregation House was built in the churchyard, adjoining the north wall, and in the room above the books then belonging to the University were kept in a great chest which was the beginning of a university library.

Another church which would have been familiar to Richard was St. Peter-in-the-East, in which also lectures were given. It is less changed than St. Mary's. The crypt dates from very early days, for it was one of the churches which Robert d'Oili in his later life restored, after he had repented of his evil deed in wresting property from the monks of Abingdon. The present chancel arch is part of D'Oili's restoration, as is also the Norman door of St. Ebbe's. This latter is all that remains to give us any idea of the beauty of the old Norman church which originally stood in this place, and where Richard may have worshipped.

If we count the bequest of William of Durham in 1249 as the foundation charter of University College, then this college ranks as the earliest in Oxford. Merton was not founded until 1274, when Walter de Merton brought his students from Surrey (where he had gathered them together into one house, under discipline) to Oxford, and established them near to St. John the Baptist's Church, which they used for their chapel and which was afterwards incorporated into the college.

Merton was a secular foundation, as was Balliol, which was founded about ten years later, and Exeter in 1314; but by the date of the foundation of Oriel (1326) Richard must have long left Oxford.

It was the custom in those early days, when the roads were far from safe, to send "fetchers," or "common carriers," to bring the students who lived at a distance under safe conduct to Oxford. These carriers had regular routes which they took early in October, for the university year began in that month as it does still. We are told that the cost of the journey was 5d. a day, which was sometimes commuted to 3d. for the poorer students, but on the return journey they seem to have had to fend for themselves; Richard certainly must have done so when he left the University by his own choice.

What a contrast to the spacious wolds and moors of Yorkshire this little city would have appeared to Richard when he first came to it: its streets and timbered houses and low Norman towers crowded between the walls, the spire of St. Mary's overtopping the rest. For a city's walls had then to be high for the sake of defence, and the church towers low and strong enough to resist the enemy. Oxford

fortification, and built above the Gate was the Bocardo prison where debtors were interned. The bag which they lowered for alms, with the cry: "Pity the poor Bocardo birds," can be seen in the illustration (p. 28) which is from an original drawing by J. B. Malchair engraved by Skelton.

Near the South Gate there stood another church dedicated to St. Michael which Wolsey afterwards pulled down to make way for his great college. The Gate itself stood where the wall of Pembroke—which is a part of the old city wall—reaches to the street. Wood thus describes it:

> The South Gate stood near to the S.W. corner of Christ Church on the descent of Fish Street, known formerly by the name of Tower Hill and Grandpont. When in its prime it was an ornament to that end of the town well guarded on each side with a large fortification, and adorned with battlements on the top; the arms of England and France quartered were engraven on a stone, having England on the upper and France on the nether part, which was contrary to all that I had before seen.

The site of the West Gate is where the streets running westwards from St. Peter-le-Bailly and St. Ebbe's now meet; St. Peter's, as its name implies, being then within the precincts, or bailly, of the castle. Near the East Gate was the other church dedicated to St. Peter, the Gate standing almost at the end of the High, at the corner of Merton Street.[1]

The Hospital of St. John the Baptist, which was afterwards incorporated into Magdalen College, was outside the city wall. The postern gate, though now blocked up, is still discernible in the outer wall of the college. Still farther eastwards, on the way to Cowley, was a hospital for lepers. It was founded by Henry I. and dedicated to St. Bartholomew c. 1126. The chapel adjoining it is still in use, and remains almost as it was in the thirteenth century, so carefully has its restoration been carried out.

We have records of sixteen churches belonging to Oxford. Four are given in Domesday, and the others in the cartularies of Abingdon, Oseney and St. Frideswide, and in a charter of Henry I.'s reign. Of these, fourteen were crowded within the city walls. Some were, however, only

---

[1] See plan of Oxford, facing p. 12 (No. 4). The other three Gates are also marked in the plan, though not indicated by any letter or number.

small chapels. One of these, dedicated to the Holy Trinity, was built over the East Gate; of another, dedicated to St. George, within the castle buildings, the crypt still remains. Several churches have entirely vanished: St. Edward's, around which the Jewries were grouped; St. Mildred's, the site of which has been traced at the north side of the first quad of Lincoln College; St. Michael-in-the-South, where the Hebrew Professor's lodgings in Christ Church now are; and St. Bodhoc, of which I can find trace neither as church nor saint. The tower of St. Martin's remains, and two old doorways of St. Ebbe's, although they are almost hidden by the singularly ugly modern encroachments; but St. Peter-le-Bailly exists only in name for the old church was demolished in 1872 when the road was widened. St. Aldate's and All Saints', though in appearance modern, compared to those of which we have already spoken, are of very ancient foundation. The present church of St. Thomas the Martyr was built in 1141 for the dependants and servants of Oseney Abbey, to which it belonged, during the years Stephen was besieging the castle, for it was then impossible for any to pass in and out. It was then dedicated to St. Nicholas of Myra, but later, when it became a parish church, it was re-dedicated to St. Thomas. Of St. Mary's, and St. Michael's by the North Gate, we have already spoken, and of St. Peter-in-the-East; all three have much left to remind us of what they were like in those early years. The present cathedral of St. Frideswide is perhaps the most altered in appearance, although the old Saxon tower remains. It was built at the end of the twelfth century by Prior Guismond (c. 1180), and was entirely cruciform in shape, like many Norman churches, and had a barrel roof much lower than the present one. The Lady chapel and the Latin chapel were later additions, the eastern aisle of the north transept being absorbed by them and extended to its present length.

Four well-known churches in modern Oxford then stood without the walls; viz. St. Mary Magdalen's, St. Cross, St. Giles' and St. Clement's. St. Cross or Holywell Church was built as a chapel of ease to St. Peter-in-the-East. Of the original building only the Norman chancel arch which Robert d'Oili restored remains. St. Clement's stood originally just beyond the bridge over the Cherwell, where, on the open space now called the Plain, a small piece of the old churchyard is left enclosed within a triangular railing. St. Mary Magdalen's was only just without the North Gate, but St. Giles' was then far beyond the walls of the city in the "pleasant fields of Beaumont." The chancel and nave belong to the close of the twelfth century, as does the tower; and in the wall of the north aisle is some beautiful arcading which was probably there when the church was given to the nuns of Godstow in 1138.

The parish church of St. Martin was the centre of the city's life. It stood at the crossing of the two main roads which ran from north to south, and west to east, hence its name Carfax, or *quatre fourqs* (*quatuor furcas*), "the four forks." Within its churchyard the Portmannimot, or Town Council, met, and without its eastern wall under a low shed, later called the "penniless bench," justice was administered. Carfax is still the place of public proclamations and until recently the citizens assembled there on Armistice Day to honour the memory of their dead.

Here also was the focus of the markets, whose booths stretched up the surrounding streets as they do in any Normandy town to-day. To mention a few: the sellers of straw and hay were to stand with their teams in the High Street, between the East Gate and All Hallows'; sellers of hogs and swine between St. Mary's and All Hallows'; the bakers and tanners and cornsellers were to take their stand in what is still called the Cornmarket, between Carfax and the North Gate. Butter, eggs and cheese, as well as meat, were sold in Butcher's Row, where the animals were also slaughtered. Not until the reign of Edward II. was slaughter forbidden within the city walls, and that only at the insistence of the University. Fish Street, as its name implies, was the place of the fish market which was held every Wednesday and Saturday and stretched right up to Folly Bridge where the Grandpont then crossed the river.

The thronged streets of mediaeval Oxford have been well described by a writer in the *Quarterly Review* for January 1892, from which I quote the following picturesque passage [1]; though the reference to the Jews dates it as

[1] My attention was drawn to this passage in the interesting history of *The Church of St. Mary the Virgin*, by the Rev. H. L. Thompson (Constable, 1903).

slightly earlier than the years during which Richard was studying there, and Exeter College, which is also mentioned, was not founded until 1314.

Within the walls of the city—in the narrow, ill-paved, dirty streets which, overhung by signs, wound through rows of tall, irregularly-built houses, whose stories rose one above and beyond the other, like inverted staircases, till they almost excluded the light of day—were herded together a motley throng, over which neither chancellor nor mayor, had they worked in harmony, could exercise any control. The rough upland folks occupied the centre of the streets with their carts and strings of pack-horses. At the sides crowded citizens in every dress, plying their various trades, chaffering with the manciples, but always keeping their bow-strings taut, ready to promote a riot by pelting a scholar with offal from the butcher's stall, prompt to draw their knives at a moment's notice. Here moved to and fro among the shops and stalls, Jews in their yellow gaberdines; black Benedictines and white Cistercians; friars black, white and grey; men-at-arms from the castle; flocks of lads of twelve to fourteen, who had entered some grammar school or religious house to pass the first stage of the university course. Here passed a group of ragged, gaunt, yellow-visaged sophisters, returning peacefully from lectures to their inns, but with their "bastards," or daggers, as well as their leather pouches at their waists. Here a knot of students fantastically attired in many-coloured garments, whose tonsure was the only sign of their clerkly character, wearing beards, long hair, furred cloaks, and shoes chequered with red and green, paraded through the thoroughfare, heated with wine from the feast of some determining bachelor. Here a line of servants carrying the books of scholars or of doctors to the schools, or there a procession of colleagues escorting to the grave the body of some master, and bearing before the corpse a silver cross, threaded the throng. Here hurried a bachelor in his cape; a regent master in his heelless shoes or "pynsons," a scholar of Exeter in his black boots, a full-fledged master, with his tunic closely fastened about the middle by a belt, and wearing round his shoulders a black, sleeveless gown. Here gleamed a mantle of crimson cloth, symbolising the blood of the Saviour, or the budge-edged hood of a doctor of law or of theology, for it was then an object of ambition to wear, not to evade, the academical dress. In the hubbub of voices which proceeded from this miscellaneous, parti-coloured mob, might be distinguished every accent, every language, and every dialect. A mediaeval university was essentially cosmopolitan, and the influx of foreigners into Oxford was very great, especially when the University of Paris was temporarily dispersed, and when the Franciscan schools were at the height of their reputation. Frenchmen, Germans, Spaniards, jostled in the streets against English, Irish, Scotch, and Welsh; Kentish students mingled with students from Somerset or Yorkshire, and the speech of each was unintelligible to the other. National hostilities, clan hatreds, local jealousies, intellectual antipathies, differences of blood, language, and race, contributed to the heterogeneous character of the university. Men of the same nationality, province, or county, congregated together, advanced under their distinguishing banners to the fray, and in celebrations of the festivals of their own patron saints found more fruitful occasions of brawling than in football or cudgel-playing.

This gives us a very good idea of the turmoil into which Richard was suddenly plunged. It can hardly have been congenial to the soul of a hermit. "Over this seething mass," the writer continues, "no control could be exercised. The students were unattached, subject to little or no discipline, residing in private lodgings, or voluntarily associated for economy in inns, hostels, entries or halls."

The history of the University at this date is one of turbulence and disorder. Constant disputes arose between the Northern and Southern nations and between English, Welsh and Irish, and as all could carry arms there were many cases of students being hurt and sometimes killed. Richard being a mere boy and under the supervision of the Hall was not so likely to get embroiled in these affrays, but the poverty of the students was pitiful. The boys were herded together in class-room and dormitory like flocks of sheep. They were not exempt from corporal punishment and were hedged in by rules and restrictions. Candles were an exorbitant price and rushlights gave little light, so the students had to go to bed with the sun and rise betimes, which in the cold of the winter mornings cannot have been pleasant. We are told how Sixtus V. as a boy was found reading by the light of one of the oil lanterns which were suspended at the crossways of the streets.

What fires there were were of charcoal or wood. There were no chimneys, and the smoke had to escape by a hole in the roof. The streets had no sidewalks and were either of mud or cobbled; open streams and gutters, called kennels, running through them which were used as

c

receptacles for every sort of refuse, either thrown from the windows above, or from the stalls of the market-sellers. The shambles alone in that crowded "Row" must have been cause enough for many plagues. There was an entire absence of cleanliness. The custom then was to strew the dining-halls with rushes, which if not renewed became a source of sickness. Even as late as the sixteenth century, when one would think men had learned wisdom, Erasmus tells us that these rushes "are occasionally removed, but so imperfectly that the bottom layer is left undisturbed sometimes for twenty years, harbouring . . ." The rest of the sentence can be left to the imagination.

It is easy to understand why there were so many outbreaks of the pestilence, and in later times an epidemic they called the sweating sickness. Illness was taken so much as a matter of course that houses were provided by many of the colleges for the masters and fellows to resort to "for the use of wholesome air in times of pestilential sickness." St. Bartholomew's Hospital was given by Edward III. to Adam de Brome for this purpose for the use of Oriel College; Magdalen had a house at Brackley in Northants; while the fellows of Merton went to Cuxham or Islip, and those of Exeter to Kidlington.

The dirt and squalor prevalent then in Oxford must have seemed strange to the many visitors who came from cities like Florence, Bologna or Pavia. There is a legend that Dante once visited the schools of Oxford,[1] and Agnellus the first Provincial of the Franciscan Friars came from Pisa.

The scholars were divided into Northern and Southern nations, and so little agreement was there between these two that one of the proctors had always to be a North-countryman, and the other a Southerner. Probably Richard found himself engaged in many a skirmish, for his northern tongue would draw great ridicule upon him, nor would he be loath to fight. And there were other interests to divert his mind from study. Not far away at Woodstock was the fascinating menagerie which Henry I. had begun when he built his hunting-seat there. Often the boy must

[1] Cf. Lyte, p. 89. He says that "Giovanni da Seravalle, Bishop of Fermo, writing in 1416, states positively that Dante studied the liberal arts at Padua and Bologna, and theology at Oxford and Paris," and gives authorities.

have escaped out of the crowded city into the surrounding woods, and there perhaps watched the boar-hunting,
or joined in stalking deer. There is no reason to think that
he was different from other lads of his time, and he may
quite possibly have looked on at bear-baitings. The age
was a rough one, and what to us seems a cruel sport was to
them an amusement. Much later Erasmus has drawn for
us an unforgettable picture of the floggings inflicted upon
boys at school. The University in its beginning was little
more than a high school, and Richard would not be exempt.

We must think of him mixing in all the rough and tumble
of life at that time, jostling his way through the narrow
streets with their overhanging gables, out through the
West Gate, past the strong towers and bulwarks of the
castle towards the beautiful Abbey Church of Oseney
which he must have loved to frequent, or to the more recent
and smaller Rewley Abbey not many paces away on the
same island. If he wandered northwards just beyond the
walls he would come to the royal palace and its gardens
and meadows; and to the south, past the old St. Frideswide's, a cruciform low-roofed Norman church with its
Saxon tower, as he neared the Grandpont which bridged
the Thames, he would come across a network of streams.
There the Black and the Grey Friars had not long built
their great barn-shaped churches, where he might listen
to their preaching and hear their disputations and lectures.

The parish churches would be almost entirely of Norman
architecture, low and rather squat. St. Mary's had its tower
and spire, but its roof was far lower than it is now. For
obvious reasons, when the dread and menace of war was
never far away, men then tried to nestle their towns low
within their walls. Even within the city walls life was
not too secure. In the narrow thoroughfares, badly paved
and badly lighted, it was an easy matter to be tripped up
and robbed. The Town and Gown rows had begun early,
for Robert of Gloucester describes the affray which took
place in 1263 when young Edward was refused admittance
into Oxford; the city and some of the students being on
the side of De Montfort against King Henry III. There
were no doubt constant bickerings in Richard's time,
but the worst and most famous fight of all on St. Scholas-
tica's Day happened thirty years or more after he had left.

From the direst straits of poverty Richard would have been exempt, but we have a picture given us of shivering students huddled round a teacher as poor as themselves in porch and doorway, and soliciting alms of the passers-by. Many who were not able to find protection in an inn, hostel or hall would have to find their own lodging, and with them things must often have gone badly.

On the whole, therefore, the five or six years which Richard spent at Oxford would be among the most varied and interesting of his life. Though he had many hardships to endure he never really suffered from poverty, as later he seems willingly to have done, nor went hungry, though cold was the lot of all. He was protected and guarded and given every opportunity for study, in which we are told "he made great progress."

CHAPTER II

OF THE INFLUENCE OF THE FRANCISCANS IN OXFORD: AND OF THE FRIARIES AND MONASTIC HOUSES THERE

The coming of the friars to Oxford—Dominicans (1221)—Franciscans (1224)—Agnellus of Pisa—Grosseteste—The building of their church—Roger Bacon: A comparison with Richard Rolle—The Carmelites, or White Friars—The Austin Friars—The Trinitarians, or Red Friars—The monastic houses—Cistercians—Benedictines—Augustinians—Bernardines—The foundation of the secular colleges of Merton and Balliol.

WE have tried in the previous chapter to sketch the material Oxford into which Richard the future hermit found himself so suddenly plunged, and which must have perplexed and dazed the boy not a little; but the determining factor of Oxford in his life was mental. It was those who were then living within her walls, rather than the city herself or the then emerging University, which shaped Richard's future. Let us therefore study Oxford shortly from this point of view.

As regards European fame Oxford was then at her zenith. It is commonly said that thirty thousand students listened to the lectures of Duns Scotus, but this number must be grossly exaggerated as the city was far too small in those days to lodge so great a concourse. Still there is no doubt that with the emigration of the English nation from the schools of Paris the numbers of scholars had greatly increased. They were gathered from all parts of the civilised world so that Oxford had become almost cosmopolitan in character.

The greatest impetus to learning in the thirteenth century was the coming of the friars.[1] Foreign students flocked

[1] For this chapter cf. *The Grey Friars in Oxford*, by A. G. Little (Oxford Hist. Soc. Clarendon Press, 1892); *The Coming of the Friars*, by the Rev. Augustus Jessopp, D.D. (Fisher Unwin); *The Franciscans in England*, 1224–1538, by Edward Hutton (Constable, 1926), a most interesting book to which I am much indebted.

to Oxford to hear famous doctors of the Dominican Order,
while among the Franciscans were Adam Marsh, called
the Illustrious Doctor, and Roger Bacon.

To quote again the unknown writer of the *Quarterly*:

As a crowded centre of population Oxford offered a great
field for their missionary labours. As a hotbed of free thought,
if not of heresy, it demanded their anxious care. As a recruiting
ground for their own order, it necessarily possessed unique
attractions. At first the Mendicants excited no hostility.
Primarily the Dominicans devoted themselves to missions
and the Franciscans to the care of the sick; but both orders
soon acquired influence as teachers. The Dominican House
became the recognised place of study for the Friars of the
Order in Northern Europe. The Franciscan School grew into
the acknowledged rival of the theological Schools of Paris.

The Dominicans were the first to arrive, about 1221.
Their ostensible purpose was the conversion of the Jews,
and therefore they first made their home in the Jewry,
but in 1259 moved to an island formed by the junction
of the Thames and the Trill Mill stream. The site is still
to be identified in the present Blackfriars Street. There
they built a stately church which was consecrated in 1262.

The Franciscans landed in England two years before
the death of their founder, on 10 September, 1224; at the
very time when Francis was wrapt in prayer on the holy
mount of La Verna, where he received the stigmata on
Holy Cross Day, just four days later than the first coming
of the friars. The Franciscan chronicler, Friar Thomas of
Eccleston, tells us that they were "charitably conveyed
across to England by the monks of Fécamp." Agnellus
had been chosen by Francis himself to be the first Provincial
Minister of England. The Pisan historian, Tronci, calls
him "Agnello degli Agnelli, Nobile Pisano." He had been
won by the preaching of Francis in 1211, when the saint
had visited Pisa, and had been professed there in the
Franciscan Convent. He seems to have been a very humble
man and, like Francis, had refused to receive priest's
orders, until commanded to do so later by the General
Chapter; but when he landed in England he was a deacon.
Only one of that little band of four was in priest's orders;
he was an Englishman, Richard of Ingworth. The other

two clerical friars were also English, but the five lay brethren who accompanied them were foreigners.[1]

The Franciscans were first housed by the Dominicans until they procured a small dwelling near St. Ebbe's Church. A year later they rented, and were afterwards given, a house belonging to Richard de Mulliner, with a strip of ground between the city wall and the present Church Street.[2] The site is not easy to identify. Agnellus, like Francis, was possessed of the spirit of holy poverty and only built when there was absolute necessity, and then with humility, and he would not allow the walls of the infirmary to be any higher than the height of a tall man.

The first call of the Franciscans in Oxford was to the sick, hence they gave great attention to the study of medicine and botany. Shakespeare draws a very true picture of them in Friar Lawrence, who, when Romeo goes to ask his aid in the early morning, is starting forth to seek for herbs, plants and stones:

> I must up-fill this osier cage of ours
> With baleful weeds and precious-juiced flowers.
> The earth that's nature's mother is her tomb;
> What is her burying grave that is her womb,
> And from her womb children of divers kind
> We sucking on her natural bosom find,
> Many for many virtues excellent,
> None but for some and yet all different.
> O, mickle is the powerful grace that lies
> In herbs, plants, stones, and their true qualities:
> For nought so vile that on the earth doth live
> But to the earth some special good doth give.
>
> Act II. Sc. iii.

The choice of Agnellus by Francis was justified, for with his humility he combined discernment. Eccleston writes in his chronicle:

Seeing how the place was increasing where the highest learning in England flourished, and where scholars from all parts were accustomed to meet, he [Agnellus] had a school of becoming dimensions built in the convent of the brethren, and besought Master Robert Grosseteste of holy memory to lecture to them.[3]

---

[1] Cf. Hutton, pp. 15 sqq.   [2] Little, p. 13.
[3] Hutton, pp. 44–5.

By his appointment of Grosseteste Agnellus conferred a lasting benefit both upon his Order and upon Oxford. There is no space here to dwell upon the far-reaching influence he had upon mediaeval thought. His greatest claim to originality lies, perhaps, in the fact that he was interested in the study of languages, and was, for those days, a Greek scholar. In pure philosophy he was content with the old Aristotelian system, and lectured in the fashion of the scholastics, which gave rise to the oft-told story of how one day when Agnellus entered the lecture-room he heard the question propounded by Grosseteste, *Utrum sit Deus?* (Whether there be a God?)

"Hei mihi, hei mihi," cried Agnellus, *"simplices coelos penetrant et literati disputant utrum sit Deus!"*

For ten years Grosseteste lectured in the school of the fratry until he was consecrated Bishop of Lincoln (in which see Oxford then was) in 1235, drawing large numbers to listen to him, and increasing the reputation of the Order by his learning and influence, so that gradually the English Franciscan company attracted to their convent some of the greatest scholars and the most learned and original men of that day. Such names as Alexander of Hales, Adam de Marisco, or Adam Marsh, Roger Bacon, Duns Scotus, and William of Ockham, conjure up controversies and disputes of absorbing and endless interest.

Under the rule of Agnellus all the buildings of the fratry were contained within the city walls. The only one of any size was the school; the chapel, or church, in the choir of which Agnellus was buried, being very simple and quite small. Afterwards it was pulled down to make room for a new and much larger church, which was begun in 1246 and dedicated in honour of Francis, whose canonisation so quickly followed on his death.

The spirit of the Order soon began to change under Brother Haymo (1238-9), who took in more land and walled it round, for he preferred the friars should have ample areas, and should cultivate them, "that they might have the fruits of the earth at home rather than beg them from others," taking advantage of the deed of Henry III., which gave the friars permission,

for the greater quiet and security of their habitation, to inclose the street which extends under the wall of Oxford, from the gate which is called Watergate (i.e. Littlegate) in the parish of St. Ebbe, up to the postern in the same wall towards the Castle; so that a crenellated wall like the rest of the wall of the same town be made round the foresaid dwelling, beginning from the west side of Watergate, and reaching southwards as far as the bank of the Thames, and extending along the bank westwards as far as the fee of the Abbat of Bec in the parish of St. Bodhoc, and then turning again northwards till it joins the old wall of the foresaid borough on the east side of the small postern.[1]

Wood thus describes Little Gate:

Little Gate, or Luttel Gate, or else Water Gate, from the common ford at Preacher's Bridge which nearly adjoined it, was used to water cattle. Through the Gate was the way which led from the City to the Black and Grey Friars. The upper chamber which lay over it was for long inhabited by scholars, which shows how full was the University, as the Gate was on a common road—a place of continual disturbance.

The church of St. Bodhoc has quite disappeared. It was given to the Friars of the Penitence of Jesus Christ, known as the "Friars of the Sack," "to make thence a chapel for themselves"; but on the suppression of the Order it passed to the Friars Minor. Bodhoc, or Budoc, was a Celtic saint like Aldate; these two being the only Celtic dedications known in Oxford.

In 1246 the friars began to build a new church in honour of their founder. It probably stood due east and west. Mr. Hutton thinks that the west end was without the old wall of the city, and that the present Church Place marks the site.[2] It was completed by 1248, and was not far from the Trill Mill stream, so called from the mill which the friars had there. For the most part this stream is now covered, but there still remains a fragment of old wall, close to where the stream runs under Quaking Bridge from the old castle mill which still remains in use. This wall may have enclosed the orchard and garden of the friary, which occupied the ground now known as Paradise Square and Penson's Gardens. The whole district has been almost obliterated by buildings and workshops, and the covering of the mill stream makes it the more difficult to trace, though the names Friars Street, Blackfriars Street and

---

[1] Quoted by Little, p. 14.   [2] Hutton, p. 45.

Littlegate Street bear their own witness. All that remains
are fragments of the old boundary walls, hidden in the
back-yards and garages, and an old bastion of the city
wall.

The friars' church was much sought after as a place of
burial, and we know that Agnellus was buried by its high
altar, his body being removed there from the first humble
chapel which he had built; and of late years a tablet erected
in honour of Roger Bacon has been built into a part of the
old city wall which is a continuation of the wall remaining
on the south side of Pembroke, but which was partly
destroyed to make room for St. Ebbe's Street. The inscription, in Latin and English, reads in its English version:

The Great Philosopher ROGER BACON known as the Wonderful Doctor, who by his Experimental Method extended mar-
vellously the Realm of Science, after a long life of untiring
activity, near this place, in the home of his Franciscan brethren,
fell asleep in Christ, A.D. 1292.

Thus tardily has Oxford recognised one of the most
astounding men who has ever graced her precincts. He may
not unaptly be compared to Leonardo da Vinci. The greatest
of all Grosseteste's disciples, under him he read Greek and
Latin, and began his study of physics and optics, which
latter was a favourite subject with Grosseteste who had a
theory that light was a constitutive principle of matter;
while both alike were devoted to the science of mathematics.
Bacon went farther than his master and learned Arabic,
which led to his devoting himself to astrology, alchemy
and magic, and following the misguided advice of Grosseteste he joined the Franciscan Order, to find that he had
entered a prison rather than a monastery.

The room in the tower which went by the name of Bacon's
study, stood at the far end of Folly Bridge. The tower was
a part of the gateway which dated from the reign of Stephen
as a watch-gate. The tradition was that Bacon used it for
his astronomical observations, and that when a greater
than he passed below it would fall. Perhaps it was there
that Bacon wrote in secrecy his three great works, the
Opus Majus, the *Opus Minus* and the *Opus Tertium*,
at the bidding of Pope Clement IV. The latter when he
was cardinal had heard of Roger from a clerk named

Raymond of Laon and thought the work he desired to see was then written, but Roger says:

> Whilst I was in a different state of life I wrote nothing on science; nor in my present condition had I ever been required to do so by my superiors; nay a strict prohibition has been passed to the contrary under penalty of forfeiture of the book and many days fasting on bread and water, if any book written by us should be communicated to strangers.

But the Pope's command was to send him a fair copy of this work of which Raymond had spoken secretly, and without any delay, in spite of any constitution of his Order to the contrary. It is one of the most pathetic stories in the history of literature, for amid great difficulties, jealousies and lack of money, Bacon obeyed.

He made himself a skilled mechanic, he constructed scientific instruments, and all his mind and heart, his insatiable curiosity, his clarity of vision, his violent desire for knowledge and for achievement he put into works written with immense speed, in less than eighteen months, for the Pope. Upon them and their success with Clement his heart must have been fixed.[1]

But when the books reached Clement he was too ill to open them and died without seeing the great work which Bacon had accomplished at his bidding, and at so great a cost.

Mr. Hutton devotes a chapter of his book to Bacon.

> He was [he says] before all things English in the character and atmosphere of his mind, which refused to wander far from useful practical knowledge and experiment. He was Franciscan chiefly, one may think, by accident and perhaps because he seemed to see in that Order, influenced as he was by Grosseteste and Peter de Maricourt, something of that future for which he sacrificed everything and to which his last gesture was a passionate greeting. Thus it was perhaps the experimentalism of St. Francis, the actual testing of the teaching of the gospel by experience, which attracted him to the Order. For in the thirteenth century he, with St. Francis, represents above all the tendency to experiment. He had a contempt for the metaphysical quarrels that everywhere surrounded him and criticised them, let us admit it, with something less than charity and with more ardour than justice. He had an instinctive dislike and mistrust of the

---

[1] Hutton, p. 144.

syllogism of the schools, the scholastic method, its verbiage and artificial precision were repugnant to him. He attempted to show that in the science of reason one ought not to follow authority. Perhaps he did not fully understand, he certainly did not appreciate, the questions which were convulsing the universities of his day. In this too he is a forerunner of the modern world. For he, too, lonely though he was, isolated as he seemed, would one day have disciples, a whole world of them, so that we are his children over near seven hundred years.[1]

And again:

He condemns utterly the teaching of the time and its methods—the endless commentaries which distort the work of Aristotle, the bad translations. Every sort of study needs reform. As for theology and ecclesiastical studies, there is too much poor philosophy in them and an absolute ignorance of those sciences so necessary to them. The *Liber Sententiarum* is more valued than Holy Scripture, and the text of the Bible is at the same time so corrupt, and the theologians so utterly ignorant of Greek and Hebrew, that all sorts of errors pass for truth. That Theology is the Queen of sciences he admits, but he maintains that it, with Philosophy and Canon Law,— the whole realm of knowledge, in fact, are but the handmaids of that divine wisdom which is contained altogether and wholly in Holy Writ, that they have but an interpretative value and duty in regard to the Scriptures.[2]

I have quoted these passages because what Mr. Hutton has said of Roger Bacon is, *mutatis mutandis*, equally true of Richard Rolle. He also was an experimentalist in his own sphere, and he shared Bacon's intense love for the Scriptures, to which we shall have to refer later. Both men are most English in their outlook on life, maintaining that theory must be subordinate to life and to experience, and that life must be judged by experience and modified accordingly.

In spite of the ever-increasing fame of the friars, and the number of disciples and learned men who crowded the churches, and the schools in the fratry, they were forbidden to lecture publicly without a dispensation; neither were they allowed to preach before the University, since they held no degree, nor without a degree in Arts were they allowed to study for the Doctorates of Theology, of Law

---

[1] Hutton, pp. 146–7.   [2] Ibid., p. 143.

South View of Bocardo or North Gate
(From a drawing by J. B. Malchair)

or of Science. But to obtain a degree in Arts it was necessary to pursue a seven years' course of study, which included the seven liberal arts and philosophy. After that seven more years were prescribed for the course laid down for a doctorate. Thus we can understand why a boy must enter the University at so early an age and also why the rule forbade the mendicant Orders from taking up secular studies. There were constant attempts on their part to get the statute changed, and for a long time dispensations were freely granted; yet the opposition of a single Master of Arts could prohibit them, and naturally the more famous the friars became the greater grew their rivalry with the University. The Dominicans made one final effort in 1311 to get the statute altered so as to admit them to become Doctors of Theology without the intermediate Arts degree, but they were defeated, and the struggle only led to the strengthening of the hands of the University.

By then the friars were falling into disfavour, and were becoming unpopular, but they had given an immense impetus to the foundation of colleges, which were based upon the monastic rule, giving their students both discipline and claustral seclusion together with a common life.

The success of the two great mendicant or preaching Orders drew other monastic communities to Oxford. In 1226 the Carmelites, or White Friars, settled outside the North Wall, near to the royal palace of Beaumont. Before they had any chapel of their own they were allowed to use what is now the southernmost aisle of St. Mary Magdalen's as their church, and the narrow passage which leads off the Magdalen Street, facing the church, to Beaumont Street, by its name, Friars' Entry, still reminds us of the path they took from their temporary convent to this chapel. About sixty years later Edward I. granted them the palace for their use.

The Austin Friars or Hermits were the next to come, and were given land beyond Smith Gate, near Wadham College. They attended lectures at first in the Franciscan schools, but later built spacious halls of their own, one for theology and another for philosophy. They became so famed for their learning and disputations that it was decreed by statute that none should take their Master's degree until he "was thought worthy, or could answer these Augustin Fryers."[1] "Doing Austins" was a common expression, and remained in use long after the dissolution of the monasteries.

The Trinitarians, sometimes called the Red Friars because of the blue - and - red cross on their habit, had their first fratry behind Merton, between what is now known as the Broad Walk, through which the Trill stream ran, and still runs only now it is covered, and the Botanical Gardens. Later they bought a chapel dedicated to the Holy Trinity, which as we have seen was a part of the East Gate. Their name was derived from this chapel; but they seem to have all died of the plague in 1349, and their convent became a hall for poor scholars.

Besides the friars the monastic Orders were plentifully represented. We have noted how the Cistercians settled on land on the Isle of Oseney and there built Rewley Abbey. At Gloucester Hall (now Worcester College) the Benedictines had their cells, each great Benedictine house being represented. The arms of five of these can still be seen over the doorways of the south side of what is now the Great Quadrangle. Originally it was part of the cloister, which luckily escaped demolition when the other side of the cloister was destroyed in the eighteenth century to make space for the new part of the college, but fortunately funds failed before they had finished and so the southern side remains much as it was. The Benedictines from Durham came in such numbers that they built later a college of their own, Durham Hall, where is now Trinity College; a part of the older buildings still fronts the Broad. Canterbury Hall was also a Benedictine foundation, although sometimes secular clergy were also admitted. Archbishop Islip of Canterbury was its founder and he appointed Wyclif as its first warden, from which post the latter was ejected on the death of the archbishop. It stood on the site of the great gate of Christ Church, which was named Canterbury Gate after the hall.

Nor must we forget the Augustinian Canons Regular who had their great monastery at Oseney; and later a smaller house at St. Mary's College, which lay west of the North Gate. In New Inn Hall Street, amid the modern buildings there can still be seen an old stone gate-

[1] *The Mirror of Oxford*, p. 58.

way, one of the entrances to Frewen Hall, which is all that remains of the old college founded in 1435; the prior who ruled it being subject to the Abbot of Oseney. It was there that Erasmus lodged when in Oxford.

The Bernardines were the last order to found a house in Oxford. They were a branch of the Cistercians and settled opposite to St. Mary Magdalen's. In 1436 Archbishop Chichele converted their house into the college of St. Bernard. It was not destroyed at the dissolution but was presented to Christ Church by Henry VIII. Sir Thomas Whyte bought it and in accordance with a strange dream founded there a college dedicated to the honour of Our Lady and St. John Baptist. Chichele's Tower Gateway still remains, and from its niche a weather-worn statue of St. Bernard looks down.

Gradually the tide of feeling turned against the mendicants, whose privileges, immunities, learning and proselytising zeal threatened to empty the churches, confessionals and the pockets of the clergy, and the Oxford halls and colleges began to pass out of their hands. Merton College, as we have noted, was a secular foundation; its founder, Walter de Merton, was careful to exclude all monastic influence, and no monk or friar was to be admitted on the foundation. Merton's aim was to have a perpetual succession of poor scholars, eager to study arts, philosophy, theology and canon law, or even civil law. He wished to protect his students against any proselytising of the friars, and to train men for the religious life in the world and not in the cloister. Thus he educated them to be parish priests, lawyers, etc. It was not meant that they should remain in college for any length of time, but that they should pass as quickly as they could through their prescribed courses and go out to serve their fellow-beings in the world at large. Balliol followed Merton (1282), and Exeter a few years later (1314). These must have been already founded when Richard came to Oxford, but it was still too early for their influence to have been greatly felt. We should imagine that the friars within whose halls and chapels the boy must often have strayed, would as well as the many monastic orders prove a great attraction to him. He came from a land of monks; Yorkshire was then more thickly sprinkled with abbeys and monasteries than any other county, and the homesick and lonely child would perhaps find in their familiar habits a certain sense of friendliness, as so often in a strange place we may feel a thrill of delight in seeing a familiar uniform which carries us back in memory to places and people we have loved.

It is possible too that the sermons to which Richard listened in the Franciscan church, built in honour of a saint to whom he must have felt drawn in an especial way, did much to inflame him with that passionate love for the Crucified which took so deep a root in his heart. We can well believe that he would flee with relief from the benches of St. Mary's, where he had to listen to lectures and controversial disputes, to find in the more simple minds of the friars some rest and solace for the vague desires and yearnings after something which he could certainly not express, and as yet but dimly understood.

CHAPTER III

THE STUDIES THEN PURSUED AT OXFORD

"He desired rather to be more fully and perfectly instructed in the theological doctrine of Holy Scripture than in physics or the study of secular knowledge."—LESSON I.

Universal use of Latin—Earliest libraries at Oxford—The *Trivium* and *Quadrivium*—Determination—Regents and Non-regents—Not known whether Richard took his degree or received orders—The catalogue of Oriel College Library and the textbooks then employed—William of Ockham and Nominalism—Summary of the great debate between the Thomists and Scotists—A modern exponent of Nominalism — How far Richard was influenced by Ockham—What led him to follow the mystic's quest and leave Oxford.

IF we were suddenly to find ourselves in Oxford of the fourteenth century the first thing by which we should be arrested would probably be the extraordinary blend of tongues. Not only did the English dialects differ from one another so greatly as almost to seem each a language by itself, but there would be the many dialects of France. We might catch snatches of the Provençal songs which the followers of Francis had learnt from his lips, or hear an Italian student singing the *canzone* of Dante or of Jacopone da Todi; and there were the strange-sounding tongues of the Eastern traders and students. But the prevailing speech among the students would have been Latin. And this to our modern ears would hardly sound like itself, for it was that delightful colloquial Latin by means of which the students of the world conversed freely with each other. Latin was obligatory in many of the hostels and halls, and was used for lectures and in all academic disputations, besides being the language of the Church.

Since Latin was thus the keystone of all learning we should expect to find a large place given to its study, yet there are very few books on grammar among the contents of the old catalogues of the college libraries. From these we can best know what books were most studied at that time and in use in the schools. One of the earliest is the catalogue of Oriel College of 1375. That library contained the books which Bishop Cobham had originally collected for the University Library which he had begun to house at St. Mary's, but when he died in 1327 the books which he had bequeathed to the library had to be pawned to pay his debts and funeral expenses. Adam de Brome, the rector of St. Mary's, and the re-founder of Oriel College, remonstrated and was told that if he liked to redeem the books they might be given to his new foundation, and this he gladly did. This catalogue is, therefore, representative of the University, and not only of a small body of scholars. Thus it is all the more surprising to find so few books on grammar or syntax. Very little pains seems to have been taken to acquire any real mastery of Latin. The formal rules of the language were taught from the works of Donatus and Priscian; the catalogue includes several portions of the latter's enormous grammar.[1]

To understand the catalogue we must remember that the course of study was then divided into the *Trivium* (or three ways), and the *Quadrivium* (or four ways). The *Trivium* comprised grammar, logic and rhetoric, and the *Quadrivium*, arithmetic, geometry, music and astronomy.

Their names were given in the old line:

Lingua, tropus, ratio, numerus, tonus, angulus, astra.

The first three years of the course was spent over the *Trivium*, after which the student became a "general sophister," and had to attend the logical "variations" which were held in the parvise, disputing, arguing, and "responding on sophisms." The parvise was a cloister or paved platform or space adjoining a church, which shows the ecclesiastical origin of these debates. There is an interesting relic of this custom in the old phrase *in parviso*, which is still retained in the Latin certificate issued to successful candidates in the examination known as *Responsions*, although the modern undergraduate translates it as "for Smalls" or "for Little-go." A year at least was

[1] The catalogue has been edited for the Oxford Hist. Soc. (1885): *Collectanea* vol. i., pp. 62–5.

spent in "variations," and then the student was allowed to "respond to the question," and became a "questionist" as well as a "sophister," and might soon after proceed to the ceremony of "determination," by which the degree of Bachelor of Arts was obtained. After "determination" the student passed on to the *Quadrivium*, i.e. study of music, astronomy, geometry and arithmetic, but there seems to have been no fixed rule as to the time at which rhetoric (which belonged to the *Trivium*), arithmetic, and natural and metaphysical philosophy should be studied.

The formal ceremonies for "determination" began on Ash Wednesday, and ended ten days before Easter, the determining Bachelor being said "to stand in Lent"; for during nine days—the first and last day of "determination," and for seven other days—he had to stand at a desk morning and afternoon, to defend the propositions he had laid down against any who chose to dispute them. If he wished to become a Master his future career would depend upon the skill with which he defended his arguments, for in those days Master was synonymous with teacher, and no one in the universities of Paris, Oxford or Cambridge could be recognised as a Master who had not actually taught in the schools. The Masters were distinguished as *Regentes* or Regent Masters who had actual management of the schools, and *Non-Regentes* or Non-Regents who had done their term of teaching.[1]

There is no allusion in any place to Richard Rolle having received the degree of Bachelor, and certainly he would have found the ceremonies attending determination extremely uncongenial, and moreover the expenses were very heavy. Besides the fees exacted, on these occasions there was a great deal of feasting, including the drinking of much wine. Richard as we know was poor, and though it was possible for a poor student to find a wealthier one to "determine" for him, it is unlikely that he would have had such a friend, or, if he had, that he would have wished to be indebted to any for such a purpose.

Neither is there evidence that Richard received minor orders while at Oxford, though the probability that he did so is great, for all students who had passed the grammatical studies were qualified to do so. From Richard's

[1] Cf. Lyte, pp. 205, 899.

later life, as a teacher, preacher, and spiritual adviser or confessor to nuns, we should infer that, like Francis of Assisi, he had received some of the minor orders, though not the higher order of priesthood. Also it is hardly likely that he would so readily have ascended the pulpit in the chapel at Topcliffe, if he had never had to practise preaching when at Oxford.

In regard to the textbooks in use, Priscian and Donatus, as we have seen, were read in the schools of grammar, and also Terence; arithmetic was chiefly the study of the *Computus*, a method of discovering Easter; logic was taught from the *Isagoge* of Porphyry, the *Summulae* of Petrus Hispanus, and the *Sophistici Elenchi* of Aristotle. In rhetoric Boethius and Aristotle were the principal text-books. Then the student passed on to music, geometry and astronomy, for which Boethius, Euclid and Ptolemy were read; and for philosophy Aristotle was the sole authority. Only after taking a Master's degree in Arts was he eligible for the higher faculties of law, theology and medicine.

This catalogue, of which the writer in the *Quarterly* gives a full account which I have abridged, throws a most useful light upon contemporary studies. It cites nearly a hundred volumes, arranged according to the subjects required for the two degrees in Arts, and the subsequent study of law and theology. Though to us it may seem a small number, it is an enormous advance upon the days when a student was dependent solely upon oral instruction, and when a MS. was considered so valuable that it was accepted by the University Chest as security for a loan. Besides the works mentioned above, there were more than twenty volumes on philosophy, yet the greater part of the catalogue is devoted to works on law and theology. There is no Greek work, and no Latin classic. Languages were still neglected, and pure scholarship unknown. It is strange that books on natural science and mathematics should be so few considering the work of Roger Bacon who had still many disciples; nor do we find any of the Arabian commentaries on Aristotle in which the contemporary Italian libraries are so rich.

Theology is the science which is best represented, for there are forty works on it to only six on law, in spite of the latter's growing popularity as a study; yet we notice with some surprise that the library contains not a single copy of the Scriptures, and Patristic literature is very poorly represented. Of the four great Doctors of the Church only Augustine and Gregory are found, and no Greek fathers; while Anselm and Hugh of St. Victor are the sole names cited among the early mediaeval theologians.

Yet traces of the ferment into which theologians in Oxford were plunged in the fourteenth century are evident, for on the one side we find the scholastic commentators on the Sentences, and on the other the great attempt of Aquinas to reconcile Aristotelian philosophy with Christian thought. Here also are the treatises which until the Reformation were to be used as the textbooks of the schools, "in which Duns Scotus enlarged the bounds of thought, incorporated the result of Byzantine logic; and began the line of reasoning which eventually undermined the Scholastic methods." Yet neither Ockham, his disciple, nor Holcot, Burleigh, or Bradwardine are represented.

From this summary we can conjecture the sort of training which Richard went through. In the *Vite* we read that "He desired rather to be more fully and perfectly instructed in the theological doctrine of Holy Scripture than in physics or the study of secular knowledge." Which sentence we must take for what it was worth, remembering that the object of the *Vite* was to uphold the piety of their saint. To judge by the catalogue from which we have quoted, Richard would not have found much instruction on Holy Scripture at that time, but of theological debates there were no end.

Thomas Aquinas had died in 1274, at the early age of forty-seven, and Duns Scotus, his chief critic, in 1308. William of Ockham—so named from a small village in Surrey—carried on the teaching of Scotus. He had been the most brilliant of his scholars; and his influence was probably the greatest under which Richard came when at Oxford. Burleigh and Bradwardine were also among Ockham's pupils, the latter being about ten years senior to Richard. It is very possible that they sat together in Ockham's lecture-rooms, absorbing this new nominalistic teaching, which underlies so much of Richard's writings, although it may have been almost unconsciously imbibed, for

Richard was too young to have fully understood the endless debates and arguments there propounded.

Burleigh and Bradwardine belonged to the secular college of Merton, founded as we have seen in 1264, for twenty students of theology or of canon law. We read that these two students mixed but little in public disputations, being "filled with fervent charity and devotion." Though neither was a member of any religious order, Richard would have had much affinity with both them and Ockham (1270–1349).

Ockham was an ardent Franciscan, of the evangelical type. Richard would find much to attract him in his teaching, both in the independent attitude of his mind and in his personal love for Christ. In politics also Ockham followed his own course and openly challenged papal authority, being at one time imprisoned at Avignon because he had espoused the cause of Louis of Bavaria against Pope John XXII. The rival Popes held Avignon from 1309 to 1378, and the unsettlement and dismay which this schism caused must have been greatly felt at Oxford, and their rival claims were hotly contested there. Richard, who all his life seemed to be up against authority, would throw himself into the controversy with all the extreme ardour of youth and ignorance; for what boy exists who does not delight in taking sides in any political campaign, and the less he knows about it the more ardent is his partisanship.

Ockham held an independent and revolutionary attitude in regard to dialectics as well as politics. He recanted his "heresies" before his death, which took place in the same year as Richard's, although he was his senior by thirty years. Ockham died in the Franciscan convent at Munich, almost immediately after his reconciliation with the Church.

He was the last of the great schoolmen and the last also of that great company of English Franciscans which included Alexander of Hales, Adam Marsh, Roger Bacon and Duns Scotus. "Is it not significant," asks Mr. Hutton, "that among these should appear already two such rebellious spirits as Roger Bacon and Duns Scotus?"[1]

The great debate between the Thomists, or followers of

[1] Hutton, p. 163.

the Italian Aquinas, and the Scotists, or adherents of the Scotsman Duns, had been dividing men's minds for many years before Richard came to Oxford, and had now diverged more or less into a party warfare. The Thomists were upheld by the Dominicans, and the Scotists by the Franciscans, each Order naturally backing their own member; the Scotists had by far the larger number of followers, and Ockham carried on the debate for his side with great brilliancy.

It all turned upon the nature of being.

The meaning and reality of genus and species, of differences and accidents, of the general terms known as Universals, became the favourite topic of the Schools. The Realists, seeking with Plato to explore a spiritual and immaterial world, found the only real existence in ideas, drawn from some source eternal and divine, in abstract, inspired conceptions of truth and goodness, of wisdom, beauty, humanity, and the like. In the visible world around them they found only more or less imperfect reproductions of these unchangeable ideas. The Nominalists, following Aristotle's method more boldly sometimes than the Church approved, maintained that these Universals, these general conceptions, were names, sounds, phrases only, which had no existence apart from the senses and experience of men, and claimed that it was with the individual intellect, and not with such impalpable abstractions, that the pursuit of the secret of existence must begin.

"The question concerning genera and species" (so ran this celebrated sentence which launched the whole debate), "whether they have a substantial existence or are found only in bare concepts of the mind; whether, supposing them to have a substantial existence, they are corporeal or incorporeal; and whether again they are found apart from things which the senses can perceive, or exist in those things, and with them and about them; I shall forbear to say. For this kind of question is a very deep one and demands a fuller investigation." [1]

Each side found vigorous advocates. The Realists, wrapped in contemplation of invisible and unsubstantial things, had little difficulty in reconciling their conceptions with the authority

---

[1] "Mox de generibus et speciebus illud quidem sive subsistant, sive in solis nudis intellectibus posita sint, sive subsistentia corporalia sint an incorporalia, et utrum separata a sensibilibus an insensibilibus posita et circa haec consistentia, dicere recusabo; altissimum enim negotium est hujusmodi et majoris egens inquisitionis."
Boethius' version of the Greek might perhaps be improved on, but it was from his version that the controversy took rise.

and traditions of the Church. When Berengar questioned the miracle of Transubstantiation, the transformation of the bread and wine into the body and blood of Christ, Realism stepped in to distinguish between the invisible substance, the Universal, which the priest could change, and the visible accidents or adjuncts which remained.[1]

Mystical experience, the realists held, is not real knowledge until it has been translated into *phantasmata* or images, so that it may behold the universal in the particular. The human mind in its natural and ordinary operation is cognisant of spiritual things only indirectly, by abstraction from sensible images, and then by way of "eminence" and of "negation"; whereas mystical knowledge is a different operation of the same faculty whereby it knows spiritual things directly, by means of purely non-material impressions received from them in some unknown manner. Thus, unless they were prepared to be illogical, the scholastics could not admit a philosophical mysticism, the mystic believing himself to be in direct communion with God, and in an immediate intuition apart from creatures; while the scholastic taught that the intellect cannot know, and therefore the will cannot love, God, except through the medium of our senses. To put it briefly: "Our sensations and our ideas are not the objects of our knowledge but the instruments or means by which we know; or rather they are themselves the knowledge."[2]

"The Nominalists, on the other hand, relied on analysis and inquiry, on arguments drawn from human perception and experience, and were led to apply the test of reason to the mysteries and dogmas of the faith."[3]

Ockham held the opinions of the nominalistic school. Nominalism had been revived by Rosellinus who flourished in 1080.[4] According to his theories, universals are simply subjective products of abstraction: they are not real things but only means, for real existence belongs only to individuals. His watchword was *Universalia post rem*. Ockham went farther and maintained that only individuals

[1] Cf. *A History of the University of Oxford*, by Sir Charles Mallet, vol. i., pp. 11–12 (Methuen, 1924).
[2] Cf. article on "Scholasticism" in the *Encyclopædia of Religion and Ethics*, edited by J. Hastings, vol. ix., p. 247.
[3] Mallet, i., p. 11.
[4] See note 2 above.

as individual things have meaning. Universals as common conceptions are abstractions made by our own understanding from these individual things, and did not exist *in re*. Therefore the alternative was that they existed *in mente*. Yet he expressly dismisses the theory that universals are fictions, or only the work of the mind. The universal is not anything really existing; but it is a *terminus*: hence his followers were at first called Terminists.

Yet Ockham claimed to be a disciple of Aristotle, and explained the *universalia ante rem* as meaning not substantial existences in God, but simply God's knowledge of things; a knowledge which is not of universals but of singulars, since these alone can exist *realiter*. But such a doctrine is widely different in spirit from the realism of Thomas Aquinas. It distrusts abstractions and makes for direct observation and inductive research.

Thus Ockham, still a scholastic, strikes the death - blow at scholasticism by giving us the scholastic justification of the empirical method of thought through the observation of individual things; the derivation of universal principles from individual experience; which was the great truth for which Roger Bacon contended.

He therefore attacked the scholastic system, for his doctrine excluded a rational theology, since all knowledge that transcends experience he assigned to truth. And since some dogmas are irrational, truth must be of a twofold nature. Thus the idea of God though not irrational is one whose truth cannot be demonstrated. We can only form the idea of God by the artifices of abstraction, and can have no knowledge of Him in Himself but only a relative notion whose truth-value remains an open question. Ockham held that the soul has a faculty of its own for apprehending super - conscious truth. Truth is therefore *secundum rationem* and *secundum fidem*.[1]

It is not difficult to see how this doctrine tended to open the way towards a less dogmatic mysticism. The scholasticism of Aquinas contained elements of mysticism; and the *Summa* includes a "Treatise on the Active and

[1] Cf. the articles on "Scholasticism" in the *Encyclopædia Britannica* (eleventh edition, vol. xxiv., pp. 346 sqq.) by Professor A. Seth Pringle Pattison; and on "Mysticism" (vol. xix., pp. 123 sqq.) by the same writer.

Contemplative Life,"[1] and a chapter concerning "Rapture"
But contemplation was understood by the scholastics to
be the conclusion of rational discourse, and not an intuitive
experience, and had little in common with mystic contemplation, as we shall see later. Bonaventura, although
called the "prince of mystical theologians," has very few
actual references to mysticism as a system, which can
scarcely be said to exist in England at that date. Although
his influence upon Richard was great, it was rather by reason
of his devout meditations upon the Passion, and his writings
concerning the love of God, than for any mystical doctrine.

Aquinas had made an attempt in the *Summa* to reconcile
philosophy and Christianity, and to show that natural
and revealed truth were complementary the one to the
other. In this immense work he advances arguments on
both sides of every question, and decides on each judicially
and in strict accordance with the doctrines of the Church.
He was constructive, whereas the strength of Duns Scotus
lay in his destructive criticism. The former builds upon a
wonderful system of theology, trying to prove the unity
between faith and science, theology and philosophy; Duns
sees no basis for truth other than the will of God, to which
the individual will of man must submit. Will is the moving
power of the intellect, not the intellect of the will. Theology
rests upon faith, and faith is not speculative but practical,
because an act of will. According to Aquinas the intellect
is the moving power of the will. He taught that moral
freedom means that by an intellectual act of analysis and
comparison various possible lines of action are revealed,
and one is seen to be the best, and the will decides on
that. But the Divine will is subject, as the human, to
a rational determination; only in God the union of reason
and will is perfect, so that God commands good because
it is good. To Duns good is so only by an arbitrary imposi-
tion. It is good *because* God wills it, though he guards
himself against the heretical idea that God could will evil;
since it is impossible to make contradictories identical.
Hence Aquinas was on the side of rationalism and Scotus
on that of scepticism.

[1] Cf. *Summa Theologica*, translated by Fathers of the English
Dominican Province, Quest. 175, p. 63; Quest. 179, art. 1, pp. 99
sqq. (Burns Oates & Washbourne, 1922).

VIEW OF UNIVERSITY COLLEGE TAKEN
ABOUT 1600

EAST VIEW OF EAST GATE
(From a sketch by J. B. Malchair)

The subject is very intricate and difficult to follow, especially for the lay mind and in so bare an outline which is all that there is space for here; but in the *Life of Fogazzaro* by Signor Gallarati-Scotti, I came across a passage which seems to elucidate it, and translate it into more modern terms. The author is speaking of the beginning in Italy "of that movement towards mysticism which was the prelude to modernism"; and he refers to Maurice Blondel's "*L'Action: Essai d'une critique de la vie et d'une science de la pratique*, which Baron von Hügel called a "great book." [1] We might class Blondel as a modern follower of the nominalistic school. The book is now out of print, but Signor Gallarati-Scotti thus sums it up:

Written in a style whose density and concentration render it extremely obscure . . . the work nevertheless remains the corner stone of that school which by assuming an attitude of determined opposition to scholastic intellectualism, and sought confirmation of the supernatural, not by means of ratiocination, but through the inner moral experience of a truth that has been "lived." According to Blondel no demonstration can possibly create in us a faith in the supernatural; such faith can spring only from a deep-seated action, from our willingness to feel faith within ourselves.

Blondel has been skilfully elucidated by a more intelligible writer, Père Laberthonnière, a priest of the Oratory. In his small book, *Le Dogmatisme moral* (1898), he gave a general outline of his mystical philosophy. Of this book Gallarati-Scotti writes:

This essay is based upon a clever analysis of the various forms of dogmatism—the empiric, which considers the world as a system of things experienced, the intellectual which considers it as a system of ideas, the sceptical according to whose teachings we are condemned to move in a world of appearances from which there is no escape, and, finally, the illusory, which, in its empiric form, consists of the belief that we draw our being from sensation, and in its idealistic form attributes an ontological value to ideas as such. According to Laberthonnière our being is not derived either from sensations or from pure thought; were this the case, if exterior reality entered into us in its finished form, there could be neither error nor illusions. If ideas were put into us, we should all think alike. But, on the contrary, truth is not outside of us but within us, and it is from the inside that "we ourselves

[1] *The Mystical Element of Religion*, i., p. 48 (Dent, 1908).

derive what our ideas contain." In order then that ideas may be our own and be really ideas, we must have "lived them."

It is therefore necessary that we find them within ourselves if we are to know God and other beings truly and well. But to find them we must lay ourselves open to them and cause them to dwell within us. To accomplish this, it is important above all things to detach ourselves from the sway of the external world of phenomena, or in other words from the illusion that being is in things external. And this can be done only by an act of the will, by dying to ourselves the death of the mystic—the death of which St. Augustine and St. Paul speak. By means of this act of the will we seek to obtain the absolute certainty that He who is that God, is neither something that may be attained by vain gropings in space, nor an idea that may be discovered by means of dialectic demonstrations, but the life of our life, the very being of our being. Thus must we deify ourselves, not in the pantheistic sense, but by the communings of our will with the Will that is Divine. Our wishes must be God's wishes; thus the act of the will becomes an act of love, of the love that has nothing in common with desire that leads us to transform the object beloved into ourselves, but rather the love that leads us to transform ourselves into the object beloved. For God is not a geometrical theorem but a living reality; we do not prove Him, rather do we desire and love Him.

And he goes on to describe love in words which are almost identical with what Rolle says of the "high love of God," of which we shall speak in a later chapter, and shall therefore postpone the rest of the quotation from Laberthonnière until then.

This system is very much the same as Richard's. In Italy it resulted in modernism, and it is therefore all the more interesting to find that Richard was not free of this charge, even in the fourteenth century. In his Postil on *Job* he complains, "*Non acceptantes me quia modernus sum*"; and because he did not follow on the beaten track his teaching seemed to the ecclesiastical minds of that day mysterious. "*Mysterium mitto modernis.*" Thus does history, especially ecclesiastical history, repeat itself, and what Signor Gallarati-Scotti writes of Fogazzaro is true of Richard, who was in his day also looked askance at by those in high authority in the Church, so that it bears quotation:

He did not pause to inquire how [his theories] could be brought into full harmony with the most profound teachings of the philosophy of the Church. . . . He felt only that the perturbation of men's consciences and the vagaries into which philosophy had fallen demanded a solution through mysticism . . . the need of finding God by casting aside empty concepts that are not life-giving. If a renewal of the catholic spirit were possible it must begin at the very root in a fuller communion between each individual and the living loving Reality; it must be an entirely inner renewal, a return to the fountain head of all that is good and of all true liberty which is with us . . . the invisible battling of the will to remain staunch to the evangelical principle, accepted not with a part alone, but with the whole being; a battling to reach that true reform which is the result of the inner purification of each individual; to discover true unity, to be free and safe.[1]

The teaching of Ockham and his exposition of nominalism had a far-reaching influence upon religious thought. We can well understand the growing attraction it would have on Richard who by this time must have been at least seventeen and probably older,[2] since no student was admitted to attend philosophical disputations until he had passed the three years' course of the *Trivium*, and entered upon the *Quadrivium*. When we are young the personality of our teacher counts for more than his actual teaching. It is to those who have inspired us to search and learn for ourselves, rather than to the teacher whose lectures have been the clearest and of most practical use, that we owe the most, and so it was with Richard. There was something in the fervent love of the Franciscan friar which held the lad's attention; some word which he let drop may have set the spark of love alight in Richard's soul, and may have stirred the spirit of revolt which lay dormant in his nature.

But whether it was Ockham's influence, and the companionship of the two students of Merton, Burleigh and Bradwardine, which incited Richard to follow the mystic's quest; or whether it was a merely boylike irritation, and reaction from the subtle scholastic arguments and disputations, or from another cause of which we shall now speak, are matters for conjecture; but the fact remains that he left Oxford suddenly before the end of his course and without taking a degree.

[1] *Life of Fogazzaro*, translated by Mary Prichard Agnetti, pp. 198 sqq. (Hodder & Stoughton).
[2] Cf. chap. i., p. 9.

CHAPTER IV

RICHARD LEAVES OXFORD AND FLEES FROM HIS FATHER'S HOME TO BECOME A HERMIT

"At length, in his nineteenth year, considering that the time of mortal life is uncertain and its end greatly to be dreaded (especially by those who either give themselves to fleshly lusts or only labour that they may acquire riches, and who, for these things, devote themselves to guile and deceit, yet they deceive themselves most of all), by God's inspiration he took thought betimes for himself, being mindful of his latter end, lest he should be caught in the snare of sinners."—LESSON I.

Richard's dislike of theological subtleties—His desire is to know God rather than what God is—Was it this which drove him from Oxford? Or did he fear the publicity of "determinating"? Or was he in some peril of soul?—His early temptations and attitude towards women—The necessity for friendship and of true friendship between men and women—He follows the call of "interior melody" and flees from his home to seek solitude, habited in his sister's dress to resemble a hermit—Reaches a church at Topcliffe on the vigil of the Assumption, where he spends the night—In the morning uninvited he preaches at mass—All are amazed at his eloquence, and the squire, John de Dalton, invites him to dinner—Overcome by shyness he hides, but on being found dines with them—Afterwards the squire offers him a cell on his own estate.

THE sentence taken from the *Vite*, which heads this chapter, is the only actual datum upon which to construct any theory as to Richard's sudden exit from Oxford. No doubt there were many influences at work. We can easily understand the irritation of theological controversy to anyone of a mystical turn of mind, and judging from the many passages scattered throughout his books it is plain that Richard would have taken no pleasure in the barren debates of the schoolmen. His desire was always to know God, rather than to know about God.

This is borne out by a beautiful passage in *The Fire* (p. 33). The chapter is headed "Concerning Heretics, and

Faith in the Trinity," but heretics are dismissed shortly:
Their "frowardness" springs from

> an untaught and inordinate mind which is blinded by desire
> of its own excellence. . . . When the Christian religion wills
> to cut away all that is contrary, and fully accord in unity of
> love, the manner of heretics and the proud [it is noticeable
> that he classes them together] is to get new opinions, and to
> make known questions, unwont and from the saying of holy
> kirk, so that those things that true Christian men hold holy,
> they joy to scatter with their vanities.

There seems here to be a reminiscence of the "questions"
which were put by the master to the "sophisters" at the
logical "variations" that, as we have seen, were held in the
parvise during the students' third year at Oxford. For at
least a year Richard had had, with the other students, to
attend these logical "variations," where they disputed,
argued and responded on sophisms.[1] We can well imagine
how distasteful this must have been to him, and his
references to such knowledge are never sympathetic.

He spends neither time nor labour in refuting heresies,
or discussing points of doctrine. His exposition of the
true faith concerning the Trinity in this chapter is as
condensed as the Athanasian Creed, and has the same
beauty and rhythm, and is of course based upon it. And
then follows this passage on the knowledge of God, one of
the most beautiful in the book:

> Thou askest what God is? I answer shortly to thee: such a
> one and so great is He that none other is or ever may be of
> like kind or so mickle. If thou wilt know properly to speak
> what God is, I say thou shalt never find an answer to this
> question. I have not known; angels know not; archangels
> have not heard. Wherefore how wouldest thou know what is
> unknown and also unteachable? Truly God that is almighty
> may not teach thee what He Himself is. For if thou knew what
> God is thou shouldest be as wise as God is: that neither thou
> nor any other creature may be.
> Stand therefore in thy degree, and desire not high things.
> For if thou desirest to know what God is, thou desirest to be
> God; the which becomes thee not. Wot thou well God alone
> knows Himself, and may know. Truly it is not of God's un-
> power that He may not teach thee Himself as He is in Himself,
> but for His inestimable worthiness; for such a one as He is,

---

[1] Cf. Lyte, pp. 205 sqq.

none other may be. Soothly if He might be truly known, then were He not incomprehensible. It is enough for thee therefore to know that God is; and it were against thee if thou would know what God is.

Although we cannot conceive what God is, yet we may know Him perfectly; as he goes on to explain:

Also it is to be praised to know God perfectly; that is to say, He being unable to be fully conceived: knowing Him to love Him; loving Him to sing in Him; singing to rest in Him, and by inward rest to come to endless rest. Let it not move thee that I have said to know God perfectly, and I have denied that He may be known: since the prophet in the psalm has said: *Praetende misericordiam tuam scientibus te*, that is to say: "Thy mercy show to them knowing Thee."

Throughout his writings there are allusions to his dislike for the formalism and the subtleties of the "philosophers." In *The Fire* there are many very notable passages. He speaks there of

those taught by knowledge gotten, not inshed, and puffed up with folded arguments (p. 142);

and in the prologue describes how love did not come to him while

given without measure to disputation; but I have felt myself truly in such things wax cold, until putting a-back all things in which I might outwardly be occupied, I have striven to be only in the sight of my Saviour and to dwell in full inward burnings.

And he continues:

Wherefore I offer this book to be seen: not to philosophers nor wise men of this world, nor to great divines lapped in infinite questions, but unto the boisterous [1] and untaught, more busy to learn to love God than to know many things; for truly not disputing but working is to be known and loved. For I trow these things here contained may not be understood of these questionaries; in all science most high in wisdom, but in the love of God most low.

Therefore to them I have not written, except, all things forgetting and putting a-back that are longing [2] to this world, they love to be given only to the desires of our Maker. First truly *they must flee all earthly dignity, and hate all pride of*

---

[1] i.e. ignorant.   [2] Belonging.

knowledge and vainglory,[1] and at the last, conforming themselves to highest poverty, meditating and praying, they be
constantly given to the love of God.[2] (p. 13.)

One chapter of *The Fire* (v.) is entirely given to the
subject: "Whether it is better to take entent to the Love
of God than to Knowledge or Disputation." The last few
sentences especially have reference to those who "only
labour that they may acquire riches":

Wherefore let us seek rather that the love of Christ burn
within us than that we take heed to unprofitable disputation.
Whiles truly we take heed to unmannerly seeking, we feel
not the sweetness of the eternal savour. Wherefore many now
so mickle savour in the burning of knowledge and not of
love, that plainly they know not what love is, or of what savour;
although the labour of all their study ought to spread unto
this end, that they might burn in the love of God. Alas! for
shame! *An old wife is more expert in God's love, and less in
worldly pleasure, than the great divine, whose study is vain.*
For why? *because he studies for vanity*, that he may appear
glorious and so be known, and *may get rents and dignities*: the
which is worthy to be held a fool, and not wise. (p. 31.)

In those days the distinction between the learned and
the ignorant was very strongly marked, and often learning
and piety were spoken of in terms which might be
interpreted to mean that they were contradictory. This
was the view of the early Franciscans and there are numerous illustrations of it in the *Fioretti*. We remember how
Brother Giles praised Bonaventura for his learning, and
the saint replied that a poor old woman could love God
better than a learned theologian. Thereupon Giles cried out
to an old woman who was passing that she loved God
better than Bonaventura.

Richard shared their dread of learning; with him it
almost amounted to dislike. Although not a Franciscan, he
was imbued with their love for God, and their delight in
poverty and simplicity; and was instrumental in spreading
the doctrines of St. Francis in the north, since he became
the most widely read of all religious writers. This is testified to by reason of the quantity of MSS. extant which

[1] I make use of italics here and elsewhere in the text to draw
attention to any special point.
[2] All quotations from *The Fire of Love* or *The Mending of Life* are
from my modernised edition of Misyn's translation (Methuen, 1914).

E

contain his writings, and by the numberless other tracts and treatises, in prose and verse, which have been wrongly fathered upon him, since his name was so familiar and his fame widely spread.

Richard fled from Oxford before his ideas had had time to ripen, but it is possible that one immediate cause was his dread of the publicity of determinating, which we have alluded to in the previous chapter.

Yet there may have been another and more cogent reason which made the boy suddenly take flight. The sentence from the *Vite* quoted as a heading to this chapter may bear several interpretations, but it is certainly capable of bearing reference to some temptation. "By God's inspiration," it reads, "he took thought betimes for himself, being mindful of his latter end, lest he should be caught in the snare of sinners."

Dr. Horstman, to whom we owe so much, speaking of this period, says:

So, conceiving that salvation was not to be obtained through dialectics and philosophy but through flight from the world, and fearing some imminent danger for his soul, he in his 19th year, when he can scarcely be supposed to have attained to classic composure and to a sense of method and investigation, left the University and returned to his father's house . . .;

and in a note he adds: "It seems that he passed through an early love with all its bodily consequences"; and he even specifies the "young woman" as being the same "who continued to haunt his imagination in the beginning of his conversation" (*sic*) — he must mean conversion.[1]

This deduction is open to question and we shall consider it later; but there is no doubt whatever that Richard, both in the *Melum* and in *The Fire*, constantly refers to some early sin. In the latter he cries: "Lord God, have mercy on me! My youth was fond[2]; my childhood vain; my young age unclean"; and in an autobiographical passage in the former speaks of some early sin—before he had entered upon his lowly life of a hermit—which caused

[1] Library of Early English Writers: *Richard Rolle*, edited by C. Horstman, vol. ii., p. vi (Swan Sonnenschein, 1895).

[2] i.e. foolish.

him deep remorse, and inspired him with a resolve "to expiate the sin which as a boy I had committed." [1]

These words may refer to some escapade as a student in Oxford, or they may be merely the exaggerated language of the saint when he repents his early misdeeds. A mystical temperament involves an emotional one, in which the senses are fully employed. There has seldom been a life of a mystic in which this note does not re-echo. Francis of Assisi and Catherine of Siena are the great exceptions. Their love for God was so pure that it never seems to have been deflected by earthly passion, so that they came out of such temptations entirely unscathed.

Yet we have always to guard ourselves against misinterpreting the speech of the mystic, remembering that the symbolism of earthly love has perforce to be used for spiritual. The reader of the Song of Solomon can infuse what he wishes into the words he reads; yet no more beautiful poem of heavenly love exists. It has been used throughout the ages to express the inarticulate love of the soul for his Beloved, and his deep longing after that which is beyond, but which is his goal; and yet the language is purely sensuous.

Richard passed through more than one temptation. In the *Incendium* [2] he relates how he rightly was reproved

---

[1] It is useless to give references to the *Melum* as there is only one MS., not even foliated; but Dr. Horstman in the introductions to his two volumes of Rolle has given many extracts, from which I quote.

I give the passage in full from the original (MS. Dd. 5.64, 2. *Incendium*, lib. i., cap. xii., fol. 20):

"Infancia mea stulta fuit, puericia mea vana, adolescencia mea immunda; sed nunc Domine ihesu inflammatum est cor meum amore sancto, et renes mei commutati sunt. . . . Verumptamen jam dudum a tribus mulieribus dignam meritis reprehensionem accepi. Una me reprehendit quia cupiens corrigere insaniam earum in superfluitate et mollicie vestium ornatum illarum immoderatum nimis inspexi; que dixit quod non debui eas tantum considerare ut scirem utrum essent cornute vel non; et ut mihi videtur bene me redarguit et erubescere fecit. Alia me reprehendit quia de mammis eius grossis loquebar quasi me delectarent, que ait quid ad me pertineret si essent parve vel magne, et hec similiter recte locuta est. Tercia me in joco tangens, quia minabar quasi rude eam tangere vellem vel tetigi, dixit, 'Quiesce frater,' quasi dixisset non pertinet

[2] See also the Early English Text Soc. (Original Series, 106), bk. i., ch. xiii., p. 25.

by three women because he used them with too great
familiarity, and they made him ashamed. The fourth woman
seems to have been a member of the house (*cui ad modum
familiaris eram*), and he excuses himself by saying that these
things happened because he was seeking their well-being
(*salutem*), and he adds: "not that I have unlawfully desired
anything of them with whom I have for some while taken
my bodily sustenance." This last woman must therefore
have been a member of the Daltons' household; perhaps
some maidservant.

It was a rough age in which he lived, and the language
which Misyn employs in relating these temptations to our
ears sounds coarse. What in another would be mere horse-
play was—as one of the women reminds him—a lapse from
his estate (*non pertinet ad statum suum scilicet heremiticum
ludere cum mulieribus*). Thence we infer that this episode
belonged to a later time, after he had left Oxford and
definitely embraced the life of a hermit.

We have here, however, sufficient evidence to prove that
Richard was not impervious to the love of women, and
suffered, sometimes unwillingly, from their attention, for
in the same chapter he says: "And therefore I trow it is
better to want their speciality than to fall into their hands,
that know not, either in love nor in despite, to keep
measure" (p. 58).

In later life he learnt how to "keep measure," and he
may have owed much to Lady Dalton, his benefactress
and constant friend. Three of his books were expressly
written for women, and there were many spiritual friend-
ships between him and devout ladies, as we shall see.

ad statum suum scilicet heremiticum ludere cum mulieribus, et
illa etiam non immerito me confudit. Debui enim magis sustinuisse
quam aliud huiusmodi intulisse. Nam rediens ad meipsum, gratias
ago Deo meo quia per illarum verba me bonum docuit, et viam
suaviorem quam antea cognovi ostendit, ut amplius operante gratia
Christi, non inveniar reprehensibilis coram mulieribus in hac parte.
Quarta mulier, cui ad modum familiaris eram, non me reprehendendo
sed quasi contempnendo, dixit, 'Nichil habes nisi pulcrum visum
et pulcrum verbum, opus nullum habes.' Et ideo melius estimo
earum specialitate carere, quam in earum manus incidere que
modum nesciunt tenere sive in amore, sive in contemptu. Michi
autem ista contigerunt quia salutem earum procuravi, non quod
in eis aliquod illicitum appetivi cum quibus sustentacionem per
aliquod tempus accepi corporalem."

But in his early books, and especially in *The Fire*, there are some very bitter references to women which may be the outcome of personal experience; e.g. there is an almost autobiographical ring in the following:

> Women if they love men are fond, because they know not to keep measure in loving; and truly when they are loved they prick full bitterly. (p. 125.)

Beauty had a strong appeal for him:

> Truly the beauty of women beguiles many men, through desire whereof the hearts of the righteous also are some time overturned, so that they that began in spirit end in the flesh. Therefore beware, and in the good beginning of thy conversation keep no speech with women's fairness lest receiving thereof the venomous sickness of lust for to proffer and fulfil foulness of mind and being, deceived knowingly and cowardly, thou be drawn away by the discomfits [1] of thine enemies. Therefore flee women wisely and alway keep thy thoughts far from them, because, though a woman be good, yet the fiend by pricking and moving, and also by their cherishing [2] beauty, thy will can be overmickle delighted in them, because of frailty of flesh. (p. 126.)

And again:

> Yet, forsooth, friendship betwixt men and women may be perilous, for fair beauty lightly cherishes [3] a frail soul, and temptation seen sets fleshly desire on fire and ofttimes brings in the sin of body and soul; and so the company of women with men is wont to happen to the destruction of virtue. And yet this friendship is not unlawful but meedful; if it be had with good soul, and if it be loved for God and not for the sweetness of the flesh. (p. 173.)

There are many beautiful passages concerning friendship in this chapter. [4] It is impossible to read it and not perceive how rich and full a nature the writer must have had. Here I can only quote a short extract:

> True friendship certain is the sadness [5] of lovers, and comfort of minds; relief of grief, and putting out of worldly heaviness; reformation of sinners; increase of holiness; lessening of slander, and multiplying of good meed. While a friend is drawn from ill by his friend by healthful counsel and is inflamed to do good when he sees in his friend the grace that he desires to have. Holy friendship therefore that has medicine

---

[1] i.e. conquests. [2] Alluring. [3] Easily allures.
[4] Bk. II., ix. [5] Constancy.

for all wretchedness is not to be despised. From God it truly is that amid the wretchedness of this exile we be comforted with the counsel and help of friends, until we come to Him. Where we shall all be taught of God, and sit in eternal seats; and we shall be glad without end in Him that we have loved, and in whom and by whom we have friends.

From this friendship I can except no man, be he never so holy, but he needs it; unless there be any such to whom not man but angels serve. There are some that joy in God's love and are so moistened with His sweetness that they can say: *Renuit consolari anima mea*: "My soul gainsays to be comforted" with worldly cheer with which worldly lovers refresh themselves. Nevertheless it behoves that in these things that, according to nature and grace, are needful to their body, and in men they be delighted. Who eats or drinks or takes recreation from heat or cold, withouten liking? Who has a friend, and in his presence and speech and dwelling with him and taking part in his good, is not glad? Sickerly none but the mad and they that want reason, for in these things and others like is the life of man comforted—although it be the holiest—and joys most quickly in God. (pp. 174–5.)

We can infer from these passages, which can easily be multiplied, that there was no room in Richard's nature for any hatred of women, in spite of the hard things he sometimes writes concerning their wiles; in this same chapter we have an example: "These ladies and women," he says scornfully, "that are called worthy, that desire to be fair for a time and everlastingly to be foul." He was no celibate by nature, but the greater love absorbed the lesser. Indeed the mystic is one who either so greatly falls in love with his Beloved that other loves seem dimmed; or else there is the conflict. Then their dilemma is that of St. Paul: torn between two; harmony can only be obtained by refusal. For such a one the solution can only be as given so vividly by the writer of the *Imitation*: *Nudus, nudum Jesum sequi.*

However conflicting may have been the causes which led to Richard's flight from Oxford before his course of study was finished, it is clear from what followed that he was following some soundless call. For he is not satisfied when he returns to his father's house, he still longs for greater solitude: that "wilderness" of which he speaks so often:

I had great liking to sit in wilderness that I might sing more sweetly far from noise, and with quickness [1] of heart I

---

[1] i.e. fervour.

might feel sweetest praise; the which doubtless I received of His gift whom above all things I have wonderfully loved. (p. 141.)

He constantly speaks of song, and of singing; it is one of the dominant notes of his mysticism, and one by which he is most easily recognised. "The high love of Christ," he says, "stands in three things: in heat, in song, in sweetness." He sings for love, as did Francis. It is possible he may have heard the songs in the Provençal tongue which, as a child, Francis had learnt from his mother, and which the French students sang as they went about the streets of Oxford, as the Italians sang those of Jacopone. Italian was a strange language to Richard and may have fallen unheeded on his ear, but he must certainly have known French, although it seems to have had but slight influence upon him considering the time in which he wrote.

But apart from any outside influence the lover naturally seeks to express his feeling in song; and Richard had an innate gift of song. One wonders if he sang his way through the villages and towns he had to pass on his long journey from Oxford back to Yorkshire. It is not likely that he had much money in his purse but probably was dependent upon the kindness and good will of strangers for a night's lodging or for a meal, which he may have requited by song.

When he reached his native wolds, and looked down upon the squat Norman tower of the old church at Thornton he must have hesitated before he descended the hill. He could hardly have expected a very warm welcome home. Evidently Neville's intention had been that he should take Holy orders, but when he had to admit that he had returned with no degree his parents' disappointment must have been keen.

But whether he was welcomed or not he does not seem to have remained at home for long. He found there nothing to satisfy him, for "he loved God more than his earthly father." Even his beloved sister "whom he loved with tender affection" could not understand his longing, which was growing stronger and stronger, to flee away to some solitary place to be alone, so as to hear "the joyful song of God's love."

The story of his flight from home is fully told in the *Legenda* and is charming in its simplicity. Like a boy his first concern is with externals. He resolves to be a hermit so he must be clothed like one. Therefore he persuades his sister in loving terms to bring him two of her dresses, one white and one grey, to a wood beside the house. She trustingly does so, knowing nothing of what was in her brother's mind. Taking them from her, he cuts off the sleeves from the grey tunic, and the buttons from the white: "et modo quo poterat albe tunice manicas consuit, ut suo proposito aliqualiter aptaretur." Which I think must mean that he sewed up the white sleeves so as to be more like those of a hermit's dress. Most pictures of the women's dress of that time show a tight-fitting under sleeve, with a long, widely flowing upper sleeve belonging seemingly to an outer gown, which sleeves would be those he sewed up. He then strips and puts the white tunic next his skin, and the sleeveless grey one over it, through the empty armholes of which he thrusts his white sleeves. (He is evidently here trying to imitate a scapular.) Then taking his father's rain-hood (capuciavitque se pluviali capucio supradicto) he covers his head with it, "so that thus in some measure, as far as was then in his power, he might present a certain likeness (confusam similitudinem) to a hermit." The rain-hood apparently does duty for a cowl.

This account is not at all unlike the description of the dress of the early Austin hermit as given in Dugdale,[1] which dress would have been familiar to Richard; for close to Thornton-le-Dale, at Kirkham, there was a house of Augustinian Canons,[2] which hermits of the Augustinian Order would often frequent. We are told that their habit was a long gown, with brown sleeves and a fine cloth hood; and under these grey garments other white ones; and Stevens notes that "when they go abroad they put on over all a sort of Cowl and a large Hood, both Black; the Hood round before and hanging down to the Waste in a Point, being girt with a Black Leather Thong."

When Richard comes from behind the shelter of the trees to show himself in this strange disguise to his sister, instead of meeting with the admiration he no doubt expected, she

[1] Dugdale, vol. vi., pt. iii., p. 1590; and cf. Stevens' *Continuation*, vol. ii., p. 215.

[2] It was founded by Walter Espec and his wife, *c.* 1121, in honour of the Holy Trinity. See Dugdale, vol. vi., pt. i., p. 207.

cries out in her amazement, "My brother is mad! My brother is mad!" She calls so loudly that he is afraid of someone coming, so he drives her off "with threats," and takes to his heels, lest he should be caught and brought back again. Truly a delightful beginning of his life as a hermit, which life he seems to have followed quite steadfastly, for we never hear of his returning to his home.

Half running and half walking, towards evening he reaches a church about twenty-four miles from Thornton if one takes a straight course over the moors. It was close to the house where a John de Dalton lived, and therefore it is thought to have been at Topcliffe, near Thirsk, in which parish there was a township of the name of Dalton. Topcliffe was a dependency of the Percys who with the Nevilles were the two oldest families of Yorkshire. The Daltons had originally been dependants of these two great families but were not now. John de Dalton is called "squire" to denote that he belongs to the gentry, but he was not technically the squire of Topcliffe.

This part of the moor lying between Thornton and Topcliffe can have changed but little since the day when Richard took his flight. Still one meets with the rough stone crosses, such as that at Stape Cross, on the moor above Newton Dale. There is something very impressive even to the ordinary wayfarer in suddenly seeing this symbol in the lone expanse of heather and bracken and gorse, with the evening shadows creeping across and blending the purple, russet and yellow all into one indescribable colour. Sometimes a shaft of sunlight through the bars of cloud will strike upon some single tuft and make it gleam like gold. As the sun drew near its setting, and the arms of the cross were outlined against a blood-red sky, Richard must have felt some premonition of the fire of love which he was to experience later in so high a degree. We may picture him in his uncouth dress kneeling at the foot of the rough granite cross, already in his thought a hermit, and vowed for ever to the service of his King who "coroned was, with thorns sore pricking."

If in later years Richard's prayers so often turned to song, there is every reason to suppose that in his youth, which is the time which we associate with verse-making, his prayers and praises fitted themselves naturally to rhythm,

The lyrics printed in this book have no dates attached. They were copied together, but they were probably composed at many different times. Nor can we rightly use the word "composed" for such spontaneous utterances. As he knelt there in speechless prayer, words such as these might take form and sing themselves to ease the pent-up feelings in his heart: [1]

> Jesus that dydest on the Rood
>   for the love of me,
> And boughtest me with Thy blood
>   Thou have mercy of me.
> What me letteth of any thing
>   for to love Thee,
> Be it me lief, be it me loth,
>   Thou do it away from me.

Or :

> In love Thou wound my thought,
> And lift my heart to Thee.
> My soul Thou dear hast bought,
> Thy lover make it be.
> Thee I covet,
> This world nought,
> And from it I flee.
> Thou art That I have sought.
> Thy face when may I see?

With some such words as these making music in his heart, or singing them aloud, we can picture the boy bounding over the moors, exultant in his sense of freedom and escape from all trammels, filled with hope; seeing visions of a wonderful future, committing his whole life with all its daily happenings into the hands of God, and filled with the desire to lift up those that were down, so that they too might share his happiness and be warmed by the fire which was enkindling him.

At vesper time he reaches a church, "on the vigil," we are told, "of the Assumption of the most blessed Virgin, Mother of God, and therein he set himself to pray." The candles are lit, and he kneels at a faldstool where he can gaze at the lamp burning before the hanging Pyx, and is

---

[1] It is not my intention to intersperse Richard's life with his lyrics, but this point cannot too early be emphasised. Though of necessity the lyrics have to be gathered together, and form a separate part of this volume, they ought really to be woven into the fabric of his life as part of its tissue, so full are they of his personal devotion to Christ.

THORNTON-LE-DALE AS IT IS TO-DAY

so lost in his prayer that he does not notice the little stir in the congregation when the lady of the manor enters with her servants for vespers. Her heart is touched by the sight of the boy in this odd dress in such deep devotion, and she will not let him be disturbed. After the service, as Richard rises, her sons who had returned from studying at Oxford recognise him as a former student whom they had known there.

We are not told where Richard spent that night, the turning-point of his life. He may have remained in the chapel watching and keeping tryst with his Beloved. It was a night in which, to use his own words, "the habitations of the lovers were builded in one"; when "first my heart waxed warm with the fire of love, and lovely ditties rose up within me." Some of his experience must have found voice when, the next morning, entirely unasked, he finds a surplice which he puts on, and sings the office of matins with the rest of the congregation. Then at mass, incited by the same sense of exaltation, after the singing of the gospel, he asks the priest for a blessing, and mounts the pulpit, where he moves his hearers to tears. The love, and penitence, and yearning of his heart have found vent in words which call forth a wonderful response, for "they all said that they had never before heard a sermon of such virtue and power."

But the sermon over, the reaction follows. He had spoken with the inspiration of the poet, and the supernatural knowledge of the mystic; stirred by his passionate love for Christ no barrier could restrain him, and he had fearlessly faced a strange congregation. But now the Divine afflatus has left him, and he becomes again a shy, timid runaway; a truant from his own home as well as from his university. Being invited by the squire to dinner he takes refuge in some garret where he hopes no one will find him. We give the rest of the tale in the words of the *Vite*. We notice that the writer interprets his shyness as humility, taking the opportunity, as is his wont, to show how the "sanctus Ricardus" thus follows the teaching of the gospel.

Therefore, after mass, the aforesaid squire invited him to dinner, but when he entered his manor he betook himself to a certain mean and old room; for he would not enter the hall, but sought rather to fulfil the teaching of the gospel, which says, "When thou art invited to a wedding, sit down in the lowest room; that when he that bade thee cometh, he may say unto thee, Friend, go up higher," and this too was fulfilled in him. For when the squire had sought for him diligently, and at last found him in the aforesaid room, he set him above his own sons at the table. But he kept such perfect silence at dinner that not a word proceeded from his mouth. And when he had eaten enough he rose, before the table was removed, and prepared to depart. But the squire who had invited him said that this was not customary, and so prevailed upon him to sit down again. When the meal was over he again wished to depart, but the squire, seeking to have some private talk with him, detained him until all who were in the room had gone, when he asked him if he were the son of William Rolle. Then he rather unwillingly and with reluctance answered: "Perchance I am"; since he feared that if he were recognised the plan on which his mind was set would be hindered. For this squire loved his father as a friend with warm affection. But Richard—newly made a hermit without his father's knowledge and against his wish—had taken this estate upon him because he loved God more than his earthly father.

And when the aforesaid squire had examined him in private, and convinced himself by perfect evidence of the sanctity of his purpose, he, at his own expense, clad him according to his wish, with clothing suitable for a hermit; and kept him for a long time in his own house, giving him a place for his solitary abode and providing him with food and all the necessaries of life. Then he began with all diligence, by day and night, to seek how to perfect his life, and to take every opportunity he could to advance in contemplative life, and to be fervent in divine love.

John de Dalton must have been a devout man, and one of some discernment to have taken so much interest in this strange lad; though no doubt he was primarily influenced by his friendship and love for Richard's father. It is therefore hardly conceivable that he would have sheltered the would-be hermit, and kept him for so long a time under his own roof, without the consent of Richard's parents; nor, considering how near Topcliffe was to Thornton, is it likely that his sojourn there could have been hidden from them, even if the boy had wished it. Probably Dalton arranged matters with William Rolle, who, if poor, may not have been altogether sorry to be relieved from the responsibility of a son who had so far done little to justify his hopes.

But as is often the case, the stranger saw farther into the heart of Richard than had his own father; and he expressed his sympathy in a way which would at once have won any lad of that age, by providing him, "at his own expense," with "clothing suitable for a hermit." John de Dalton seems to have had unusual understanding of youth, perhaps because his own sons had been at Oxford. They had known Richard there, and may have told their father of events and happenings of which we know nothing. Whatever they said must have redounded to Richard's credit, otherwise the squire would not have welcomed him so willingly into his house, nor set aside a place for his "solitary abode"; as it is in the original: "et ipsum in domo sua diu retinuit, dans sibi locum mansionis solitare."

CHAPTER V

RICHARD DWELLS WITH THE DALTONS: LIVES HARDLY AND IS TEMPTED

*"Because there are many steps preparatory to the kindling of this love—as, for example, those things which diminish and remove the loves opposed to it—therefore this saint wore down the lusts of the flesh ; . . . He spurned the world too with its riches, being content with only the bare necessaries of life, that he might more freely enjoy the delights of true love. For these reasons, therefore, he mortified his flesh with many fasts, with frequent vigils, and repeated sobs and sighings, quitting all soft bedding, and having a hard bench for a bed, and for a house a small cell ; fixing his mind always on heaven, and desiring to depart and be with Christ his most sweet Beloved."—*LESSON V.

Yorkshire from early times was sought out as a solitude for hermits—The islands of Coquet and Farne—SS. Cuthbert, Henry, Bartholomew—Richard's attraction towards the solitary life and praise of it—He accepts the squire's offer of a cell on his estate and begins there his life as a hermit—The life of voluntary suffering and penance has been in all ages the means to attain union with God—Richard treads the *via purgativa*—His advice to others concerning fasting, watching, and hardships and his own practice—Tempted of the devil and by the powers of evil—They attack him through others by calumny and detraction — This time of conversion "wherein he was truly turned to God" lasted for three years until the "opening of the heavenly door."

RICHARD was not original in his choice of a hermit's life. From the thirteenth century onwards, we find records of an enormous number of hermitages and anchorages. From the tabulated lists in Miss Clay's book on *The Hermits and Anchorites of England* they seem to have been most plentiful in the fourteenth century, and by far the greatest number are found in the northern counties. In Yorkshire alone she notes a hundred. It was not surprising that the wild spaces of that great and sparsely inhabited county should attract solitaries, for it was easy to find there remote and quiet spots far from the haunts of men and yet within distance of one of the many abbeys and priories which were scattered over the three Ridings where the hermit could find a confessor and hear mass.

Farther north the islands of Farne and Cocket, or Coquet, had been renowned from very early times for their hermit saints.[1] We have only to recall the names of Aidan, Bishop of Lindisfarne, and Cuthbert who succeeded him; but two years later the latter resigned his bishopric, to live as a hermit on one of the small islands of Farne, dying there in 687. The Isle of Coquet lay to the south of Farne Island, and when St. Cuthbert visited it he found it inhabited by many hermits; but there is little knowledge to be gained of them until much later, in the twelfth century, when the fame of St. Henry spread; he died on the island in 1127, quite alone. A beautiful story is told of his death, how far away other hermits heard the singing of a choir, and when it ceased a bell tolled. They hastened to the hermitage but could find no one living; only seated on a stone in his cell was the dead body of the saint, stark and cold, and beside him burnt a candle lit by no human hand.

We know too of Bartholomew who lived on one of the Farne Islands for over forty-two years, and whose life was told by Gaufridus. He also died in solitude. The monks from Lindisfarne had administered the last holy rites and left him, and when they returned they found his body lying near to the stone coffin which the old hermit had lengthened with his own hands, as when it was brought to him he found it was too short.

Guthlac (d. 714) lived in the fenny marshes of Croyland near his sister; and three centuries later Godric dwelt at Finchale, which valley he had discovered in a forest north of Durham. There he made a cave in the earth near the bank of the River Wear. A spot is still pointed out as "St. Godric's Garth." He protected the birds, tamed "serpents," and made the stags and wolves and other beasts obey him. For sixty years he dwelt at Finchale and thousands of pilgrims resorted to his shrine. And still nearer to Richard's time there was the famous Robert of Knaresborough. He was a citizen of York and died in 1218. Richard must have heard many a tale told about him. His cave lay about a mile below the castle of Knaresborough under a rock. After his death Brother Ive, another hermit, lived there, and others after him. His chapel became a place of pilgrim-

[1] See *The Hermits and Anchorites of England*, by R. M. Clay, in "Antiquary" series Methuen, (1914).

age and it is quite possible that Richard was numbered among the pilgrims who frequented it; many miracles of healing we are told were wrought there.

It was not unnatural that a lad of Richard's independent character should choose for himself the life of a solitary; although Yorkshire was famed at that time for the number of its monastic houses. There were fourteen great abbeys, one of which, Byland, was in that part of the North Riding which is most closely associated with Richard's name. There were besides ten priories, thirty friaries, thirteen cells and twenty collegiate churches. Yet Richard, in spite of having in Oxford come under Franciscan influence at its best, was not attracted towards any institutional life.

He has much to say in praise of the "solitary or hermit's life" in *The Fire*, especially in chapters xiii. and xiv. from which I quote:

Some [he says] have been, and peradventure are yet alive, that alway set life in common before solitary life, against whom there is not mickle to dispute, because that life only they praise, the which they either covet to keep, or at least know full little. Truly they praise not solitary life for they know it not.

And he explains the true meaning of Eccles. iv. 10, *Vae soli*, i.e. without God:

He truly is alone with whom God is not.

Forsooth he that chooses solitary life for God, and leads it in good manner is not near woe but fair virtue; and the Name of Jhesu shall continually delight his mind; and the more men dread not to take that life which is without the solace of man, the more shall they be gladdened with the comfort of God. Ghostly visitations ofttimes they receive, the which set in company they know not at all. Therefore it is said to a beloved soul, "I shall lead her into the wilderness, and there shall I speak unto her heart." [1]

Some truly are taught by God to desire (the) wilderness for Christ, and to hold a singular purpose; the which forthwith, that they may more freely and devoutly serve God, forsaking the common clothing of the world, despise all transitory things, and cast away temporal things; and excelling in height of mind they desire only everlasting joy, and are only given to devotion and contemplation, and every effort of their life they cease not to give to the love of Christ.

The righteous hermits . . . live in the charity of God and

---

[1] Hos. ii. 14. I have slightly altered and abbreviated the foregoing passage.

of their neighbour; they despise worldly praise; as mickle
as they can they flee man's sight; they hold ilk man more
worthy than themselves; they continually give their minds
to devotion; they hate idleness; they manly gainstand fleshly
lusts; they savour, and burningly seek, heavenly; earthly
they covet not, but forsake; in sweetness of prayer they are
delighted. Truly some of them feel the sweetness of eternal
refreshment; and with chaste heart and body, with the unde-
filed eye of the mind, behold God and the citizens of heaven.
(pp. 59–60.)

But the hermit's life is great only "if it be greatly done."
It has to be strengthened first by hardship.

Because by the bitter drink of penance they have loved
great labour, they are now set afire with the love of high
contemplation, and alone are worthy to take heed to God,
and to bide the kingdom of Christ.

And he cites St. Sampson and the "blessed Maglorius."
They were both in turn bishops of Dol, in Brittany. The
latter when a very old man left Dol to seek a quiet spot
in Jersey, and there lived as a hermit until the outbreak
of a plague when he healed many, but died probably of
the same sickness. Richard continues:

Saint Cuthbert, also, went from his bishopric to an anchorite's
life.
Therefore if such men have done thus for to have more
meed, who of good mind will be hardy to set any state in holy
kirk before solitary life? Truly in this they occupy themselves
with no outward things, but only take heed to heavenly contemplation; and that they be continually warm in the love
of Christ, and set worldly business perfectly behind.
Wherefore a heavenly noise sounds within them, and full
sweet melody makes the solitary man merry; for clatterings
distract them who are set among many, and but seldom suffer
them to think or pray. Of which solitary the psalmist speaks
in the Song of Love, saying: "I will go into the place of the
marvellous tabernacle, into the house of God." And he describes
the manner of going, in rejoicing and songs of praise, saying:
In voce exultationis et confessionis; that is to say: "In voice
of gladness and shrift." And that loneliness withouten noise
and bodily song, is needful to that—that man may receive
that songful joy, and hold it in joying and singing—he openly
shows in another place: *Elongavi, inquit, fugiens; et mansi in
solitudine*. That is to say: "Fleeing by myself, I have with-
drawn, and in [the] wilderness I have dwelt."
In this life truly he is busy to burn in the fire of the Holy

F

Ghost, and into the joy of love to be taken and comforted by God to be glad. For the perfect lonely man hugely burns in God's love; and while in surpassing of mind he is rapt above himself by contemplation, he is lift up joying unto that sweet and heavenly noise.[1] (pp. 60–2.)

It is clear from this, although he was writing many years after he had left his father's house, that Richard's longing for a hermit's life was very deep; yet even as a hermit he strikes out a free and independent course for himself. He attaches himself to no eremitical Order; although later, when he wrote the *Regula Heremitarum*, he had certainly the hope of forming some community of hermits; but that is a very different thing from submitting to the rule of another. His rules are self-imposed. He wishes to seek God in solitude, undisturbed by the routine and work of a religious house, and also he would be free of all mundane concerns such as food, clothing, etc., neither had he the wherewithal to procure such for himself without the distraction of begging.

All these considerations no doubt weighed with him, although when the squire talked with him after supper he may only have been conscious of his desire to escape from the ties and interruptions of his life at home; to be entirely free and at rest to listen to the songs of love which were flooding his soul. It seemed to him as if his thought was turned into song and his mind was changed into full sweet sound. It was this which had made him flee across the moors, singing his songs of love, and take refuge in the chapel, where he could spend the night undisturbed; and this interior melody had forced him, in spite of his natural sensitiveness and shyness, to ascend the pulpit and preach his impassioned sermon.

What therefore could be more welcome than John de Dalton's offer to give him a solitary place apart in his own house and provide food and all the necessaries of life? It must have seemed to the lad almost as the finger of God, and he gladly accepts, for this is exactly what he longs for: quiet to listen and to rest in the "high love of Christ";

[1] This should be compared with the passage from St. Augustine's *Enarration on Psalm xli.*, quoted by Abbot Butler in *Western Mysticism: The Teaching of SS, Augustine, Gregory and Bernard on Contemplation*; with "*Afterthoughts*," p. 29 (Constable, 1928).

"which love soothly stands in three things: in heat, in song and in sweetness. And I am expert in mind that these three cannot long remain without great rest" (p. 66).

Richard's life as a hermit seems to have developed somewhat slowly. First he is evidently one of the members of Dalton's household; though probably living a studious life, spending much time in prayer and in the chapel, and perhaps feeding apart. Later he has removed some distance from the manor house, for in Lesson VIII. we are told that "a certain lady [probably Lady Dalton herself] was drawing near to death—in whose manor Richard had a cell but a long way off from the family, where he was wont to live alone and give himself to contemplation."

Still later in life, when he has removed to Richmond, he appears to be living the solitary life of a normal hermit, in a cell quite unattached. Perhaps this earliest period of his life is of the most interest; when, as he says, "turned to Christ with all my heart I am tied first by true penance" (p. 78). These are the days of effort and struggle when "seeking to forsake all things that long to vanity, I shall be ravished to sing in songful and tuneful melody." But before he can sing the songs of Sion he must, in the language of the mystic, tread the purgative way, or as it is sometimes called, the way of negation.

In the early stages of every life which has an objective this path has to be taken; for there are always temptations to be attracted by other things and allured towards other interests, whether the way chosen leads to political or social fame; towards the attainment of wealth, or scientific discovery; or whatever it may be. Perhaps the purgation or negation—whichever term we like to use—is the sharpest for those who are urged by the desire of creating, and are continually goaded by the effort to embody in some actual material, whether it be words, stone, paint, or sound, the vision of which they catch fleeting glimpses.

The attainment of this union with the Divine is potentially within the reach of all; but the achievement is so exacting and so arduous that few have persevered in the quest. Because it is possible for everyone the lives of the mystics are of perennial interest. For the mystic is one who counts all things as loss so that he may win Christ. He is content to give all, that he may possess All; to strip himself that he may follow the naked Christ; to empty himself that Christ may have space. Of necessity the first part of this journey must lie along the road of negation, or mortification, by which alone it is possible to enter into close union with God. Not only must the soul be tested by temptation, but it has to be mortified and purified by voluntary penance.

However greatly the modern mind may rebel against the idea of voluntary suffering, alike in non-Christian and Christian mysticism it appears to be the sole means of attaining to any close communion of the soul with that which lies beyond. To the Christian it is in addition the effort of the lover to share in the sufferings of his Beloved; to partake of His Passion.

Through all the ages this has been so. It is no outworn method practised by the saints of mediaeval days. We have but to remember the recently published biographies of such men as Charles de Foucault and Father William Doyle, S.J. The latter, perhaps, appeals to us the most, being nearer to our own lives. He lived a normal, cheerful life, beloved by all, and if it had not been for his sudden death in the trenches, so that he had no opportunity of destroying his private journals, none would have guessed of the physical austerity which lay hidden beneath his friendly gaiety. It is a fact the value of which must be tested to be experienced. Arguments concerning it will neither convince us nor prove its truth, and if our courage shrinks from personal experience then we must needs rest upon the testimonies of the saints of all ages. The form such sufferings take depends largely upon temperament; thus we have the repugnant asceticism of St. John of the Cross, of Suso and, in a lesser degree, of Tauler, but to the joyous nature of St. Francis it was a sheer delight to chastise brother ass, Poverty was his bride, whom he embraced with song.

But Richard apparently found no joy in mortification. It seems to be one of the distinguishing marks of what we may call the English type of mysticism that voluntary suffering is not unduly stressed. A certain amount of bodily penance was in the Middle Ages an ordinary part of the Christian's life; there was nothing abnormal or unusual in it, although it might be, and very often was, exaggerated. It is noticeable, however, that when Richard refers to such things as watching, fasting and penance, he is always, in his advice to others, on the side of moderation.

Here, for instance, is his advice concerning fasting:

In meat and drink be thou scarce and wise. Whiles thou eatest or drinkest let not the memory of thy God that feeds thee pass from thy mind; but praise, bless, and glorify Him in ilka morsel, so that thy heart be more in God's praising than in thy meat, that thy soul be not parted from God at any hour. Thus doing, before Christ Jesu thou shalt be worthy a crown, and the temptations of the fiend, that in meat and drink awaits most men and beguiles them, thou shalt eschew. . . . The unwise and untaught, which have never felt the sweetness of Christ's love, trow that unwise abstinence be holiness; and they trow they can not be worthy of great meed anent God unless they be known as singular of all men by scarceness and unrighteous abstinence.

But truly abstinence by itself is not holiness, but if it be discreet it helps us to be holy. If it be indiscreet it lets holiness, because it destroys discipline, without which virtues are turned to vice. If a man would be singular in abstinence he ought to eschew the sight of men and their praising, that he be not proud for nought and so lose all: for men truly ween they be holiest that they see most abstinent, when in truth ofttimes they are the worst. (p. 210.)

It is very certain that he esteems fasting of little account compared with the love of God; it is safe only for the lover to fast, otherwise it only tends towards vainglory. In other words, fasting is useless and worse as an end in itself, but as the outcome of love it has worth.

He continues:

He certain that has truly tasted the sweetness of endless love shall never deem himself to pass any man in abstinence, but the lower he supposes himself in abstinence anent himself, the more he shall be held marvellous anent men. The best thing, and as I suppose pleasing to God, is to conform thyself in meat and drink to the time and place and estate of them with whom thou art; so that thou seem not to be wilful nor a feigner of religion.

And what could be wiser advice than this:

Truly it is wholesome counsel that they that fast little give preference to them of greater abstinence, and since they may not do so great abstinence be sorry in mind. And they that are of great abstinence should trow others higher in virtue; whose virtue, in which they surpass, is hidden to men, whiles *their* virtue, that is to say abstinence, is praised of many. But unless it be dight with meekness and charity before Christ, it is nought.

But far above fasting or any penance that is seen of men he sets love:

Truly the virtue of others is the more in that it is not seen of men. Who may know how much love a man has anent God, how great compassion anent his neighbour? And doubtless the virtue of charity surpasses without comparison all fasting or abstinence, and all other works that may be seen; and oft it happens that he that before men is seen least to fast, within, before Christ, is most fervent in love.

It behoves him truly to be strong that will manfully use the love of God. The flesh being enfeebled with great disease ofttimes a man cannot pray, and then mickle more he cannot lift himself to high things with hot desire. I would rather therefore that a man failed for the greatness of love than for too mickle fasting; as the spouse said of herself: *Nunciate dilecto quia amore langueo*; that is: "Show thyself to my love for I long for love." (pp. 211–12.)

This chapter of *The Mending of Life* from which I have quoted is headed: "Of the Setting of Man's Life," and it should be compared with *The Form of Living* (chap. vi.) where he speaks of "temperance and discretion in meat and drink": "Both come to one end, excess and over-fasting; for neither is God's will—and that many will not suppose for anything one may say. . . ." This book was written for a nun of Ainderby, Margaret Kirkby, and he counsels her to beware of over-great abstinence which causes tremblings, "as if thou wert ready to give up the ghost. And wit thou well thou didst sin that deed . . . I counsel thee that thou shalt eat better and more, as it comes, that thou be not beguiled." But "afterward when thou hast proved many things, and overcome many temptations, and knowest better thyself and God than thou didst, then if thou seest that it be to be done, thou mayst take to greater abstinence. And meanwhile thou mayst do privy penance which all men need not know." He wisely says: "Righteousness is not all in fasting or in eating; but thou art righteous if contempt and praise, poverty and riches, hunger and need, or delights and dainties be all alike to thee. If thou takest these with love of God I hold thee blessed and high before Jesus." [1]

He more than once speaks of the wisdom of sitting to pray, lest the body become unduly weary and should hinder rather than help the soul, and he himself is seated when he receives the great mystical experience which he fully records, and which will be given in detail in the following chapter.

But we must bear in mind that this wise counsel was the result of his more mellowed judgment. *The Fire, The Mending* and *The Form* were all written later, long after these first years of his hermit's life, during which he was purified and tried by penance. He was no sparer of himself in these years as we can gather from the many glimpses of his life which he gives in the *Melum*.

The compiler of the *Vite* is content to say what might be said of any holy man: "He mortified his flesh with many fasts, with frequent vigils, and repeated sobs and sighings; quitting all soft bedding and having a hard bench for a bed, and for a house a small cell." In the *Melum* we have a more individual account. It is clearly a youthful writing, and has the personal subjective note which we usually find in youth. Dr. Horstman thinks it was written when Richard was twenty-six years of age, during a time of mental stress and conflict when his ideas were as yet confused, and he was seeking to defend himself against his detractors and against calumny. We find here no trace of joy in the austerities which he undertakes, which were in a measure the harder because he was then living within the reach of the ordinary comforts of life, perhaps under the same roof as the squire and his lady.

I quote the following passages from the *Melum* together, although possibly some may refer to the short period after Richard left the Daltons, when Dr. Horstman thinks he mixed freely with men and women in order to teach and preach. In any case they show that his life was never one of ease, and that in spite of the moderation he preaches to others his own personal asceticism severe. He practises great poverty and self-abnegation; he suffers the extremes

[1] *The Form of Perfect Living*, edited by Dr. Hodgson, pp. 38 sqq. (London, Baker, 1910).

of heat and cold, sometimes having only rags to cover him
and not even water to drink. Here are his own words:

Finally, dwelling among the rich, rotten rags hardly covered
me, and in my nakedness I was annoyed with the bites of
flies which no comfortable covering prevented from walking
over me, and my skin became rough with ingrained dirt; and
yet in warm weather I was tormented by the heat among men
who were enjoying all the shade that they desired; and my
teeth chattered with the cold while they were indulging in
rich adornments and rejoicing in superfluities: although
nevertheless they loved not the Giver of these things.

And this also must refer to a later experience:

I give glad praise to the Lawgiver, and with joy, without
sadness or languor, I lift up my soul to the Light because now
I have no power at all, nor have I anything which I receive
except what others beg for the poor; and I do not get food
when I want but as men are willing to give me. I am not
ashamed to be abased among the poor by the powerful and
to suffer from hunger. While those who flourish like the grass
make holiday, I am tortured with thirst, unpitied by the
worldly, nor have even water to quench it, while they drink to
excess; but their happiness is shortlived.

No wonder that his health is undermined and that he
suffers from excruciating headaches.

Indeed I have so weakened my flesh, and suffer so from
headaches in consequence, that I cannot stand, so bad are
they, unless I am strengthened by wholesome food.

The Sequence in the mass for his feast is full of references
to this time of purgation.

Uitam illam hic mercatus,
carnis tulit cruciatus,
datus penitencie.

.   .   .   .

Amor thema fit doctrine,
et celestis discipline,
cor uertens in faculam.

.   .   .   .

Studet, legit, scribit et suplicat,
deo totum se factis dedicat,
mundi dolos et carnis abdicat
ut hostes nequissimos.[1] Etc.

---

[1] See Dr. Woolley's *Officium*, p. 36.

Which may be translated thus:

He purchased here the heavenly life, he bore the torments of the flesh; he gave himself to penitence.

Love he made the theme of his teaching and of heavenly discipline, turning his heart to a torch.

He studies, reads, writes and prays, by his deeds he wholly gives himself to God; he renounces the snares of the world and the flesh, which he holds [as] his most noxious enemies.

It is undeniable that suffering undertaken voluntarily and against all common sense solely for the love of God, is a supreme venture of faith, and has strange and often far-reaching results. It seems as if the barriers which hedge us in in this world are broken. Like St. Paul, men are conscious that they "wrestle not against flesh and blood, but against spiritual wickedness in high places." In mediaeval times this wickedness seemed sometimes to assume material forms, and thus arose the sundry legends of attacks of demons, which figure also in the life of Richard the hermit. Certainly, if we believe in a personal devil, we can easily conceive that few things would cause him greater anger than to see men and women trying to curb and subdue the physical side of their nature, which is the very avenue by which he hopes most easily to lead his victim astray.

In the *Vite* we have two accounts of Richard's personal contact with the devil. The first belongs to this time, for it evidently took place just at the beginning of his conversion, and is taken "from a writing in the saint's own hand found after his death in a small volume of his works." [1] The story referred to in this lesson is found in the Thornton MS. under the title: *Narracio. A tale that Richard Hermit made.*

There is another copy in MS. Harl. 1822, which is slightly earlier than the Thornton. In it the *Narration* forms the last paragraph of the *Oleum Effusum*, to which it is appended as an example of the virtue of the Name of Jesus, and is thus introduced:

Soothly I have no wonder if he tempted, falls, that puts not the name of Ihesu in lasting mind . . . for there may no wicked spirit noy where Ihesu is mickle in mind or named in

---

[1] See Lesson VII., p. 305.

mouth; therefore the name of Ihesu is busily to be held in mind.

And the scribe continues straightway this tale of Richard's:

When I had taken my singular purpose and left the secular habit, and I began more to serve God than man, it fell on a night as I lay in my rest, in the beginning of my conversion, there appeared to me a full fair young woman the which I had loved before, and she loved me not a little in good love. And when I had beholden her, and I wondered why she came so in the night in the wilderness, suddenly without more speech, she laid her beside me. And when that I felt her there, I dreaded that she should draw me to evil, and said I would rise up and bless us in the name of the Holy Trinity; and she strained me so stalwartly that I had no mouth to speak, nor no hand to stir. And when I saw that I perceived well that there was no woman but the devil in shape of a woman. Therefore I turned me to God and with my mind I said: "O Ihesu, how precious is Thy blood," making the cross with my finger in my breast; and as fast, she wax weak and suddenly all was away. I thanked God that delivered me, and soothly from that time forth I forced me to love Ihesu; and ay the more I profited in the love of Ihesu, sweeter I found it; and from that day it went never from my mind, therefore blessed be the name of Ihesu in the world of worlds. Amen.

Here, clearly, we have the conflict in Richard's mind between earthly and heavenly love. From time immemorial it has been the great struggle of the mystic, and it has constantly been misinterpreted because of the difficulty of finding fitting symbols for supernatural love, so that men have turned to the great Hebrew love song to find expression for a love which transcends all human experience. True love is of the will, yet the emotions must play a large part, and the mystic is one who is peculiarly susceptible to the emotional element, and who is therefore especially liable to be tempted keenly through the sensuous side of his nature. A vivid consciousness of a personal God is his dower, and a subdual of the sensual so as to leave free and unimpeded course for the spiritual, is one of the initial struggles, depicted in some form or another, in the life of every mystic.

In Richard's case the struggle seems to have been sharp, but of brief duration, for all his allusions to such temptations refer to his early life, as does this *Narration*.

In the famous fifteenth chapter of the *Incendium*, which

begins, *"Cum infeliciter florerem et in juventus vigilantis adolescentie jam advenisset"*—which chapter is often found as a separate tract in the early printed editions of Rolle's Latin works, and in some MSS. under the title of the whole work, *Incendium Amoris*—the opening paragraph seems to have reference to this experience:

When I was prospering unhappily, and had attained to youth of wakeful age (*vigilantis adolescentie*), the grace of my Maker was near, the which restrained the lust for temporal shape, and turned it into a spiritual embrace to be desired; and lifting my soul from low things has borne it to heaven, so that I might truly burn with desire for the everlasting happiness, more than I ever before was gladdened by carnal company, or by worldly softness. (p. 69.)

This was probably what he calls the beginning of the change of his life and of his mind, which he describes in the chapter headed "Conversion" in *The Mending of Life*. He asks:

What is turning to God but turning from the world and from sin; from the fiend and from the flesh? What is turning from God but turning from unchangeable good to changeable good; to the liking beauty of creatures; to the works of the fiend; to lust of the flesh and the world? Not with going of feet are we turned to God, but with the change of our desires and manners.

.   .   .   .   .   .

To be turned from the world is naught else but to put aback all lust, and to suffer the bitterness of this world gladly for God; and to forget all idle occupations and worldly errands, in so mickle that our soul, wholly turned to God, dies pithily to all things loved or sought in the world. Therefore being given to heavenly desires they have God evermore before their eyes, as if they should unwearily behold Him. (p. 198.)

.   .   .   .   .   .

And there are many lettings [1] so that the eyes of our heart may not be fixed on God; of which we put some: abundance of riches; flattering of women; the fairness and beauty of youth. This is the threefold rope that scarcely may be broken [2]; and yet it behoves to be broken and despised that Christ may be loved.

He that desires to love Christ truly, not only without

---

[1] i.e. hindrances.   [2] Eccles. iv. 12.

heaviness but with a joy unmeasured, he casts away all things that may let him. And in this case he spares neither father nor mother, nor himself; he receives no man's cheer; he does violence to all his letters [1]; and he breaks through all obstacles. Whatever he can do seems little to him so that he may love God. He flees from vices as a brainless [2] man, and looks not to worldly solace, but certainly and wholly directed to God, he has nearly forgotten his sensuality. He is gathered all inward and all lifted up into Christ, so that when he seems to men as if heavy, he is wonderfully glad. (p. 199.)

This passage has an autobiographical ring in it, and in *The Fire* he quite simply gives his own experience:

If I will truly show the process it behoves me preach solitary life. The spirit forsooth has set my mind on fire to have and to love this, the which henceforth to lead according to the measure of my sickness I have taken care. Nevertheless I have dwelt among them that have flourished in the world, and have taken food from them. Flatterings also, that ofttimes might draw worthy fighters from high things to low, I have heard. But these out-casting for the sake of One, my soul was taken up to the love of my Maker; and desiring to be endlessly delighted with sweetness, I gave my soul up, so that in devotion she should love Christ. The which she has forsooth received of her Beloved so that now loneliness appears most sweet to her, and all solace, in which the error of man abounds, she counts for nought. (p. 69.)

Neither did calumny deter him:

This have I known, that the more men have raved against me with words of backbiting, so mickle the more I have grown in ghostly profit. Forsooth the worst backbiters I have had are those which I trusted before as faithful friends. Yet I ceased not for their words from those things that were profitable to my soul; truly I used more study, and ever I found God favourable. I called to mind what is written: *Maledicent illi, et tu benedices*, that is to say: "They shall curse him, and thou shalt bless." (p. 70.)

Certainly Richard used himself manfully, as he adjures others to do; he is never weary of cautioning those who are "newly turned," for he knows by his own experience the necessity of fleeing all occasions of sin. He exhorts them with their will to "avoid words, deeds, and sights stirring to ill. The more unlawful a thing is, the more it is to be

---

[1] i.e. hinderers.   [2] Some editions read *quasi ebrius*.

forsaken." Even those who "have long done well sometimes are drowned [by riches and women] in the worst dykes."

The fiend is never tired of bringing old sins to mind, and "the desolation of the contrite" causes unprofitable desires that had been quenched to stir themselves.

> Among these it behoves the penitent manfully to use himself, and to take ghostly armour to gainstand the devil and all his suggestions; and to slake fleshly desires and ever to desire God's love; and to go not from Him, despising the world. (p. 200.)

This time of purgation, of hardship and pain of body and mind Richard endured for nearly three years; but:

> In process of time great profit in ghostly joy was given me. Forsooth three years, except three or four months, were run from the beginning of the change of my life and my mind [i.e. his time of conversion] to the opening of the heavenly door, so that the Face being shown the eyes of the heart might behold and see by what way they might seek my love and unto Him continually desire.

We have now reached the time in Richard's life when he enters upon his mystical experiences, and begins to savour the joy of divine contemplation. This we must speak of in the next chapter.

CHAPTER VI

OF RICHARD'S MYSTICAL EXPERIENCES AND HOW HE ATTAINS
TO THE HIGH LOVE OF CHRIST WHICH STANDS IN HEAT,
SONG AND SWEETNESS

*"And while my whole heart and all my desires were engrossed in
prayer and heavenly things, suddenly, I know not how, I felt within
a symphony of song, and I overheard a most delightful heavenly
harmony, which remained in my mind. For straightway, while I
meditated, my thoughts were turned into melody of song, and for
meditation I, as it were, sang songs. And that music voiced itself
even in my prayers and psalmody ; and by reason of the interior
sweetness which was outpoured upon me, I was impelled to sing what
before I had only said."*—LESSON IX.

Richard's attraction for us—Simplicity of holiness—Definition
of mystical contemplation—Symbolic projection and self-identification with the object translated into terms of mysticism—Divine
union possible only by means of self-negation—Richard's description
of his experiences difficult to fit into any recognised scheme—He is
akin to the doctors of the early Church — Modern writers on
mysticism—Mgr. Farges' account of mystical contemplation and
how far Richard's experiences correspond to the threefold way of
Purgation, Illumination and Union—He likens this union to Heat,
Song and Sweetness—The Holy Spirit is our guide, and inspires our
souls with this holy wisdom, which is mystical contemplation.

THE lives of the saints should be of perennial interest
since it is to that high vocation that we are called, yet often
they are not so; and especially is this true of the lives of those
whom for want of a better term we may call mystical saints.
Their lives attract us sometimes almost against our better
judgment, so repellent are the austerities which many
practised, and so often does their conduct towards others
seem so greatly lacking in charity as to appear almost
unchristian.

But none can say that this is the case with Richard.
His attraction for us is that of sympathy; his experiences
have been shared by many another of like temperament.
He is indeed a great exponent of what has been rightly
called sanctified common sense. He is not deflected by
trying slavishly to imitate the lives of others, nor is he

ever a tame follower of the advice of others as regards the secret things of the soul, but he continually strives to keep himself free from worldly distractions, and alert to the voice of the Holy Spirit of God. Is it untrue to say that in much so-called saintliness there is the effort to vie with those who have passed through life in the odour of sanctity, and whom God has led, each in His especial way; whereas surely true sanctity consists in the humble and simple effort to wait upon God's will in the trivial details of life? True holiness is indeed so simple and often so seemingly prosaic, that it is seldom recognised until the saint has passed from our midst, and then we find that this humble life has left behind it a strong persuasive attraction which has in some strange way a constant influence upon our lives.

So far Richard's life has not had any special marks of holiness; he seems rather to have followed the promptings of his own will, in leaving Oxford and running away from his home, and if he had not found a kind friend in the squire, who was, fortunately for Richard, his father's friend also, the lad would probably have been sent back again. But these three years of stern effort and perseverance in prayer, against distractions and temptation, bear their fruit and he begins to have strange mystical experiences. I shall use the terms "mystical" and "mystical experience" in the same sense as Abbot Butler gives to them in his book on *Western Mysticism*.[1] He uses the word "mystical" in "its proper traditional, religious sense, given in the beginning by Dionysius, viz. 'the secret knowledge or perception of God in contemplation.'" He holds that "mystical experience is not the vision of the Divine Essence, but it is a perception of His Being and Presence, experimental and direct, which in one way or another the mystics do claim as the culmination of their experiences in the higher kinds of contemplation."

He thus enlarges upon it:

So that the prayer of loving attention of faith is not only infused but mystical: but nothing less than it is mystical. "Mystical experience" should be usefully restricted to that experimental perception of God, however expressed, that is

---

[1] See "*Afterthoughts*," p. lxxix. I should like to acknowledge here my indebtedness to this book.

the real claim of the mystics in their higher states of contemplation and the assertion on the validity of which depends the religious and philosophical importance of mysticism so called. (pp. lxxxiv–v.)

For the clearer definition of mysticism we owe much, and shall in the future owe still more, to what is named the New Psychology, which has given us a categorical explanation in scientific terms of what the mystic has described.

The better modern writers on psychology steer clear of the mud-banks of Freud and Jung, with their obsession of sex, and the unsavoury pathology of some French psychologists, their whole tendency being to look forward rather than back; to reveal life as a progress with a definite purpose, which is the achievement of unity. In particular the principles of symbolic projection, and of self-identification with the object towards which each individual strives, have far-reaching results and are of the greatest importance in the study of mysticism; though it is impossible to do more than to allude to them here.

We cannot get away from the fact that as individuals we are dominated by something which lies beyond; with which we identify ourselves, and yet to which we can never wholly attain nor possess; nor indeed can we find symbols by which we can define this goal. Only in flashes do we catch glimpses of our vision—it may be in the beauty of a sunset, in a vernal wood, in some great poem or drama; or perhaps most nearly in music. Then we realise that our goal is in very truth a part of our being; after which we yearn and by which we are possessed. And it is this, after which we strive, that gives to our life its unity.

Translated into the language of the mystic, the object with which we seek identity and into which we seek to project ourselves is God, as revealed to us by Christ. He dwells in us and we in Him. Thus the mystic is the only person who can reasonably and safely experience this union, achieved by self-identification and expressed by symbolic projection, in which we both possess, and are possessed by, the object of our endeavour. The Incarnation, by means of which God has become identified with man, has removed the barrier between God and man. *Because* God first loved us, we dare to love Him; and the soul may fearlessly adventure forth on that high quest of union with God. Indeed absolute unity is only possible between the Maker and the made; between God and man.

And this union with the Divine is both the goal and the achievement of the mystic. It is the fulfilment of the prayer which Christ offered to His Father on the last night of His earthly life.

Holy Father, keep through thine own name those whom thou hast given me, that they may be one, as we are. . . . Neither pray I for these alone, but for them also which shall believe on me through their word; that they all may be one; as thou, Father, art in me, and I in Thee, that they also may be one in us . . . that they may be one, even as we are one. I in them, and thou in me, that they may be made perfect in one. (St. John xvii. 11, 20–3.)

Dame Julian of Norwich, who had a great metaphysical trend, seems almost to be defining this principle of projection when she writes:

High understanding it is inwardly to see and know that God, which is our Maker, dwelleth in our soul; and a higher understanding it is inwardly to see and know that our soul, which is made, dwelleth in God's substance. I saw no difference between God and our substance, but as it were all God; and yet mine understanding took that our substance is in God; that is to say, that God is God, and our substance is a creature in God.

And again:

And our faith is a virtue that cometh of our Nature-substance into our Sense-soul by the Holy Ghost; in which all our virtues come to us: for without that no man may receive virtue. For it is nought else but a right understanding, with true belief, and sure trust, of our Being: that we are in God, and God in us, Whom we see not. And this virtue with all other that God hath ordained to us coming therein, worketh in us great things. For Christ's merciful working is in us, and we graciously accord to Him through the gifts and the virtues of the Holy Ghost.[1]

This accords with Abbot Butler's "own belief." He thinks that rigid methods of speculative authority are being applied too greatly.

[1] *Revelations of Divine Love*, edited by Grace Warrack (Methuen, 1923). See pp. 130–1.

G

We all believe that the Holy Ghost is really and in His substance dwelling in the souls of the just, of all who are in God's grace and friendship. We know that He sheds abroad in the hearts of such the love of God, and with love the other infused virtues and the gifts and fruits of the Spirit, and that all prayer and contemplation is due to His working in us, and that the mystic experience and union is the culmination of the working of the Holy Ghost in souls conspicuously generous in self-denial and in devotion, and pliable in responding to His inspiration and guidance. We know that all true mystical graces are the working of the Holy Ghost.[1]

The same idea as that of Dame Julian underlies the following passage from a recent book of Essays [2]:

Mysticism rests on the gallant faith of Plato, that the "completely real can be completely known" and that only the completely real can be completely known. Complete knowledge is the complete unity of knower and known, for we can in the last resort only know ourselves. . . . At the core of our personality is a spark lighted at the altar of God in Heaven—a something too holy ever to consent to evil, an inner light which can illuminate our whole being. To purify the eyes of the understanding by constant discipline, to detach ourselves from hampering worldly or fleshly desires, to accustom ourselves to ascend in heart and mind to the Kingdom of the Eternal values which are the thoughts and purposes of God, this is the quest of the mystic and the scheme of his progress through his earthly life. It carries with it its own proof and justification in the increasing clearness and certainty with which the truths of the invisible world are revealed to him who diligently seeks for them. The experience is too intimate, and in a sense too formless to be imparted to others. Language was not made to express it, and the imagination which recalls the hours of vision after they have passed, paints the vision in colours not its own. . . . But the revelation was real and it is here and here only, in the mystical act *par excellence*, the act of prayer, that faith passes for a time into sight. Formless and vague and fleeting as it is, the mystical experience is the bedrock of religious faith. In it the soul, acting in a unity with all its faculties, rises above itself and becomes a spirit and therefore asserts its claim to be a citizen of heaven.

Abbot Butler stresses this point:

The feature which marks off true mysticism from the counterfeits which so often, especially in these our days,

---

[1] See "*Afterthoughts*," p. 1.
[2] *Outspoken Essays*, by Dean Inge, (Second Series), p. 14 (Methuen).

masquerade in its name [is the purification of the soul]. . . . It is the constant teaching of the great mystics that there can be no progress in prayer without mortification; no contemplation without self-denial and self-discipline seriously undertaken, no real mysticism without asceticism, in its full sense of spiritual training.[1]

Richard, as we have seen, tried to purify his mind, and detach his desires from the world and the flesh, since the only possible way for man to attain to union with the Divine is by means of negation of self. It is the first stepping out upon that threefold way along which the mystic must pass; but it is better to think of this way of purgation, illumination, and union in the terms of states or stages.

In the fifteenth chapter [2] of *The Fire of Love*, which we shall quote in full later, Richard has given us an account of his mystical experiences. Here a definite time is assigned by him to each state. He tells us that "*three years, except three or four months*, were run from the beginning of the change of my life and of my mind to the opening of the heavenly door, so that, the Face being shown, the eyes of the heart might behold and see by what way they might seek my Love, and unto Him continually desire." This must be said to refer to the time of purgation of which we spoke in the last chapter, when, as the lesson says, "He wore down the lusts of the flesh, so that he might more freely enjoy the delights of true love."

Then: "The door yet biding open, *nearly a year* passed until the time in which the heat of everlasting love was felt in my heart."

And he continues: "Truly in this unhoped for, sensible, and sweet-smelling heat, *half a year, three months*, and *some weeks* have out run, until the inshedding and receiving of this heavenly and ghostly sound," which he describes.

He tells us that one night as he sat in the chapel before supper,[3] he beheld "above" him the noise as it were of

[1] *Western Mysticism*, p. 32.

[2] This famous chapter is found in many printed Latin versions of Rolle's Latin works, and in some MSS. under the title of the whole book, *Incendium Amoris*. In its separate form it is slightly longer. Cf. for example, La Bigne's *Bibliotheca Patrum Maxima*, vol. xv. (Cologne, 1618).

[3] The "night before supper" may be taken as the night of Wednesday in Holy Week, before the *Cena Domini*; but though it would

readers, or rather singers; and also felt within him "the noise of song"; and his "thought was changed to a continual song of mirth."

A little later he says:

> Wherefore from the beginning of my changed soul unto the high degree of Christ's love . . . in which degree I might sing God's praises with joyful song, *I was four years and about three months.*

These divisions of time do not seem exact and are at first sight confusing.

We have first, "three years except three or four months," by which Richard seems to refer to his actual time of purgation, when he was turned to God. Then nearly a year passes until he experiences the *heat* of everlasting love." This experience lasts for half a year, three months and some weeks; and the whole ground seems to have been covered by the "four years and about three months" (p. 72).

Having reached the state of song, the ecclesiastical music of the Imitation, or the "liking heavenly melody which *dwelt*" with him in his mind, he tells us that: "with the first disposition of love [surely the experience of heat of which he also speaks in the prologue] gathered into this degree [i.e. the melody], she bides to the very end."

Though there is a formlessness about Rolle's definitions, so far as they can be said to be definitions, and though he wrote before men had thought of bringing mystical experiences into any scheme or classification, we find that all unconsciously he has trodden the well-worn path of the recognised mystic, though the divisions of time may seem unusual. First *Purgation* which lasted for nearly three years, then the state called *Illumination*, when the Face was shown so that "the eyes of the heart might behold and see by what way they might seek my Love, and unto Him continually desire." In his case this was accompanied by the heat, "*fervor*" or fire of Love, in which state he dwells for a year

seem a natural night on which to have such an experience there is nothing in the Latin to suggest it. MS. Dd. 64, 2 reads: "Dum enim in eadem cappella sederem et in nocte ante cenam psalmos prout potui decantarem quasi tinnitum psallencium vel pocius canencium supra me ascultaui."

and a half, until he attains to the state of *Union* with God.
What else can he mean but this when he writes:

Forsooth [the soul] profits not a little set in these degrees
in this life, but she ascends not into another degree, but as it
were confirmed in grace, as far as mortal man can, she rests.

Yet we must not expect to find in Rolle's own descrip-
tions any dividing line between these states or any chart
which we can use for our own guidance. For such we must
go to the Spanish mystics; St. Teresa and St. John of the
Cross are our classic guides along the mystic path. They
wrote with such explicitness, and yet with a wealth of
beauty, and with such convincing candour that they have
never ceased to be our standard. But Richard very seldom
makes the effort to clarify his thought or arrange his
ideas in order. No doubt this is partly due to his impatience
of and reaction from the scholastic method, but largely it
arises from what we may call an untidy mind. He could and
did experience, and of his experiences none can write more
beautifully. He pours forth the melody that surges in his
heart in impassioned words, which rush out, tumbling
over each other in their eagerness; but he fails to give us
any clear account or to differentiate between one stage
and another. As in his own uncultivated wolds there are
no dividing walls or barriers to mark the road, all is free
trackless space. Those not in sympathy with this attitude,
the poet's attitude, of mind, find his redundancies weari-
some, often even irritating; yet herein lies both his weak-
ness and his fascination. His absence of method produces
a certain sense of freshness and truthfulness, for a too
clearly defined exposition of mystical experience is to
some minds a deterrent; since what in reality could be more
labyrinthine and devious than the mystic's progress, or,
to regard it from another aspect, the lover's chase after
his Beloved?

Richard in his lonely corner of Yorkshire probably died
without ever having heard of the tanner's daughter at
Siena, whose name was to become a spiritual force almost
equal to that of Francis, already a canonised saint. Close
to Assisi, at Foligno, Blessed Angela was living, who with
Bridget of Sweden and the Abbess Gertrude at Helfta
was at that time experiencing strange revelations, visions

and ecstasies. Though Richard may not even have known their names, yet waves of thought are spread by unknown means, nor can we in this life hope ever to gauge the mysteries of prayer.

It was indeed an age of great lovers of God, and what we have learnt in these last ten years of scientific discovery may be to us symbolic of great spiritual facts. Thoughts, as well as words, may be conveyed by invisible means, and Richard was stirred by the same wave of passionate love and devotion, although in the expression of his love he is far removed from these mystics whose names we have cited. Nor has he much in common with Tauler or with Suso who were also contemporary with him.

He tells of no direct revelations or visions such as these were given, nor, as we have seen, can he give us any systematic account of mysticism. His works bear no trace of any philosophic or scientific treatment of contemplation; they are not the outcome of intellectual knowledge but the expression of religious experience. He desires rather to know God, than to know about God; to contemplate rather than discourse upon contemplation. He shows far greater kinship with the great doctors of the early Church who are indeed his spiritual ancestors.

Abbot Butler finds in the teaching on contemplation of the three great doctors, Augustine, Gregory and Bernard, a type of mysticism that differentiates it from other types of mysticism, earlier and later. It may be described as

pre-Dionysian, pre-scholastic, non-philosophical; unaccompanied by psychophysical concomitants, whether rapture or trance, or any quasi-hypnotic symptoms; without imaginative visions, auditions, or revelations; and without thought of the Devil.

(Which his note explains as meaning there was not that abiding sense of the danger of the intervention of the devil which recurs so often in later mystics.)

It is a mysticism purely and solely religious, objective and empirical; being merely, on the practical side, the endeavour of the soul to mount to God in prayer, and seek union with Him and surrender itself wholly to His love; and on the theoretical side, just the endeavour to describe the first-hand experiences of the personal relations between the soul and God in contemplation and union.

This might with equal truth have been written of Richard Rolle.

And the abbot continues:

> . . . real religious mysticism is not a philosophy; it is an experience. . . . Mysticism as such has nothing to say to philosophy; some mystics . . . have held philosophies, . . . but most mystics . . . have been devoid of anything that deserves the name of philosophy. For like religion, mysticism is not the privilege of the intellectual, but is within the reach of the poor and unlearned and the little ones of Christ; and without any doubt it is most commonly and most successfully cultivated by those who know not its name. . . . Mysticism finds its working expression not in intellectual speculation but in prayer.[1]

This applies in every respect to Richard and to his writings; both his treatises on contemplation, which make up the greater part of his prose, and his lyrics; yet it would be well for the sake of clarity to see a little more precisely how his mysticism fits into the recognised scheme of the mystical way.

It is best to go to the authorities in the Latin Church for a well-grounded estimate of mysticism, for none can deny that, as a whole, they have greater experience and a clearer understanding of this subject than we have to-day in the Church of England, since in that Church there has been no intermission of monasticism; and monasticism is indeed the mainspring of the mystical life and supplies it with vital force and energy. Besides which their study has been constantly devoted to mystical theology, more especially of late years, and the greatest names among the mystics, both in past ages and in modern times, have been enrolled within the Latin Church.

I shall be content here to refer to Mgr. Farges' treatise which has been recently translated under the title *Mystical Phenomena*.[2] It is based upon a seven-years' course of lectures on ascetic and mystical theology which he gave at

---

[1] *Western Mysticism*, p. 187.

[2] The full title is: "*Mystical Phenomena compared with their Human and Diabolical Counterfeits*. A treatise of Mystical Theology in agreement with the principles of St. Teresa set forth by the Carmelite Congress of 1923 at Madrid, by Mgr. Albert Farges; translated from the Second French Edition by S. P. Jacques" (Burns, Oates & Washbourne, 1926).

the University Seminary at Angers; which seminary he had founded in 1898. The book was first published in 1920, but in a later edition of 1923 the results of the great Carmelite Congress at Madrid in that year are summarised and commented upon, and the various controversies, notably that on *The direct apprehension of God in the mystical state*, are referred to in the appendices which are given in this translation. This book has to some extent superseded Père Poulain's *Les Grâces d'Oraison*,[1] of which ten editions have appeared between the years 1902 and 1922, and which has been translated into German, Italian, Spanish as well as English.

Mgr. Farges is a supporter of Poulain but an opponent of Abbé Auguste Saudreau, whose books *Les Degrés de la Vie Spirituelle* (1891), *La Vie d'Union à Dieu, et les moyens d'y arriver* (1901) and *L'Etat Mystique* have also been recently translated into English.[2]

Mystical Phenomena repays study, and contains a most useful and enlightening bibliography, for we are often strangely ignorant of the mass of modern books on mysticism which are poured forth yearly from the continental press, although a great many have become familiarised in translations.

In recent years there has been much controversy over "Active" or "Acquired" Contemplation as opposed to "Passive" or "Infused" Contemplation. Canon Saudreau asserts that contemplation should be the normal issue of a spiritual life seriously led, and is therefore possible to all devout people, and in his last book, *The Life of Union*, he quotes many theological writers to prove his point. In 1901 Père Poulain had contradicted this theory in *Les Grâces d'Oraison*; and Mgr. Farges supports him, opposing Saudreau and what may now be called the Dominican view, as led by Père Lagrange. The Jesuits have now joined in the dispute, their leader being of course Père Poulain, and they oppose the Dominican position.

Père Poulain clearly contends that there is a fundamental distinction between ordinary prayer, and extraordinary

---

[1] *The Graces of Interior Prayer* (London, 1920).

[2] Under the titles: *Degrees of the Spiritual Life* (1907), *The Mystical State* (1924), *The Life of Union with God* (1927), all published by Burns, Oates & Washbourne.

or mystical prayer. He thus defines the latter: "Supernatural acts or states are called mystical which our own efforts and industry are unable to produce, even feebly; even for a moment." He thinks that mystical prayer, although the reward of previous endeavours, is a thing that can in no way be achieved, but is wholly given. Like Mgr. Farges he distinguishes between acquired, or non-mystical contemplation, and infused, or mystical contemplation.

Mgr. Farges is insistent that these two kinds of contemplation, having been introduced and become a part of the vocabulary of mystical theology for the last three centuries, must be distinguished and these terms employed. He takes St. Teresa as the authority upon whose definition of mystical contemplation he bases his argument. She writes, in a letter to Fr. Rodrigo Alvarez: "I call mystical that which no skill or effort of ours, however much we labour, can attain to, though we should prepare ourselves for it; and that preparation must be of great service." [1]

To quote Mgr. Farges' own words:

The essential phenomenon of all mystical life is a most complex phenomenon which is known to theologians by the one word *contemplation,* or the infused prayer of contemplation. Its more adequate and complete formula should be this: *the intimate union of the soul with God through infused prayer of contemplation.* (p. 37.)

This infused, or as it is often called passive, contemplation, must be distinguished from acquired contemplation, which is the highest degree of ordinary prayer, and is also called by some writers the prayer of simplicity or of simple regard. This form of contemplation is common to all pious souls and is often exemplified in the story, told under different forms, of the peasant who was found sitting before the Tabernacle and when asked by the priest what he said to God, replied, "I just sits and looks at Him, and He looks at me."

Both these degrees of contemplation belong, according to Mgr. Farges, to

the third period, when the pure love of God opens for the soul the vast field of the perfect life, known as the *unitive*

---

[1] Cf. *Mystical Phenomena,* p. 10.

way. To please God—this is the habitual yearning of such a soul. All other selfish motives are effaced, or at least subordinated to this one desire. Although the soul has not yet achieved union with eternal blessedness, and is still far short of so doing, nevertheless this state is like a far-off foretaste thereof; it is a final stage, a state of relative repose on this earth, and thus we may rightly call it the unitive and perfect life. (pp. 5–6.)

But this way

branches off in two different directions, both of which lead the soul towards its ever-closer union with God, but by different methods and roads. The one is *active*, and calls for our own efforts at all costs; the other *passive*, under the hand of God, in a very short moment, and calls only for our consent. The former is the ordinary and longer road, the other a "short cut." In the one we walk on foot; in the other God bears us on wings of His grace, without any merit of our own, other than our readiness to be led. (p. 6.)

Later he emphasises the point that this passive or infused contemplation

is *not simply a higher* and eminent *degree* of ordinary prayer. Otherwise contemplatives, when they enter this new way, would not have the sensation so often described by them, of entrance into a sphere altogether new, astonishing, incomprehensible; but on the contrary, they would have the feeling of what has been, at least in part, *a former experience*. (p. 44.)

. . . If the soul [he had said earlier] follows the ordinary ways of Providence, it remains always *active* and master of itself, without any suspension of its powers; on the other hand, in the extraordinary ways, it becomes at certain moments *passive* in the hands of the Holy Spirit, who takes possession of it, suspends its powers more or less, and acts in it and through it. Such, for example, are the mystical phenomena of infused recollection, of the prayer of quiet, full union, ecstasy, raptures, and, so much the more, visions, prophecies, and all the other marvellous happenings which depend in no way on the will of souls thus favoured, but solely on the good pleasure of God. . . . They are gifts of God entirely gratuitous, because they are necessary neither to salvation nor to that Christian perfection towards which we ought to strive, but are infused by His grace into certain privileged souls. (p. 7.)

He elsewhere defines the two kinds of gifts of God: the *"gratis datae*, which are given gratuitously, without any

merit on our part, for the advantage of our neighbour—
such as prophecy, the gift of tongues, etc.—and those
described as *gratum Deo facientes*, which are intended for
our personal sanctification, and whose increase in our soul
must always be merited." [1] He excludes the former kind of
gifts, and states that contemplation is not given us for
our neighbour's advantage, *gratis data*, but for our own
sanctification, *gratum faciens*.

He also excludes all those graces of sanctification which
being "*invisible or unconscious*, escape the observation or
experience of the contemplative. . . . In such a case the
novelty, being in his regard unconscious, could not bring
about any of that unrest and astonishment, or those
torments described by S. Teresa and all the mystical
saints." The soul must be "conscious of being passive in
the hands of God, of receiving into itself an infused power,
raising it to supernatural and superhuman acts of knowledge
and of love. It is the *sensation of the Divine*, or the experimental knowledge of the action of God in our souls." [2]

In the light of these definitions let us now read Richard's
own description of the various mystical states he experienced and of his entrance into what is technically
known as infused or passive contemplation.

I give the passage in full (chap. xv., pp. 70 sqq.):

And in process of time great profit in ghostly joy was given
me. Forsooth three years, except three or four months, were
run from the beginning of the change of my life and of my mind,
to the opening of the heavenly door; so that, the Face being
shown, the eyes of the heart might behold and see by what
way they might seek my Love, and unto Him continually
desire. The door forsooth yet biding open, nearly a year passed
until the time in which the heat of everlasting love was verily
felt in my heart.

I was sitting forsooth in a chapel, and whiles I was mickle
delighted with sweetness of prayer or meditation, suddenly
I felt within me a merry and unknown heat. But first I
wavered, for a long time doubting what it could be. I was
expert that it was not from a creature but from my Maker,
because I found it grow hotter and more glad.

---

[1] They are defined by Thomas Aquinas as: "Gratia *gratum faciens*
est per quam ipse homo Deo conjungitur, et *gratis data* per quam
unus homo alteri ad salutem cooperatur" (*Summa*, I. ii., Quest. cxi.,
Art. 1).

[2] Cf. pp. 44–6.

Truly in this unhoped for, sensible, and sweet-smelling heat, half a year, three months and some weeks have out run, until the inshedding and receiving of this heavenly and ghostly sound, the which belongs to the songs of everlasting praise and the sweetness of unseen melody; because it may not be known or heard but of him that receives it, whom it behoves to be clean and departed [1] from the earth.

Whiles truly I sat in this same chapel, and in the night before supper, as I could, I sang psalms, I beheld [2] above me the noise as it were of readers, or rather singers. Whiles also I took heed praying to heaven with my whole desire, suddenly, I wot not in what manner, I felt in me the noise of song, and received the most liking heavenly melody which dwelt with me in my mind. For my thought was forsooth changed to a continual song of mirth, and I had as it were praises in my meditation,[3] and in my prayers and psalm saying I uttered the same sound: and henceforth, for plenteousness of inward sweetness, I burst out singing what before I said, but forsooth privily, because alone before my Maker. I was not known by them that saw me as, peradventure, if they had known me, they would have honoured me above measure, and so I should have lost part of the most fair flower, and should have fallen into desolation.

In the meanwhile wonder caught me that I should be taken up to so great mirth whiles I was in exile; and because God gave gifts to me that I knew not to ask, nor trowed I that any man, not the holiest, could have received any such thing in this life. Therefore I trow this is given to none meedfully, but freely to whom Christ will; nevertheless I trow no man receives it unless he specially love the Name of Jesu, and in so mickle honours It that he never lets It pass from his mind except in sleep. I trow that he to whom it is given to do that, may fulfil the same.

Wherefore from the beginning of my changed soul unto the high degree of Christ's love, the which, God granting, I was able to attain—in which degree I might sing God's praises with joyful song—I was four years and about three months. Here forsooth, with the first disposition of love gathered into this degree, she bides to the very end; and also after death she shall be more perfect: because here the joy of love or burning of charity is begun, and in the heavenly kingdom it shall receive its most glorious ending. And forsooth she profits not a little, set in these degrees in this life, but she ascends not into another degree; but, as it were confirmed in grace, as far as mortal man can, she rests. . . .

---

[1] i.e. separated.

[2] p. 71.—This use of "beheld" is not uncommon in M.E. Cf. also Rev. i. 12, "I turned to see the voice that spake with me."

[3] The Latin reads: "et quasi odas habui meditando."

Continually with joy shall I give thanks because He has made my soul in clearness of conscience like to singers clearly burning in endless love; and whiles she loves and seethes in burning, the changed mind, resting and being warmed by heat, and greatly enlarged by desire and the true beauty of lovely virtue, blossoms without vice or strife in the sight of our Maker; and thus bearing praise within herself, gladdens the longer with merry song and refreshes labours.

Many and great are these marvellous gifts, but among the gifts of this way none are such as those which full dearly in figure confirm the shapeliness of the unseen life in the loving soul; or which so sweetly comfort the sitter, and being comforted, ravish him to the height of contemplation and the accord [1] of the angels' praise.

Behold, brethren, I have told you how I came to the burning of love, not that ye should praise me, but that ye should glorify my God, of whom I received ilk good deed that I had; and that ye, thinking that all things under the sun are vanity, may be stirred to follow, not to backbite.

It is clear from this account that Richard was conscious of receiving some infused gift, for he says, "I felt in me the noise of song," and "my thought was forsooth changed to continual song." He knew it came from above, for "I beheld above me the noise . . . of . . . singers," and recognises it is a gift from God (the *gratum faciens*). "God," he says,

gave gifts to me that I knew not to ask, nor trowed that any man, not the holiest, could have received any such thing in this life. Therefore I trow this is given to none meedfully, but freely to whom Christ will; nevertheless I trow no man receives it unless he specially love the Name of Jesus, and in so mickle honours It that he never lets It pass from his mind except in sleep.

Surely this is an extraordinarily simple yet striking definition of passive or infused recollection or quiet, of which St. Teresa later is to give us her famous exposition, and which she classes as supernatural. Mgr. Faiges thus differentiates between passive and active recollection:

In active recollection, it is by means of personal effort and initiative that we bring our freedom into action. In passive recollection, it is by willing compliance with the good pleasure of God. The soul lets itself go voluntarily, and freely abandons itself to the action of divine grace, for it still could, at least in the initial stage, turn away and become distracted, and thus break the charm. (p. 121.)

---

[1] i.e. harmony.

It is obvious that rest, i.e. freedom from exterior interruptions, is very necessary if the soul is to remain in a
state of contemplation, and on this Richard often dwells,
as in the following passage:

As I forsooth, seeking in scripture, might find and know,
the high love of Christ soothly stands in three things: in heat;
in song; in sweetness. And I am expert in mind that these
three can not long remain without great rest. For if I would
contemplate standing, walking, or lying, methought I lacked
full mickle thereof in myself and me-seemed desolate; wherefore, constrained by need, that I might have and abide in
high devotion, I chose to sit. The cause of this I know well;
for if a man stands or walks for some time, his body waxes
weary and so the soul is let, and in a manner irks for the
charge, and he is not in high quiet and, it follows, not in
perfectness; for, after the philosopher, the soul is made wise
sitting or resting. He therefore that as yet is more delighted
in God standing than sitting, may know that he is full far
from the height of contemplation.

And he enlarges on it:

The soul goes up into this height whiles, [soaring by excess,[1]]
it is taken up above itself, and heaven being open to the eye
of the mind, it offers privy things to be beheld. But first
it behoves to be exercised busily, and for not a few years,
in praying and meditating, scarcely taking the needs of the
body, so that it may be burning in fulfilling these; and, all
feigning being cast out, it should not slacken day and night to
seek and know God's love.

And thus the Almighty Lover, strengthening His lover to
love, shall raise him high above all earthly things and vicious
strifes and vain thoughts, so that the wicked and dying flies
of sin lose not the sweetness of the ointment of grace [since
dead, they become as nought [2]]. And henceforward God's
love shall be so sweet to him, and shall be also moistened with
sweetness most liking, and he shall taste marvellous honey,
that in himself he shall feel nought but the solace of heavenly
savour shed into him, and token of high holiness. Truly fed
with this sweetness he desires ever to wake, inasmuch as he
feels verily the heat of endless love burning his heart, nor
goes it away, enlightening the mind with sweet mystery.
(pp. 136–7).

---

[1] The Latin reads: "Exit autem in hanc excellenciam animus
dum [per excessum euolat] et supra se rapitur, et oculo mentali
apertum celum secreta offert intuenda."
[2] Cf. Eccles x. 1.

Here we have evidently Richard's description of Divine Union or Mystical Contemplation as defined by Abbot Butler.[1] It is not feigned for it has been won at the cost of much spiritual labour and bodily privation: "first it behoves to be exercised busily for not a few years in praying and meditating, scarcely taking the needs of the body"; and it necessitates quiet and abandonment to God, so that "it should not slacken day nor night to seek and know God's love."

Richard constantly likens this union to ghostly song, which is generally accompanied by a most "merry heat," and "sweetness" which is both the cause of the heat and song, and is also caused by them:

"For heat and song truly cause a marvellous sweetness in the soul; and also they may be caused by full great sweetness" (p. 67).

These three, *heat, song* and *sweetness*, are especially characteristic of Richard, and we shall speak of them more fully in the next chapter, where we shall try to gather together Richard's own definitions of mystical contemplation and of love. The melody or song from the passages we have cited, and which could be greatly multiplied, seems to be the strand of this threefold cord which is most intimately connected with the state of Divine Union; but the three are never absent from what Richard tells of his mystical states. As Mgr. Benson has aptly said, "they first follow one another, and then combine, like a chord played arpeggio, and then held down."[2]

We must give one more impassioned passage where Richard struggles to express this Union which cannot be told in words. It is in the chapter we have just quoted on "The Contemplative Life."

Truly the lover of the Godhead, whose inward parts are verily thirled with love of the unseen beauty and who joys with all the pith of his soul, is gladdened with most merry heat. Because he has continually given himself to constant devotion for God, when Christ wills, he shall receive—not of his own meed but of Christ's goodness—a holy sound sent from heaven, and thought and meditation shall be changed into song, and the mind shall bide in marvellous melody.

---

[1] See p. 82 supra.
[2] *A Book of the Love of Jesus*, by R. H. Benson, p. 221 (Pitman).

Soothly it is the sweetness of angels that he has received into his soul and with the same song of praise (*eadem oda*), though it be not in the same words, he shall sing to God. Such as is the song of the angels so is the voice of this true lover; though it be not so great or perfect, for frailty of the flesh that yet cumbers. *He that knows this, knows also angels' song, for both are of one kind, here and in heaven.* Tune pertains to song, not to the ditty that is sung. This praising and song is angels' meat; by which also living men, most hot in love, are gladdened, *singing in Jesu*, now when they have received the doom of endless praise that is sung by the angels to God. It is written in the psalm: *Panem angelorum manducavit homo*, that is to say: "Man has eaten angels' bread." And so nature is renewed and shall pass now into a godly joy and happy likeness, so that he shall be happy, sweet, godly, and songful, and shall feel in himself lust for everlasting love, and with great sweetness shall continually sing.

Soothly it happens to such a lover what I have not found expressed in the writings of the doctors: that is, this song shall swell up in his mouth, and he shall sing his prayers with a ghostly symphony; and he shall be slow with his tongue, because of the great plenty of inward joy, tarrying in song and a singular music, so that that he was wont to say in an hour scarcely he may fulfil in half a day. Whilst he receives it soothly he shall sit alone, not singing with others nor reading psalms. I say not ilk man should do this, but he to whom it is given; and let him fulfil what likes him, for he is led by the Holy Ghost; not for men's words shall he turn from this life. In a clear heat certain shall he dwell, and in full sweet melody shall he be lift up. (pp. 137–9.)

This is clearly an account of a grace to which none can attain by their own effort. It is the Divine Wisdom for which the writer of the Book of Wisdom prayed:

I loved her above health and beauty, and chose to have her instead of light: for the light that cometh from her never goeth out. (Wisd. vii. 10.)

For she is a treasure unto men that never faileth: which they that use become the friends of God, being commended for the gifts that come from learning. (14.)

For wisdom is more moving than any motion: she passeth and goeth through all things by reason of her pureness.

For she is a breath of the power of God, and a pure influence flowing from the glory of the Almighty. . . . (24, 25.)

And being but one she can do all things; and remaining in herself she maketh all things new; and in all ages entering into holy souls she maketh them friends of God and prophets. (27.)

Throughout the whole Book of Wisdom we find wonderful

echoes of this mystical contemplation, which very much later St. Teresa and St. John of the Cross were to define; but I do not think that anyone apart from the writers of the Canticles and of the Gospels and Epistles of St. John has captured the spirit of love and of wisdom, and imprisoned it in words more beautifully than Richard Rolle. He is, to use his own expression, *inebriated*, or as Misyn always translates it, *moistened* with the love of God.

And Richard ends this chapter by speaking thus of Wisdom:

A fair visage has he whose fairness God desires, and keeps in himself the unmade wisdom. Wisdom truly is drawn from privy things, and the delight thereof is with the lovers of the everlasting; for she is not found in their souls that live on earth as they delight.[1] She dwells in him of whom I spake, because he melts wholly in the Christ's love and all his inward members cry to God. This cry is love and song, that a great voice raises to God's ears. It is also the desire of good, and the affection for virtue. His crying is outside of this world because his mind desires nothing but Christ. His soul within is all burnt with the fire of love, so that his heart is alight and burning, and nothing outward he does but that good may be expounded. God he praises in song, but yet in silence: not to men's ears but in God's sight he yields praise with a marvellous sweetness.

---

[1] Latin: "in terra suaviter viventum." Misyn: "þat likandly lyfis."

H

CHAPTER VII

OF THE UNION OF THE SOUL WITH CHRIST: AND HOW PERFECT LOVE STANDS IN HEAT AND SONG AND SWEETNESS: AND OF THE THREE DEGREES OF THIS LOVE

"Then he began with all diligence, by day and night, to seek how to perfect his life and to take every opportunity he could to advance in contemplative life and to be fervent in divine love. And to what excellent perfection he at length attained in this art of fervent love for God he himself records, not for boastfulness nor to seek vainglory, but rather after the example of the glorious and humble apostle Paul. . . . So too this holy hermit Richard . . . tells to what high and sweet delights he attained by contemplation, so that others may obtain hope of likewise advancing in acts of contemplation and love for God. . . ."
LESSON IV.

Richard describes this Divine Union to which he has attained as High Love of God—It is a generating love; born of suffering, whose pivot is the will of God—It is experienced as heat and light—His similarity to the later Spanish mystics—Both describe love as fire and flame—Examples given—The imagery of music especially characteristic of Richard—His definition of Heat and Song and Sweetness, and how great rest is necessary to enjoy them—The three degrees of Love: Insuperable, Inseparable, and Singular, as given in *The Mending*, in *The Form*, and in *The Commandment of Love*—The heavenly melody or song, which belongs more especially to the last degree—Love is diffusive, unitive and transformative — Comparison with Mgr. Farges — Seven experiments by which we can tell if we have attained to Singular love —Richard answers the questions: What is love? Where is love? How we shall love God stalwartly, devoutly and sweetly? — His rhapsodies of love and similes — Perfect love includes our neighbour—This heat and song and sweetness can never cease—Death is the gate to joy: therefore he longs for death, which shall be for him "as heavenly music."

RICHARD nearly always speaks of mystical contemplation in terms of love. "To me it seems that contemplation is the joyful song of God's love taken into the mind with the sweetness of angels' praise." Correctly speaking love is the goal of mystical contemplation, but with Richard these two are inextricably involved, in spite of the fact that he writes a chapter on Love, and another on Contemplation, in *The Mending*. *The Fire of Love* is really a book of contemplation; his lyrics are songs of "love-longing," expressing his yearning after Union with God. Love is the keynote of all he writes, but when his feelings cannot be contained he breaks forth into lyrical rhapsodies as we often find in *The Fire*, but these are not in the actual form of verse as are the lyrics. To say, as M. Joly does, that "Le mysticisme, c'est l'amour de Dieu," or that the mystic is "one who has fallen in love with God," is, of course, inadequate as a definition, but is very true as a *description* of Richard's mysticism.

He is most akin with the Spanish mystics of a later date, and shares with them their dislike of abstractions and metaphysical subtleties. Owing but little to his immediate predecessors, he drew largely upon the Scriptures and the writings of the doctors of the early Church, as did the Spaniards.

This mystical love, although it is a personal love for the Beloved, is not selfish or merely emotional; it is supernatural. The will is its pivot, and the will must be purified and strengthened by suffering. All mystics are emphatic on this point. They teach it, if not by words, by their lives. Richard dwells but little upon pain because when he writes he has attained to the way of Union, and his book on contemplation, which he names so fittingly *The Fire of Love*, is not so much a guide for others as the expression of his own intimate experience of love.

Mgr. Farges in his latest work [1] has pointed out that the chief virtue of the Unitive Way is the Union of perfect Love, or "the blending of our life with God through our Lord Jesus Christ." It is this love which Richard never tires of describing under the terms of heat, sweetness and song. He tries by these figures to convey what in the language of psychology we should call the *projection* of the soul into God, and her *identification* with God through the humanity of Christ; so that henceforth God and the soul are one. [2] "Love truly suffers not a loving soul to bide in itself, but ravishes it out to the Lover; so that the soul

---

[1] *Les Voies Ordinaires de la Vie Spirituelles* (trans. 1927; Burns, Oates & Washbourne).

[2] See supra, chap. iv.

is more there where it loves, than where the body is, that by it lives and feels" (*The Mending*, p. 230). And in *The Fire* he says: "A better dwelling-place nor sweeter found I never, for it has made me and my love one, and made one out of two" (p. 187).

Some have tried to convey this sense of Union in terms of light and radiance, and have told us how they have felt themselves irradiated by a supernatural brilliance which seemed to bathe their whole being in a veil of light, so that they were clothed in light "as it were with a garment." But whether the experience comes by means of light or heat, it is the same Spirit who inspires our soul, "and lightens with celestial fire":

> Thy blessed unction from above
> Is comfort, life, and fire of love.

The experience must take a different form according to the temperament of the one who receives it. In every case with this sense of light or of heat there flows into the heart an overwhelming sweetness and joy. And it is a generating joy, which inspires, and does not rest in its own satisfaction. As Père Laberthonnière (from whom we have already quoted) expresses it:

> It is by loving that we get beyond ourselves, that we lift ourselves above our own temporal individuality. It is by loving that we find God and all other beings, that we rediscover ourselves. Nor do we find God and all the other beings and our true selves for any purpose other than to love again. And thus it is ever, without pause or ending. There is no end to love, for it is self-generating, it is eternally reborn from itself, eternally renewed and expanded. Love is at once light, heat and life.[1]

Love therefore to the mystic is no soft indulgence to lull the heart to rest, but a burning fire to inspire it to work out his salvation; a fire which is inflamed by the contemplation of the cross of Christ.

As Mgr. Farges says, the Union which was the object of Christ's prayer before His Passion is not that passive or mystical union in which the powers are suspended, but pure love which lives only for the glory of God; so that we try to unite our lives, as did Christ, with

[1] Cf. *Life of Fogazzaro*, p. 290.

God, "as far as the difference in nature and substance will allow a human being to do."

This Divine Union to which Richard attained finds perhaps its fullest expression in *The Fire* and in the lyrics, both of which were written not so much for the instruction and help of others as to ease his heart of this consuming love. But such intimate love of a personal Christ can only be had at the price of suffering and struggle. The soul must be purged by interior trials, by calumny and misunderstanding, and consequent loneliness. By such things it is detached from the exterior world which becomes of less and less importance, and as the love for self dwindles the love for God grows. The Carthusian motto "Stat crux dum volvitur orbis" is to the mystics a great reality. Their hearts are drawn upwards by aspiration and remain fixed upon the cross, while the world revolves as a globe below.

Richard speaks of love as a mystery, which most certainly it is, for the soul "would hie the quicklier to do God's will if she should perceive any hard thing she might offer for that cause."

Pain, hardness, suffering must be where love is, but it is turned to delight when borne for love's sake. Love is the true philosopher's stone by which the dross of pain is converted to the gold of endless joy in the Beloved, for this supernatural love eliminates pain.[1]

In his earlier book, the *Melum*, we find, as we should expect, the note of suffering more in evidence, but there is none of the agonising experiences of mental and spiritual torture which is so marked a feature in the life of St. Teresa, and which leave us aghast at the needless pain which they depict. Take for example this passage:

I know not who could have invented such torture for one who felt bound to obey the counsel given her by her confessor, for she would have thought her soul was at stake had she disobeyed him.

and we know that here, as in many other such references, she is speaking of herself.

"Such torture" would have been impossible in Richard's

[1] We have a striking witness to this in the life of Sadhù Sundar Singh. Cf. *The Gospel of Sadhù Sundar Singh*, by Dr. Friedrich Heiler. See especially pp. 171 sqq. Abridged translation by Olive Wyon (Allen & Unwin, 1927).

case. Apart from the fact that, unlike Teresa, he was under no vow of religious obedience, his nature would have prohibited him from following direction which his conscience told him was mistaken. Love was alike his guide and his goal. He goes straight towards his Beloved by the urge of love. "Truly in the sweetness of high love the conscience shines."

Thus he is led by love to the source of all love. His outlook is objective rather than subjective. Although constantly harassed by temptations they seldom come to him under the veil of sanctity, as they so often seem to have done to the saintly women who have left their records behind them. We have no trace in Richard of any undue dependence upon direction. He speaks of the "shrift father," but always in connection with sin, never with direction. In our modern usage of the word "confession" when we mean "shrift," or the sacrament of penance, we have confused the issues. Richard himself became in later life "confessor" to the nuns at Hampole, but we have no certain evidence that he was a priest; for direction and absolution were then held always as two distinct things. Surely the most important virtues for a confessor are simplicity and all lack of scrupulosity, and in these Richard must have been accounted great, and perhaps we may hold this as not the least of the claims he has upon our sympathy to-day.

Though there is a gentler element in Richard than in St. John of the Cross, they are alike. St. John depicts mental agony in abundance, but as with Richard it is the suffering and thirst of the soul after God; it is not the cry of a soul tortured by the clumsy knife of an earthly surgeon, as with St. Theresa, but that of a Prometheus Bound, and his four books read like a great spiritual drama. There is no dramatic element in Richard yet he is nearer to St. John than to Teresa. Though there is little likelihood that the Spanish mystic ever read the writings of the Englishman who so long preceded him, yet the likeness to Richard in his description of love in *The Living Flame* is so striking as to be worth comparing.

First let us read what Richard says in his prologue to *The Fire*:

More have I marvelled than I showed when, forsooth, I first felt my heart wax warm, truly, and not in imagination, but as if it were burned with sensible fire. I was forsooth amazed as the burning in my soul burst up, and of an unwont solace; ofttimes, because of my ignorance of such healthful abundance, I have groped [1] my breast seeking whether this burning were from any bodily cause outwardly. But when I knew that it was only kindled inwardly from a ghostly cause, and that this burning was nought of fleshly love or concupiscence, in this I conceived it was the gift of my Maker. Gladly therefore I am molten into the desire of greater love; and especially for the inflowing of this most sweet delight and ghostly sweetness; the which, with that ghostly flame, has pithily [2] comforted my mind.

If he had not known it he would have thought it impossible for any man to feel such an experience in this world:

First truly before this comfortable heat, and sweetest in all devotion, was shed in me, I plainly trowed such heat could happen to no man in this exile: for truly so it enflames the soul as if the element of fire were burning there. Nevertheless, as some say, there are some, burning in the love of Christ, because they see them despising this world, and with busyness given only to the service of God. But as it were if thy finger were put into fire it should be clad with sensible burning, so, as beforesaid, the soul set afire with love, truly feels most very [3] heat; but sometimes more and more intense, and sometimes less, as the frailty of the flesh suffers.

But none could suffer it for long:

O who is there in mortal body that all this life may suffer this great heat in its high degree, or may bear for long its continual existence? Truly it behoves him fail for sweetness and greatness of desire after so high an outward love; and no marvel though many, passing out of this world, full greedily would catch it and yearn after it with full hot desire; so that unto this honey-sweet flame with wonderful gifts of mind he might yield his soul, and so be taken and forthwith enter the companies of them that sing praises to their Creator withouten end. (pp. 11–12.)

And now compare St. John of the Cross. He is speaking of the awakening of God in the soul, and the soul's consequent awakening to the realisation of God's presence within it:

Then occurs the most delicate touch of the Beloved, which the soul feels at times, even when least expecting it, and which

---

[1] i.e. searched.   [2] To the core=Lat. *medullitus*.   [3] Real.

sets the heart on fire with love, as if a spark had fallen upon
it and made it burn. Then the will in an instant, like one
roused from sleep, burns with the fire of love for God, praises
Him and gives Him thanks, worships and honours Him, and
prays to Him in the sweetness of Love. (Cant. xxv. 5.)

And again in *The Living Flame*, paraphrasing the stanza:

> O sweet burn
> O delicious wound,
> O tender hand, O gentle touch
> Savouring of everlasting life
> And paying the whole debt,
> In destroying death thou hast changed it into life,

he comments:

This is an infinite Fire of Love, so when God touches the
soul somewhat sharply, the burning heat within it becomes
so extreme as to surpass all the fires of the world. This is why
the touch of God is said to "burn," for the fire there is more
intense and more concentrated, and the effect of it surpasses
that of all other fires . . . the burning of fire does not distress
(the soul) but gladdens it, does not weary but delights it and
renders it glorious and rich. This is the reason why it is said
to be *sweet*. (ii. 3–4.)

And this again recalls Richard:

When a soul is on fire with love . . . it will feel as if a
seraph with a burning brand of love had struck it, and penetrated it, already on fire, as glowing coal, or rather as a flame,
and burns it utterly. And then in that burn the flame rushes
forth and surges vehemently, as in a glowing furnace or forge.
. . . Then the soul feels that the wound it has received is
delicious beyond all imagination. . . . It feels its love to
glow, strengthen, and refine itself to such a degree as to seem
to itself as if seas of fire were in it, filling it with love. . . .
In this state of life, so perfect, the soul is as it were keeping
a perpetual feast with the praises of God in its mouth, with a
new song of joy and love. . . .[1] (ii. 10–11.)

The heat of love is, of course, a common simile with
many mystical writers, more especially with St. Bernard;
and sweetness is also often employed as descriptive of
mystical states, but in his use of song and of music to
express his union with God Richard is almost unique.
With him the "inshedding and receiving of this heavenly

[1] Cf. *The Living Flame*, edited by Lewis and Zimmerman, pp. 33,
55 (Baker, 1912).

and ghostly sound" followed his first experience of "the heat of everlasting love" which rested with him for about nine months.[1] It is possible that he may have borrowed this simile from Augustine who also uses it,[2] but that seems doubtful. It seems too spontaneous and too much a part of Richard's nature to be borrowed. It is a theme upon which he most constantly dwells, and he also speaks of contemplation as *musica spiritualis, invisibilis melodia, canticum spirituale, sonus coelestis, iubilatio, canorus iubilus, clamor*; and in his English works there are many references to this heavenly "myrth" and "melodie," and "soun of heaven"; and, as we have already seen, he identifies contemplation with this divine melody.

In chapter xiv. of *The Fire* he explains what he means by this *calor* or *fervor, canor* and *dulcor*. Yet, before we begin to read what may appear to be a definition, let us guard ourselves against thinking that any statement which Richard seems upon some sudden impulse to give is complete. We seize upon it with delight as upon a plank in a morass, only to find our hopes shattered; for he has turned aside to another thought, or breaks out into some rhapsody of love. He must be free of any such trammel as an exact and comprehensive definition, and to try to formulate one from anything he says is as difficult and impossible a task as it would be to imprison into musical notation the song of the nightingale; to which bird he compares himself:

> In the beginning of my conversion . . . I thought I would be like the little bird that languishes for the love of his beloved, but is gladdened in his longing, when he that it loves comes, and sings with joy, and in its song also languishes, but in sweetness and heat. (p. 190.)

He seldom goes back upon what he has said, but he often modifies or enlarges upon it, so as to make his meaning obscure.

[1] See *The Fire*, chap. xv., as quoted on p. 83.

[2] "Abbot Butler says: The imagery of music to express the mystic experience occurs (so far as I know) only here in Augustine [i.e. *Enarration on Psalm xli.* 4], though it is employed by other mystics, as Richard Rolle"; and he cites the well-known passage from cap. xv. of the *Incendium*. Cf. *Western Mysticism*, p. 29. We shall refer to this later in speaking of Richard's debt to Augustine—see p. 134.

A modern French writer who has recently translated *The Mending of Life* describes Richard's style by this apt simile: "Nous dirions volontiers qu'il est clair par places, comme est claire l'eau de la petite rivière que les arbres surplombent et qui est tachée par le soleil de larges plages lumineuses."[1]

Dr. Horstman, who always thinks of Richard Rolle as a typical "Saxon," gives this interesting and true account of the workings of his mind:

> The Saxon, kept from satisfaction, is in perpetual unrest, perpetually consumed by the *trieb* which he resists; a prey to confused feelings and conceits which throng upon him and rapidly succeed each other; of unbounded imagination; his mind is too full, too embarrassed to find expression, to sift, arrange, and lay clear its conceptions; too restless to follow and develop a particular object until it is properly brought out and perfected. His ideas, born in the immediate truth of his own sensation and experience, are right enough; he is an original thinker and has plenty of common sense; his difficulty lies in the forming.[2]

Therefore for our own enjoyment of Richard we had better steer as clear of definitions as he did, but such as he has given us I shall now try to set forth.

He tells us that "seeking in Scripture" he found "the high love of Christ soothly stands in three things: in heat, and song, and sweetness," and that

> in these three that are tokens of most perfect love, the highest perfection of Christian religion without all doubt is found; and I have now, Jesu granting, received these three after the littleness of my capacity. Nevertheless I dare not make myself even to the saints that have shone in them, for they peradventure have received them more perfectly. Yet shall I be busy in virtue that I may more burningly love, more sweetly sing, and more plenteously feel the sweetness of love. (p. 66.)

And then he goes on to define these three:

> Soothly, *heat* I call it when the mind is truly kindled in love everlasting; and the heart in the same manner, not hopingly

---

[1] See *Du Péché à l'Amour Divin, ou l'Amendement du Pécheur* (p. 41), par Léopold Denis, S.J. (Desclée, 30 rue Saint-Sulpice, Paris, 1927).

[2] Vol. i., p. v.

but verily, is felt to burn. For the heart turned into fire gives the feeling of burning love.

Song I call it when in a soul the sweetness of everlasting praise is received with plenteous burning, and thought is turned into song; and the mind is changed [1] into full sweet sound.

These two are not gotten in idleness, but in high devotion; to the which the third is near, that is to say *sweetness* untrowed. For heat and song truly cause a marvellous sweetness in the soul; and also they may be caused by full great sweetness. (p. 67.)

And in his commentary on the Canticles he thus expresses how this gift of *song* acts upon him who receives it:

Now he does not say his prayers but, in a condition of mental exaltation and a rapture of love, he is carried away beyond himself with a marvellous sweetness and is enabled in a wonderful manner to sing to God with a spiritual instrument.

But for the enjoyment of these three gifts rest is essential. In many places he stresses this point, e.g. in the chapter from which we have cited (see p. 94).

And in *The Form* he asks:

In what state may men love God most? I answer in such state as it be that men are in most rest of body and soul, and least occupied with any needs or business of this world. For the thought of the love of Jesus Christ and of the joy that lasts aye seeks outward rest, so that it be not hindered by comers and goers, and occupation of worldly things; and it seeks within great silence from the annoyances of desires, and of vanities and of earthly thoughts. And especially all who love contemplative life, they seek rest in body and soul. For a great Doctor says: "They are God's throne who dwell still in one place, and are not running about but in sweetness of Christ's love are fixed."

He gives his own experience:

And I have loved for to sit, for no penance nor fantasy, nor that I wished men to talk of me, nor for no such thing, but only because I knew that I loved God more, and longer lasted within the comfort of love, than going, standing or kneeling. For sitting am I in most rest and my heart most upward.

---

[1] Some MSS. read *immovatur* = tarries or dwells in.

It is curious how often he refers to "sitting," and yet he seems conscious that it is his own idiosyncrasy, for he adds: "But therefore, peradventure, it is not best that another should sit, as I did and will do till my death, save he were disposed in his soul as I was." [1]

From the passage which we have just cited *sweetness* seems to be always the concomitant of *heat* and *song*; at once the cause and the effect, and can therefore hardly be thought of as existing apart, *per se*.

We shall find this note of song and melody in the joy of love in all Richard says or sings, beside it the progress of the soul is of minor importance. It is God rather than the soul which is the theme of all he writes; even when he speaks of actual sin it is from the objective point of view, and with no morbid dwelling upon or analysis of self. The more we read his works the more noticeable this seems, especially in comparison with contemporary continental writers, and with later English mystics. He appears to be one of the most objective mystical writers of whom we have knowledge.

Love, according to Richard, is possessed of *three degrees*, which correspond to those given us by Richard of St. Victor in *De gradibus caritatis*; to which the Victorine has added a *fourth*, viz. "Love Insatiable." Between the two Richards there is great similarity of thought, and to that we must return in the following chapter, on the sources upon which Rolle drew. We find these degrees described most clearly in *The Mending, The Form*, and more briefly in *The Commandment of Love to God*. These passages I shall now cite in full.

(1) *The Mending*.[2]

There are soothly three degrees of Christ's love, by one or another of which he that is chosen to love profits. The first is called, unable to be overcome; the second, unable to be parted; the third is called singular. [3]

Then truly is love *unovercomeable* when it can not be overcome by any other desire. When it casts away lettings, and

---

[1] I quote from Dr. Geraldine Hodgson's edition of *The Form of Living*, etc., pp. 70–1 (Baker, 1910).

[2] Chap. xi., pp. 230 sqq.

[3] Cf. *The Form of Living*, where these degrees are called "*Insuperable, Inseparable*, and *Singular*."

slakes all temptations and fleshly desires; and when it patiently suffers all griefs for Christ, and is overcome by no flattery nor delight. All labour is light to a lover, nor can a man better overcome labour than by love.

Love truly is *undeparted* when the mind is kindled with great love, and cleaves to Christ with undeparted thought. Forsooth it suffers Him not to pass from the mind a minute, but as if he were bound in heart to Him it thinks and sighs after Him, and it cries to be holden with His love that He may loose him from the fetters of mortality, and may lead him to Him Whom only he desires to see. And most this name JESU he in so mickle worships and loves that It continually rests in his mind.

When therefore the love of Christ is set so mickle in the heart of God's lover and the world's despiser that it may not be overcome by other desire of love, it is called *high*. But when he holds undepartedly to Christ, ever thinking of Christ, by no occasion forgetting Him, it is called *everlasting* and *undeparted*. And if this be high and everlasting, what love can be higher or more?

Yet there is the third degree that is called *singular*. It is one thing to be high, and another to be alone; as it is one thing to be ever presiding, and another to have no fellow. Truly we may have many fellows and yet have a place before all.

Truly if thou seekest or receivest any comfort other than of thy God, and if peradventure thou lovest the highest, yet it is not singular. Thou seest therefore to what the greatness of worthiness must increase, that when thou art high thou mayest be alone.

Therefore love ascends to the singular degree when it excludes all comfort but the one that is in Jesu; when nothing but Jesu may suffice it. The soul set in this degree loves Him alone; she yearns only for Christ, and Christ desires; only in His desire she abides, and after Him she sighs; in Him she burns; she rests in His warmth. Nothing is sweet to her, nothing she savours, except it be made sweet in Jesu; whose memory is as a song of music in a feast of wine. Whatever the self offers to her [besides] it or comes into mind, is straightway cast back and suddenly despised if it serve not His desire or accord not with His will. She suppresses all customs that she sees serve not to the love of Christ. Whatever she does seems unprofitable and intolerable unless it runs and leads to Christ, the End of her desire. When she can love Christ she trows she has all things that she wills to have, and withouten Him all things are abhorrent to her and wax foul. But because she trows to love Him endlessly she steadfastly abides, and wearies not in body nor heart but loves perseveringly and suffers all things gladly. And the more she thus lives in Him the more she is kindled in love, and the liker she is to Him.

No marvel loneliness accords with such a one that grants no fellow among men. For the more he is ravished inwardly by joys, the less is he occupied in outward things; nor is he let by heaviness or the cares [1] of this life. And now it seems as if the soul were unable to suffer pain, so that not being let by anguish, she ever joys in God.

(2) *The Form of Living.*[2]

Three degrees of love I shall tell thee, for I would that thou mightest win to the highest. The first degree is called *Insuperable*. The second *Inseparable*. The third is *Singular*.

(1) Thy love is *Insuperable* when nothing that is contrary to God's love overcomes it, but it is stalwart against all temptations, and stable, whether thou beest in ease or in anguish, or in health or sickness; so that men think that thou wouldest not, even to have all the world without end, make God angry at any time; and thou wert liefer if so it should be, to suffer all the pain and woe that might come to any creature, before thou wouldest do any the thing that should displease him. In this manner shall thy love be Insuperable, that nothing can bring it down, but it may aye spring on high. . . .

(2) *Inseparable* is thy love when all thine heart and thy thought and thy might is so wholly, so entirely and so perfectly fastened, set and established in Jesus Christ that thy thought comes never from Him, never departs from Him, sleeping excepted; and as soon as thou awakest thine heart is on Him; saying *Ave Maria* or *Gloria Tibi Domine* or *Pater Noster* or *Miserere mei Deus*, if thou hast been tempted in thy sleep; or thinking on His love and His praise as thou didst waking. When thou canst at no time forget Him, waking or sleeping, whatso thou dost or sayst, then is thy love *Inseparable*. . . .

(3) The third degree is highest and most wondrous to win. That is called *Singular*, for it has no peer. *Singular* love is when all comfort and solace is closed out of thine heart, but of Jesus Christ alone. Other joy it delights not in. For the sweetness of him that is in this degree is so comforting, and lasting in His love, so burning and gladdening, that he or she who is in this degree can as well feel the fire of love burning in their soul, as thou canst feel thy finger burn if thou puttest it in the fire. But that fire, if it be hot, is so delectable and so wonderful that I cannot tell it.

---

[1] i.e. charges.

[2] Chap. viii., pp. 46 sqq. In my quotations from Dr. Hodgson's edition of *The Form* I have allowed myself licence occasionally to retain the word in the original, and in some places to punctuate differently; I have also inserted numbers—or used italics—when it seemed advisable for the sake of clearness.

Then thy soul is Jesu loving: Jesu thinking: Jesu desiring: only in the desire of Him breathing: to Him singing: of Him burning: in Him resting. Then the song of loving and of love has come; then thy thought turns into song and into melody; then it behoves thee to sing the psalms which before thou saidst. Then thou must be long about few psalms; thou wilt think death sweeter than honey for then thou art full sicker [1] to see Him whom thou lovest. Then mayest thou boldly say: "I languish for love"; then mayest thou say: "I sleep and my heart wakes."

In the *first degree* men may say: "I languish for love," or "I long in love"; and in the *second degree* also; for languishing is when men fail for sickness, and they who are in these two degrees (fall) from all covetousness of this world, and from lust and liking of sinful life, and set their will and their heart to the love of God—therefore they may say "I languish for love"; and much more that are in the second degree than in the first.

But the soul that is in the *third degree* is all burning fire, and like the nightingale that loves song and melody, and falls (dies) for great love; so that the soul is only comforted in loving and praising of God, and till death come, is singing ghostly *to IHESU*, and *in IHESU*, and *IHESU*, not bodily crying with the mouth—of that manner of singing I speak not, for both good and evil have that song.

And this manner of song have none unless they be in this *third degree* of love, to the which degree it is impossible to come but in a great multitude of love. Therefore if thou wilt wot what kind of joy that song has, I tell thee that no man wots, save he or she who feels it, who has it, and who loves God singing therewith. One thing I tell thee, it is of heaven and God gives it to whom He will, but not without great grace coming before. Who has it, he thinks all the song and all the minstrelsy of earth naught but sorrow and woe (compared) thereto. In sovereign rest are they that may get it. . . .

In the *first degree* are many; in the *second degree* are full few; but in the *third degree* are scarcely any; for ay the greater that the perfection is the fewer followers it has.

In the *first degree* men are likened to the stars; in the *second* to the moon; in the *third* to the sun. Therefore says S. Paul: "Others of the sun, others of the moon, others of the stars"; so it is of the lovers of God. In this *third degree,* if thou mayst win thereto, thou shalt know more joy than I have told thee yet.

And there follows, as a specimen of the songs of love, the

---

[1] Dr. Hodgson translates *syker*=of sighs. I take it to be the northern form, *sicker*=sure.

lyric which is given on p. 224, "When wilt thou come to comfort me?" We notice that the song of the third degree of love is of heaven, and "God gives it *to whom He will, but not without great grace coming before.*" Richard has many a time shown that this grace is the result of painful discipline; but when the soul has attained to the third degree then it seems as if she *were unable to suffer pain.* All pain is now turned to joy by her love.

Is it surprising that to savour love like this the soul must cease from the love of this world?

O my soul, cease from the love of this world and melt in Christ's love, that always it may be sweet to thee to speak, read, write, and think of Him; to pray to Him and ever to praise Him. O God, my soul, to Thee devoted, desires to see Thee! She cries to Thee from afar. She burns in Thee and languishes in Thy love. O Love that fails not, Thou hast overcome me! O everlasting Sweetness and Fairness, Thou hast wounded my heart, and now overcome and wounded I fall. For joy scarcely I live, and nearly I die; for I may not suffer the sweetness of so great a Majesty in this flesh that shall rot.

All my heart truly, fastened in desire for JESU, is turned into heat of love, and it is swallowed into another joy and another form. Therefore O good Jesu have mercy upon a wretch. Show Thyself to me that longs; give medicine to me hurt. I feel myself not sick, but languishing in Thy love. He that loves Thee not altogether loses all; he that follows Thee not is mad. Meanwhile therefore be Thou my Joy, my Love, and Desire, until I may see Thee, O God of Gods, in Syon.

In *The Commandment of Love* he puts it more briefly:

And that thou mayst come to the sweetness of God's love I set here three degrees of love in the which thou be waxing.[1]

The first degree is called *Insuperable*, the tother *Inseparable*, the third *Singular*.

Thy love is *insuperable* when no thing may overcome it; that is neither weal nor woe, ease nor anguish, love of flesh nor liking of this world; but ay it lasteth in God though it were tempted greatly; and it hateth all sin, so that no thing may slake that love.

Thy love is *inseparable* when all thy thoughts and all thy wills are gathered together and fastened wholly in Jhesu Christ, so that thou may no time forget Him, but ay thou thinkest on Him; and therefore it is cleped inseparable for it may not be departed from thought of Jhesu Christ.

That love is *singular* when all thy delight is in Jhesu Christ,

---

[1] i.e. growing.

and in none other thing findest comfort or joy. In this degree is love stalwart as death, and hard as hell; for as death slays all living things in this world, so perfect love slays in a man's soul all fleshly desires and earthly covetousness. And as hell spareth not to dead men, but tormenteth all that come thereto, so a man that is in this degree of love, not only he forsaketh the wretched solace of this life, but also coveteth to suffer pain for God's love.[1]

In *The Fire* yet another definition is given of the *strength* of love:

Love forsooth has a diffusive, unitive and transformative strength.[2] In *Diffusion*[3] truly: for it spreads the beams of its goodness not only to friends and neighbours, but also to enemies and strangers. In *Union*[4] truly: for it makes lovers one in deed and will; and Christ and every holy soul it makes one. He truly that draws to God is one spirit, not in nature but in grace, and in onehood of will. Love has also a *Transforming*[5] strength, for it turns the loving into the loved, and ingrafts him. Wherefore the heart that truly receives the fire of the Holy Ghost is burned all wholly and turns as it were into fire; and it leads it into that form that is likest to God. Else had it not been said: *Ego dixi dii estis et filii Excelsi omnes*; that is to say: "I have said ye are gods, and are all the children of the high God." Forsooth some men have so loved each other that they nearly trowed there were but one soul in them both. (pp. 80–1.)

These three degrees of love, viz. insuperable, inseparable— —or to use the English words: unovercomable, undeparted —and singular, are the same as the degrees which Mgr. Farges differentiates as belonging to the Unitive Way,[6] viz.:

(i.) Habitual forgetfulness of self in order to think only of the glory of God.

(ii.) Habitual pursuit of the greater glory of God.

(iii.) A constant state of indifference to anything else.

And he adds another:

(iv.) The choice between two things, which are equally pleasing to God, of that one which will be more crucifying to self.

---

[1] I have modernised this from MS. Rawl. A. 384, printed by Horstman, vol. i., pp. 62 sqq.

[2] MS. C. "lufe forsoth has strength in spreding, in knytynge and turnynge."

[3] Spreading.   [4] Knitting.   [5] Turning.

[6] See *Ordinary Ways of the Spiritual Life*, p. 77.

This last degree is really included in what Richard calls *Singular* love; for in that degree the soul desireth to suffer pain for love of God; though he would hardly, being of an objective turn of mind, have stopped to weigh which of two things would be most crucifying to self. Indeed one questions whether his love of God was not of too wholesome a nature to imagine that what would be most crucifying and painful to self would, for that reason, be the more pleasing to Christ who was crucified for man; though Richard's love for God causes him to embrace pain which comes naturally, with a true delight, for through pain we grow in love. *Singular* love means simply that there is no delight for him save in Christ. All earthly comfort is as naught, "and now it seems as if the soul were unable to suffer pain," and death will seem "sweeter than honey."

In *The Form* (chap. x.) he gives seven *experiments* by which we may know if we have attained to Singular love. These are:

(i.) When all desire of earthly things is slaked in him.

(ii.) A burning yearning for heaven. For when men have felt aught of that savour, the more they have the more they covet; and he that nought has felt, nought he desires. Therefore when anyone is so much given till the love thereof, that he can find no joy in this life, he has token that he is in charity.

(iii.) If his tongue be changed, and he that was wont to speak of earthly things, now speaks of God and of the life that lasts ay.

(iv.) He gives himself entirely to God's business and not to earthly.

(v.) When the thing that is hard in itself, seems light for to do; the which love makes. For as Austin says: "Love it is which brings the thing that is far near-to-hand, and the impossible to the openly possible."

(vi.) Hardness of thought to suffer all anguish and noys that come; without this all the other suffices not. For whatso befalls him shall not make a righteous man sorry. For he that is righteous he hates nought but sin, he loves nought but God and for God; he dreads nought but to wrath God.

(vii.) Delight in soul when he is in tribulation, and he makes praise to God in the anger (pain) that he suffers. And this shews well that he loves God, when no sorrow may bring him down. For many love God while they are in ease, and in adversity they grumble and fall into such mickle sorryness, that scarcely any may comfort them, and so slander they God striving and fighting against His judgments. And that is a caitiff praise that any wealth of the world makes; but that praise is of mickle price that no violence of sorrow can do away.[1]

This chapter of *The Form* should be read in full.[2] It begins thus:

Thou speakest so much of love tell me: What is love? and Where is love? And how shall I love God verily? And how may I know that I love Him? And in what state can I love Him most?

And he answers:

Thy first asking is: What is Love?
And I answer: Love is a burning yearning after God with a wonderful delight and certainty. God is light and burning; light clarifies our reason, burning kindles our desires, that we desire naught but Him. Love is a life, coupling together the loving and the loved. For Meekness makes us sweet to God; Purity joins us to God; Love makes us one with God. Love is the beauty of all virtues. Love is the thing through which God loves us and we God, and each one of us another. Love is the desire of the heart ay thinking til him that it loves; and when it has that it loves, then it joys and nothing can make it sorry. Love is yearning between two, with lastingness of thought. Love is a stirring of the soul for to love God for Himself, and all other things for God; the which love when it is ordained in God, it does away all inordinate love in anything that is not good. But all deadly sin is inordinate love for a thing that is naught; then love puts out all deadly sin. Love is a virtue which is the rightest affection of man's soul. Truth may be without love, but it cannot help without it. Love is perfection of letters, virtue of prophecy; fruit of truth, help of sacraments; stabiling of wit and knowledge; riches of poor men, life of dying men. See how good love is!

And his similes are remarkable, and remind us of the Sadhù Sundar Singh.

We shall afforce us to clothe us in love, as iron or coal does in the fire; as the air does in the sun; as wool does in the dye. The coal so clothes itself in fire that it is fire. The air so clothes

---

[1] This is modernised from the version given in MS. Dd. 5.64, printed by Dr. Horstman, vol. i., pp. 43 sqq.
[2] Chap. x., p. 55.

itself in the sun that it is light. And the wool so substantially takes the dye that it is like it. In this manner shall a true lover of Jesus Christ do: His heart shall so burn in love that it shall be turned into the fire of love, and be as it were all fire; and he shall so shine in virtues that no part of him shall be murky in vices.

The second asking is: Where is Love?

And I answer: Love is in the heart, and in the will of man; not in his hand nor in his mouth, that is to say, not in his work but in his soul . . . when he forsakes the world only for God's love, and sets all his thought on God, and loves all men as himself. And all the good deeds that he may do, he does them with intent to please Jhesu Christ, and to come to the rest of heaven. Then he loves God; and that love is in his soul, and so his deeds shew without. . . . No thing that I do without proves that I love God; for a wicked man might do as much penance in body, as much waking and fasting as I do. How may I then ween that I love, or hold myself better for that that ilk man may do? Certes, whether my heart loves God or not wots none but God, for aught that they may see me do. Wherefore love is verily in will, not in work save as a sign of love. For he that says he loves God, and will not do in act what is in him to show love, tell him that he lies.

The third asking is: How shall I verily love God?

I answer: Verray love is to love Him with all thy might *stalwartly*; In all thy heart, *wisely*; In all thy soul, *devoutly and sweetly*.

Stalwartly can no man love Him, but he be stalwart. He is stalwart that is meek, for all ghostly strength comes of meekness. On whom rests the Holy Ghost? In a meek soul. . . . And he that loves God perfectly, it grieves him not what shame or anguish he suffers, but he has delight, and desires that he were worthy for to suffer torment and pain for Christ's love; and he has joy that men reprove him and speak ill of him.[1]

As a dead man, whatsoever men do or say, he answers nought; right so, whoso loves God perfectly, they are not stirred by any word that man may say. For he or she cannot love that may not suffer pain and anger for their friend's love. For whoso loves, *they have no pain*.[2] . . . In nothing

---

[1] Cf. this from Douce MS. 322, Bodleian: "Through two things principally may a man know whether he be meek or no: Let his heart be not moved though his own will be contraried or againsaid, and when he is despised and falsely challenged and dislandered, yet his will stand unmovable from desiring of wrath, and his mouth be shut from unmeek answer."

[2] Cf. supra, p. 101.

may men sooner overcome the devil than in meekness, which he mickle hates. . . .

Also it behoves thee to *love God wisely*; and that thou canst not do but if thou be wise. Thou art wise when thou art poor and without covetousness of this world, and despisest thyself for the love of Ihesu Christ, and expendest all thy wit and all thy might in His service.

And here is another of Richard's similes which are not unlike those of the Sadhù:

If thou saw a man have precious stones, that he might buy a kingdom with, if he gave them for an apple as a child will do, rightwisely might thou say that he was not wise, but a great fool. Just so, if we will, we have precious stones; poverty, and penance, and ghostly travail; with the which we may buy the kingdom of heaven.

And if thou have *sorrow for thy sins*, and for thou art so long in exile, out of thy country, and forsakest the solace of this life; thou shalt have for this sorrow the joy of heaven. And if thou be in travail and punishest thy body reasonably and wisely . . . for the love of Ihesu Christ, for this travail thou shalt come to rest that lasts ay, and sit in a settle of joy with angels. But some are that love not wisely; like til children that love more an apple than a castle.

And if thou wilt love Ihesu verily thou shalt also love *devoutly and sweetly*. *Sweet love* is when thy body is chaste and thy thought clean. *Devout love* is when thou offerest thy prayers and thy thoughts to God with ghostly joy, and burning heart, in the heat of the Holy Ghost, so that men think that thy soul is as it were drunken for delight and solace of the sweetness of Ihesu, and thy heart conceives so mickle of God's help, that thee thinks that thou mayest never be from Him departed. And then thou comest into such rest and peace in soul, and quiet, without thoughts of vanity or of vice, as if thou wert in silence and sleep, and set in Noe's ship, so that nothing may hinder thee from devotion and burning of sweet love. From (the time) thou hast gotten this love, all thy life, till death come, is joy and comfort; and thou art verily Christ's lover, and He rests in thee, whose stead is made in peace.

The fourth asking was : How thou might know that thou were in love and charity?

I answer: That no man wots on earth that they are in charity, save it be through any privilege or special grace that God has given to any man or woman, that all others may take ensample by. . . . A man wots not whether he be worthy hatred or love, but all is reserved uncertain till another world.

Nevertheless, if any had grace that he might win to the third degree of love which is called *Singular*, he should know that he were in love. But in such manner is his knowing that he might never bear himself the higher, nor be in the less care to love God; but so much the more that he is sure of love, will he be busy to love Him and dread Him that has made him swilk (like this), and done that goodness to him. And he that is thus high, he will not hold himself worthier than the sinfullest man that walks on earth.

Then there follow the seven *experiments* by which to test whether we have this singular love, which we have cited; as also the answer to the question: *And in what state can I love Him most ?* [1]

The soul that has attained to this highest degree of love Richard likens to a "pipe of love." "The which soul knowing the *mystery of love*, with a great cry ascends to his love." Here indeed we have what he elsewhere speaks of as Love entering boldly into "the bedchamber of the Everlasting King," [2] where is the espousal bed of Christ and the soul. That "settle of love" of which Richard so often sings in the lyrics:

> The settle of love is lift high,
>   for in til heaven it ran. . . .
>
> .   .   .   .   .
>
> The bed of bliss it goes full nigh,
>   I tell thee as I can;
> Though us think the way be dregh,[3]
>   love couples God and man.

This is the *mystery of the kingdom* which is the supreme quest of the mystic. Here alone, in Christ, can the soul find rest. "Nothing is sweet to her, nothing she savours, except it be made sweet in Ihesu, whose memory is as a song of music in a feast of wine." A truly haunting phrase and worthy to be placed beside the Canticles.

Nor do I know of anyone outside the writer of Solomon's Song who has more beautifully expressed this inexpressible love of the thirsting soul:

O sweet Ihesu, I bind Thy love in me with a knot unable to be loosed, seeking the treasure that I desire, and longing I find, because I cease not to thirst for Thee. Therefore my sorrow vanishes as the wind, and my meed is ghostly song that

[1] See supra, pp. 114 sqq.   [2] Cf. *The Fire*, p. 233.   [3] i.e. long.

no man sees. Mine inward nature is turned into sweet song, and I long to die for love. The greatness of the gifts delights me with light, and the tarrying of love punishes me with joy, whiles they come that receive me, and in receiving refresh.

But those things want that my Beloved shall show to me, longing: they wound me, so that I languish, and they heal not yet my languor fully, but rather increase it; for love growing, languor is also increased. (p. 165.)

And again:

Alas what shall I do? How long shall I suffer delay? To whom shall I flee that I may happily enjoy that I desire? Needy am I and hungry, noyed and dis-eased, wounded and dis-coloured for the absence of my love; for love hurts me, and hope that is put back chastises my soul. Therefore the cry of the heart goes up, and amongst the heavenly citizens a songly thought runs desiring to be lifted up to the ear of the most High. And when it comes there it proffers its errand and says:

O my love! O my honey! O my harp! O my psaltry and daily song! When shalt Thou help my heaviness? O my heart's rose, when shalt Thou come to me and take with Thee my spirit? Truly Thou seest that I am wounded to the quick with Thy fair beauty, and the longing relaxes not but grows more and more, and the penalties here present cast me down, and prick me to go to Thee, of whom only I trow I shall see solace and remedy. But who [meanwhile] shall sing me the end of my grief and the end of mine un-rest? And who shall show to me the greatness of my joy and the fulfilling of my song, that from this I might take comfort and sing with gladness, for I should know that the end of mine unhappiness and that joy were near? (p. 150.)

And here he actually breaks into verse; it is the only place in *The Fire* where he does so:

> O deus meus,
> O amor meus
> Illabere mihi,
> Tua caritate perforato,
> Tua pulcritudine vulnerato,
> Illabere, inquam,
> Et languentem.

which Misyn thus translates:

O my God! O my Love! into me glide; with Thy charity thirled; with Thy beauty wounded:
Slide down and comfort me, heavy;

and the original Latin continues in prose [1]:

> give medicine to me, wretched; show Thyself to Thy lover.
> Behold in Thee is all my desire, and all my heart seeks.
> After Thee my heart desires; after Thee my flesh thirsts.
> And Thou openest not to me but turnest Thy Face. '
> Thou sparrest Thy door, and hidest Thyself; and at the pains
> of the innocent Thou laughest.

. . . Come into me, my Beloved! All that I had I gave for
Thee, and that I should have, for Thee I have forsaken, that
Thou in my soul mightest have a mansion for to comfort it.
Never forsake Thou him that Thou feelest so sweetly glow
with desire for Thee; so that with most burning desire I desire,
to be ever within Thy halsing. [2] So grant me grace to love Thee,
and in Thee to rest, that in Thy kingdom I may be worthy for
to see Thee withouten end . . . . (p. 21.)

And again in *The Mending* he cries:

O sweet and true Joy, I pray Thee come! Come, O sweet
and most desired! Come, my Love, that art all my comfort!
Glide down into a soul longing for Thee and after Thee with
sweet heat. Kindle with Thy heat the wholeness of my heart.
With Thy light enlighten my inmost parts. Feed me with
honeyed songs of love, as far I may receive them by my powers
of body and soul. (p. 230.)

In the chapter (xi.) from which we have already quoted,[3]
he gives perhaps his most complete description of his
burning love, of which he never tires of singing. In it he
rises to an ecstasy, and cannot find words by which to
express what this love is which seems to wound and tear
his heart. Like the lark, he soars and sings; and every now
and again, also like the lark, when singing, he drops down
into fields of prose. The whole chapter should be read
in order to understand this curious medley of prose and
poetry; of common sense and rhapsody, which is one of
his special characteristics. Here only the most striking
passages can be quoted:

Charity truly is the noblest of virtues, the most excellent
and sweetest, that joins the Beloved to the lover, and ever-

---

[1] "Consolare medicina tu miseri; ostende te amanti; ecce in te est
omne desiderium meum, omne quod querit cor meum," etc. Dr.
Horstman takes this absence of rhythm as one of the proofs of the
later date of the *Incendium*, since the *Melum Contemplativorum*, a
much earlier work, is constantly broken up into verse.

[2] i.e. embrace.   [3] See supra, p. 109.

lastingly couples Christ with the chosen soul. It re-forms in us the image of the high Trinity, and makes the creature most like to the Maker.

O gift of love, what is it worth before all other things, that challenges [1] the highest degree with the angels! Truly the more of love a man receives in this life, the greater and higher in heaven shall he be. O singular joy of everlasting love that ravishes all His to the heavens above all worldly things, binding them with the bands of virtue.

O dear charity, he is not wrought on earth that—whatever else he may have—has not thee. He truly that is busy to joy in thee, is forthwith lift above earthly things. Thou enterest boldly the bedchamber of the Everlasting King. Thou only art not ashamed to receive Christ. He it is that thou hast sought and loved. Christ is thine: hold Him, for He cannot but receive thee, whom only thou desirest to obey. For withouten thee plainly no work pleases Him. [2] Thou makest all things savoury. Thou art a heavenly seat; angels' fellowship; a marvellous holiness; a blissful sight; and life that lasts endlessly.

O holy charity, how sweet thou art and comfortable; that remakest that that was broken. The fallen thou restorest; the bond thou deliverest; man thou makest even with angels. Thou raisest up those sitting and resting, and the raised thou makest sweet.

And the following passage explains why every mystic finds it impossible to give any clear account of his progress in the experience of God's love:

Thus truly Christ's lover keeps no order in his loving nor covets no degree, because however fervent and joyful he be in the love of God in this life, yet he thinks to love God more and more. Yea, though he might live here evermore yet he should not trow at any time to stand still and not progress in love, but rather the longer he shall live the more he should burn in love. God truly is of infinite greatness, better than we can think; of un-reckoned sweetness; inconceivable of all natures wrought; and can never be comprehended by us as He is in Himself in eternity.

And he again breaks forth into a rhapsody of love:

O merry love, strong, ravishing, burning, wilful, stalwart, unslakened, [3] that brings all my soul to Thy service, and suffers it to think of nothing but Thee. Thou challengest for Thyself all that we live; all that we savour; all that we are. [4]

---

[1] i.e. claims.
[3] Inextinguishable.

[2] Cf. 1 Cor. xiii.
[4] Cf. Rom. xiv. 8.

Thus therefore let Christ be the beginning of our love, whom we love for Himself. And so we love whatever is to be loved ordinately for Him that is the Well of love, and in whose hands we put all that we love and are loved by. Here soothly is perfect love shown; when all the intent of the mind, all the secret working of the heart, is lifted up into God's love, so that the strength and mirth of true love is so great that no worldly joy . . . is lawful or delights it.

And here we have the same selfless love as St. Francis Xavier expresses in his well-known hymn.

Although there were no torments for the wicked, nor no meed in heaven, should be trowed for chosen souls, yet shouldst thou never the sooner loose thee from thy Love. More tolerable it were to thee to suffer an untrowed grief than once to sin deadly. Therefore thou truly lovest God for Himself and for no other thing, nor thyself except for God; and thereof it follows that nothing but God is loved in thee. How else should God be all in ilk thing if there be any love of man in man?

And compare this passage from *The Fire*:

For truly if we love God rightly we would sooner lose great meed in heaven than once sin venially; for most righteous is it to ask no meed of righteousness but the friendship of God, that is Himself. Therefore it is better ever to suffer tormentry than once, wilfully and knowingly, to be led from righteousness to wickedness. (p. 39.)

Then again he soars upward, singing thus of love:

O clear charity, come into me, and take me into thee, and so present me before Thy Maker. Thou art savour well tasting; sweetness well smelling; and pleasant odour; a cleansing heat, and a comfort endlessly lasting. Thou makest men contemplative; heaven's gate thou openest; the mouths of accusers thou sparrest; thou makest God be seen, and thou hidest a multitude of sins. We praise thee; we preach thee; by the which we overcome the world; in whom we rejoice, and by whom we ascend the ladder of heaven. In thy sweetness glide into me: and I commend me and mine unto thee without end.

And in *The Fire* he gives us this prayer for love:

Lord Ihesu, I ask Thee, give unto me movement in Thy love withouten measure; desire withouten limit; longing with outen order; burning withouten discretion. Truly the better the love of Thee is, the greedier it is; for neither by reason is it restrained, nor by dread thronged, nor by doom tempted. No man shall ever be more blest than he that for greatness of love can die. No creature truly can love too mickle. In all other things all that is too mickle turns to vice, but the more the strength of love surpasses, the more glorious it shall be. (p. 78.)

This perfect love embraces the love of our neighbour, for Richard, though carried away by excess of love, never forgets the earth from which he has taken flight, and constantly breaks off from his most impassioned utterances to give us some homely advice or warning. He is emphatic that all true love of God must include the love of man, since we dwell in God and God in us.

Therefore [he says], if our love be pure and perfect, whatever our heart loves it is God. Truly if we love ourself, and all other creatures that are to be loved, only in God and for God, what other in us and in them love we but Him? For when our God truly is loved by us with a whole heart and all virtue, then, without doubt, our neighbour and all that is to be loved, is most rightly loved. If therefore we shed forth our heart before God and in the love of God being bound with Him, and holden with God, what more is there by which we can love any other thing?

Truly in the love of God is the love of my neighbour. Therefore as he that loves God knows not but to love man, so he that truly knows to love Christ is proved to love nothing in himself but God. Also all that we are loved or love—all to God the Well of love we yield: because He commands that all the heart of man be given to Himself. All desires also, and all movings of the mind, He desires be fastened in Him. He forsooth that truly loves God feels nothing in his heart but God, and if he feel none other thing nought else has he; but whatso he has he loves for God, and he loves nought but that God wills he should love: wherefore nothing but God he loves and so all his love is God. (p. 87).

And he thus sums up all that he has said of heat and song and sweetness, in this account of a man who is perfectly turned to Christ:

He despises all passing things, and he fastens himself immovably to the desire only of his Maker, as far as he is let by mortality, because of the corruption of the flesh. Then no marvel, manly using his might, first, the heaven as it were being opened, with the eye of his understanding he beholds the citizens of heaven; and afterward he feels sweetest heat as it were a burning fire. Then he is imbued with marvellous sweetness, and henceforth he is joyed by a songly noise.

This therefore is perfect charity, which no man knows but

he that receives it; and he that has received never leaves it: sweetly he lives, and sickerly shall he die. (p. 89.)

Naturally, and like all true mystics, he longs for death—that lowly door through which we must pass to reach the Hall of Everlasting Love.

And I spake thus to death:
O Death, where dwellest thou? Why comest thou so late to me, living but yet mortal? Why halsest thou not him that desires thee?
Who is enough to think thy sweetness, that art the end of sighing, the beginning of desire, the gate of unfailing yearning? Thou art the end of heaviness, the mark of labours, the beginning of fruits, the gate of joys. Behold I grow hot and desire after thee: if thou come I shall forthwith be safe. Ravished, truly, because of love, I cannot fully love what I desire after, until I taste the joy that Thou shalt give to me.

.   .   .   .   .   .

Therefore truly I long after love the fairest of flowers, and I am inwardly burnt by the flame of fire. Would God I might go from the dwelling of this exile. . . . Now, grant my best Beloved, that I may cease; for death, that many dread, shall be to me as *heavenly music*. Although I am sitting in wilderness yet I am now as it were set stable in Paradise, and there sweetly is sounding a loving song in the delights that my Love has given me. (p. 74–6.)

Here again we note the blending of the three: the burning of the flame; the heavenly music; and the sweet sound of the song of love.

CHAPTER VIII

THE SOURCES UPON WHICH RICHARD DREW

" Yet wonderful and beyond measure useful was the work of this saintly man in holy exhortations, whereby he converted many to God : and in his sweet writings, both treatises and little books composed for the edification of his neighbours; which all sound like sweetest music in the hearts of the devout."—LESSON VI.

Difficulty of ascertaining the sources which Richard drew upon until we have further knowledge—Some however are unmistakable —Holy Scripture, especially the Psalter, and Canticles contained in the Breviary—The Prymer—The Book of Job—The Wisdom and Song of Solomon—Ecclesiastes—Ecclesiasticus—His knowledge of the Fathers—Similarity between Augustine and Richard—Both use the imagery of music—Yet Richard flees "the outward songs that are wont in the kirks"—Heavenly music—A digression—Other points of contact between Augustine and Richard—Isidore— Influence of St. Bernard—Devotion to the Holy Name—St. Bernard's famous Sermon xv. on the Canticles—Both Bernard and Bonaventura very popular in Yorkshire—Bonaventura's *Life of Christ*— His treatises on love compared with Richard's—Hugh and Richard of St. Victor—Anselm's influence upon English mysticism very great, especially in the south, where Anglo-Norman French prevailed—Yorkshire not affected, and Rolle is singularly free from French influence—St. Edmund Rich—Paraphrased in some of Richard's lyrics—John Hoveden's Latin poems in honour of Our Lady—Imitated by Richard in his youth—Devotion to Our Lady in the thirteenth century—Its reticence—Love to her never divorced from love to her Son.

MISS HOPE ALLEN, an American student, who is one of the greatest authorities on Richard Rolle, has for long been making researches among the MSS. said to contain his works, and we look for her book [1] giving us the canon of his authentic works with great eagerness. Until it appears little can be said with any completeness as to his sources. On the other hand, with the publication of Miss Allen's book, when scholars set to this task there will always be the danger of ascribing to Richard knowledge which he did not possess. This has been the tendency all

[1] See page 320.

down the ages; as we are only too conscious of with certain Shakespearian students who find elaborate reasons and recondite sources for much which, most probably, came spontaneously to the poet's mind.

We have always to bear in mind that Richard suffered from what I have called an untidy mind. Such a one may read widely, and assimilate much of what he reads, but he would find it very difficult to say from whence he drew any particular idea. Moreover, the speed with which one thought suggests another makes it most difficult for minds like Richard's to disentangle their ideas, or to find in well-arranged and tabulated pigeon-holes what first suggested to them a certain line of thought or put certain expressions into their minds. Their writings are apt to be confused, full of repetitions and often redundant.

But there are some sources upon which Richard drew about which there can be no question. Their influence is stamped upon the English works which have been gathered together by Dr. Horstman, and many of which have now been republished in modern English; as also upon his *Incendium Amoris* and *De Emendatione Vitae*, of which we have English translations. Moreover we have his lyrics to guide us. There is little doubt that many anonymous translations of parts of his most popular Latin writings exist, buried in unknown MSS. or embodied in other books, such for example as *The Poor Caitiff*, which was for long ascribed to Wyclif, but which is in reality a medley of writings; but until these have been investigated we must leave them out of account.[1]

First and foremost Richard was imbued with love of the Scriptures. Oxford may have inspired him with this love; for by a regulation of Grosseteste, the first morning lecture had to be upon the Bible.[2] His books abound in quotations from the Scriptures, in which his mind was soaked. As we should naturally expect, they are largely

---

[1] My authority is Miss Hope Allen, who writes: "A medium by which some of his most characteristic passages were current in an English translation was the immensely popular compilation known as the *Poor Caitiff*, which included anonymous translations from several of Rolle's writings." See article in *Mod. Lang. Review*, 1919, vol. xiv., pp. 320 sqq.

[2] Cf. *Cambridge History of English Literature*, vol. ii., chap. ii., p. 44, by the Rev. J. P. Whitney.

taken from the lessons and psalms in the Breviary, which of course greatly differed according to the dioceses and orders. He usually contents himself with vague references, e.g. "as it is written," or "as saith the psalmist," and probably relied largely upon his memory, for his quotations very often do not correspond either to the Vulgate translation, nor to the *Vetus Itala*. What Dr. White says of St. Bernard's variations from the Vulgate may be said with equal truth of Richard: "He probably used an old Vulgate text which had preserved a certain number of old Latin readings, as so many of the Vulgate MSS. did; and also he often quoted from memory, or a slip of the pen on the part of the saint or his copyists" would account for the differences.[1]

In *The Mending* he exhorts us not to be

negligent in meditating and reading Holy Scripture; and most in those places where it teaches manners, and to eschew the deceits of the fiend; and where it speaks of God's love and of contemplative life. Hard sayings may be left to disputers and to wise men used for a long time in holy doctrine. (p. 225.)

He himself seems to have especially loved the Psalter, the Book of Job, the Lamentations, the Canticles and the Book of the Wisdom of Solomon, Ecclesiastes, the Proverbs and Ecclesiasticus, and of course he frequently quotes from the Gospels and Epistles in the New Testament. He has written commentaries and postils [2] upon the Book of Job, the Lamentations, the Canticles and on Proverbs, and was the first to translate the Psalms into English, forestalling Wyclif, with whom he would have had much in common. Wyclif was only twenty-four when Richard died and there is likelihood that they may have met, since the former was born near Richmond, where Richard went in later life, when he had become known; and very probably he met the boy John before the latter went to Oxford,

---

[1] See preface to "De Diligendo Deo," edited by W. W. Williams, p. vii, in *Select Treatises of S. Bernard of Clairvaux* (Camb. Univ. Press, 1926).

[2] *A postil* is, properly speaking, a marginal note, as a *gloss* is a word inserted between the lines; but both words were used alike for a series of such comments, and are practically synonymous with *commentary. Enarration,* which is used largely in speaking of the commentaries of the early Latin Fathers, means really an exposition.

where afterwards he was to gain fame as Master of Balliol.

There is a very early translation of the Psalter in English verse which is extant in three northern MSS., all, Dr. Horstman [1] thinks, belonging to Yorkshire, and in comparing these with the later prose translation, which is certainly by Richard, we find many points of resemblance, sometimes whole verses in almost identical words, so that it is clear that the writer in prose is greatly indebted to the writer in verse. Dr. Horstman says: "The greater freedom from French words, and the archaic character of the older Psalter, do not necessarily imply another author. In a transition time an author may write very differently when a young man and when advanced in years. The metrical Psalter might well be the work of his youth, his first attempt." He also thinks that the seeming archaism of the language is due to the fact that the translator utilises glosses containing words which were "no longer understood." "Other words the translator seems to have formed himself by literally translating Latin terms in the manner of the old glosses," and he cites *locupletare*, glossed as stedful, *impetus* as sithcoming, sithstreme, etc.

There is a note in the fly-leaf of the Egerton MS. 614 in a later hand to the effect that this Psalter was translated by Richard of Hampole. It reads: "Videtur hoc Psalterium in Linguam Anglicanam transtulisse et versibus haud elegantibus concinuisse Ricardus de Hampole, vero nomine Rollus, Gente Anglius, Eboracensis Com. Ord. Augustini Eremita, in cenobio Hampoliense, prope Doncastriam vixit. Obiit anno 1349." The Harl. MS. 1770 is marked as belonging to the Abbey of Kirkham, close to Thornton-le-Dale, and is written in a northern hand *c.* 1380. The first part contains the Latin Psalter with a French translation in parallel columns, the English metrical Psalter following. Dr. Horstman says: "The question is one of great difficulty, and I cannot now attempt to solve it." It would be an interesting point to solve, and perhaps with our greater knowledge one not impossible for the scholar to-day. The author of the later prose translation and commentary is indisputably Richard. This was edited as far back as

[1] MSS. Vesp. D. vii., Egerton 614, and Harl. 1770. Cf. Horstman, ii., p. 129, and see note, p. 130.

1884 by Mr. Bramley [1] from a northern MS. of University College, Oxford. It contains also the Canticles and the Magnificat. In his prologue to the translation Richard writes:

In this work I seek no strange English, but the lightest and commonest that is most like til the Latin, so that they who know no Latin, by the English may come til many Latin words. In the translation I follow the letters as mickle as I may; and there [2] I find no proper English I follow the writ of the words, so that they who read it they need not there dread erring.

which lets in an interesting light upon his method of translation. He continues:

In expounding I follow holy doctors, for it may come into some envious man's hand, that knows not what he should say; that will say that I wist not what I said, and so do harm til himself and til others, if he despise the work that is profitable for him and others.

This Psalter was the earliest biblical book to be translated into English prose after the Conquest. The upper classes were mainly French-speaking until about the year 1350. There was naturally greater contact between Normandy and the southern counties of England than there was with the northern, and for that reason we have this revival of the vernacular earlier in the north than in the south, Richard being the pioneer. His translation, according to Miss Deanesley, "became the standard English version of the Psalms." [3] It was copied throughout the fifteenth century by scribes of different dialects, and as it followed the text the most closely, it was the natural book to be used by the Lollards when they wished to insert their own teaching into the gloss. It was probably to protect the

---

[1] *The Psalter with a Translation and Exposition in English by Richard Rolle of Hampole*, edited by H. R. Bramley, p. 4 (Oxford, 1884).

[2] i.e. where.

[3] Cf. *The Lollard Bible*, by Margaret Deanesley, p. 231 (Camb. Univ. Press). There is an interesting reference to this Psalter in *The Mirror of Our Lady*: "Of psalmes I have drawen but few, for ye may have them of Rychard hampoules drawynge, and out of Englysshe bibles if ye haue lysence therto." *The Mirror of Our Lady* was written for the nuns of Syon College, who for long possessed the MSS. of Richard's *Incendium*, and seem still to have a traditional love for him. Cf. E.E.T.S., Extra Series, 19 (1873), p. 31.

K

book from such interpolations that the copy of the Psalter at the nunnery of Hampole was kept in chain bonds, as the writer of the metrical preface tells us:

> Therefore a worthy holy man: called Richard Hampole,
> Whom the Lord that all thing can : taught loyally in His school,
> Glosed the Psalter that sues here : in English tongue sickerly,
> At a worthy recluse prayer : called Dame Margaret Kirkby.
> This same Psalter in all degree : is the self in soothness
> That lieth at Hampole in surety : at Richard's own buryness,[1]
> That he wrote with his own honds : to Dame Margaret Kirkby,
> And there it lieth in chain bonds : in the same nunnery.

Richard has evidently to protect himself against the "envious man" who is ready at every turn to misrepresent him and accuse him of false doctrine, and certainly if he had lived later his free spirit might have found points of contact with Wyclif, but he shows no sign in any of his writings of swerving from his allegiance to Holy Church.

It is interesting to find that Dr. Littledale knew this work of Richard's, and quotes it frequently in his own commentary upon the Psalter which he began with Dr. Neale, who died before its completion. It does not appear that the latter had any knowledge of Rolle, for he is one of the additional authorities cited by Dr. Littledale in his preface to vol. ii.[2]; he adds this note:

> Richard Rolle of Hampole, the Yorkshire hermit, preacher, poet and saint . . . wrote a terse mystical paraphrase which often comes very little short of the beauty and depth of Dionysius the Carthusian himself. I have cited it with frequency, proportioned rather to its merit than its bulk.

This Psalter of Richard's is largely based upon Peter Lombard's, whose fame rests upon his *Sententiae*, a book very often quoted in the Middle Ages. Peter's commentary is chiefly taken from Augustine, Cassiodorus, the Venerable Bede and Haymo of Halberstadt, with pithy remarks of his own. Probably Richard's sources were the same, which accounts for the similarity between the two.

Besides commentating on the Psalms, Richard adds a gloss on the Canticles from the Old Testament, and on the Magnificat; the other New Testament Canticles being only found in some Lollard adaptations of the Psalter. The Old

---

[1] i.e. burial-place.

[2] *Commentary upon the Psalter*, by Neale and Littledale, vol. ii., p. ix.

Testament Canticles are very commonly found in mediaeval commentaries on the Psalter, since they were a part of the Breviary, being included in the Office for Lauds. All breviaries differ, and Dr. Littledale, in the preface from which I have quoted, gives us a list of seventy-seven canticles from the Mozarabic Breviary, of which four only are taken from the New Testament. The more usual custom was to choose one for each day of the week, the Benedicite being recited on Sunday; on Monday, the Song of Isaiah (Is. xii.); Tuesday, of Hezekiah (Is. xxxviii. 10–20); Wednesday, of Hannah (1 Sam. ii. 1–10); Thursday, Exodus (Exod. xv. 1–18); Friday, Habakkuk (Hab. iii. 2 to end); and on Saturday, the Song of Moses (Deut. xxxii. 1–43). We notice that most of Richard's quotations from these books are to be found in one of these canticles. He would have known the Breviary well, even though he may not have recited all the Divine Office, though there is no reason to suppose he did not. The common manual of prayer for the devout laity was the English Prymer. Of this we have many copies extant; well-worn little books possible to carry about in the pocket. But only three MSS. of the Prymer of the Use of York, which would probably be the one best known by Richard, appear to exist.

Some are beautifully illuminated,[1] and many contain the music to which the Psalms, etc., were chanted. Mr. Bishop says that, "from the fact that almost all mediaeval prayerbooks in manuscript or in print agree in containing a definite series of devotions with or without varying additions, we may feel sure that but one prayerbook was in common use in the Middle Ages, and this book we may believe to have been the Prymer."[2] It is found in both English and Latin. The MS. versions almost invariably contain:

1. The Hours of the Blessed Virgin.
2. The seven Penitential Psalms.

[1] For example: MSS. Harl. 1251, a tiny volume with seventeen full-paged pictures of saints; Harl. 1663, a fat little book without illustrations but with music; and two very beautiful French MSS. Add. 16997, fol. 119; and Egerton 1070, which is especially interesting for its heraldic illuminations; and a great many others might be mentioned.

[2] See Mr. Bishop's essay on *The Origin of the Prymer* (E.E.T.S., Original Series, 105 (1895), p. xxxix).

3. The fifteen Gradual Psalms.
4. The Litany.
5. The Office for the Dead.
6. Commendations.

We also find in many Prymers the Hours of the Passion, based upon and following the model of the Hours of the Divine Office.

Apart from the Psalter and the Divine Office, and Manual of the Prymer, we find that Richard, judging from his own works,[1] had an especial affection for the Book of Job, the Wisdom and the Song of Solomon, Ecclesiastes and Ecclesiasticus.

His commentary upon Job is named from its opening sentence the *Parce mihi Domine*. It is based upon the nine lessons of the *Dirige*, which are directed to be read at the Matins Office for the Dead. They are called the *Dirige* from the first word of the antiphon: "*Dirige, Domine Deus meus, in conspectu tuo viam meam.*" This piece is of undoubted authenticity since the author calls himself "*Ricardus heremita*"; but *Pety Job*, beginning "*Parce mihi domine*," which is a poem in twelve-line stanzas made upon Richard's *Postillae super Lectiones mortuorum*, is written by an East Midland poet of a much later date.

Richard may have made the selection of extracts from St. Gregory's *Moralia* (viii., cap. 26), taken from the same chapters of Job as the *Dirige* and which is usually named *Moralia in Job*; but it is not an original work.

The Canticles were always a storehouse for mystical writers from which to draw their text. Richard wrote many *Postillae super Cantica*, mostly upon chapter i. 1, 2 and 3. That on the *Oleum effusum nomen tuum* was translated into English under the title: *Of the Virtues of the Holy Name of Ihesu*, but probably not by Richard himself.[2] The English version is some two hundred words shorter than the Latin.

[1] A list of these will be found in appendix ii.

[2] The English tract known as *Oleum Effusum* which Horstman prints as Rolle's (vol. i. p. 186) under the title *Encomium nominis Jesu*, is unlikely to be his. In style it is like Walter Hilton, and is attributed to Hilton by J. E. Wells. (See his *Manual of the Writings in Middle English*, p. 463, where he says it is "improperly attributed to Rolle.")

The English tract of which we have often spoken, *Ego dormio et cor meum vigilant*, though it takes this verse from the Canticles as its title, is not really a commentary, but a eulogy of the love of Christ and of the Passion. Twice over in it Richard breaks into verse.[1]

Dr. Horstman in his list of Richard's Latin writings cites also a small tract on the Lamentations of Jeremiah, and another on Psalm xx. He may also have been the author of a short piece on Contemplation based upon Prov. xxxi. 10, *Mulierem fortem quis invenit*, which is found in MS. 77 of St. John's College, Oxford.

Of "holy doctors" Richard cites many in his English books. In *The Form* there are six references to Augustine, and he quotes SS. Bernard and Jerome. In a tract on Daily Work,[2] St. Gregory is mentioned six times, and SS. Isidore, Jerome, Ambrose and Bernard, and in the tract on Grace,[2] SS. Anselm, Isidore and Augustine. These references to the fathers and doctors of the Church are very common in mediaeval writings and I do not think they necessarily imply that the writer had read the works of the men he cites. In a fourteenth-century tract on *The Dread and Love of God*[3] the references are given carefully in the margin, but Richard gives us no such aid, and it would be only time wasted to try to trace these sayings. Moreover there exist many MSS. which contain collections of "Sayings from the Fathers," and from "Holy Doctors," and I think it is quite possible these were drawn upon, rather than the writers themselves.[4]

The fact that works by Augustine and Bernard were often ascribed to Richard goes to show that there was much

[1] Cf. part ii., p. 226.
[2] These two tracts are of doubtful authenticity. In style they are not unlike *The Dread and Love of God*, where also many names of fathers and doctors are cited. Miss Deanesley says that quotations from the fathers in the Latin tracts occur only in those of which the authorship is doubtful.
[3] I modernised this under the title *Contemplations of the Dread and Love of God*, from the Harl. MS. 2409 (Washbourne, 1916).
[4] There are three such collections in the Bodleian Library at Oxford, viz. MSS. Bod. 938 (now S.C. 3054), Laud. 210 (S.C. 1292), and Rawl. C. 285, in which there are many quotations from SS. Austin, Gregory, Jerome, Bernard, Anselm, besides the gospels and St. Paul. It is more than likely that Richard had recourse to such collections, other MSS. being probably inaccessible.

resemblance between them, and Richard has many points in common with Augustine whom he must certainly have read. Dr. Horstman thinks that an English translation in rhythmical prose of a *Meditacio S. Augustini*, found in MS. Harl. 1706, is his. The Meditation was wrongly ascribed to Augustine, as indeed were many of his then reputed works, e.g. the *Soliloquies*, and the *Meditation upon the Passion*. There is no doubt that Richard was greatly influenced by the latter and incorporates some lines of it into his lyric, "My King that water gret." [1] Considering Richard's great love for the Psalms, and the fact that he translated them and glossed them probably more than once, there is every reason to think that he knew Augustine's commentaries, more especially as he repeatedly quotes from Augustine in his other writings. Dr. Horstman has no doubt upon this point, and Dr. Geraldine Hodgson has drawn parallels between Richard and Augustine in his *Enarratio in Psalmum xli.* [2]

As we have already noted, Abbot Butler has drawn attention to the similarity between them as regard to their use of the imagery of music. [3] He quotes a remarkable passage from Augustine's Enarration on Psalm xli. 4.

This psalm is sung as "a Psalm for Understanding" (title). For what understanding is it sung? Come, my brethren, catch my eagerness; share with me in this my longing; let us both love, let us both be influenced with this thirst, let us both hasten to the well of understanding. . . . He is both the Fountain and the Light; for it is "In Thy Light that we shall see Light." . . . There is, then, a certain light within, not possessed by those who understand not . . .

and so on, too long to quote. But he continues (§ 9):

. . . It was going up to the tabernacle (i.e. the church) the psalmist arrived at the house of God; . . . by following the leadings of a certain delight, an inward mysterious and hidden pleasure, as if from the house of God there sounded sweetly some instrument; and he whilst walking in the tabernacle,

---

[1] See part ii., p. 226.

[2] *The Sanity of Mysticism*, chap. xv., pp. 157 sqq.

[3] St. Augustine wrote six books upon music: on the duration of syllables, their value and their combinations: the effects of rhythm and variations of method and forms of verse were all exactly explained. And this was only a part, for six other books to follow should have treated of melody.

hearing a certain inward sound, led on by its sweetness and following the guidance of the sound, withdrawing himself from all noise of flesh and blood, made his way on, even to the house of God. . . . In the house of God there is a never-ending festival; the angelic choir makes an eternal holiday, the presence of God's face, joy that never fails. From that everlasting, perpetual festivity there sounds in the ears of the heart a mysterious strain, melodious and sweet, provided only the world does not drown the sounds. As he walks in this tabernacle, and considers God's wonderful works for the redemption of the faithful, the sound of that festivity charms the ears and bears the *hart* away to the *water-brooks*.[1]

Abbot Butler adds this note on the long passage he has quoted, which forms indeed a commentary upon Richard's mystical experience.

In § 2 St. Augustine sets in the forefront the vague yet intense longing for something not clearly known, yet strongly desired, which is the motive power impelling one, destined to ascend the Mount of Contemplation, to embark on the dark and difficult way that lies before him. The mystics are all agreed as to the necessity of this great desire as the condition of success in the pursuit of the Contemplative life. Here too is emphasised that characteristic doctrine of the mystics—the special inward light enlightening with spiritual understanding the minds of those who cultivate the inner life. In § 3 is set forth as a preliminary condition of contemplation the necessity of the destruction of vices in the soul and the elimination of imperfections. Herein lies the feature which marks off true mysticism from its counterfeits. It is the constant teaching of the great mystics that there can be no progress in prayer without mortification. . . .

Then Augustine speaks of his search for God—"'that if I could I might not believe only, but might also see somewhat,'" which the abbot says is the "fundamental Postulate of mysticism": that it is possible in this life to see somewhat of God—to have an experimental perception of Him. To attain to this the mind must "mount up above itself to where God dwells." St. Augustine finds that that which gives to the soul its final uplift to the mystic height, is the thought of the holiness of God's faithful servants; this the abbot thinks is "unique."

The more normal teaching of the mystics, that God is found

---

[1] *Western Mysticism*, pp. 26–9.

within the soul, is of course also taught by St. Augustine in various places. . . .

And so he comes to the mystic experience itself. Then is he struck dumb with astonishment. It is as if some strains of the music of the heavenly festival reached the ear of the heart, leading him by a mysterious inward delight. And led on by the sweetness of this inward sound, withdrawing himself from all noise of flesh and blood, charmed by that melodious strain that comes from the court of Heaven, he is borne along to the "water-brooks," that is, to the inward sweetness of God.

In § 10 St. Augustine thus describes his actual experience:

But seeing that the corruptible body presseth down the soul, even we have in some way dispersed the clouds by walking as longing leads us on, and for a brief while we have come within reach of that sound, so that by an effort we may catch something from that house of God, yet through the burden of our infirmity we sink back to our usual level . . . for he that was led on by delight of that inward, spiritual sound to feel contempt for exterior things and be ravished by things interior, is but mortal man still; is still in peril in the midst of the offences of this world. . . . Lo, we have been gladdened by certain inward delights; with the mind's eye we have been able to behold, though but with a momentary glance, something not susceptible of change; why dost thou still disquiet me? Why art thou still cast down? For thou dost not doubt of thy God. . . . Why do I disquiet thee, but because I am not yet there, where that delight is, to which I was rapt as it were in passing. . . .

And the abbot comments: "In this passage Augustine has described the phenomena of actual mystical experience"; the act of contemplation being here characterised as "the 'perception of Something Unchangeable' accompanied by a wondrous inward joy; but after the brief moment of realisation the soul, weighed down by the burden of its infirmity, sinks back to its own level and normal experience. . . . Here is emphasised what is the testimony of all the mystics as to the transient nature of the act of contemplation." [1]

Dr. Horstman takes the awakening in Rolle of *canor* as parallel with Bede's description of Cædmon. "He learned to sing not from man nor as taught by any man,

[1] *Western Mysticism*, pp. 33–4.

but by the help of God he received a free gift of song";
and adds:

This canor—this divine melody chiming from above and
resounding in his breast which henceforth is full of delightful
harmony, so that his thought, his very prayers, turn into
songs to Jesus or Mary, and that he now modulates what
before he used to say—what can it mean but the awakening
of his poetical powers, which to him appear a miraculous
gift imparted at the height of the ecstasies? [1]

But surely here he misses the point. It is "heavenly
music" of which Richard speaks,[2] the "mysterious strain"
of Augustine, "melodious and sweet provided only the
world does not drown the sounds." Richard complains
that people came asking him to sing in the kirk not understanding this "ghostly song":

Because in the kirk of God there are singers ordained in
their degree, and set to praise God and to stir the people to
devotion, some have come to me asking why I would not sing
as other men when they have ofttimes seen me in the solemn
masses. They weened forsooth I had done wrong, for ilk man,
they say, is bound to sing bodily before his Maker, and yield
music with his outward voice. I answered not thereof, for they
know not how I gave forth melody and a sweet voice to my
Maker; but, because they could not understand by what way,
they weened that no man might have ghostly song.
Therefore my soul has found boldness to open my music
a little that is come to me by burning love; in which I sing
before Jesu and sound notes of the greatest sweetness. Also
the more they have stood up against me, because I fled the
outward songs that are wont in the kirks, and the sweetness
of the organ that is heard gladly by the people; only abiding
among these either when the need of hearing mass—which
elsewhere I could not hear—or the solemnity of the day asked
it on account of the backbiting of the people.
Truly I have desired to sit alone that I might take heed to
Christ alone, that had given to me ghostly song, in the which
I might offer Him praises and prayers. They that reproved me
trowed not this, and therefore they would have brought me
to their manner; but I could not leave the grace of Christ
and consent to fond men that knew me not within. Therefore

---

[1] Vol. ii. p. vii. (note 2).
[2] In the previous chapter we dealt fully with Richard's use of
canor, and can only here give some of the references in *The Fire*;
which might be multiplied greatly (pp. 66, 67, 76, 144, 145, 150,
181, 190, 191, etc.).

I let them speak, and I did that that was to do after the state in the which God had set me. (pp. 132–3.)

This distaste for the music of "outward song" in the kirks is an interesting point with Richard, and one upon which he dwells elsewhere, in a passage also worth quoting. He is anxious to stress the point that it is not organ music.

Other men's words break and destroy their prayers, and this forsooth happens not to the perfect. They truly are so stabled that by no cry or noise, or any other thing, can they be distracted from prayer or thought, but only cut off by such from song. For truly this sweet ghostly song is specially worth because it is given to the most special.[1] It accords not with outward songs, the which in kirks and elsewhere are used. It discords mickle from all that is formed by man's outward voice to be heard with bodily ears; but among angels' tunes it has an acceptable melody, and by them that have known it, it is commended with marvel.[2]

See and understand and be not beguiled, for to you I have shown, to the honour of Almighty God and to your profit, why I fled strangers in the kirks, and for what cause I loved not to mingle with them, and desired not to hear organ players. Truly they gave me letting from songful sweetness, and gart (made) fail the full clear song. And therefore marvel not if I fled that that confused me; and in that I had been to blame, if I had not left what would have put me from so sweet song. Forsooth I had erred if I had done otherwise; but well I knew of whom I received it. Therefore I have alway conformed me to do His will, lest He should take from me, being unkind, that He gave to me kindly. I had great liking to sit in (the) wilderness that I might sing more sweetly far from noise, and with fervour of heart I might feel sweetest praise; the which doubtless I have received of His gift whom above all things I have wonderfully loved.

Truly my heart has not yearned in bodily desire, nor have I conceived this comfortable song that I have sung, singing in Jesu, from a creature. Therefore love has brought me thereto, that I should not stand in the plight in which the unworthy are cast down; but that I should be raised above the height of all seen things, and from heaven should be kindled and lightened to praise God, whose praising is not comely in the sinner's mouth. (pp. 140–1.)

---

[1] There is some corruption here in the English translation. The Latin reads: "Ita enim stabiliti sunt, quod nullo clamore vel tumultu aut quacumque alia re distrahi poterunt ab oracione vel cogitacione, set tantum a canore per talia diuelli. Istud namque dulce canticum spirituale quidem et speciale valde quia specialissimis] datum."

[2] Admiration.

Moreover Richard tells us in *The Form of Living* that "the special gift of those that lead a solitary life is for to love Ihesu Christ," and he that "mickle loves, him list oft sing of his love, for joy that he or she has when they think on that that they love, especially if their lover be true and loving." [1]

And in his commentary on the Canticles, as we saw in the last chapter, he writes of the lover as being "in a condition of mental exaltation and a rapture of love," so that "he is carried away beyond himself with a marvellous sweetness and is enabled in a wonderful manner *to sing to God with a spiritual instrument.*"

> Soothly [he says in a passage already quoted] it is the sweetness of angels that he has received into his soul. . . . Such as is the song of angels so is the voice of this true lover. . . . He that knows this, knows also angels' song, *for both are of one kind, here and in heaven.* Tune pertains to song, not to the ditty that is sung. This praising and song is angels' meat, as it is written in the psalm: *Panem angelorum manducavit homo.* (p. 138.)

Here again he is at one with Augustine.

It has been the thought of many that music will be the universal language by which all men shall converse together in the courts of heaven; and surely this is not fantastical but most reasonable. "Death," says Richard, "shall be to me as heavenly music." Why? Surely because it is for him the entrance to the city of music.

Music is the outcome of intense feeling; the natural medium of praise and rejoicing. Nature is full of music. Apart from the song of birds and incessant hum of insects there is the music of wind; sometimes a gentle singing among the rushes; the soughing of a rush of wind through fir-trees, or the blasts of some mighty storm amid the mountains; or there is the song of water, as it gurgles through the stones of a mountain stream, or laps against the sand upon the seashore, or the roar of the waves, or the rush of some mighty waterfall. Countless indeed are the instruments which nature employs, and can there be an end to the music of the spiritual world?

Even here on earth music is the most symbolic, the least material of arts. It is not permanent, but passes as the bird

[1] See Horstman, vol. i., p. 29.

who wings its flight from the darkness through the lighted hall back again to the black night. To be musical it must be transient, yet it seems to have power for the short moments it endures to uplift the soul to another plane. To those who have the hearing ear, music is more than beautiful melody, it is a mystical experience. Music is indeed the most mystical of all arts because song is always the expression of love; and love is the material from which the immaterial is fashioned. And if you should ask how can this be, I would refer you to the fragrance of a flower. Music is like fragrance: evanescent, intangible, but with a subtle influence upon our memory that nothing else has. Listening to some melody our sense of space and time merges into an everlasting present. And what else can eternity be? Heaven can be naught else but the eternal presence of God.

Craving the reader's pardon for this digression we must return for a moment to Augustine. There is no doubt that Augustine had a great attraction for Richard. It is possible that the latter's *Rule for Hermits* owes something to Augustine's so-called "Rule," though he never drew up a Rule properly so called, but his Epistle 211 contains practical advice to a community of nuns on their daily life; and his Sermons 355 and 356 describe the common life he led with his clerics at Hippo. These latter were the basis of the Rule of the Augustinian Canons, and it is possible that Richard in later life joined the Order of the Augustinian Hermits, sometimes wrongly called Friars, but we shall have to consider this point later.[1]

In the passages we have cited we can see a close kinship between Augustine and Richard in their general mystical characteristics, and still closer is the likeness to a work now considered spurious which was very widely read in the thirteenth century, the *Meditationes et Soliloquia*. Some scholars think it was compiled by Hugh of St. Victor from the *Confessions*, and an application of the Rule of St. Augustine. For several centuries it retained the name *Soliloquies*. Not unlike in nature, both Richard and Augustine having gone through much moral stress and temptation, dwell upon the yearning desire they have for God, and upon the need of purification and of purging the soul of sin before they can hope to find God. They are alike

[1] See p. 181 infra.

also in their rapturous joy in the love of God, and constantly use the term "inebriated" (which Misyn always translates "moistened") in reference to this love. Augustine in his *Confessions* speaks of that wondrous sweetness, which were it perfected in him, he says, "I know not what else the life to come will be." But naturally the parallels seem closer in the original Latin than in English translations.

Dr. Horstman in his list cites many works which have been fathered alike upon Richard, Augustine and Bernard; which shows that there was some resemblance between them. He also includes (vol. ii., p. 377) a translation of a meditation wrongly attributed to St. Augustine, and which was then popular and is found in many English MSS. It is a free translation, made in rhythmical prose, and Horstman thinks it "is possibly" by Richard; beyond a doubt Richard knew Augustine's reputed meditation on the Passion, of which he incorporates a verse into his lyric in the *Ego Dormio*.

We also find a translation of the *Consilia Isidori*, another popular devotional book at that date, ascribed to Richard, and, as we have seen, he took extracts from the *Moralia* of St. Gregory when he wrote on Job. There are few safer methods of coming to any right judgment in tracing influences in these early times than taking a survey of the contents of the various MSS. and tracing from them what books were most popular. The actual MSS. now in our possession are posterior to Richard, most of them containing works ascribed to him; but they are a gauge as to what writers were then most read. I give a list of the contents of one such MS. (Vesp. E. 1, Brit. Mus.) as an example.[1] It will be seen that it contains many of the Latin tracts then attributed to St. Bernard and St. Bonaventura, which had so great an influence upon Richard, and through him upon contemporary religious thought in England; and also the *cursus* of the *Jesu dulcis Memoria*.

We are only beginning to clear the ground of the many mistakes which have been made concerning Rolle during the last fifty years; and one is in attributing to him the inception, in England, of the devotion to the Holy Name. There is no doubt that he gave it great impetus by his own

[1] See appendix iii., p. 319.

devotion to a personal Christ, which breathes through all his writings and which is one of the fundamental notes in Christian mysticism; but that devotion had been already deeply rooted in England in the thirteenth and fourteenth centuries by extracts and translations from the works of SS. Augustine, Anselm, Bernard and Bonaventura.

The nucleus of this devotion is to be found in St. Bernard's fifteenth sermon on the Canticles on the Name of Jesus; and to the hymn, or rather poem, then attributed to him, *Jesu dulcis Memoria*. His authorship of this poem is, however, impossible, since it has been found in a MS. of the eleventh century; and St. Bernard was only born in 1091.[1]

This hymn became immensely popular and was translated and paraphrased, and expanded many times in Middle English so as to form a rosary. It did much in setting the type of mysticism which was so largely developed by Rolle; but it was known before the time of his boyhood, for two lyrics in imitation of it occur in the famous collection of Middle English lyrics in MS. Harl. 2253, which is dated *c*. 1310.[2]

In one of the Prymers in the British Museum [3] there is an old prayer to the Name of Jesus which, judging from his lyrics, must have been familiar to Richard. It reads:

Ihesu my lord; ihesu my god; ihesu my creature; ihesu my sauour; ihesu my blis; ihesu my succour; ihesu my helpe,

---

[1] I owe this fact to the courtesy of the late Rev. G. H. Palmer, Mus.Doc. Dom Pothier of Solesmes (at present the Abbot of La Wandrille, in Normandy) made this discovery, and ascribes the poem to a Benedictine abbess (see *La Revue du Chant Grégorien*, xᵉ année, p. 147). Yet before the finding of this early MS. M. Hauréau wrote: "La pièce (i.e. le jubilus *de nomine Jesu*) composée de quarante-huit strophes de quatre vers commence *Jesu dulcis memoria*; ou bien encore *Dulcis Jesu memoria* . . . n'offre aucun trait original. L'inspiration en est pieuse, d'une piété vive et soutenue; mais ce qui fait le mérite d'un poème: l'invention, le charme de style, le judicieux emploi des figures, tout cela manque dans cette amplification mystique." And he points out that no editor attributed the poem to St. Bernard until Gillot, in 1586; and all the MSS. which ascribe it to Bernard are of the fourteenth and fifteenth centuries. "Mabillon," he notes, "a judicieusement pensé qu'un tel écrivain ne devait pas être considéré comme auteur certain d'un si méchant poème." (*Des Poèmes Latins attribués à Saint Bernard*, par B. Hauréau (Paris, 1890), pp. 63 and 65.)

[2] See also p. 288 (pt. ii.).

[3] MS. 27, 948, fol. 63.

ihesu my comforth; ihesu my myrthe; ihesu my solas; ihesu my ledur; ihesu my techer; ihesu my counselour; ihesu my maker; ihesu my founder; ihesu my mercy: ihesu haue mercy, ihesu lord mercy, ihesu, ihesu graumercy. Fader, Sone and holy ghost iii persones and oo god graumercy. amen.

Every one of these titles (except "ihesu my founder") is used by Richard. We shall find later that nearly every lyric of chapter iii., part ii. of this volume is centred upon the Name of Jesus. And besides the lyrics, one of his best-known Latin tracts is entirely devoted to the praise of the Holy Name. It forms a part of the *Postillae super Cantica*,[1] and is a commentary on the second verse of the Vulgate translation of the Canticles.

This is most certainly influenced by St. Bernard's famous Sermon xv., which should be read in full. It has been translated by Mr. S. J. Eales, from whose edition I quote short extracts.[1] It is entitled:

> *In what manner the name of Jesus is a salutary medicine to the faithful Christian in all adversities*. . . . The Name had been poured forth . . . not only poured [*fusum*], but poured forth [*effusum*]; for the impouring [*infusum*] was already achieved. Already the heavens possessed it; already it had been made known to angels. . . . *Thy Name is as oil poured forth*.

Why oil? he asks.

> . . . as far as I am able to judge, the reasons are these three: that it gives light; it gives nourishment; and it anoints. It maintains flame; it nourishes the flesh, it relieves pain; it is light, it is food; and it is medicine. . . . (p. 83.)

and it follows closely the *cursus Jesus dulcis Memoria*:

"As honey to the mouth, as melody in the ear; as song of gladness to the heart, is the Name of Jesus. . . ."

To speak of this devotion to the Name of Christ as a "cult" is, at this early date, misleading. The "cult" came much later with St. Bernardine of Siena, who in the fifteenth century used to stir people's devotion by his symbol of the Holy Name painted upon a board, with rays of light surrounding it; a sign constantly seen to-day fastened

---

[1] Cf. p. 127 supra. The *Postillae* are found in MS. C. C. C. Oxford 193: and in the MS. Vesp. E. 1 at the British Museum (an abridgment of the latter is MS. 127 of St. John's College, Oxford).

[2] See *Cantica Canticorum*, by Samuel J. Eales (Elliot Stock, 1895).

above the doors of houses in Italy. In its first beginning
it was no specific manner of worship, but only the expression
of especial devotion to the Person of Christ Incarnate;
as here it is the humanity of Christ which Bernard would
impress upon his hearers:

Nothing is so powerful as the Name of Jesus to restrain the
impulse of anger, to repress the swelling of pride, to cure the
wound of envy, to bridle the impulse of luxury, and to extin-
guish the flame of fleshly desire, to temper avarice and put to
flight ignoble and impure thoughts. . . . Why? . . . For
when I utter the Name of Jesus I set before my mind not only
a Man, meek and humble in heart, moderate, pure, benign,
merciful, and in short conspicuous for every honourable and
saintly quality, but also in the same individual the Almighty
God, who both restores me to spiritual health by His example,
and renders me strong by His assistance. All these things are
said by me when the Name of Jesus is pronounced. From
Him, inasmuch as He is Man, I derive an example; inasmuch
as He is the Mighty One, I obtain assistance. Of His example
I make, as it were, medicinal and salutary herbs, as His help
is an instrument to prepare them; thus I obtain a remedy of
power such as none among physicians is able to compound. . . .
(p. 84.)

Whence [he exclaims in the same sermon] do you suppose so
bright and so sudden a light of faith has been kindled in the
whole world except by the preaching of the Name of Jesus?
. . . Is any of you sad? Let Jesus come into your heart; let
His Name leap thence to your lips, and behold, when that
blessed Name arises, its light disperses the clouds of sadness,
and brings back security and peace. Is any falling into crime,
or even in his despair rushing upon death? Let him call upon
that life-giving Name, and does he not speedily begin to
breathe again, and revive. . . .

and so on.

We could find many similar passages in Richard. In
The Form (chap. ix.) he writes:

If thou wilt be well with God, and have grace to rule thy
life and come to the joy of love, this name JESUS, fasten it so
fast in thy heart that it come never out of thy thought. And
when thou speakest to Him, and through custom sayest
Jesus, it shall be in thine ear joy; in thy mouth honey, and in
thine heart melody: for men shall think joy to hear that name
be named, sweetness to speak it, mirth and song to think it.
If thou thinkest on Jesus continually, and holdest it firmly,
it purges thy sin and kindles thy heart; it clarifies thy soul,

it removes anger and does away slowness. It wounds in love and fulfils with charity; it chases the devil and puts out dread; it opens heaven, and makes a contemplative man.

Have in mind Ihesu, for all phantoms and vices it puts out from the lover. And hail oft Mary, both night and day. Mickle love and joy shalt thou feel if thou wilt do after this lore.

And in *The Fire* he thus describes what this "joying in Jesu" means to him:

. . . unto the time I can clearly see my Beloved, I shall think of His full sweet Name, holding it, joying, in my mind.

And no marvel that he be glad thereof in this life that has lust ever to fulfil the desires of His Maker. Nothing is merrier than JESU to sing, nothing more delightful than JESU to hear. Hearing it truly mirths the mind; and song up-lifts it. And truly, whiles I want this, sighing, and heavy as it were with hunger and thirst, methinks myself forsaken. Forsooth when I feel the halsing and kissing of my Love, with untold delight as it were I overflow; whom true lovers, for love only of His unmeasured goodness, set before all things. Coming therefore into me, He comes inshedding perfect love. My heart also He refreshes, giving perseverance. He warms me, and also makes fat, all lettings to love putting away. (pp. 109–10.)

and again: "O good Jesu, Thou hast bound my heart in the thought of Thy Name, and now I can but sing it"; and in *The Mending* (chap. xl.) there are many references to his joy in the Holy Name; "that I may sit and rest, joying in Thee, Jesu."

The mediaeval devotion to the Holy Name is analogous to belief in the Presence of Christ in the Blessed Sacrament. It was based upon the words of St. Paul (Phil. ii. 8–11):

Being found in fashion as a man, he humbled himself, and became obedient unto death, even the death of the cross.

Wherefore God also hath highly exalted him, and given him a name which is above every name:

That at the name of Jesus every knee should bow, of things in heaven, and things in earth, and things under the earth;

And that every tongue should confess that Jesus Christ is Lord, to the glory of God the Father.

As God tabernacled in man in the Person of Jesus Christ, so does He tabernacle in the Blessed Sacrament. There, as has been truly said: "Our Lord enters into relation with locality for us." He focuses His Humanity

L

there, upon the altar, in the Bread and Wine, under which He veils His Godhead; so that we worship Him there in the same way as we should have worshipped Him upon earth, when His Divinity was veiled in a human body for three-and-thirty years, since God can be seen only by spiritual vision and handled only by the touch of faith. Both the repetition of the Holy Name of Jesus, and the Presence of Christ upon the altar, are a means of making more real to mind and spirit the actual and eternal presence of God in the person of Christ, although the latter in a higher and more objective degree.

For since the soul of man is an enigma, invisible and intangible to its possessor, the body being but the outward sign; therefore as long as this life lasts man must be content to rest in sacraments, the essence of which must of necessity be indefinable.

Might not these words of Richard when he invokes the Holy Name be used with an even fuller meaning in Presence of the Blessed Sacrament?

O good Jesu, who shall grant me to feel Thee, that now may neither be felt nor seen? Shed Thyself into the entrails of my soul. Come into my heart and fill it with clearest sweetness. Moisten my mind with the hot wine of Thy sweet love, that forgetful of all ills and all scornful visions and imaginations, and only having Thee, I may be glad and joy in Jesu my God. Henceforward, sweetest Lord, go not from me, continually biding with me in Thy sweetness; for Thy presence only is solace to me, and Thy absence only leaves me heavy.

And in the last and highest degree of love, inseparable or undeparted "when the mind is kindled with great love, and cleaves to Christ with undeparted thought . . . as it were bound in heart to Him," Richard says:

And most this name JESU he, in so mickle worships and loves that It continually rests in his mind. . . . Nothing is sweet to her (i.e. the soul), nothing she savours, except it be made sweet in JESU; whose memory is as a song of music in a feast of wine.[1]

This devotion to the Person of Christ in the Holy Name is also testified by the custom in these early MSS. of

[1] Other passages from this chapter have been quoted on pp. 109–10, 120–2 supra, and should be read again in this connection.

writing Jesu in much larger letters, as is so often found when that Name denotes the yearning after God, as here: "All my heart truly fastened in desire for JESU is turned into heat of love"; and in the passage just cited.

It is not surprising that we should meet with St. Bernard's writings, in Latin, as well as in English translations, in so large a number of MSS. in our libraries, when we remember that St. Bernard had in 1131 sent his secretary William with twelve monks from Clairvaux to establish houses of the same Order in England. He fixed upon Yorkshire, always a refuge for hermits and monks because of its vast spaces of uncultivated and waste land. Within twenty years five of the great Cistercian abbeys were founded: Rievaulx, Kirkstall, Byland, Jervaulx and Roche. Of these there is little doubt that Richard would know Byland, not far to the east of Topcliffe, and Fountains, an earlier foundation, a little farther off on the south-east, and in later years Roche, which was within easy distance of Hampole, and in their libraries he would find copies of the founders' tracts and sermons.

About a century later a Franciscan saint, Bonaventura, was appointed to the See of York (1265), but he begged the Pope, Clement IV., who had formerly been papal legate to England, for his release. His refusal of the archbishopric must have been much debated in the monasteries of Yorkshire and probably increased the popularity of his works. Miss Deanesley speaks of his *Life of Christ*, written originally for the instruction of a woman, as the one most used for translation throughout Europe. "It contains quite as much homily as actual narration. Many verse translations of the part on the Passion are frequent, but there was no complete prose translation before Wyclif. It was used by Rolle and quoted in his *Meditation on the Passion of Our Lord*, which is a more fervent and glowing work, and of course further from the original." [1]

The third chapter of Bonaventura's *Life of Christ* is translated under the title *The Rule of the Life of Our Lady*,[2] and an abridged prose translation of his *Meditationes Vitae Christi* is found in the Thornton MS. under the title of *The Privity of the Passion*. It contains chapters 74–92 of the

[1] Cf. *The Lollard Bible*, pp. 152–3.
[2] See MSS. Harl. 1022 and Bod. 938.

Meditationes, and is divided into parts to correspond with the Hours of the Passion. This is printed by Horstman (vol. ii., pp. 198 sqq.). Another very free translation of a part of the *Meditationes* is found in an east midland MS. called *Meditations of the Supper of Our Lord*. There are also two other pieces not in a northern dialect, based upon *The Privity of the Passion* (Horstman, i., pp. 83 and 92), which are ascribed to Richard. They are full of rhyme, assonance and poetical ornament and are to be associated with *The Talking of the Love of God*, which, as we shall see presently,[1] is influenced by Anselm. There is yet another *Meditation on the Passion and Three Arrows on Doomsday*, which Horstman says misleadingly is "certainly a work of Rolle's"[2] (vol. i., p. 112). This must not be confused with a later piece under the same title, *The Three Arrows on Doomsday*, contained in many southern MSS. and which has been ascribed to Wyclif, and certainly cannot be by Rolle. Probably neither of these *Three Arrows* is by Richard, the first is unlike in style, and the second is too late in date. The English tract on Daily Work (see p. 133 supra) which is sometimes called *The Mirror of Discipline* is really based upon Bonaventura's *Speculum Disciplinae ad novitios*, though it is not intended for religious, and there are similar writings by Hugh of St. Victor and St. Bernard.

Bonaventura also wrote two treatises on love. The first of these, *De Triplice Via*, was mistakenly called the *Incendium Amoris*, in confusion with Richard's treatise, and a part of the latter's prologue was inserted into Bonaventura's *De Triplice Via*.[3] The other, entitled *De Perfectione Vitae*, contains a good deal which is similar to

---

[1] See p. 155 infra. Miss Peebles in her article in vol. ix. of Bryn Mawr College Monographs, p. 85, says that "*The Talking of the Love of God* is an imitation of Rolle's *Meditatio de Passione Domini*."

[2] A few lines are closely parallel to a short lyric on the Passion, beginning:

"Unkind man give keep to me;
And look what pain I have suffered for thee. . . ."

The prose passage begins: "Now understand thou unkind man . . ." (see vol. i., p. 119), but neither the lyric nor the prose tract is thought to be by Rolle.

[3] See note (p. 243) in my edition of *The Fire of Love*.

Richard in thought, as well as to Augustine. Here, for example, is what he says on prayer:

> The love of God vivifies prayer. . . . It sometimes happens that the mind is rapt out of itself, when we are so inflamed with heavenly desires that everything earthly becomes distasteful, and the fire of divine love burns beyond measure, so that the soul melts like wax, and is dissolved, ascending up before the throne of God like the fumes of fragrant incense. Again it sometimes happens that the soul is so flooded with divine light, and overwhelmed by the vision of God's beauty, that it is stricken with bewilderment and dislodged from its bearings. And the deeper it sinks down by self-abasement in the presence of God's beauty, like a streak of lightning, the quicker it is caught up and rapt out of itself. Finally it occurs that the soul, inebriated by the fulness of interior sweetness, utterly forgets what it is and what it has been, and is transported into a state of ineffable beatitude and entirely permeated with uncreated love.[1]

In *The Triple Way* Bonaventura distinguishes six stages or degrees of perfect charity; they are sweetness, yearning, satiety, spiritual inebriation, security and tranquillity. These are more or less in agreement with Richard's three degrees, love insuperable, inseparable and singular, but the Italian has a clearer mind and a greater gift for exposition and classification. But indeed it would be almost impossible not to find many parallels in the writings of men of like mind, inspired by the same fervour of love for God. But the likeness lies in the substance rather than in the style; songs of love having of necessity much resemblance to one another.

We find a closer similarity, both of style and thought, between Richard and the two great Victorines, Hugh and Richard. The philosophical and theological school of St. Victor was founded at the convent of St. Victor (hence its name), close to Paris, by William of Champeaux, who, being unable to withstand the brilliant attacks of Abelard, had resigned his chair at Notre-Dame. St. Bernard took a lively interest in it and indirectly influenced its teaching; and Bonaventura had an especial admiration for Hugh, whom he called "alter Augustinus." In his classification of theologians according to their threefold interpretation of the Scriptures (i.e. allegorical and spiritual,

[1] Chap. v. of *De Perf. Vitae*. Opera Omnia, tom. viii.

moral, and mystical) as Doctors, Preachers and Con-
templatives he gives Augustine as the chief example of the
Doctors, Gregory of the Preachers, and Dionysius of the
Contemplatives, and then says:

"Anselm follows Augustine; Bernard follows Gregory;
and Richard follows Dionysius, for Anselm excelled in
reasoning, Bernard in preaching, Richard in contemplation; but Hugh in all these."

Hugh (1096–1141) was of noble birth and entered St.
Victor *c.* 1115, St. Bernard surviving him by twelve years.
He was a philosopher as well as mystic; yet knowledge to
him was only the vestibule of the mystic life. In his description of the stages in the ascent of the soul to God he
closely follows Augustine, holding that by *cogitatio* we see
God in the material world; by *meditatio* we find Him in
the interior soul; and by *contemplatio* we have a supernatural intuition of Him. In his interpretation of Scripture
his thought dwells perpetually in a world of allegory.
In this he has no resemblance to Rolle although some
similarity to the writer of *The Prick of Conscience*, and
this may have led critics to lay undue emphasis upon
his influence. Hugh of St. Victor more truly than St.
Bernard may be said to be the founder of what was
regarded as the orthodox science of mysticism; even in
his doctrinal works there is a mystical element, and
the love of God pervades them all. One of his most
beautiful mystical writings was in praise of love, *De Laude
Caritatis*, and this has more in common with Richard
the Hermit.

The influence of the Victorines upon Rolle leaves great
scope for study, but it is a subject for the Latin scholar,
since Rolle's Latin writings would have to be read carefully
besides the works, which are enormous in bulk, of Hugh and
Richard of St. Victor. Miss Deanesley sees "a considerable
resemblance between Rolle's style and thought in the
Incendium" and the mystical works of Hugh, and cites the
word "arrha" as used by both to express the sweetness
granted to the contemplative while still on earth; both
have the same fondness for alliteration, and in her edition
of the *Incendium* she gives parallel passages. But such
evidence is inconclusive, for we have also to consider
Rolle's earlier Latin works and the likeness between the

Melum and the *Amor Dei* and the works of Hugh may be found to be small.

The popularity of the Victorines in England can be tested by the number of translations we find of these works. *The Soul's Ward* is a rendering, with many variations and additions, of a part of one of Hugh of St. Victor's Latin treatises [1]; as is also a short Kentish version added to the *Ayenbite of Inwit*. This latter is of course connected with *The Prick of Conscience*, and I am inclined to think that the supposed indebtedness of Richard to the Victorines is based partly upon his mistaken authorship of this poem.

Richard of St. Victor (d. 1173) was a pupil of Hugh, and became prior in 1162. He was born in the north country and his writings were more widely read in England than were Hugh's. One small work which begins "A grete clerk that men call Richard of Saynt Victor" is often attributed to Rolle, but it is only a fragment of about one hundred and twenty words.[2] His best-known treatises were the *Benjamin Major* and *Benjamin Minor*. The latter was freely translated and abridged and is found in many English MSS. It has been modernised [3] and it is therefore easy to compare it with Richard Rolle. It had great influence upon one type of English writings which were in turn influenced by the pseudo-Dionysius, whose works were first translated into Latin by Erigena. They are: *The Epistle of Discretion in Stirrings of the Soul*; *A Treatise of Discerning Spirits* (these two are printed in *The Cell of Self-knowledge*); *The Divine Cloud of Unknowing*; *Dionese Hid Divinity*; and *The Epistle of Privy Counsel*.

The *Benjamin Minor* seems strangely dissimilar from Rolle's writings. Its style is most affected, and the influence of the Neoplatonist terminology as well as of the works of the pseudo-Dionysius can be clearly detected. But a better book for comparison is his treatise, *The Four Degrees of Fervent Love*, which naturally has more likeness to Rolle. It has been lately translated into French

---

[1] *De Anima et Ejus ad Sui et ad Dei Cognitionem et ad Veram Pietatem Institutione* (lib. iv., c. 13–15).

[2] It is found in MS. Dd. 5.64 (Camb.), and Wells says: "Possibly by Rolle."

[3] In *The Cell of Self-knowledge*, edited by Edmund G. Gardner (Chatto & Windus, 1910).

by M. l'Abbé Leclef, and in the same year (1926) Père Denis, S.J.,[1] translated Rolle's *De Emendatione Peccatorie*, (*The Mending of Life*). Père Denis draws parallels between the hermit's three degrees of love and Richard of St. Victor's, stating that the former has borrowed phrases from the latter, and quotes a passage from *The Mending* which is practically identical with one in St. Victor. It runs: "Sed aliud est esse summum atque aliud esse solum: sicut et aliud est semper praesentem esse et aliud consortem omnino non admittere. Possumus enim et praesentes esse et multos socios habere et prae omnibus quidem superiorem locum tenere." The parallel passage from the Latin of *The Mending* is: "Aliud est solum esse, et aliud summum esse: sicut aliud est semper praesidens esse, et aliud consortem non admittere. Possumus enim multos socios habere, et tamen prae omnibus superiorem locum tenere."

The likeness is so great as to suggest that the scribe inserted this passage, possibly from memory, from St. Victor's book, and this supposition is strengthened by the fact that this passage is not found in two well-known MSS. of the *Emendatio*. We found the same thing in the prologue to *The Fire*, which was inserted into Bonaventura's *De Triplice Via*; or the scholar may discover that the opposite has occurred here, and that Rolle and not Richard of St. Victor was the original author. In any case these apparent superficial similarities are much less important than is the texture and whole idea which underlies a book. The striking point about Richard of St. Victor's mysticism is his similes, especially in his book on *The Four Degrees of Love* where he speaks of mystical love or contemplation as being the espousal of the soul with God. I quote from the French translation:

Au premier degré se font les fiançailles, au deuxième on célèbre les noces, au troisième le mariage se consomme, au quatrième il porte ses fruits. Au premier degré la bien-aimée s'entend dire: " Je te fiancerai à moi pour toujours; je te fiancerai à moi dans la justice et le jugement, dans la grâce et la tendresse; je te fiancerai à moi dans la fidélité" (Hos. ii. 19–20). Au deuxième degré on célèbre les noces à Cana en

---

[1] Both are published by Desclée (Paris, 1926) in "Editions de la Vie Spirituelle."

Galilée, et il est dit à l'âme: "C'est moi qui suis ton époux, et tu ne cesseras de me suivre" (Jer. iii. 14, 19). Du troisième degré il est écrit: "Celui qui s'unit au Seigneur est un seul esprit avec Lui" (1 Cor. vi. 17). Du quatrième: "Nous avons conçu, nous avons été en travail, et nous avons enfanté l'esprit" (Is. xxvi. 18).[1]

And again, compare the following with Rolle's three degrees of love, insuperable, inseparable and singular; and draw, if you can, parallels.

Au premier degré Dieu vient dans l'âme, et l'âme rentre en elle-même. Au deuxième degré, elle s'élève au-dessus d'elle-même et est attirée jusqu'à Dieu. Au troisième degré l'âme élevée jusqu'à Dieu pénètre entièrement en lui. Au quatrième degré, pour plaire a Dieu, elle sort et descend au-dessous d'elle-même.

Both Hugh and Richard of St. Victor insist upon the knowledge of self as the way to knowledge of God. "The way to ascend to God," says Hugh, "is to descend into oneself." And Richard here continues:

Au premier degré l'âme rentre en elle-même, au deuxième elle va au-delà d'elle-même. Au premier degré elle arrive jusqu'à elle-même, au troisième elle arrive jusqu'à Dieu. Au premier degré elle rentre en elle à cause d'elle, au quatrième elle en sort pour l'amour du prochain.

A far more fundamental influence not only upon Richard but upon the whole trend of English mysticism was that of St. Anselm (1033–1109).

His famous works [writes Mr. J. R. Green in a well-known passage of his history] were the first attempts of any Christian thinker to elicit the idea of God from the very nature of the human reason. His passion for abstruse thought robbed him of food and sleep. Sometimes he could hardly pray. Often the night was a long watch till he could seize his conception and write it on the wax tablets which lay beside him. But not even a fever of intense thought such as this could draw Anselm's heart from its passionate tenderness and love. Sick monks in the infirmary could relish no drink save the juice which his hand had squeezed for them from the grape-bunch. In the later days of his archbishoprick a hare chased by the hounds took refuge under his horse, and his voice grew loud as he forbade a huntsman to stir in the chase, while the creature

---

[1] *Les Quatre Degrés de l'Amour Ardent*, traduction de M. l'Abbé Ed. Leclef, pp. 27, 30 (Desclée, Paris, 1926).

darted off again to the woods. Even the greed of lands for the Church to which so many religious men yielded found its characteristic rebuke as the battling lawyers saw Anselm quietly close his eyes in court and go peacefully to sleep.[1]

Anselm's actual stay in England during his tenure of the See of Canterbury was comparatively short. He began while there to write the *Cur Deus Homo* (*c.* 1089) upon which Grosseteste lectured in Oxford. This book remained the textbook upon which the scholastics built their arguments, and much has been written of his influence upon scholasticism. When forced from the abbey of Bec to succeed Lanfranc at Canterbury he had brought a large number of MSS. with him and also many of his monks among whom were copyists. He did all in his power to promote learning during the turbulent years of William Rufus' reign while he remained in England; and his monks restored the Benedictine tradition in the south where their monasteries became again seats of learning.

Anselm's famous saying: "neque enim quaero intelligere, ut credam; sed credo ut intelligam," expresses his mystical tendency, and Professor Schofield thinks that his influence upon English mysticism has never been gauged,[2] while Miss Allen in an interesting essay [3] writes thus:

It is true that he had little concern with the development of mystical theology, but in the growth of the mystical type of personal devotion his share seems to have been great; and this, rather than metaphysics or visions, was to the last the principal element of English mysticism. Parts of his prayers and meditations may almost be said to set the type for the characteristics of English mysticism, and they even contain references to the Name of Jesus, the devotion which was later to be so popular in England.

Quite possibly the prayer cited on p. 158 may have been by Anselm. Migne [4] prints prayers and meditations which represent Anselm's own devotions and these, as Père Ragey in his interesting life of the saint notes, would in

[1] *History of the English People*, by J. R. Green, pp. 137–8 (Macmillan, 1892).

[2] *English Literature from the Norman Conquest to Chaucer*, by Professor Schofield, p. 33 (London, 1906).

[3] "Mystical Lyrics of the *Manuel des Péchiez*," in *Romanic Review*, vol. x., pp. 183 sqq.

[4] Also cf. Migne, vol. clviii.

his personal intercourse with his brother monks and with others, have stimulated this type of devotion. Certainly his prayers were more often copied than any other of his writings, and spread everywhere. We have several such manuals in our libraries, well-worn little books of a size that could be easily carried in the pocket.[1]

Two of Anselm's meditations have been ascribed to Rolle; and there has always been confusion between Augustine and Anselm in early MSS. Miss Allen notes that some of Augustine's meditations are also attributed to John, Abbot of Fécamp, who was neighbour to Anselm while the latter was at Bec; but it is more probable that John borrowed from Anselm. Many meditations and prayers gathered under Augustine's name have no claim to be his but really belong to Anselm; while others, on the contrary, said to be by Anselm are not his.

Anselm's influence has also been traced on several alliterative and lyrical writings in prose of the south-western dialect belonging to the thirteenth century. They are *The Orisoun of Our Lord*; *The Lofsong of Our Lord*; and *The Wohung of Our Lord*.[2] These are full of reminiscences of the prayers and meditations of Anselm. Two of them were combined and abridged in a later writing, *The Talking of the Love of God*, which is an imitation of Rolle's *Meditation on the Passion*, though not his.[3] Mr. Wells thinks that they also bear marks of the influence of Hugh of St. Victor, and of other French writers in Latin.[4]

These tracts are earlier than Richard and, being written in the south, show a much stronger French influence, and are closely related to the secular love-lyrics of the time; they bear more resemblance to the *Ancren Riwle*, and may be by the same author as the Rule.[5] Rolle, writing in the north where Norman influence had hardly penetrated, is, considering the date at which he wrote, singularly free from any strong influence of the French lays and love-

---

[1] MS. Harl. 2882 is a good example. Cf. also *La Vie de S. Anselme*, by Père Ragey (Paris, 1891).

[2] See *Old English Homilies*, printed by Morris, E.E.T.S., No. xxix.

[3] My authority is Miss Peebles, in an essay published in the Bryn Mawr College Monographs, vol. ix., p. 86, note.

[4] *Manual of the Writings in Middle English* (1050–1400), by J. E. Wells (Oxford Univ. Press, 1916).

[5] Cf. Wells, *Manual*, p. 529.

songs. There is scarcely a trace of knightly flavour in his lyrics.

The absence of French influence upon Rolle is perhaps partly accounted for by the patriotic love of the Yorkshire-man for his county which is still as strong to-day. We have no evidence of Richard either translating from Anglo-Norman French, or using it himself.

But in the south we find the opposite. The dread of provincialism made men more anxious to learn French than to drop it. This preserved rather than lessened the national dignity; and was also of use since the dialects differed so greatly in their pronunciation, if not in their spelling, that men in the south found it hard to understand those from the north. Higden (d. 1364) in his *Polychronicon* describes the Yorkshire dialect as almost unintelligible, and when leave was given to laymen to administer baptism in English the qualification, Peckham (d. 1292) tells us, was added, "vel aliter in lingua materna secundum patriae consuetudinem," which is significant.

We also read that in the monastic houses of St. Peter's, Westminster, and St. Augustine's, Canterbury, only French is to be spoken in cloister and chapter house; and the monks make their profession in French and Latin, but the lay brothers may use English.[1] All of which is a commentary upon Rolle's avoidance of French and his use of either Latin or English. But we must not forget that, unlike Grosseteste, St. Edmund and many other famed English religious writers, he had never visited the schools at Paris.

SS. Augustine, Anselm, Bernard and Bonaventura seem to have been the primary influences upon Richard, and their thought and words are woven into the web of his thought and writings; next to them come the Victorines, who may have had more direct influence than we can at present trace. These he read in Latin, for since he was a pioneer in the use of the vernacular, naturally there were

---

[1] Cf. *The Customary of the Benedictine Monasteries of St. Augustine, Canterbury, and St. Peter's, Westminster,* edited by Sir Edward Maunde Thompson for the Henry Bradshaw Society, London, 1902. ". . . suam confestim peticionem faciet Gallica, si noverit, vel eciam patria lingua" (i., p. 276). "Vel eciam Gallice sic dicat. . . . Aut saltem patria lingua dicat hoc modo: Hic frere N. byhote stedevastnesse and chaste lyf, fore God and alle hys halewen, and þat hic sal ben bousum and liven withouten proprete al my lyf tyme" (ii., p. 228).

no writers in English who affected him as a medium for religious instruction. All that was then being written in English were long epics like the *Cursor Mundi*, or *The Prick of Conscience*, so often fathered upon Rolle; and there was Robert Mannyng, a monk in the Gilbertine priory at Sempringham, who made a free translation of Waddington's *Manuel des Péchiez*, which he called *Handlyng Synne*; but none of these can be said to have influenced him in any way.

But there were two Englishmen then who, unlike the Victorines, lived in England although they wrote in Latin, to whom Richard seems indebted, and who may be said to have had a superficial influence upon him. Both were ecclesiastics; Edmund Rich, who preceded him in Oxford, where he lived a life renowned for its saintliness, and John Hoveden, chaplain to Queen Eleanor, who was mother to Edward I.

Edmund Rich was born *c.* 1170, and taught at Oxford about 1202 until 1222 when he became treasurer at Salisbury Cathedral, and about ten years later was elected to the See of Canterbury; he died at Pontigny *c.* 1240. The *Speculum Ecclesiae* is the only literary composition of his which has come down to us. The date of his writing it is not known, but he dedicated it to the Cistercian monks of Pontigny with whom he took refuge. He was greatly beloved and the esteem in which he was held is testified by his canonisation only six years after his death. His work became immensely popular and many translations of it were made into French and English in prose and in verse. A northern translation which is found in the Thornton MS. and has been ascribed to Richard, is, however, merely a *copy* of a translation which is possibly southern, and its date is 1350, which precludes Richard's authorship.[1] Another English version of the first part of

---

[1] Dr. Horstman prints the Thornton version of the *Mirror* (vol. i., p. 219) and adds this note: "The *Speculum* is the great storehouse from which R. Rolle derived some of his favourite subjects and ideas; and though the translator's name is not given in either manuscript, it is highly probable that R. Rolle himself is the translator: at least its northern origin is beyond doubt." But this has been disputed by Herr Konrath; and the borrowings from the *Speculum* are also found in *The Prick of Conscience*, which poem Horstman attributed to Rolle; hence perhaps this misstatement.

the *Speculum* is found under the title *How a Man shall live perfectly*. It was circulated largely in an Anglo-Norman form, being best known in the south where almost every monastery possessed a copy. Besides as the prose translations we find two translations in verse in the Vernon MS.; one being called *The Spore of Loue*, or *The Prikke of Loue*; and metrical paraphrases of it are numerous.

The reason of its popularity was not far to seek, for it is a storehouse of prayers and ejaculations to be said when awaking, retiring to rest, if awake in the night, etc., and one of the most popular was the prayer for friends, kindred and others, adaptations of which are still often used. It runs:

In manus tuas, domine, & sanctorum angelorum tuorum, commendo in hac nocte (vel die) animam meam et corpus meum, et patrem et matrem, fratres et sorores, amicos, familiares, propinquos, parentes, benefactores meos, et omnem populum catholicum. Custodi nos, domine, in hac nocte (vel die) per merita & intercessionem beate Marie et omnium sanctorum, a viciis, a concupiscenciis, a peccatis et temptacionibus diaboli, a subitania et improvisa morte, et a penis inferni. Illumina cor meum de Spiritu sancto & de tua sancta gracia: et fac me semper tuis obedire mandatis, & a te numquam separari permittas; qui viuis et regnas deus, etc.[1]

The Morning Prayer, thanking God for His mercies, was also very popular, and of it many versions exist. Two of these have been attributed to Rolle: "Almighty God in Trinity," and "Lord God Allwielding"; and will be found in the second part of this book (pp. 293–4). Another version beginning: "I thank Thee, Lord God, full of might,"[2] though having much resemblance to the *Speculum*, is really closer to the English tract on Daily Work, to which reference has already been made. Neither the tract nor the paraphrase appears to be characteristic of Rolle.

And besides prayers there were meditations for each of the seven hours; chapters upon the seven deadly sins; the seven evangelical virtues; and the seven gifts of the Holy Ghost; the Commandments, Creed, Sacraments, etc.

[1] MS. Thornton. Cf. Horstman, vol. i., p. 222.
[2] Printed in *The Middle English Penitential Lyric*, by Frank Allen Patterson, Ph.D., p. 120 (Columbia Univ. Press, 1911); also in *The Minor Poems of the Vernon MS.*, Pt. II., by F. J. Furnivall (E.E.T.S., 117, 1901).

Thus it was a storehouse not only for Richard but for religious folk generally. As Dr. Patterson justly says:

It was one of those books that precede public thought. England was at that time approaching the full development of mysticism. St. Edmund's Mirror was just in advance of its age; it was filled with a mystic fire and devotion that appealed to Richard Rolle and his followers, for in it they found many of their ideas. With the spread of mysticism the *Speculum* became almost a handbook of religious devotion, and as such it was often rendered into simple English prose for the use of the unlearned. [1]

John Hoveden (d. 1275) was one of the first prebendaries of the collegiate church of Howden (from which place he took his surname), in the East Riding, which was founded 1266. His poems are written in the style of Bonaventura, many being in direct imitation, and are pathetic and often estatic praises of the Blessed Virgin. The longest, containing four thousand verses in rhyming couplets, is called: *Philomela sive meditatio de nativitate, passione et resurrectione Jesu Christi*, and is based upon Bonaventura's *Philomela praevia temporis amoeni*. He wrote many others, all in Latin, one of which was included in Bonaventura's works, so great was the likeness between them.

In his youth Rolle wrote a Latin poem in honour of Our Lady beginning: *Zelo tui langueo virgo speciosa*, which is an imitation of the *cantus Philomela* ascribed to Bonaventura, but in which the influence of Hoveden can be traced. The last two stanzas are given us by Horstman, [2] and run:

Praefulgenti virgini do praeconia,
Et dignentur imprimi floris gaudia,
Amans intus ardeo, vincens vilia,
Zelo tui langueo, virgo regia.

Virgo decora, pari fine vivens pure dilexi,
Squalentis heremi cupiens et in arvis haberi
Per cytharam sonui coelicam subjectus amori;
Virgo quam cecini, animam sublima Ricardi.

which last verse proves his authorship.

Richard tells us that he came to the love of Jesus through devotion to His Mother, in a passage in the *Melum*,

---

[1] Patterson, p. 27. [2] Vol. ii., p. xxxvi, note 3.

which is found in several MSS. as a separate extract. His extraordinary use of alliteration is lost in translation so I give the original.

Amicam autem adamavi in quam angeli omnipotentes anhelant aspicere et mirificam Mariam misericordiae matrem mulcebam mihi in mollitie melliflua; nec despexit dilectationem quam detuli, at potius procuravit a piissimo ut animus ornaretur ad amicabiles amplexus intimi amoris. Illam utique habui adjutricem quae oravit amatorem eterni ne abicerer ab electione amantissima; alioquin non amassem altissimum ardenter, nec suscepissem suavitatem sonantis citharae, neque caperer ad concentum canorum; quoniam illa ardentissima erat in amore, et omnes amicos citus accendit ad amandum. Pulcherrima profecto puella clericulos cupit sibi conformari quos secum communicandos capiat ut quemamodum illa castissima continuabatur, ita et ipsi sine concupiscentia carnali consistant. Hanc amavi a juventute mea, et jam in jubilum geror sine gemitu, nec abstulit aliena quod ipsi obtuli ab initio, virginitatem videlicet, ut vivam virtuose et vestiar virtutibus, et ex quo jussus fuero finire praesentem peregrinationem in aulam, adsumar aeternitatis ad inhabitandum cum angelis quorum consortium continue concupisco.[1]

In the thirteenth century devotion to Our Lady was coming into greater prominence, largely through the influence of the French *Puys,* or contests of songs, which were made at the *fêtes* held in honour of the Blessed Virgin. These *fêtes* originated in Normandy owing to a legend, related by Wace, how in the eleventh century Our Lady appeared to some sailors whom she saved in a storm, and told them to found a *fête* at Caen in honour of the Conception, giving them explicit directions. Later

---

[1] This passage is quoted from Miss Allen's *Mystical Lyrics*, p. 169, and is taken from C.C.C. Oxford MS. 193, fol. 234 (of which I have modernised the spelling). The whole article is very interesting in its bearing upon Richard Rolle. She writes: "In the lyric to the Son in the *Manuel,* we see expressed just such a concentration on the thought of Christ and emotional absorption in His Sacred Humanity as was the special characteristic of Rolle, and after him, of the general mystical movement in England. In this type of devotion the lyrics of the Harl. MS. (273) had appeared as pioneers, and since they seem to antedate Rolle, they were pioneers of mysterious origin. Other evidence has now appeared showing that Rolle was born into an environment in which there were influences already making strongly towards mysticism, and that even the type to which he was to give such vigorous and abundant expression was already in process of formation" (pp. 169–70).

the composition of poems in her honour became one of the characteristics of these feasts, and a class of religious poetry called *Puys* which were connected with them grew up in France.[1]

In the thirteenth century collections of miracles of Our Lady were written in England—they had long been common in France—and the *Cursor Mundi* had a long dedication in her honour, which began thus:

> Whoso will of her fairness spell
> Find he may enough to tell
> Of her goodness, of her trouthhood,
> Men may find, about to spread;
> Of ruth, of love and charity
> Was never her equal, nor ever shall be. . . .

This spirit of devotion to the Blessed Virgin showed itself also in architecture, for by the end of the twelfth century large Lady chapels were added at the far eastern end of our cathedrals, as at Gloucester and Chichester.[2] Though Richard wrote no English poem in direct honour of Our Lady, his love for her is never absent in his love for Christ; for of her was born Jesus, the Saviour. He expresses the typical English devotion to the Mother of God:

> Ihesu Christ, saint Mary's sone

> .   .   .

> Ihesu Christ, my God veray,
> That of our dear Lady was born . . .

or:

> Hail Ihesu, the blessed flower
> Of thy Mother, Virgin.

Only in the later versions of the long poem on the *cursus* of *Jesu dulcis Memoria* do we find verses inserted directly addressed to Our Lady, beseeching her to intercede for man with her Son.

There is a very beautiful poem of the early fourteenth century, beginning:

> Stand well, Mother, under rood,
> Behold thy Child with glad mood,

---

[1] Cf. Patterson, pp. 40 sqq.
[2] Cf. *Gothic Architecture in England and France*, by G. H. West, pp. 48, 52 (Bell & Sons, 1911).

M

where she expostulates with her Son for hanging there, and suffering so much torment; and he answers:

> Mother, if I thee durst tell,
> If I ne die, thou goest to hell;
> I thole death for man's sake.

and again:

> Mother, I may no longer dwell;
> The time is come, I go to hell.
> I thole this for thy sake.

In England the love for Our Lady lost nothing by the recognition of her complete humanity. She, as much as St. John and as that other Mary weeping at the foot of the Cross, must be redeemed by the death of her Son. When Richard mentions the Mother of God, we find always a note of tender love and reverence in what he says, but direct references to her are few. He counsels us, first to fasten the Name JHESU so fast in our hearts "that it come never out of thy thought," and then "hail oft Mary, both day and night."[1]

Mary seems to be never separated in his thought from her Son, and we find the same in early paintings. Very few frescoes and pictures of the thirteenth and fourteenth centuries are found of Our Lady apart from Christ. Either the Divine Child rests within her arms, or she stands in sorrow at the foot of the Cross, or else she is depicted clasping in her arms the dead body of her Son. In some very early pictures, even as she lies upon her bed of death, Christ is seen beside her receiving her soul as typified by a tiny swaddled infant.[2]

This type of devotion to Mary, the spotless maiden and Mother of God and perfect embodiment of human love with its infinite capacity for human suffering and sacrifice, is one of the most beautiful characteristics of our early English mystical writers.

---

[1] *The Form of Living*, chap. ix.
[2] These I have seen in Italy but not, as far as I recollect, in England, where the art of painting was much later of development.

CHAPTER IX

THE LATTER DAYS AND DEATH OF RICHARD

"*Also this holy hermit, Richard, out of the abundance of his charity, used to show himself very friendly to recluses, and to those who were in need of spiritual consolation, and who suffered disquiet and vexation in soul or body through the malignant work of evil spirits. God granted him singular grace in helping those who were troubled in that way. . . .*

. . . . . .

"*After this the saint of God, Richard, betook himself to other parts ; doubtless through the providence of God, so that dwelling in many places he might benefit many unto salvation, and sometimes also that he might escape impediment to contemplation, as we read in the book of the 'Lives of the Fathers' that many of the most holy fathers in the desert used to do.*"—LESSON VIII.

Richard compared with Shelley—His attacks upon the abuses in the Church which bring upon him ecclesiastical condemnation—The backbiting and slander of his foes—His life as a hermit derided—He defends himself—Preaches, writes, and counsels others, more especially women, for whom he begins to write in English—His power of doing two things at the same time—He calms a lady, in whose manor he had a cell, in the agony and delirium of death—He is said to have put demons to flight—A crisis in his life—He becomes conscious of his gift of healing—Feels the call to go and minister to others—He leaves the Daltons and is heard of next in Richmondshire—Cure of the Lady Margaret, an anchoress at Ainderby—Parallel to cures in modern psychotherapy—Two types of character, extrovert and introvert—Richard belongs to the former type like St. Paul—Clang association—Although a hermit Richard wanders from place to place and mixes with others—The Order of Augustinian Hermits—The elasticity of their Rule—Was Richard attached to them?—Possibility that he received priest's orders later in life—No proof he did not—The friaries belonging to the Austin Hermits or Friars which Richard may have visited—Tickhill was not far from Hampole—Richard becomes spiritual adviser to the nuns of the priory at Hampole—Description of Hampole as it is now—The old Irish hermit's song gives a picture of Richard's life in his cell at Hampole—He writes *The Commandment of Love to God*, probably his last prose tract, for a nun of the priory there—Extracts from it showing that he has attained to a ghostly joy and peace which it is beyond the reach of men to disturb—Death comes to him during a violent outbreak of the plague—The upheaval that followed it prevented his canonisation—Many miracles were wrought at his shrine and are related in the lessons of the Office—Estimate of his influence.

163

IN his youth Richard seems to have had an impetuous and headstrong disposition, united to the passionate emotionalism of the poet. It is possible to trace a resemblance—a strange one when we consider the difference of religious profession—between him and another member of University College who, four centuries later had also to leave Oxford without taking a degree. Yet allowing for the great divergence of religious opinions and of time there is much of the same spirit in Shelley as there was in Richard. In both we find the same enthusiasm and high courage in defence of the needy and down-trodden, and neither hesitates to draw upon himself misconception and calumny by upholding what he deems to be true; nor does either scruple to attack those in high places and in authority. During those first years after he had returned from Oxford Richard was in open revolt, as was Shelley, against all abuses. It is the effusion of youth. He wishes to reform everything, and tilts at everyone, from the king downwards. The *Melum*, probably his earliest work, and the most autobiographical, though really in praise of contemplation, is full of strictures on the abuses in the Church, which certainly in those days cried out for criticism. He attacks, sometimes very bitterly, the prelates and clergy whose lives were often an open scandal. He refers to this also in the *Incendium*, when speaking of those who sin grievously in regard to women: "and most," he says, "that have taken Holy orders, and go to women as wooers, saying that they languish for their love, and are near to fainting for the desire they have and the strife in their thought; and thus they lead them, being light and unstable, to wretchedness in this life, and also in the life everlasting" (p. 174).[1]

But what chiefly provokes his wrath is the formalism of the clergy, the *"ministerium mechanicum"*; he declaims against the worldliness of the seculars and monks; against the prelates who prohibit hermits from preaching and send other, unfit, persons:

"They forbid excellent men to preach and allow others

---

[1] Dr. Horstman in his packed prefaces gives us many excerpts from the *Melum*, the *Postillae on Job*, the *Regula Heremitarum*, etc., from which I quote. See especially Horstman's introduction to vol. ii.

to do so who have no mission from God; they reject the hermits."

> Woe be to the priest [he exclaims in his *Postillae on Job*] who with such zeal and clamour exact tithes and payments for sacraments, and take so little care of the souls of their parishioners. They are prompt to demand money, but seldom or never do they preach: they excommunicate those who deprive the Church of her rights, but it is they themselves who are in the first place self-excommunicated because they do not rule the Church as they are bound to do. (ii., p. xxi.)

It was to be expected that his greatest enemies should be among the professional Christians whom he had so fiercely chastised. Of these he writes:

"Such great hatred and envy I did not find in, nor suffer from any, as from those who were called disciples of Jesus Christ."

They ridiculed him as a saint without miracles; found fault with his idle inactivity, his contemplation without works, his independence without obedience. They despised him as a layman, and questioned his learning. Yet he speaks of their learning as "a laborious acquisition not infused, and in the pride of their elaborate argumentations they looked down on me, saying what school was he at and who was his teacher?"

They said that he could not preach, and despised his words because he was poor and had no reputation among the great. His teaching is to them a mystery: "*Mysterium mitto modernis*"; and they say that he errs in his interpretation of Holy Scripture. Even thus early he is rejected because he is classed as a modernist. "*Non acceptantes me quia modernus sum*" (Job). He is an innovator, and an upstart; an *homo novus*.

In the *Melum* he directly challenges his bishop, who, Horstman thinks, is probably the great detractor to whom the whole book is addressed. "Behold," he writes, "a youth, animated with a righteous zeal, rises up against an elder, *a hermit against a bishop*; and against all, however great soever, who affirm that the heights of sanctity consist in exterior acts" (ii., p. xxii).

Hermits were not in favour, and were often prohibited from preaching by those in prelacy. In the register of Archbishop Melton of York (1317–42) there is an order (dated August 1334) forbidding "anyone to listen to the teaching of Friar Henry de Staunton, hermit." He was probably one of the Augustinian Hermits who had a house at York, on the banks of the Ouse, near the Ouse bridge. This house was founded as early as 1278, and they owned a library of 646 volumes before the Dissolution. If Richard had had access to this library he would not have lacked for books. Dr. Horstman says, "We may readily suppose that this hermit was a disciple or follower of Richard Rolle"; but we know nothing more of him than this entry. Possibly Richard was also at some time, probably at the beginning of his hermit's life, inhibited from preaching, which may have given an added bitterness to his attack. Later in life he becomes far less polemical, for he learns that love conquers all pain, and calumny only drives him closer to Christ.

But there was much to excuse his early bitterness, for evidently his enemies did their best to poison his friends and patrons against him. He tells us that those he thought were his true friends became his worst detractors; yet he will not divulge their names. "Derisiores et detractores non divulgavi ad dampnum, necnon et amavi eos qui me arguerunt et ostenderunt odia, ut ab omnibus abominarer." They even try to lure him into sin, so that they may have cause to drive him from the houses of those he loves, and since he was dependent upon the kindness of those he met with for his sustenance, they did him grievous injury.[1]

But this must have been after he had left the shelter of the Daltons and mixed more freely with others. The *Melum* shows that even when living a life of strict contemplation he tries his utmost to win souls. There are many passages of exhortation in that book.

O come, ye youths and maidens and learn from me how to love. Forsake the impure love of one another and embrace eternal love. O maidens, do not hanker after men, do not adorn yourselves for men, to tempt them; lo Christ, most lovely of all the Sons of men, the King of Heaven, desires your beauty, woos your love; He loves maidens chaste and poor,

---

[1] Cf. Dr. James's article on the "Catalogue of the Library of the Augustinian Friars at York" (*Fasciculus*: J. W. Clark).

he wants love, not passion. He will adorn you with a wonderful crown, a worthy diadem, with shining garments, and her that now languishes for Him in love He will requite with everlasting sweetness.[1]

Even when with the Daltons his private character is attacked. Because he lives in the house of the rich, he is called a glutton: "My detractors say that I am led astray by the pleasures in which the rich delight, and am unworthy of God." He is accused, like Christ, of being a wine-bibber, and eating with sinners; and it is said that his contemplation was feigned and arose from over-eating.

"Speaking like sophists they affirmed that on account of the food I had taken I continued to sit (at table?); and they ascribed to drink what the most Holy bestowed; and many asserted that I underwent penance in public to win applause from the people."[2]

To a nature as shyly sensitive and affectionate as was Richard's such misrepresentation and calumny must have been peculiarly hard to suffer with patience. Much of the chapter on Friendship in *The Fire* seems to have been wrung out of his personal experience. The real hardship of his life, and the voluntary discomforts and pain he bore, have been already dwelt upon in a previous chapter; where we noted that to bear privations, and willingly suffer from hunger and cold is always harder when within reach of the ordinary comforts of life.

Nothing provokes the lovers of ease and pleasure more than to see another practising that which they have not the courage to attempt. Thus it was only natural that those in high places in the Church, who wished for a life of selfish ease and licence and feared discovery, should aim their darts against one who preached so high an idealism,

---

[1] The alliteration in the *Melum* is unique. I quote these passages as examples (abridged from Horstman, ii., p. xx):

"Heu, dominae tam dulces diligunt indigne et dirae dilectioni deditae domantur et mentem immunditiae maculant amore, manentes in morsu multiplicis maeroris, languendo ad lubricium in lugubri labore, quae Deum diligere devote debuerunt et hymnum extendere amoris aeterni, in Jesu qui se gerit jugiter jubilantes!"

"Heu, virgines et viduae vilissime venduntur, vacillant et ventilant vadentes vitiatae, ornantur ob oscula," etc.

[2] ii., p. xxiii.

and who lived upon the same plane as his teaching. "His system," says Dr. Horstman in a remarkable sentence, "was hostile to kind, and he who forsakes kind is forsaken by kind, and liable to fall maybe as Joseph by the wife of Potiphar; the whole world becomes his enemy." [1] And for a time this seems to have been the case with Rolle, for in the epistle which he wrote for a young priest, perhaps for his fellow-student, Dalton's son, he asks him to be careful to whom he shows it lest it should be made the occasion for some fresh slander.

"You must use no common discretion not to expose my youth to the attacks of biting envy by showing this little book to everyone."

Though he thus attacks others in the *Melum*, and defends himself against his detractors in the *Regula*, as he enters more deeply into the spirit of the eremitical life, and is "truly turned to God," he ceases to let the backbiters and calumniators trouble him so greatly. Yet never until quite late in life in the solitude of his cell at Hampole, do his enemies cease to sting him, and all his life he is tempted to defend himself and retaliate, if not openly at least in the silence of his thought; for such is the ever-abiding temptation of the sensitive; but we do not doubt that he learned through love to control his sensitiveness for the service of others.

His first sermon in the chapel on the Daltons' estate had moved many to tears; "and they all said that they had never before heard a sermon of such virtue and power"; and very soon he seems to have attracted those living around and who were known to Lady Dalton. Unless ordained, hermits were not generally allowed to preach inside a church, but are represented in early illuminations as preaching from some pulpit set up in the churchyard, or they would draw a little band of listeners round them as they spoke in open spaces in the streets or elsewhere. In the first fervour of his conversion Richard may have preached at Topcliffe, as he certainly seems to have done later, and aided others by his holy exhortations of which the lesson speaks, "whereby he converted many to God"; but it was his "sweet writings, both treatises and little books," which "he composed for the edification of his

[1] ii., pp. xxii–iii.

neighbours," which mostly occupied him in his first hermitage.

Women seem to have been chiefly attracted by him, and it was for them that he began to write in English those "little books . . . which all sound like sweetest music in the hearts of the devout." One of the sweetest-sounding of these, full of alliteration and of verse, was the *Ego Dormio*, written for a nun at Yedingham, which convent was quite close to his old home at Thornton, and often, we should imagine, those who knew him there as a boy would be drawn by all they heard to come and visit him and ask his counsel; for the lesson narrates that "out of the abundance of his charity this holy hermit used to show himself very friendly to recluses and to those who were in need of spiritual consolation." There is an interesting story told us in Lesson VI. which excites great wonder in the narrator, and also incidentally shows the friendly terms on which he was with the Daltons. It describes how he was sitting in his cell after dinner one afternoon when the lady of the house came, "and many other persons with her, and found him writing very quickly." They ask him to desist from writing and to speak to them on holy things, which he immediately did, exhorting them most eloquently to virtue and to renounce worldly vanities and stablish the love of God in their hearts. Yet in no way on account of this did he cease from writing for two hours, without interruption, but continued to write as quickly as before; and we are told that "the spoken words differed utterly in meaning from those which he wrote."

Naturally in those days this was looked upon as a miracle, "and in no wise possible unless the Holy Spirit had at that time directed both his hand and tongue"; and there seems to be a reference to it in Richard's own words in *The Fire*:

Therefore their thoughts are made sweet in His service because studying and meditating on scripture and also writing they think on their Love, and they go not from their wonted voice of praise. That forsooth shall be considered marvellous, when one mind shall fulfil and take heed to two things in one time: that is, it offers worship and love to Jesu in singing and joying in mind, and together with that, it understands that that is in books; and neither hurts the other. (p. 161.)

The story is thus summed up in the Respond to Lesson VII.:

> Mentem simul diuersis applicat,
> manu scribens uerbis edificat
> actum mentis sic deus duplicat,
> audientes uerbi uis attrahit,
> nec loquela scribentem distrahit.[1]

In the same lesson it is written how the saint

was sometimes so absorbed in spirit while he prayed, that once when his cloak with which he was clad was taken from him, he did not feel it; and when, after patching and stitching it, they replaced it on him, he did not notice it.

His power of calming those in delirium is also noted, and we are given a lurid account of the death of a certain lady, evidently Lady Dalton—"in whose manor Richard had a cell, but a long way off from the family—where he was wont to live alone and give himself to contemplation." We infer from this that Richard had after a time removed from the room which the squire had set apart for him in his own house—as is noted in Lesson IV.—and had gone to a more solitary place where he was wont to live alone and give himself to contemplation. There they sought him out and begged him to come to the manor, for a multitude of horrible demons had invaded the room where the lady lay, "and when she saw them visibly" it was little wonder that "she fell into great fear and trembling."[2]

Here we are at once reminded of the pictures in the old block-books of the *Ars Moriendi*, where the temptations of the dying are always represented by visible demons.[3]

When Richard had "come to her consolation and admonished her holily, and had urged her to set all her hope in the superabundant mercy of God and in His over-flowing grace," he prayed that the demons should no longer trouble her; and all the terrible troop was put to flight. But the writer of the *Vite*, most likely one of the nuns at Hampole, is not content to leave it there, but adds this vivid

---

[1] *Officium*, p. 37. "He gives his mind to different things at the same time. With his hand he is writing edifying words, and God so duplicates the action of his mind that the force of his words holds his hearers, while his speaking does not interfere with his writing."

[2] For the full account in the lesson see appendix i.

[3] One such picture is given in my edition of *The Craft of Dying* (Longmans, 1917).

touch: "All the bystanders saw that in the rush-strewn floor of the room where the demons had passed the rushes seemed to be burnt and reduced to black ashes, and in these ashes there were marks impressed like the hoof-prints of oxen."

A prosaic explanation of this might be that Richard had taken incense with him to exorcise the evil spirits, and that the rushes had caught fire. Anyhow he had angered the demons so greatly that they at once followed him to his cell; but by prayer he again put them to flight.

At the beginning of his conversion a tale has been told of the appearance of a beautiful woman in his cell who tempted him, and just as that was probably a symbolic way of recounting his early temptations to set earthly love above heavenly, so here it seems that he realised, perhaps for the first time, his power to calm the minds of those in distress and to heal also their bodily ills. It was a distinct crisis in his life. As he returns to his solitary cell it seems to be filled with those principalities and powers of which the writer of the Epistle to the Ephesians speaks; and he finds he must wrestle against spiritual wickedness in high places.

Any special gift which oversteps the threshold between the material and spiritual must bring with it peculiar temptations. Very often it has been the experience of those who have had hands laid upon them in healing, or have been anointed when ill with holy oil, that a deadly spiritual conflict ensues, out of which the soul emerges strengthened and healed, even though the bodily sickness may not be removed. Mix with the throng at Lourdes, and you will find on talking to those countless sick who lie awaiting the will of God, that it is the spiritual and not the bodily miracles which are of most importance in their eyes. They may remain still crippled, or bound to beds of pain, but their souls have found wings whereby to fly in the service of God.

So Richard finds his cell filled with those demons of pride, vainglory and superiority. With his quick imagination he sees all the pitfalls that may await him if he goes forth to exercise this power which he has discovered in himself. Is this gift of God or of the devil? Must he exercise it for others outwardly, or could he not rightly hide it away?

The temptation to withhold it and withdraw himself into a deeper solitude, to spend all his efforts in writing and reading, in prayer and in more intense contemplation must have been strong. No one could have shrunk more greatly from any sort of publicity, and from laying himself open to misunderstanding and ridicule; but the call has come, as it came to Suso, to Catherine of Siena and to so many others. He must let the light of that flame which burns in his heart shine forth to kindle others to love as he has learnt to love. He must leave the calm solitude of his cell and the chapel where he had loved to spend the nights in prayer, where he had heard mass, confessed and communicated, and wander forth among strangers, wherever he feels that God calls him.

And at once he falls under the condemnation of his critics. They can countenance a hermit who secludes himself in one place, or the friar who attaches himself to some Order with a special dress, and status, but this man who wanders from one house to another, is no hermit. Some called him hypocrite, others *tutannus*, scamp, or as we might say to-day, tramp.

In Lesson VIII. there is a paragraph which seems almost of the nature of a defence against those who were disposed to class Rolle among the *girovagi* or wandering hermits. The latter were one of the pests of the Middle Ages. Rolle himself thus refers to them in *The Fire*: "I speak not of runners about that are the slander of hermits" (p. 64). These *girovagi* are thus condemned by St. Benedict in his Rule:

> The fourth kind of monks are called *Girovagi*, who spend all their lives long wandering about divers provinces, staying in different cells for three or four days at a time, ever roaming, with no stability, given up to their own pleasures and to the snares of gluttony and worse in all things than the Sarabites. Of the most wretched life of these latter [he adds] it is better to say nothing than to speak.

which indeed makes his condemnation all the graver.

They might be described as a species of religious tramp, who did no work but preyed upon the credulity of the people, wandering from place to place and never refusing, but often demanding, hospitality.

The lesson states that the saint of God betook himself

to other parts, saying that he left "through the providence of God, so that dwelling in many places he might benefit many unto salvation," which one cannot doubt was his reason; and it also defends him against those who had maligned him thus:

For frequent change of place does not always come from inconstancy, as is the accusation of certain who are given to quick and perverse judgment of their neighbours, but whose crooked interpretations and habits of detraction ought not to make a sensible person neglect those things which he has found by experience to be good and conducive to virtue.

After the death of Lady Dalton to whom his prayers had brought peace, and his words consolation to her friends —since he was able to assure them that "she was saved, and after quitting this life she would be a joint-heir in the kingdom of heaven"—he leaves Topcliffe and goes to Richmondshire. He was drawn there by "urgent and most practical reasons"; but the only clue we have to these reasons is the account of the illness of the Lady Margaret, "who had once been a recluse at Ainderby, in the diocese of York." This lady had been known to Richard for some time, and it was for her he wrote *The Form of Living*, at the end of which book he thus addresses her:

Lo, Margarete,[1] I have shortly said thee the form of living; and how thou may come til perfection, and to love Him that thou hast taken thee til. If it do thee good, and profit til thee, thank God and pray for me. The grace of Ihesu Christ be with thee and keep thee.

And it is the same Margaret Kirkby who is mentioned in the prologue to the Psalter, which apparently he wrote for her at her own request.[2] She appears to have been an enclosed anchoress and her cell was originally at East Layton, but she had permission to change her anchorage to "a place near the parish church of Aynderby, where she may see and hear the solemn sacrament of the Lord's altar, which in her present place of enclosure she is unable to do, and to dispense her from her vow of dwelling perpetually at Laton." The low side window is still there, through which she may have looked. Laton was near to

---

[1] In one MS. the name "Cecil" is substituted for "Margarete."
[2] Cf. p. 129 supra.

Hampole in the East Riding, and there may have been some connection between the anchorage there and the Cistercian convent, for in 1348 a Margaret la Boteler, nun of Hampole, was enclosed there. Miss Clay suggests [1] that she was Margaret la Boteler of Kirkby; in which case she must have returned to her first anchorage where she had been originally enclosed, but the lesson goes to prove that she was still at Ainderby when Richard died.[2]

There seems to have been a very close and lasting spiritual relationship between the Lady Margaret and Richard. The lesson (viii.) recounts how she was seized with a sudden grave illness on Maundy Thursday, and remained speechless for thirteen days.

Now a certain goodman of that town [York], knowing that the holy hermit Richard loved her with a perfect affection of charity—since he was wont to instruct her in the art of loving God, and to direct her by his holy teaching how to order her life—quickly hastened on horseback to the hermit, who was then living twelve miles from the dwelling of the recluse, and besought him to come to her with all speed. . . . And when he came to the recluse he found her unable to speak, and troubled with very grievous pains. And as he sat by the window of her dwelling [3] and they were eating together, it befell at the end of the meal that the recluse desired to sleep; and so, oppressed by sleep, she drooped her head at the window where Richard reclined; and after she had slept thus for a short time, leaning slightly upon Richard, suddenly a violent convulsion seized her in her sleep with fearful

---

[1] *Hermits and Anchorites*, p. 143 and note. All these places can be clearly seen in Speed's map by means of a good magnifying glass. Thornton (in the dale) must not be confused with the Thornton near Pickering or any of the other Thorntons in the map. The former lies in a direct line with Topcliffe which is farther west; Ainderby is almost due north, and Richmond some miles towards the north-west. There are many Kirkbys marked, two are near Richmond, and a South Kirkby close to Hampole (spelt Hampell in the map). We cannot say from which Kirkby Margaret took her name. It meant "the place of the kirk." Hampell or "Hampole" lies almost midway between Doncaster and Pontefract. A place called Claton (which may be the same as Laton) lies close to Hampole, and to the east is Fyshlake, the scene of one of the miracles.

[2] Cf. p. 308, infra.

[3] Every anchorage had two windows; the one looking into the church and the other facing outwards to give air. It was at this latter that Richard would be seated outside the cell when no one might enter.

vehemence, so that it seemed as if she wished to break the window of her house.

In the midst of this convulsion she suddenly awakes from sleep and begins a verse of the compline hymn which Richard finishes.

And the same thing happens again, only the second time she is so violent that Richard tries to hold her with his hands "lest she should rend herself, or strive in any way to injure the house, [when] she suddenly slipped from them, and in her fall was shaken out of sleep and thoroughly awakened."

Here clearly we have a case of a typical epileptoid seizure cured by powerful suggestion, which might be paralleled any day in modern psychotherapy; and from this and the other episodes we have cited from the *Vite* we see at once that Richard would prove an extremely interesting study for the modern psychologist. It is not my purpose here to go into this in any detail, but I have permission to quote a letter written in answer to my inquiries from one who is an expert on this subject, and from whom I have learnt much in regard to the psychology of religion [1]; for it seems to me that no study of mysticism can afford to omit some reference to a science which bears so closely a relation to it as does psychology.

The modern psychologist distinguishes between two types of character: the extrovert and the introvert. In the first there is a tendency to dissociation of ideas, and in the latter a tendency towards a neurosis in which the sense of conflict is very marked. We saw this in St. Teresa when earlier we drew a comparison between her and Richard. But no sane person can be a pure extrovert or a pure introvert; for the former would act before he thought, which would be most dangerous; and the latter, like Hamlet, would be prohibited from all action by thought.

Richard is a very interesting example of an extrovert. Like St. Paul he comes directly under the influence of Christ without thinking about it or debating, though, as with St. Paul, there is the sense of conflict between his higher and lower nature, between earthly and spiritual love; and in both we have a sudden conversion by which the

[1] The Rev. L. W. Grensted, Chaplain of University College, Oxford.

whole outlook on life was changed. With the introvert such sudden conversions are non-existent, since he is already aware of all that has been taking place within; the emphasis with such a one is on the intellectual side, with the extrovert it is on the side of the affections.

The extrovert is also very susceptible of control by apparently separate groups of impulses, and has the power of dissociating his ideas. This is most clearly marked in Richard who had apparently an abnormal faculty for doing several distinct things at the same time, as we have seen in the account which the *Vite* gives. On this Mr. Grensted comments:

(1) He may have been, like some chess players, a man of immense orderliness of ideas and quickness of reaction, capable of holding many things in his mind at once, and thus able to write and to talk intelligently in apparent simultaneity, but really switching over from one to the other with great speed. I see no sign in his works that this was really the case.

(2) He may have been a definite hysteric, i.e. capable of functioning in two ways with more or less independence. Quite probably he was capable of automatic writing, i.e. while he talked and presumably thought about his conversation, his hand would continue to write. What he wrote would be a medley of spiritual and moral maxims without much system or order, but in general line with the main impulse of his life. A good modern example is Vale Owen, who had not, however, the power of criticising afterwards what he had written. I think that Rolle's writings show very distinct traces of this kind of mentality. They are very lacking in structure. My impression is that he wrote under a strong impulse, and probably collected and arranged the best parts of his first draft as best he could. The fact that his works are comparatively short, points in this direction. I should imagine that he had qualities which he did not preserve. And therein he shows his essential sanity.

In the story of his cure of the Lady Margaret the pious narrator tells us how Richard promised her that she should never again suffer the torment of this illness "so long as I remain in mortal life." When, therefore, after several years her malady returned, she sent her servant to Hampole, where Richard then "led a solitary life," to inquire of the nuns there what had befallen him. The servant learnt "that the saint was dead to this world; and after diligently enquiring the hour of his passing, he found that the aforesaid illness had returned to the recluse shortly after the hour of Richard's departure." Later the anchoress removed to Hampole to be near Richard's burial-place, "and never afterwards was she afflicted with the suffering of this horrible illness."

To quote again from Mr. Grensted's letter:

> The Lady Margaret is of course a typical hysteric and a much more unhealthy one. The whole picture is just like the modern cases, and the cure is simply by powerful suggestion (though Rolle himself did not know that). I do not suppose the story of her relapse at Rolle's death is true—it is such an easy bit of popular legend—but it may be. I believe telepathy and thought transference would quite well account for it. If she knew, subconsciously, that Rolle was dead the suggestion of relapse would be very powerful indeed.

It is also interesting to note that what the psychologist calls "clang association" is strongly exemplified in Richard. His love of assonance and alliteration has already been dwelt upon, only we must remember that alliteration was very strongly marked in all early English poetry, and he is to a great extent following the tradition. But the extreme cases in the *Melum*, of which we have quoted instances, are unique, and a marked characteristic of Rolle's style. So far as they go they certainly confirm the view of his mentality given above.

Judging from the *Vite* we gather that Richard spent the next years passing from place to place, and not always remaining apart in a cell. In the *Melum* he writes:

> As Cain was made a fugitive and vagabond upon the earth . . . so I in this exile have no certain dwelling-place. From place to place I pass, as long as Almighty God deigns to direct His servant.

He was still young, for in the early Latin tract entitled *Judica me Dous* he speaks of the usefulness of seeing many places in youth so as the better to choose the one best suited for himself:

> O good Ihesu, if I am called a hermit though unworthy of the name, there neither will be, nor will deserve to be, any scandal when they hear that sometimes I change my bodily dwelling-place, or pass from one cell to another; for I am no more obliged to remain in one hermitage than in another. Hence let it not be thought useless if in my youth I should

N

see many places, so as to be able to choose one from among those best suited to my condition.[1]

It may have been during these years that he mixed freely with others in order to preach his doctrine of love and joy. There is a passage in the *Melum* where he says:

I was seen in company with the worldly, and was familiar with the houses of the rich, yet I rarely joked with girls, and would speak with women concerning faith in our Maker; sometimes playing and laughing with the rest, as it seemed to them, but inwardly praising. For this was the object that I thus should wander forth, so that I might teach all that they should love their Maker; let go vanities and the snares of destruction, and seek to serve God rather than men; and to savour heavenly things, and despise earthly.[2]

Horstman seems to suggest that he left his cell with the Daltons quite early in life, almost immediately after the mystical experiences which he describes in *The Fire*, and which lasted not more than four years. He apparently bases this upon these references in the *Melum* to a life lived more in the world than in the cell; but the compilation of this more or less autobiographical work may have been spread over a long period, and it is difficult to make any deduction until we can have the whole book in print. It is clear from the *Regula*, which is undoubtedly an early work, that he tried to get others to join him, and intended to form a community of hermits under a Rule, and to revive the old anchoritical life, but none were willing:

Alas, miserable that I am [he cries], so lonely am I that thus I can find no one in my day who desires to come with me and sitting and in silence will yearn after the joys of eternal love.[3]

For this was his most ardent desire, not preaching:

It is good to be a preacher; to exert oneself, to go hither and thither, and be weary for the salvation of souls; but it is better, safer and sweeter by far to pass one's life in contemplation, to feel the nearness of eternal sweetness, to sing the joys of eternal love, and to be rapt in the praise of the Creator by the pouring forth of heavenly songs.[4] (*Melum.*)

---

[1] Horstman, vol. ii., p. xvi, note.   [2] Ibid. p. xvii.
[3] Ibid., ii., p. xvii.   [4] Ibid., p. x, note 3.

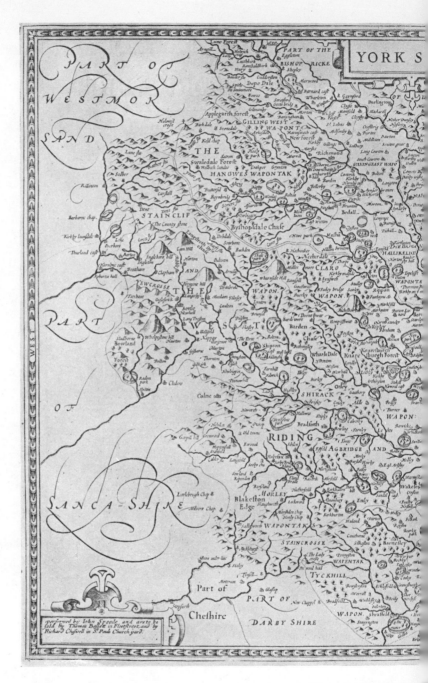

MAP OF YORKSHIRE

SPEED'S ATLAS, 1676

In all probability the *Regula* was based upon the so-called Third Rule of St. Augustine, whose writings on Community Life were compiled, many being included which are now discredited. The Third Rule in forty-five sections has come down to us in full, and proved more prolific in giving birth to new Orders than even the Benedictine Rule. It was especially popular in England where he was so greatly revered. Yet St. Augustine never wrote a Rule properly so called, but one epistle (211) is a long letter of practical advice for the religious women under his direction, not binding them to strict enclosure, but requiring them to renounce all individual property; and two of his sermons (355 and 356) describe the common life he led with his clerics at Hippo. He also wrote a treatise: *De Moribus Clericorum*. These were taken as a model for all clergy living in community, especially those attached to collegiate churches. Thus arose the very widely spread Order of Augustinian Canons. Augustinian was a generic name, and included the Hermits, more commonly called Augustinian or Austin Friars, the Premonstratensians, the Trinitarians, and the Gilbertines. These last are of especial interest as being the only purely English monastic Order. It included both men and women; the monks following the Augustinian Rule and the nuns the Cistercian. There were many Gilbertine houses in Yorkshire; and their founder, Gilbert of Sempringham, enclosed his first seven nuns, so he tells us in his Rule, "not expecting that they would come out again or that more would join them." [1]

The name Augustinian Hermit seems also of very wide application; and hermits who could not otherwise be described were often called Augustinian. In 1244 the Pope had united many hermits into communities, giving them this designation. It is difficult to find much information about them except in Hélyot.[2] They were rightly called hermits because they lived in cells, although with a common

---

[1] See a reference to this in Miss Allen's article on *The Origin of the Ancren Riwle*, reprinted from the *Publications of the Modern Language Association of America*, xxxiii. 3, p. 479; and cf. Dugdale, vii., p. xix.

[2] *Histoire des Ordres Monastiques*, etc., in eight volumes, vol. iii., pp. 7 sqq. (Paris, 1792).

chapel, and under a common Rule, as do the Camaldolese Hermits to-day, yet they are often mistakenly spoken of as friars. Their habit was first grey, with a white scapular. They wore no cord round their waist, as did the Friars Minor; but later they conformed to the habit of the latter, which led to confusion between them. These hermits were most widely spread on the Continent. The Hermits of Toulouse were united under a common Rule, in 1243, by Pope Innocent IV. who allowed them to take the Rule of St. Augustine. A later Pope (Alexander IV.) in 1254 divided all the Orders of hermits who had been included under Augustinian into four provinces; viz. France, Germany, Spain and Italy. They became very numerous, especially in Spain and Italy, and as early as 1287 an Augustinian Hermit was chosen for the office of sacristan to the papal chapel, and was responsible for having a consecrated Host always in readiness for the Pope's viaticum; which custom I believe still holds to-day. Hélyot does not mention England in his account, but Stevens states that in the year 1252 Lanfranc of Milan, the first General of the Order, had, before the confirmation of the Pope, sent some Augustinian Hermits to England on the bidding of St. Augustine himself, who had appeared to him when in an ecstasy. They first found a dwelling in Wales, and "afterwards Humphrey Bohun, Earl of Hereford and Essex, gave them a House, and a beautiful Church, remarkable for a Spire of Wonderful Workmanship in London."

They soon made their mark in Oxford, where they settled in that same year, and became renowned for their learning. Stevens gives a list of thirty-nine Austin Hermits who became famous. Robert Waldeby, first a student at Toulouse, was later made Archbishop of York, and another of the same name, John Waldeby, was a Doctor of Divinity at Oxford, and died at York in 1393; Robert Worsop was a friar at Ticul (Tickhill), not far from Doncaster, where he died 1350: both these latter may have been known to Richard. There were two other houses of Austin Hermits in Yorkshire besides Tickhill; one being in Hull and one at York itself. To the library belonging to the latter reference has been made. Another hermit, William Langham, is mentioned by Stevens as the author of *The Remedies against Temptation*, a book which

Wynkyn de Worde printed *c.* 1506 and wrongly ascribed to Rolle.[1]

It is therefore not difficult to see why Richard has been called an Austin Hermit, nor have we any real proof that he was not attached in some way to that Order. When, as a boy, he borrowed his sister's tunics, he was clearly trying to imitate their early dress, and his first dream of gathering others around him under a Rule must have been inspired by this popular Order. What Dr. Frere says of the Augustinian Canons is equally true of the Hermits:

> The adoption of the Rule of St. Augustine was a very simple matter and involved probably no change in the existing arrangements. The Rule as compiled out of St. Augustine's letter does not enter into details, nor prescribe *minutiae*, as does the Rule of St. Benedict, which is a real Rule. Every House of Canons Regular must have had its own customs to regulate daily life, service governments, etc. . . . and there was no difficulty in superimposing the Saint's Rule, and thus gaining the prestige of being Augustinian.[2]

It is quite possible, as the note in the Egerton MS. leads us to suppose, that Richard attached himself in this way to the Augustinian Hermits, whose Rule seems equally elastic as that of the Augustinian Canons. The fact that he never dwelt for any length of time in a friary or hermitage belonging to the Order, but preferred to live independently in some cell of his own choosing, "his only Abbot being Love," may not have precluded him from being recognised as one of their Order, considering the elasticity of the Rule of the Augustinians.

We must now come to the question whether Richard ever received priest's orders. He must have been in minor orders before he entered on the *Quadrivium* in his course at Oxford, and there seems to have been no barrier put in his way when he ascended the pulpit in the Daltons' chapel; from which we should suppose that he was recognised as having some status above that of a mere layman. Certainly on that occasion he gave them little time for thought; but after the sermon he is not rebuked in any

[1] Cf. Stevens' Continuation of Dugdale's *Monasticon*, vol. ii., pp. 215 sqq.

[2] See an article by Dr. W. H. Frere on the Augustinian Canons in the *Fasciculus* of J. W. Clarke (Camb. Univ. Press, 1909).

way, but on the contrary "all said that they had never before heard a sermon of such virtue and power"; which seems rather to indicate that it was not his first attempt at preaching, and that he may have been so far in training for the priesthood when a student as to have been practised in it.

As Dr. Horstman shows by quotations from the *Melum*, *Cupienti Mihi*, and the *Rule for Hermits*, he decries preaching, and also complains that being but a hermit he was forbidden to preach; and certainly in his earlier life we can gather from references in the *Incendium* and the *Melum* that he was not then ordained or else surely he would not be constrained to hear mass if he could have "said" it.

. . . they have stood up against me because I fled the outward songs that are wont in the kirks, and the sweetness of the organ that is heard gladly by the people, only abiding among these either when the *need of hearing mass*—which elsewhere I could not hear — or the solemnity of the day asked it on account of the backbiting of the people.[1]

which implies that if the people had not seen him at mass on such *dies solempnis*, they would have contemned him for breaking the Rule of the Church.

In the epistle to a parish priest, which goes by the name of *Cupienti Mihi*, he writes as if he were intending later to take Holy orders.

Know ye that I have extracted the following from the words of the fathers . . . in order that what I am *not yet* compelled to say in publick preaching, I may at least show forth in writing to you, upon whom is laid the necessity of preaching.

And in the *Regula* he counsels the hermit thus:

With consent of the bishop let some other priest be chosen, either from a neighbouring monastery or church, old, wise, and mature in character and good judgment, to whom the hermit may speak concerning confession and spiritual edification, yet rarely; and from whom he may seek counsel in doubtful matters and consolation in sorrows; whose counsels as well as precepts, in matters which are not contrary to God or his present rule, let him heartily obey, imitating the Lord, of whom it is said: He was made obedient unto death.[2]

Here Richard, in describing what the priest may do for the hermit, is drawing a picture of how he himself was

---

[1] *The Fire*, p. 133. [2] Horstman, vol. ii., p. x, note.

constantly to act in later life; giving counsel to nuns and anchoresses, and consoling their sorrows.

It was not unusual for hermits to be priests. In Stow's *Chronicle* in connection with the anchorites at Westminster we read:

"The same day the King (Richard II.) went towards Westminster . . . after which he spake with the Anchore, to whom he confessed himself."

And again of Henry V., who visited a recluse at Westminster: "and laying bare the sins of his whole life, was washed in the laver of repentance." [1]

Certainly Richard seems to have some official connection with the nuns of Hampole, whose custom it was to choose a confessor from the Friars Minor; and, as we have seen, the Friars Minor and the Austin Friars were often confused, and spoken of as if belonging to the same Order. It has been argued that if he had ended his days as a priest there would have been some reference to it in the Office. He is there called *sanctum heremitam Ricardum*; *sancti Dei Ricardi*; and *beati Ricardi heremite*; but never *sacerdotus* or *presbyter*.[2] But here again it may have been so well known a fact that it was not thought necessary to state it, but was taken for granted.

Moreover the tracts and counsels he left for the service of recluses and others seem hardly like the advice of a mere layman, nor would his exhortations have had as much weight if that were so; and in some MSS. there is joined to the *Cupienti Mihi* another tract instructing parish priests how to hear confession, beginning "Istis jam dictis." It would seem strange that a layman should instruct the clergy on such a subject.

It is not unusual for men of saintly character who, having refused to take orders in early life because of the sense of their great unworthiness, and finding that their usefulness was impeded by their inability to administer the Sacraments, consented in later life to be ordained; as,

[1] Edition 1631, p. 288.

[2] e.g. p. 78, *Officium*: "Pauper olim heremita" in the Sequence; p. 81, *Secret*: "beati Ricardi heremite precacio sancta"; p. 82, Lesson: "Sancti deo tam care dilecti Ricardi"; p. 84, Lesson relating vision a woman had of Richard: "Dum ergo jaceret in lecto vidit in plena vigilia sanctum heremitam Ricardum in habitu heremite griseo."

for example, quite recently was the case with Charles de Foucault.

As a priest Richard might have felt that his words would carry more weight, and he could be of greater service to the nuns at Hampole, if he could give them shrift and say mass for them, as well as be their spiritual adviser, which latter he certainly was; although I have not been able to trace the word "confessor" used in this connection, which would of course prove this point beyond a doubt. Until we have further evidence it must be left a matter for what has well been named "intellectual conjecture." The evidence against it is only negative, and I think it may remain for the present an open question. It seems certainly *possible* that he died in priest's orders, and I am inclined to add, probable.

It is not possible to say where Richard lived from the time he left the Daltons until he went to Hampole. He seems to have been dependent upon different people at different times; and in the passage we have quoted from *Judica me Deus* he says that he passed from one cell to another; "for I am no more obliged to remain in one hermitage than in another"[1]; from which we may infer that he sometimes stayed in the hermitages of the Austin Hermits. They had, as we shall see, three houses, called friaries, in Yorkshire. That in York itself was close to the Ouse bridge, and if he visited them he would have had access to their many MSS. It is quite possible that he wrote while there the *Commentary on the Psalter*, which he compiled later for the Lady Margaret. He was constantly in touch with her, and on first leaving the Dalton estate had gone to some place "twelve miles from the dwelling of the recluse" at Ainderby.

There exists abundant evidence to prove the popularity of his writings among the monks and friars at York. Very shortly after his death, while Spofforth was Abbot of the Benedictine Abbey of St. Mary (1405–21), the *Incendium* was in use as a monastic textbook at the abbey.[2] Also the will of Lord Scrope (1415) mentions the *Incendium*, as well as "an exposition on *Judica me Deus*, which Richard the hermit composed and wrote." This book is said by the

[1] Cf. p. 177 supra.
[2] See Miss Deanesley's edition of the *Incendium*, p. 53.

scribe to be copied from a book in the possession of a hermit at Tanfield [1] whom he (the scribe) had visited at Christmastide in 1409.

He was not continuously wandering, as the *girovagi*, neither could he have been a recluse, i.e. canonically enclosed in a cell, as was Margaret.

I was wont [he says] to seek rest, although I went from place to place; for it is not ill for hermits to leave cells for a reasonable cause, and afterwards, if it accord, to turn again to the same. Truly some of the holy Fathers have done thus, although they have therefore suffered the murmuring of men, nevertheless, not of the good. (*The Fire*, p. 70.)

And in the following passage we have proof of how he moved "from place to place," and why:

Eaten have I and drunken of this that seemed best, not because I loved pleasantness, but because nature must be sustained in the service of God and in the praise of Jesu Christ; conforming myself in good manners to them with whom I dwelt for Christ; and that I should not feign holiness where none is, nor that men should praise me too mickle where I was full little to be praised. From divers, also, I have gone, not because they fed me commonly or in hard measure, but because we have not accorded in manners, or for some other reasonable cause. Nevertheless I dare say, with blessed Job: "Fools have despised me; and when I have gone from them they have backbitten me" [1]; nevertheless they shall be ashamed when they see me that have said that I would not abide but where I might be delicately fed. (p. 54.)

Here he seems to be describing his manner of bearing himself when he mingled and lived among others. He does not go about with a long face, if he were to do so he would be called a hypocrite.

The holy lover of God shows himself neither too merry nor full heavy in this habitation of exile, but he has cheerfulness with ripeness.[2] Forsooth some reprove laughter and some praise it. Laughter therefore which is from lightness and vanity of mind is to be reproved, but that truly that is of gladness of conscience and ghostly mirth is to be praised; the which is only in the righteous, and it is called mirth in

---

[1] Tanfield is marked in the map as a few miles north-west of Topcliffe, and the hermitage there may have been known and visited by Richard during his stay at Topcliffe.

[2] Job xix. 18. [3] *Maturitate*.

the love of God. Wherefore if we be glad and merry, the wicked call us wanton; and if we be heavy, hypocrites.

And what an insight into character is shown in the following, and how true it is:

Seldom truly can any man trow good in another that he finds not in himself; and he thinks the sin into which he stumbles belongs to another. For this is the deed of the wicked; they hold that if any follow not *their* life, that he is wrong and is deceived.

And the reason is because the wicked man has forsaken meekness. The degrees of meekness are given:

. . . to hold the eyes low, not high; to have a measure in speech, and not to pass it; to hear gladly their betters and those more wise; and to will wisdom should be heard from others, rather than from themselves. Not to take the time of speaking too soon. Not to go from common life. To set others before thyself; to know thy frailties and to deem thyself worse than all others.

And he adds:

If truly I wished to come among men, I have desired that I might sit last in number, and be held least in opinion, and so all my joy should be in Christ Jesu; and thus I should take no heed to man's praising or blaming, but with busy devotion I should desire after God. (pp. 45–6.)

Far to the south, in the West Riding, and almost on the borders of Nottinghamshire, there was another house of the Austin Friars at Tickhill, which is close to Hampole. It was founded in the beginning of Edward II.'s reign. And in Hull also the Austin Friars had a house, at the east end of Trinity Church, founded *c.* 1317.[1] There is no trace and not much likelihood of Richard having gone so far eastwards as Hull, but there is every probability that he would have known Tickhill, nor is it unlikely that it was from there he moved to Hampole; perhaps at the invitation of the prioress of the convent.

The priory at Hampole, or Hanepole, or Hampell,[2] had been founded more than a hundred years earlier. William de Clarefai and his wife Avicia de Tannais, or Tany, who were evidently of French extraction, built them a house *c.* 1170, for fourteen or fifteen nuns belonging

[1] Cf. Stevens' Continuation of Dugdale, vol. ii., p. 214.
[2] As it is named in Speed's Atlas.

to the Cistercian Order. At this time the Cistercians were more popular than any other Order in the north; and in Yorkshire, besides the many monasteries there were twelve houses for women, although none of them were large. We read that the nuns were directed to choose their confessors from the Friars Minor [1]; and we have already noted that there was constant confusion between the Friars Minor and the Austin Friars. The priory was dedicated to Our Lady and is thus referred to in the prologue to Richard's Psalter:

In Yorkshire this nunnery is; whoso desires it to know,
Him there no way goes amiss; these be the places all on row.
Hampole, the nunnery hight; between Dancaster and Poumefreyt.

It stood in a pleasant vale, lying east and west, in a fine country, and was upon the high road leading from Wakefield to Doncaster, about four miles from the latter. In the *Monasticon* it is said that the "town of Hanepole" was given to the nuns.[2] There seems to have been no parish church and the people dwelling there would have been served from the nuns' chapel. It is still a tiny hamlet, with neither shop nor inn—only a post office. Miss Deanesley gives a detailed description of the few remaining stones left in the village, some of which have been built into the gable of the school, and a local tradition regards these as having been taken from the site of Richard's cell.[3] The priory probably stood on the banks of a little stream. A more picturesque description is given by the late Mgr. Hugh Benson, who writes:

Of the nunnery there are now no certain traces, except where a few mounds in the meadows by the stream below the hamlet mark its foundations, and beyond a few of its stones built into the school-house. The few grey stone houses nestle together on the steep slope in a shallow nook in the hill, round an open space where the old village spring still runs. There is no trace of Richard's cell; but, in spite of the railway line in the valley, the place has a curious detached air, lying, as it does, a complete and self-contained whole, below the Doncaster road, fringed and shadowed by trees, and bordered with low-lying meadows rich, in early summer, with daisies and

---

[1] Cf. *Victorian History*, iii., pp. 163 sqq.
[2] Dugdale, vol. vi., p. 1589.
[3] Deanesley, *Incendium*, p. 39.

buttercups, and dotted with numerous may-trees; the farthest horizon from the hamlet is not more than a mile or two away.[1]

We can think of Richard dwelling in his cell near the priory, but whether as a lay hermit, and only able to teach and give them counsel by speech, help them by his writings and songs, or whether in the capacity of their shrift father he now had authority to hear their confessions, and administer the Sacraments to them, we cannot certainly tell. This ancient hermit's song, taken from an Irish MS.,[2] gives so graphic a picture of the hermit's life that it appears to have been written by one who had made experience of that life. It seems not inappropriate to quote it here:

All alone in my little cell, without a single human being in my company: beloved has been the pilgrimage before going to the tryst with Death.

A hidden secluded little hut, that my evil may be forgiven: a straight unblemished conscience towards holy Heaven.

Sanctifying the body by good habits, trampling like a man upon it: with eyes feeble and tearful for the forgiveness of my passions.

Passions weak and withered, renouncing this wretched world; pure living thoughts, as it were a prayer to God.

Wailings with eagerness towards cloudy Heaven, sincere truly devout confessions, swift showers of tears.

A couch cold and fearful, as it were the lying down of a doomed man: a short sleep as in danger, frequent early outcries.

My food with my station,[3] beloved has been the bondage: my dinner, doubtless, would not make me ruddy.

Dry bread weighed out; well we lower the face,[4] water of the many-coloured slope, that is the drink I would quaff.

A bitter meagre dinner; diligently feeding the sick; keeping off strife; keeping off visits; a radiant smooth conscience.

. . . . . .

---

[1] *A Book of the Love of Jesus*, p. 226.

[2] Translated by Dr. Kuno Meyer. From *Ériu; the Journal of the School of Irish Learning*, Dublin, vol. ii., pp. 55 sqq. (David Nutt. 1905).

[3] i.e. "food such as befits my station."

[4] In giving thanks.

Stepping along the paths of the Gospel; psalm-singing at every
Hour; an end to talk, to long stories; constant bending of
the knees.

My Creator to visit me, My Lord, my King: my mind to go
out to Him in the everlasting Kingdom in which He is.

.   .   .   .   .   .

All alone in my little cell, all alone thus; alone I came into the
world, alone I shall go from it.

If by myself I have transgressed from pride of this world, hear
me wail for it all alone, O God!

Miss Deanesley thinks that Richard wrote the *Incendium*
while at Hampole; of it she says: "The main purpose
of the book is to vindicate the life of a hermit, not only
from the charge of vagabondage and laziness, but of in-
feriority to an active prelate or monk."

But Richard himself tells us the purpose of this book:
"And since I here stir all manner of folk to love, and am
busy to show the hottest and supernatural desire of love,
this book shall bear the name: *Burning of Love.*" Though
it is possible *The Fire* belongs to this time, I am inclined
to place it among his earlier books, written perhaps when
dwelling at the hermitage at York or Tickhill. For now
he has finished with any attempt to justify himself in the
eyes of others, and the book which really belongs to these
later years is *The Commandment of Love to God* which was
expressly written for a sister at Hampole.[1]

Most of his later writing is in English, which he had begun
to use for the sake of the Lady Margaret and for other recluses
and nuns. He most certainly, as we have seen, translated
the Psalter for Margaret of Kirkby, as he writes this
Commandment of Love to God for another woman at this
nunnery where he was so much beloved. During these years
many of his lyrics may have been put into writing, although
some were composed much earlier. Just as a troubadour
sang his songs of earthly love and prowess for the ladies of
the court, so perhaps Richard indited these heavenly love-
songs, that these ladies, in the court of their king, might
have songs which they could easily recall to mind, to sing
to their Lover.

[1] The *explicit* in MS. Dd. 5. 64 reads: "*Explicit tractatus Ricardi
Hampole scriptus cuidam sorori de Hampole.*"

In some ways *The Commandment* is the most touching of all Richard's writings. His love has hardened and strengthened, "it is stalwart as death and hard as hell," and has now become a destructive force against evil. To be perfect it must be "a wilful stirring of our thoughts to God." There can be no place for backbiting, or any envy or despite in the heart that loves God truly, "for it will make place for nothing that is against the love of Jesus Christ." "As death slays all living things in this world, so perfect love slays in a man's soul all earthly desires and covetousness. And as hell spares nought til dead men, but torments all that come theretil, so a man that is in this degree of love, not only forsakes the wretched solace of this life, but also he desires to suffer pines (torments) for God's love." [1]

There are many reminders of the lyrics in this tract, more especially of "Love is Life"; for example, compare the following with stanzas 9 and 15 [2]: "For all earthly love is passing, and wites soon away; all the delights of this world are faint and false, and failing in most need; that begin in sweetness, and their ending is bitterer than gall."

Richàrd now experiences the loneliness which comes with middle age, when vitality burns lower, and youthful keenness of interest slackens.

"If thou canst not live without fellowship, lift thy thoughts to heaven, that thou mayst find comfort with angels and saints"; and his comment is a revelation of his own experience; "the which will help thee to God, and not hinder thee as thy earthly friends do."

Often he has to restrain himself from going forth from his cell to serve others, and from speech, for a greater love constrains him. "If ye list to speak," he counsels, "forbear it at the beginning for the love of God; for when thy heart feeleth delight in Christ, ye will not list to speak or jangle but of Christ. If thou thinkest it weary to sit by thy lone, exercise thyself stalwartly in His love; and He shall so stably set thee that all the solace of this world shall not move thee hence, for ye will have no lust thereof."

The whole epistle seems to read as a description of his own life:

[1] My quotations are modernised from Horstman, vol. i., pp. 61 sqq.
[2] Infra, pp. 252, 256.

When thou art by thyself, be ever, until sleep come, either in prayer or in good meditation. And ordain thy waking and thy praying and thy fasting, that it be in discretion; not over-mickle nor over-little; but think ay that of all things God most desires the love of man's heart. . . . And therefore seek more to love Him than to do any penance; for unskilful penance is little worth or nought, but love is ever the best, whether thou dost much or little penance.

He is now beyond the reach of scandal, for

being inwardly given to the love of Ihesu Christ, that for ghostly joy of thy soul nought that men may say or do can make thee sorry, so that thy thought within be fed only in the sweetness of Christ's love; not in delight of earthly ease, nor in praise of men—*if they begin to speak good of thee*—nor in idle joy. Trust in God that He will give til thee the things that thou prayest Him skilfully in reason. Skilful prayer is to Christian men's souls, to seek and ask, night and day, the love of Ihesu Christ that they may love Him verily, feeling comfort and delight in Him, casting out worldly thoughts, and evil and ill busyness. And sicker[1] be thou if thou covet His love truly and lastingly, so that no desire of thy flesh, nor angers[2] of the world, nor speech nor hatred of men, draw thee again, and cast thee not into any business of bodily things: thou shalt have His love, and find and feel that it is more delectable in one hour, than all the wealth that we see here until doomsday.

The words I have italicised are illuminating, for now at last, as his life draws to its close, he begins to taste the rare and strange joy which comes to those who spend their lives in prayer, of being of service to the souls of men; though, to all good men, such praise must be full of humiliation as intense as is the joy.

There is a charming passage about Our Lady seeking her Son, "when He was willed from her; . . . but she found Him not for all her seeking and sorrowing, til at the last she come intil the temple"; and of the herdsmen that sought, "and found Him lying in a crib between two beasts"; and the three kings who "found Christ swaddled in clouts, simply, as a poor bairn." "Thereby," he exhorts, "understand that whiles thou art in pride and vanity thou findest Him not. How mayst thou for shame, that art but a servant, with many clothes and rich, follow thy Spouse and thy Lord, that went in one kirtle; and thou trailest as much behind thee as all that He had on. Therefore I

---

[1] i.e. Sure.   [2] Troubles.

counsel thee that thou part with them ere thou and He meet, that He reprove thee not of outrage; for He will that thou have that thou hast mastery of, and no more."

He cautions against the dread of pain and annoyance: "commit all to God's will and thank Him ay for all He sends"; and take care not to be "one without and another within, as hypocrites do, the which are like to a sepulchre that is painted richly without, and within rotteth stinking bones. . . . Thine habit saith that thou hast forsaken the world. . . . If thy body be clothed without as thine order will, look that thy soul be not naked within, that thine order forbiddeth."

And he draws a pattern for character, to which, out of much stress and weariness, we feel that he, "the saint of God," has by now attained.

Be debonair and meek to all men, let nothing bring thee to ire or envy; dight thy soul fairly, make therein a tower [1] of love to God's Son, and make thy will be as desirous to receive Him as gladly as thou wouldest be at the coming of a thing that thou hast loved most of all things. Wash thy thoughts clean with love - tears, and burning yearning, that He find nothing foul in thee: for His joy is that thou be fair and love-some in His eyes. The fairhead of the soul that He coveteth is that thou be chaste and meek, mild and suffering; never irk to do His will, ay hating all sin. . . .

He tells this nun for whom he writes:

Purchase thee the well of weeping, and cease not until thou have Him; for in the heart where tears spring, there will the fire of the Holy Ghost be kindled: and then the fire of love, that shall burn in thy heart, will bring to nought all the rust of sin, and purge the soul of all filth; as clean as the gold that is proved in the furnace.

This Fire of Love, of which he has never ceased to teach and sing, is the refiner's fire. First it must burn and scorch the soul with hot flames, until, purified by long purgation, it so enlightens the soul that there, as in a mirror, men can see the image of Christ; the Name of Jesus.

The illuminator of *The Desert of Religion* has portrayed Richard's love for this Name by painting the sacred monogram in letters of gold upon his breast, to which he makes the saint point with his right hand. As he ends this,

_____
[1] MS. Rawl. A. 359 reads "throne."

probably his last epistle, Richard urges again in burning words this love for Jesu the Incarnate Son of God; this Name which betokens His humanity:

One thing I counsel thee: that thou forget not this Name IHESU, but think It in thy heart night and day as thy special and dear treasure. Love It more than life, root It in thy mind. Love Ihesu for He made thee and bought thee full dearly. Give thy heart to Him for it is His debt. Therefore set thy love on His name, Ihesu, that is Heal. There may no ill thing have dwelling in the heart where Ihesu is holden in mind truly.

In this epistle, as in that of another great mystic, there is the note of farewell. Richard, like St. Paul in his last Epistle to Timothy, seems to realise that his course is finished. He also might have said, "I am ready to be offered and the time of my departure is at hand."

An old writer in a book, a fragment of which alone has come down to us,[1] teaches men how to die; and says thus:

But these holy men that loved and dreaded God, out of three deaths have passed. Twain, for they be dead unto sin, and dead unto the world; and they abiden the third death; that is departing of the body and soul. Betwixt them and paradise is but a little wall, which they pass through thought and desiring.

Before death called him, Richard had passed through this wall. In his early life he had longed for death—as so many long in youth—as an escape. He cries to God to take him out of this world, where love for God is dead.[1] But in *The Fire* it is the yearning of the heart after that treasure which he has amassed in a life of service:

For all that I had in this world or of this world is ended, and nought is left but that Thou lead my soul to another world where my treasure is most precious and my substance richest, and unfailingly abides. Wherefore I shall live without default; I shall joy without sorrow; I shall love without irksomeness; and loving Thee, seeing Thee, and joying in Thee, I shall be endlessly fed. Thou truly art my Treasure, and all the Desire of my heart; and because of Thee I shall perfectly see Thee, for then I shall have Thee.

And I spake thus to Death:
O Death, where dwellest thou? Why comest thou so late

---

[1] The Tower of all Towers, printed in *The Craft of Dying*, p. 129 (Longmans, 1917).

O

to me, living but yet mortal? Why halsest thou not him that desires thee?

Who is enough to think [1] thy sweetness, that art the end of sighing, the beginning of desire, the gate of unfailing yearning? Thou art the end of heaviness, the mark [2] of labours, the beginning of fruits, the gate of joys. Behold I grow hot and desire after thee: if thou come I shall forthwith be safe. Ravished, truly, because of love, I cannot fully love what I desire after, until I taste the joy that Thou shalt give to me. If it behoves me, mortal—because forsooth it so befalls—to pass through thee as all my fathers have gone, I pray thee tarry not mickle; from me abide not long! Behold, I truly languish for love; I desire to die; for thee I burn; and yet truly not for thee, but for my Saviour Jesu, whom, after I have had thee, I trow to see withouten end.

O Death, how good is thy doom to needy man, whose soul, nevertheless, is made sweet by love; to the man, forsooth, truly loving Christ and contemplating heavenly things, and sweetly burned with the fire of the Holy Ghost. After death he is taken soothly to songs of angels; because now being purged, and profiting, he dwells in the music of the spirit. And in melody full marvellous shall he die, the which when alive thought pithily upon that sweet Name; and with the companies meeting him, with heavenly hymns and honour, he shall be taken into the hall of the Eternal Emperor, being among heavenly dwellers in the seat of the blessed.

To this has charity truly brought him, that he should thus live in inward delight, and should gladly suffer all that happens, and should think on death, not with bitterness but with sweetness. Soothly then he trows himself truly to live, when it is given him to pass from this light.

. . . Therefore truly I long after love, the fairest of flowers, and I am inwardly burned by the flame of fire. Would God that I might go from the dwelling of this exile! . . . Now grant, my best Beloved, that I may cease; for death, that many dread, shall be to me as heavenly music. Although I am sitting in wilderness, yet I am now as it were set stable in Paradise, and there sweetly is sounding a loving song in the delights that my Love has given me. (pp. 74–6.)

The unknown writer of *The Tower* expresses the same thought:

Death is the running brook that departed from life. Death is on this half, and life on the other half. . . . But the wise men of this world call this death, life, and the death, that these good men call the beginning of life, they clepen the end.

---

[1] Lat. *excogitare*, i.e. find out by thinking.
[2] Lat. *meta* = goal, or turning-point.

Death seems to have come to Richard in ministering to others when the plague, or the Black Death, as it was called, which was continuously ravaging the country, broke out with great violence in Yorkshire early in 1349, and raged there for several months. In York itself according to old documents three-fourths of the inhabitants died; and in the East Riding sixty parish priests out of ninety-five were swept off by this terrible sickness.

It was not likely that Richard would have safeguarded himself when the plague invaded Hampole, nor did it spare the little nunnery there. In the records of the priory there is a long gap in the names of the prioresses. Maud (1348) is not succeeded until after 1380. This is accounted for by the upheaval followed by this great outbreak, owing to which Richard's canonisation was never proceeded with; for there were hardly sufficient clergy left to attend even to the most urgent needs of the people, and the convents and monastic houses were greatly depleted. The few nuns left at Hampole began to draw up the Office. The *Vite* were probably compiled first, and the *Miracula,* or lessons drawn up for the octave of the feast, date some thirty years later; yet miracles must have been known of earlier; for we have the evidence of the cure of the Anchoress Margaret which has been cited as given us in the *Vite.*

The actual dates of only two miracles are recorded: the Feast of the Epiphany, 1381, and the Feast of the Assumption, 1383. The first miracle of which we are told in the *Miracula* was experienced by a certain householder called Roger. Richard had appeared to him in his dreams and conversed with him; and later Roger had a vision of the saint when he was wide awake, and was "inspired" by him "with a spirit of holy devotion, and inflamed by the love of God"; so that he resolves to build a shrine in the church of the nuns of Hampole over the spot where Richard had been buried.

The second lesson describes what happened:

One day, therefore, while he was occupied with the aforesaid work of piety, and had got ready twelve oxen for drawing, it happened that when he had reached the gate of the churchyard at Hampole carrying great stones, his poor beasts by an unhappy accident turned aside from the path, and the cart collided with the side-post of the gate and cast the said stones with great force upon Roger himself. Yet he was in no wise hurt by this, nor felt any shaking or pain of body; and though his foot was very tightly jammed by the stones, he was able to get it out without injury to foot or leg. And, indeed, that this miracle should not be forgotten, one of these stones was set up at the gate of the churchyard, so that those coming that way might see it; and another is placed on the tomb of the saint.

Twenty-five other accounts of healing are recorded. In two of these Our Lady appears leading the blessed hermit, Richard, by the hand; both being cases of women, vexed with demons, who had lost the power of speech. The greater number of miracles recorded are those of the curing of the deaf, and of demoniacs afflicted with dumbness; there are two cases of blindness, and three in which the person is thought to be dead and is restored to life. In one of these latter the sufferer is a boy of five, who was choked by an apple. For three days he was thought to be dead, but is revived by a denarius placed upon his head as an offering to the saint. It is noticeable that the cures which were wrought at a distance, and not by a visit to the shrine itself, are always accompanied by the promise of money or of a candle. We find this same expression "measured for a candle" in many early accounts of miracles; notably in that of St. Thomas of Canterbury [1]; and the custom is in full force to-day. To pray to St. Antony, for example, without the promise of a candle worth a certain sum — whether large or small is immaterial — has been proved to be of little use. This is of course considered gross superstition by the many; but if thought of more deeply we can see that the candle only represents the humility necessary for a real act of faith. Most of the miracles performed by Our Lord demanded some such simple outward act as a token of the inward and spiritual grace which He was ready to bestow upon the humble and simple of heart.

The dwelling-place of those who were healed is not always recorded, but there is mention of many villages round about: Sprotborough, Wrangbroke, Morehow, Fishlake, near Thorne, and Sutton, besides four cases from

[1] See *St. Thomas of Canterbury; his Death and Miracles*, by Edwin Abbott (Black, 1898).

York, one from Durham, and two as far distant as Worksop and Leicester. Most cures are wrought by a pilgrimage to the shrine, as was the case in these two from Worksop and Leicester, though the distance made it no easy task in those days. There is one curious account of a bedridden man being told by a voice in the night to send a candle weighing one and a half pounds to be burnt before the image of Our Lady at Hampole by his wife and family; which he does. Then, while he is left alone in the house, Richard appears to him and asks him where the pain is, and touching the spot heals him. And another worth recording in which a demoniac and dumb woman falls asleep at the saint's tomb, when he appears with Our Lady in a vision of such dazzling brightness that the woman is nearly blinded. They tell her to ask the priest to whom she confesses, and she will be healed in mind and body; which she does and is cured.

Whether we believe these miracles or not, they are evidence—as are the miracles at the tomb of Sœur Thérèse of Lisieux to-day—that the sanctity of Richard was honoured and recognised as something beyond common experience, and that he was held in extreme love and reverence

"How often," I asked a Breton peasant of the poorer class, who had travelled the long road from her home to Lourdes, "have you been here?"

"Eight times."

"And why?"

"Because I love Our Lady so much," she answered simply.

There is no other answer to the enigmas of life but this of the poor peasant. Death has no power over those who love.

As will have been seen, I have hardly touched in the foregoing pages upon what may be called the historical background of Richard's life. The years in which he lived were full of events yet these seem to have passed unheeded by Richard. Born in the reign of Edward I. he was not yet thirty when Edward II. was foully murdered, and Edward III. had still many years to reign when Richard died. It comes almost as a surprise to read that not far from Topcliffe, near the great abbey of Byland which had only lately been completed, and which Richard must surely have visited, one autumn day in 1322 the country echoed to the sounds of warfare. Edward II.'s army was in full retreat, being harassed by the Scots, and there the two armies met and fought, the English being completely defeated. Some say that Edward was actually dining with the abbot when the news of the disaster reached him, and that he had only time hastily to mount and take flight southwards, when the Scots came swarming down upon the abbey. The fugitives must have passed and perhaps taken refuge at the famous castle of Topcliffe, yet no hint of war is found in what Richard writes; even in the first years of his hermit life he lived aloof, cut off from the turmoil of the world around.

Only a few scattered references in his Psalter to passing events may be traced.[1] The papal disputes, and the removal of Clement V. to Avignon under the protection of the French king, must have stirred other minds besides the ecclesiastical, for the English could hardly have welcomed the spiritual leadership of one who was dependent upon their hereditary foe. The newly awakened nationalism must have found complete sympathy in Richard, and although as yet the movement of revolt had hardly filtered into the Church, yet the germs were soon here of the great struggle which was to follow later, and result in the upheaval which we call by that much-abused word the "Reformation." If Richard had lived a century and a half later we wonder on which side he would have been.

He was a visionary, as we should expect, and sees farther than his contemporaries, and he influenced and shaped men's thoughts; yet no call came to him to bestir himself, as it did to Catherine at Siena who was in the thick of the fray. But it is untrue to say, as some have, that he was infected by Lollardry. The stress the early Lollards laid in their teaching upon love and spiritual freedom, and

[1] There is a reference in Psalm i. 8 to a pestilence, which may have been an outbreak of the plague which is recorded in 1316: and an allusion to the ill princes, "and such are our princes now that lead their life in filth of sin," in Psalm civ. 28, which may refer to Mortimer and his intrigue with the queen in 1325–6. Again in the commentary on Psalm lxxxviii. 39 there is an obvious reference to the murder of Stapledon, at Cheapside, in 1326. Cf. Bramley, pp. xv–xvi, and p. 60.

their practical care for the sick, and the reverent burying of the dead, would have attracted Richard; and he in his turn would attract them when, later, they became known in England. By that time they had become a sect, instead of being, as at first was the case, a religious Order, and they eagerly appropriated Richard's doctrines as their own; and, which was the more misleading, interpolated passages expressing their own doctrines into the hermit's works. Thus his name was smirched by their later heretical opinions which would have been entirely alien to him. Perhaps it was partly for this reason that he was never canonised. If so it is all of a piece with his life, which was ever pursued by calumny and backbiting.

He was one of those men who are to be found in every generation; impatient of restraint they must develop their genius in their own way. That Richard did so at a great cost no one can doubt. Loved by the few but hated by the many, he must have suffered all the torture of a temperament unusually sensitive to adverse criticism. Yet he never allows himself to be hindered by fear of this, nor hesitates to break through all barriers and restraints when possessed by the love of God, but when the divine afflatus leaves him he retires into himself and is a prey to desolating self-consciousness. It is indeed one of the commonest traits of the mystic, the very essence of whose belief makes him strive to purge away all that hampers union with God, and thus by self-abnegation and humility to fit himself to be a channel, necessarily an empty channel, through which the grace of God can be imparted to others: but the message delivered he sinks back, as the seaweed on the edge of the strand when the wave which had lifted it up and spread out its tiny tendrils, flows back again into the ocean.

To us he will always remain an example of the power of love to overcome the depression which slander brings upon a sensitive temperament, and to uplift the mind into an atmosphere of joy and song. His writings more than most men's are the expression of his character; and this perhaps is the secret of their endurance.

I do not think they will appeal to the scholar. His discursiveness and lack of method; his curious Latinity; looseness of style and carelessness of construction, are not faults to be easily tolerated by a scholarly mind. The poet (i.e. the poet who is made) may read Rolle's verse with a kindly amusement mingled with contempt. The theologian may find in his works the germs of many heresies, for Rolle was never a favourite with the ecclesiastics of his own day; though he would probably find far more supporters now than he did in the fourteenth century. The modern novelist may, in the words of the *Westminster Gazette*, "seize upon Richard as an owl seizes on a mouse,"[1] and in these days when psycho-analysis is run to death it is possible that the hermit may become a popular study for a psycho-analytic novelist.

But such things do not endure. And what is it in Rolle's work that makes for endurance? What is his real appeal to us to-day? It seems to me that it is twofold. First he appeals to those of a literary and artistic temperament. The purity and simplicity of his English, both of his prose and verse, attracts all who seek for purity of language and of style. What he wishes to say he says simply and straightforwardly. He does not strain a point, as so many of these early mystical writers do, or seek after some learned illustration. He is content with simple similes, as of the nightingale, or the topaz stone.[2] He writes to make himself understood, and not to show forth his learning, so that we are spared the constant quotations and references to learned authors which bespatter the pages of contemporary writers.

And his influence was far-reaching. We find the same note of simplicity in many who followed him: Dame Julian of Norwich and Walter Hilton; the anonymous authors of *The Cloud of Unknowing*, and of that poetic piece *The Talking of the Love of God*, all write in the same simple way. We might with truth say that incidentally we owe to him the purity of the language of our English Bible, for his influence was not least upon Wyclif. Thus English literature as a whole owes him a debt which cannot be

---

[1] See *Westminster Gazette* for 2 May, 1914.

[2] Cf. *The Fire*, p. 68: "Truly they [i.e. the contemplative] are like the stone that is called topaz the which is seldom found, and therefore it is held most precious and full dear, in which are two colours: one is most pure even as gold, and the other clear as heaven when it is right. And it overcomes all the clearness of all the stones; and nothing is fairer to behold. But if any would polish it, it is made dim, and truly if it be left to itself its clearness is retained,"

too much emphasised: and it is surely a healthy sign in literature that we should be recalling to mind these old writers and constantly publishing fresh editions of their books.

But there is another appeal which is to many stronger than the literary and artistic, for it is the mystical and religious element in Rolle which secures him most readers to-day. Religion and mysticism must last so long as this earth remains inhabited, and just because Richard's mysticism is individual and free from artificiality, it naturally appeals most strongly to his compatriots. We have dwelt already upon his prevailing note of Love, and on his delight in song and his joyousness. A mystic, indeed, enjoys as no other man can enjoy; for every moment that passes is fraught with the will of God. Like the yellow primrose, the passing moment contains for him all the wonders of heaven. Any instant he may make some great discovery in that spiritual world in which he breathes. The mystic is indeed the great adventurer. Life to him can never be dull, for he lives not in time, but *sub specie aeternitatis*; and when he dies, death will be to him, to quote from Rolle's own words in the *Incendium*, "as the melody of music; although I be sitting here in solitude, already I am there in paradise, sweetly intoning a song of love in the delights which my Beloved has given to me." [1]

---

[1] "Mors, quam multi metuunt, mihi esset ut melos musice, quanquam iam tanquam in paradiso positus, subsistam, sedens in solitudine, illic suauiter sonans amorosum canticum in deliciis quas dedit mihi dilectus."—*Incendium* (MS. Dd. 5.64, cap. xvi., *fol.* 29⁰⁴).

VIEW OF OSENEY ABBEY

PART II
THE LYRICS

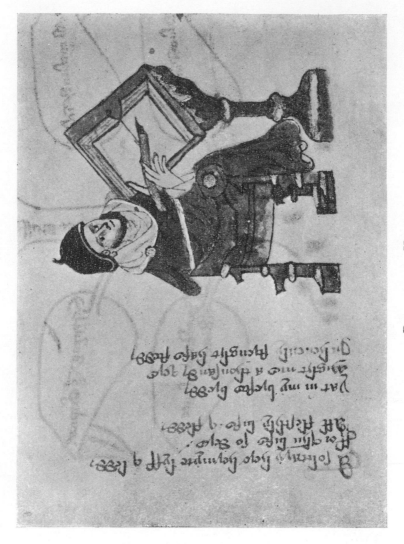

RICHARD THE HERMIT

(From MS. Stowe, 39 fol. 16v.)

PART II—THE LYRICS

CHAPTER I

THE MSS. OF MOST IMPORTANCE FOR THE STUDY OF THE LYRICS

BEFORE we discuss the poems ascribed to Richard Rolle it is advisable to give some description of the MSS. in which they are found. Then we can better gauge the evidence for their authenticity.

Dr. Horstman in his two volumes of Yorkshire writers, which he entitled *Richard Rolle of Hampole and his Followers*, thought that by collecting all the northern MSS. he would be able to gather from them all the English works, in prose and verse, of Richard Rolle. He found it a most difficult task since Rolle's name, he says,

was so associated with a certain class of literature that all works of that character, or found in certain collections (as MS. Harl. 1706) were readily ascribed to him, while some of his genuine works soon ceased to be recognised as his. His works got mixed up with those of his followers, especially W. Hilton and Wicliffe, and the more easily because both writers not only followed in his steps but freely borrowed from him (several of the supposed tracts of Wicliffe begin with the same words as works of R. Rolle and Hilton's style and manner is almost identical with his). Or translations and imitations of his work assumed his name. . . . In fact there is hardly a religious work in early English that has not been ascribed to him. How are we to get at his real works and to sever the corn from the chaff? The principal test is the dialect. As Rolle never—excepting the years of his studentship left the precincts of Yorkshire, living first in the northern, at last in the southern parts of that country, it is obvious that he can only have written in the northern dialect—unlike Wicliffe, who though a northerner, from his long residence in the South adopted the southern speech, and W. Hilton who, though originally writing in northern English, gradually admitted the mixed forms of the neighbourhood where he resided (Thurgarton in Notts.). Indeed all the genuine works of Rolle have been traced in northern texts, exhibiting the same pure northern forms, the same vocabulary. It follows that works which on closer examination are found to be of midland or southern origin cannot be his, hence many works in Tanner's list must be rejected. Nor can even northern texts which give translations of his Latin works be accepted as his if they are found seriously to misunderstand the meaning . . . which is the case in several of the pieces in MS. Thornton, though here given with his name. On the other side we may safely ascribe to him those northern texts which in the MSS. are found mixed up with works of his and contain the same peculiarities of language and style, the same cadenced prose, etc., though not bearing his name. The only possible means of approximately arriving at the truth is, therefore, to follow up the northern MSS. which contain, or may contain, his works.[1]

To a certain extent this was an excellent device, for no work of Rolle's is likely to be found only in a southern or midland MS., and as a fact none such exists. All his poems contained in southern MSS. are also found in northern MSS.; and northern forms occur even in southern and midland MSS. when the rhyme demands it. We may therefore safely state that there is no poem attributed to Rolle existing in any purely southern or midland dialect. All such bear evidence of being copied from a northern original by a southern or midland scribe.

Dr. Horstman's error lay in ascribing many works to Rolle just because they were found in these northern MSS., which did indeed contain many of his genuine writings in prose and verse, but this fact is not in itself sufficient proof. We have also to test them by their style, diction, thought, and similarity to other works which have been ascertained to be genuinely Rolle's; and the difficulty of attaining to certainty is enormously enhanced by the fact that no autograph copy of any one of Rolle's works has been as yet discovered.

The MSS. which we must examine are:

A. Northern MSS.

MS. Thornton (Lincoln Cath. MS. A. 5.2. Formerly A. 1.17).

MS. Dd. 5.64 (Camb. Univ. Lib.).

MS. Reg. 17. B. xvii. (Brit. Mus.). Written by a southern scribe.

[1] Vol. ii., pp. xxxix–xl. I give the quotation in full as Dr. Horstman's volumes have been for long out of print, and until Miss Allen's work appears they must remain the standard for all students of Rolle.

B. SOUTHERN MSS.

> MS. Vernon (MS. 3938) (Bodl. Lib., Oxford).
> MS. Simeon (MS. Add. 22283) (Brit. Mus.).
> MS. Add. 37787 (Brit. Mus.).
> MS. Pepys 2125 (Magd. Coll., Cambridge).
> MS. Lamb. 853 (Lambeth Palace Library).

A. NORTHERN MSS.

The two most famous northern collections of poems which Dr. Horstman prints in his *Yorkshire Writers* are: The Thornton MS. in the Lincoln Cathedral Library; and a very valuable small volume in the University Library at Cambridge, which contains nothing besides pieces, in prose and verse, attributed to R. Rolle.

These two volumes are of almost the same date. The Thornton MS. is ascribed by Dr. Horstman to 1430–40, and by later scholars to 1430–50 [1]; the authorities in Cambridge fix the date of their MS. as "quite early fifteenth century." It is probably older than the Thornton MS. and may have been written as early as 1400. They are very unlike in appearance, the Thornton MS. being a bulky cumbrous volume, carelessly written in cursive hand and on paper; whereas the small Cambridge book is beautifully and clearly written in black letter, upon parchment. To describe them more in detail:

THE THORNTON MS.[2]—This MS. contains romances and other poems and prose works, chiefly in English, copied by Robert Thornton, who came from East Newton in Ryedale, near Helmsley, Yorkshire. There are several autograph colophons.

The date is 1430–50, which is confirmed by the watermarks in the paper which are identical with another MS. in Thornton's hand in the British Museum, MS. Add. 31042.[3]

It is a thick volume of 322 leaves, of which the last eight are torn, being mere fragments, small folio in size ($11\frac{1}{2}$ in. by $8\frac{1}{4}$ in.), and is written throughout on paper in

---

[1] Cf. *New Palæographical Society Series*, ii., plate 45.

[2] Its pressmark is properly Lincoln Cath. MS. A. 5.2 (formerly known as A. 1.17).

[3] We owe this discovery to Mr. Beazely, who has traced the watermarks of the early books which are written on paper.

a carelessly formed cursive script which varies in size. Occasionally the copyist has amused himself by practising letters down the side of a blank column. The initials are usually in red, sometimes flourished with inks of other colours. The first letter of each half-line and the colon marking the division are often heightened with strokes of red ink.

It is not unlike the Auchinleck MS. in Edinburgh, for it also contains a prose life of Alexander, the *Morte d'Arthur* in English verse, a curious medley of romances and religious works in prose and verse, and a collection of medicinal recipes, occasionally in Latin but mostly in English. The Latin verses which have been attributed to Rolle by Horstman are found in the Thornton book, and the Psalter of St. Jerome and Latin litanies of the saints. These Latin hymns are very untidily written, perhaps by Thornton in his old age, for they occur at the end of the volume. The book remained in the Thornton family until the late sixteenth or seventeenth century.

This MS. contains thirteen lyrics attributed to Rolle, which are scattered throughout the volume, and not given consecutively, as in the Cambridge MS. They are:

fol. 191:

   (1)   *"Lorde Gode Ihesu cryste, Godd Almyghty."* [1]

   (2)   "Almighty god in trinite
             Inwardly I thank þe."

   (3)   "Lord God alweldande,
             I beteche to daye into þi hande."

   (4)   "Schelde us fra þe paynes of hell."

(Nos. 2, 3, 4 are written straight on as one poem.)

fol. 192:

   (5)   "Ihesu that diede one the rude for þe lufe of me."

   (6)   *"Ihesu of whayme all trewe luffe sprynges."*

(Followed by the prose treatise "Of the vertuȝ of the haly name of Ihesu.")

fol. 211:

   (7)   *"Ihesu crist saynte Marye sŏne."*

(Written in double columns.)

[1] Italics denote that the poem occurs only in the MS. which is being described.

fol. 211ᵛ (col. 2):
    (8)   "Fadir and son and haly gaste."
(Not complete.)

fol. 213:
    (9)   "When Adam dalfe, and Eue spane."

fol. 213ᵛ:
    (10)   "Ihesu Criste, have mercy one me."
(Six lines.)

fol. 219:
    (11)   "Ihesu thi swetnes, wha moghte it se."

fol. 222:
    (12)   "þi Ioy be ilke a dele, to serue thi Godd to paye."

(It includes "All vanytese forsake" which begins at stanza 13.)[1]

THE CAMBRIDGE MS. DD. 5.64 is a small octavo volume of 142 pages, written on parchment in beautiful black letter. The greater part of the book consists of Rolle's Latin and English tracts, but the last eight pages contain verse, written as prose, under the title (in red letters): HIC INCIPIUNT CANTUS COMPASSIONIS XTI ET CONSOLACIONIS ETERNI (*fol.* 134); and on *fol.* 141ᵛ is the *explicit*, also marked by red letters:

EXPLICIUNT CANTICA DIUINI AMORIS SECUNDUM
RICARDUM HAMPOLE

The Cambridge University Catalogue omits the words "Hic incipiunt" and considers all these lyrics as one poem, but within this *incipit* and *explicit* there lie two short prose extracts and eleven lyrics. These latter are:

fol. 134:
    (1)   *"Unkynde man gif kepe til me*
          and loke what payne I suffer for þe."

fol. 134ᵛ:
    (2)   *"Lo leman swete now þou may se*
          þat I haue lost my lyf for þe."
    (3)   *"My trewest tresoure sa trayturly was taken."*

---

[1] I have not included in this list the fragment of *The Prick of Conscience*, beginning:
      "The begynnyng es of thre."

P

fol. 135:
(4)   "*Ihesu als þow me made & boght.*"

(5)   "When Adam delf & eue span, spir if þow wil spede."

fol. 136:
(6)   "All synnes sal þou hate, thorow casting of skylle."

fol. 136ᵛ:
(7)   "*Mercy es maste in my mynde.*"

fol. 137:
(8)   "Ihesu god son, lord of mageste,
         send wel to my hert anly to couayte þe."

fol. 138:
(9)   "Loue es lyf þat lastes ay, þar it in crist es fest."

fol. 140:
(10)   "*Heyle ihesu my creatowre, of sorrowyng medicyne.*"

fol. 140ᵛ:
(11)   "All vanitese forsake, if þou his lufe will fele."

fol. 142:
(12)   "þi ioy be ilke a dele to serue thi godd to paye."

After the *explicit* at the foot of *fol.* 141ᵛ there is another rubric on the following page: ITEM SECUNDUM EUNDEM RICARDUM. "þy ioy be ilk a dele, to serue þi god to pay," and at the end, written in red letters: "All vanites forsake if þou hys lufe wil fele &c. ut supra"; referring back to the previous lyric, showing that we have the correct order of the poems in the Thornton MS.

The volume ends with a fragment of Richard of St. Victor's *Benjamin Minor*, or work on contemplation, in an English translation, of which only twelve lines are given, the rest being torn off. The first leaves are written in a clear black letter, as is all the latter part of the book including the poems; but *ff.* 17–100 are in another and more careless hand.

Whereas the Thornton MS. is evidently a collection made at different times and containing an extraordinary variety of subjects, the Cambridge MS. bears the impress of having been transcribed in some conventual house, since it is entirely restricted to religious pieces. The care of the handwriting and the fact that it is entirely restricted to Rolle's writings, suggests that it may have been copied by one of the nuns of the Cistercian convent to whom Rolle ministered.

These two are the only pure northern MSS. we have containing works by Richard Rolle, and are therefore of outstanding importance. There is, however, another MS. commonly called northern and of an earlier date, being ascribed to the late fourteenth century, known as *MS. Reg. 17. B. xvii.*

The catalogue in the British Museum describes it thus: "Theological works in prose and verse; chiefly in Northern English"; and gives a full list of contents (vol. ii., pp. 288–9).

It is a quarto (7¾ in. by 5½ in.) and consists of 108 leaves written on vellum, mostly in black letter, of the late fourteenth century.

For our purpose its most important contents are:

Art. 1. A copy of *The Lay Folk's Mass Book.*"

Art. 2. "þo passion of Ihesu and of his moder," in a northern dialect written by a west-midland scribe, beginning: "Ho so says þis with gode wille," and containing an introductory verse to

Swete Ihesu now wil I synge,

which is also included in the Vernon MS. where it is placed at the end; and the three poems on *The Prick of Conscience,* which Horstman ascribes (mistakenly) to Rolle.[1]

fol. 36:　(1)　"Alle mighty god in trinite
　　　　　　　fader and son & holy gost."

fol. 101:　(2)　"*Grete ferly hit is why men þat frasten
　　　　　　　þo world, so mykel þer inne traysten.*"

fol. 104ᵛ:　(3)　"*Alle wandreths, welthis & lykingis
　　　　　　　by chaunce or happe on þis lyue hyngis.*"

These are written in the dialect of Yorkshire but by a southern scribe; and the two latter are found only in this MS.

There is little likelihood of any of the poems in this volume being genuine works of Rolle's, as we shall see later, but Horstman has this note, delightfully vague:

This Manuscript vellum, 4°, one of the earliest containing works of Rolle, does not give the author's name, except that

---

[1] "I think R. Rolle's authorship is unquestionable" (vol. ii., p. 36): but none of these poems is the least like, either in style or theme, to Rolle, and I think his authorship can be dismissed on the same grounds as *The Prick of Conscience.* They are not therefore included in this volume.

the two Latin tracts (*Spec. peccatoris* and *Emend. pecc.*) are ascribed to him by a modern hand. The dialect is mixed and impure. However the contents have a close relation to R. Rolle and his favourite themes, *and very likely he is the author of most of them* [1]; though it is difficult to decide what he may have to do with the N. 2 and 3 (i.e. 'Swete Ihesu' and a poem on the *Spec. Mundi* of Alquin), which were originally composed in a southern dialect."

B. SOUTHERN MSS.

Although there are only two pure northern MSS. which contain the writings of Rolle, there is an important group of southern MSS. in which we find copies of northern poems and of Rolle's English prose works. [2] To these reference will have constantly to be made, and they are therefore included here. They are:

MS. Vernon (Bodl. Lib., Oxford).
MS. Simeon and MS. Add. 37787 (Brit. Mus.).
These three are very similar in content.
MS. Pepys 2125 (Magd. Coll., Camb.).
MS. Lambeth 853.

THE VERNON MS.—Bernard's catalogue of 1697 thus describes it: "A vast massy MS. for the most part in English verse, contayning the Biblical history from Genesis to the Revelation, and the history of all things and Persons in the Missal or Liturgy as saints & others by way of Meditation." [3]

If this were an accurate description it would certainly be even vaster than it is. It measures $22\frac{1}{2}$ in. by 15 in. and contains 412 leaves of thick vellum. The verse is written in triple columns and the prose in double. Some leaves are illuminated with small pictures representing the life of Our Lady and of Christ's infancy, and nearly all contain initial and marginal illuminations. It was presented to the Bodleian Library by Colonel Vernon in 1677, and dates from the latter half of the fourteenth century (1370–

[1] Vol. ii., p. 1, note. The italics are mine.
[2] Therefore in this section italics do not denote that the poem occurs only in the MSS. described.
[3] Cf. also *The Annals of the Bodleian*, by W. D. Macray, pp. 144–5 (Clarendon Press, 1890).

1385). The list of contents is given on the first few pages, and contains 161 "articles."

In the Summary Catalogue it is numbered MS. 3938, but the description has not yet been printed.[1]

The most important are:

The Southern English *Legendary* or *Lives of the Saints*.
The Northern Homily Collection.
The Prick of Conscience.
The Prick or *Spur of Love*, being a translation from Bonaventura's *Stimulus Amoris*
Piers Plowman (proving that this MS cannot be earlier than 1362); and for our purpose
Rolle's English Tracts, copied by a southern scribe, viz.:

fol. 338:
The *Form of Living*, called here "þe fourme of parfit liuyng."

fol 338v:
The *Ego Dormio*: which immediately follows on *The Form*, without being distinguished as a separate tract.

fol. 334 (col. 1):
The *Commandment of Love*, beginning: "þe communde-ment of god is þat we lufe oure lord," etc., but it is a poor version, altered and curtailed, and many passages are omitted.

Besides the lyrics in *The Form*, and the *Ego Dormio*, the following have been ascribed to Rolle:

fol. 114v (col. 1):
"Ihesu crist my lemmon swete."

fol. 114v (col. 2):
"Fadur and sone and Holigost
Lord to þe I crie and calle."

fol. 116v (col. 1):
"Ihesu þi swetnesse whose miht hit se."

(Copied by a southern scribe from a northern poem.)

fol. 298 (col. 2):
Songs of Love-longing, beginning:
"Swete ihesu now wol I synge
To þe a song of loue longinge."

fol. 334 (col. 1):
"Vnkuinde mon ȝif kep to me."

(Standing at the end of "A tretis how God apered to an holi man," and followed by "þe commundement," etc.)

---

[1] A brief list of contents was written by J. O. Halliwell in 1848.

MS. SIMEON.—The companion volume of the Simeon MS. is thus described in the catalogue of the British Museum (MS. Add. 22283):

It contains early English poems and prose treatises, transcribed about 1380–1400, and closely agreeing with portions of the somewhat earlier Vernon MS. in the Bodleian Library. The volume is very imperfect and at present consists of only 172 leaves, 177 are wanting at the beginning, and 30 in the middle; and it is incomplete at the end. The verse is in three columns, the prose in two.

Large folio, vellum, 1350–1400. Being thus incomplete it does not contain the verses on *fol.* 114ᵛ of the Vernon MS. or *fol.* 116, nor "Unkind man give keep to me" on *fol.* 334; *The Commandment* on the same folio being likewise missing.

But whereas in the Vernon MS. there are only twenty-eight hymns and religious songs, the MS. ending after "A Prayer to the Trinity" (No. 28), there are in the Simeon MS. two extra leaves, *ff.* 134–5, containing:

"Who so loueth endeles rest," and a poem entitled *A Morning Thanksgiving and Prayer to God*, beginning: "I þonke þe lord god ful of miht (*fol.* 134, col. 2).

This is a paraphrase upon a tractate called *A Mirror of Discipline or Our Daily Work*, commonly thought to be by Rolle, and the only copy of these verses known to exist; yet it is southern, therefore, if Rolle's, it can only be a *copy* of a northern MS.

In *The Annals of the Bodleian Library*, p. 145, it is stated that this MS. is "apparently the work of the same scribe" as the Vernon MS. It was presented to the British Museum by Sir John Simeon not very many years ago, towards the end of the nineteenth century, and hence its name.

MS. ADD. 37787 is similar to these and is thus described in the British Museum Catalogue: "Prayers and meditations in Latin and English, partly in verse." Many of the English articles are also in the Vernon MS. Vellum, 187 leaves, 7¾ in. by 5½ in., early fifteenth century. Originally bound in oak boards covered with red vellum, which is now worn away. It is a small, rather dumpy quarto, beautifully written, in black letter for the most part, and with illuminated initials. It was bought at the Amherst sale in 1909, and was therefore unknown to the earlier critics. It contains the *Songs of Love-longing* (*fol.* 146ᵛ) and two copies of "Fadur and sone and holygost" (*fol.* 16, 143ᵛ), the first copy being imperfect.

This volume has passed through many ownerships. The first owner was John Northewode, a monk at Bordesley; his inscription within an illuminated border is found on *fol.* 183, but no date given. Later it belonged to Lady Peyto, who died 1487.

It is evidently copied by a southern scribe, with a tendency to midland forms.

MS. PEPYS 2125, AT MAGD. COLL., CAMB.—This MS., like the last, was not known to Dr. Horstman, nor can I discover any written description of it, or of how it passed into the possession of Pepys. It is entitled *Old English Devotional MSS*. It has not been foliated and it is therefore difficult to give references. It contains a part of Bonaventura's *Vita Christi*, translated into English prose, which is also found in MS. Harl. 1022, to which it is similar, containing also the *Benjamin Minor* of Richard of St. Victor and English tracts of Rolle, viz.:

The Form of Living, which is imperfect, but which gives two versions of chapter i.

The Commandment of God (complete), entitled "A good rule for men þat desirin to lyf perfect life"; and

The Ego Dormio.

We find in it therefore the *Lyrics* from the prose tracts; but the importance of this MS. as regards Rolle lies rather in the extracts from Bonaventura (an interesting version of *The Privity of the Passion* is included) and Richard of St. Victor, two authors well known to Rolle, and translations from whose writings are often found in juxtaposition to his own works. It has been dated as "late" fifteenth century, and is written by a southern scribe, with a tendency to midland forms.

THE LAMBETH MS. 853 is dated *c.* 1430. It is a southern MS. but contains some northern poems copied by a southern scribe. Those of importance to the study of Rolle are the versions of:

fol. 14: "Ihesu þi swetnes who so myȝte it se,"
and of:

fol. 90ᵛ: "Loue is lijf þat lastiþ ay,"

and written here as a part of the same poem:

(*fol.* 90ᵛ)

> "Ihesu godis sone þou art
> lorde of moost hiȝ magiste."

They are certainly written by a southerner, but contain northern forms.

I have in every case consulted and transcribed from the actual MS., but most of them have been printed either in whole or part. The Thornton MSS. Cambridge, Dd. 5.64, and Reg. 17. B. xvii., are printed in Dr. Horstman's two volumes; and parts of the Thornton, Vernon and Lambeth MSS. useful for the study of Rolle are included in the publications of the Early English Text Society.

CHAPTER II

POEMS FORMERLY AND WRONGLY ASCRIBED TO ROLLE

RICHARD ROLLE'S reputation has for many years been based on a poem which almost all scholars now agree is not his, and since his name has been entangled with the works of other writers, it seems better before we discuss his lyrics to clear the ground of these spurious poems. The doubtful poems will be considered later.

An external and conclusive proof is almost non-existent, and we have constantly to bear in mind the wise warning of Professor Cook who, in speaking of the authorship of *The Dream of the Rood*, says:

> A certain scepticism is almost obligatory upon the student; for with every poem assigned to an author upon insufficient grounds, the possibility of new combinations favourable to the admission of still another poem is increased, until one might end by imputing practically the whole of Old English poetry to a single author.[1]

Until recent years *The Prick of Conscience* has always been associated with Rolle's name, though it is difficult to understand how anyone who has read even a part of *The Prick* with care, and who is conversant with the genuine prose and verse of Rolle, can ascribe this didactic and moralising poem to his pen. Miss Hope Allen was the first to expose this error.[2] She states that only four out of the thirty-one MSS. which have been compared,[3] and these not the best, ascribe the poem to Rolle; and that his

[1] *The Christ of Cynewulf*, p. lxv (Ginn & Co., 1900. Athenæum Press).

[2] See her essay on *The Authorship of the "Prick of Conscience,"* p. 122 (Radcliffe College Monographs, No. 15. Published by Ginn & Co., 1910),

[3] Dr. Carlton Brown in his *Register of Middle English Religious and Didactic Verse* (Oxford, 1916–20. Bibliographical Society), lists eighty-two MSS., besides numerous fragments and variants (vol. ii., p. 328).

traditional authorship rests largely upon the passage in Lydgate's *Fall of Princes*:

> In moral mateer ful notable was Goweer
> And so was Stroode in his philosophye
> In parfight lyvyng which passith poysye
> Richard hermyte contemplatyff of sentence
> Drowh in ynglyssh the prykke of conscience.

which at most can mean only that Richard translated or compiled *The Prick*.

No reference to *The Prick* is found in the *Officium*; nor is there any likeness between that poem and any genuine work of Rolle's. One of the most marked features of his style is the constant alliteration. Miss Allen notes only twenty examples of alliteration in the whole of this lengthy poem of 4812 couplets. Rolle is wonderfully simple and free in his manner of writing, and his style is utterly unlike the pompous and didactic tone of this unknown author, who delights to quote in Latin, and to show his learning by constantly dragging in famous names as his authorities.

But the strongest of all arguments against Rolle's authorship is the absence of all lyrical or mystical elements in *The Prick*. It would surely have been impossible for Richard, the hermit, full, as we have seen, of delight in music, and steeped in the love of an ever-present and personal God, to keep that which was a very part of his nature out of his verse, and especially out of a poem of this length.

Miss Allen thinks that the author of the *Speculum Vitae* or *Mirrour of Life* was probably the writer of *The Prick*. The former poem has been ascribed to William of Nassington; but there were two Williams of Nassington in the fourteenth century, either of whom might have been the author; and she concludes: "Whether William of Nassington or some one else proves to be the author of the *Speculum Vitae*, it is possible that that author may be found to be also the author of the *Prick of Conscience*"; from which guarded statement few can dissent.[1]

---

[1] Miss Allen attributes the omission of Rolle's name from "Histories of English Mysticism" to this mistaken association with *The Prick of Conscience*; but probably it has been largely due to the great difficulty in finding his works outside the MSS. The Early English Text Society edited Misyn's translation of his *Fire of*

Another work attributed to Rolle is that known as *The Lay Folk's Mass Book*, which begins:

> þo worthiest þing most of goodnesse
> In al þis world is þo messe.

There are many MSS. of it. Dr. Carleton Brown cites nine.[1] Of these the MS. Reg. 17. B. xvii. has been printed by Horstman,[2] and Canon Simmons has edited it with three other texts.[3] The poem is almost certainly a translation from the French and the name of the translator is given in the MS. Reg. 17. B. xvii.:

fol. 3, l. 18:

> In boke fynde I of ane
> dam Jeremy was his nam
> a deuoute mon & a religyus,

and in l. 30 the writer says:

> In till englishe þus I draw hit.

This Jeremy is identified by the editor with Jeremiah, Canon of Rouen, who was in Rome with Archbishop Thurston of York, and perhaps owing to this was appointed Archdeacon of Cleveland, in the See of York, about the year 1170. He would therefore be familiar with the Use of Rouen which is the one referred to in the book; and if he wrote it, French would be the language he would naturally use. Moreover it must have been translated from either French or Latin, but since it was for the lay (lewyd) or unlearned folk there would have been no object in using Latin.

Love and Mending of Life in 1896, just two years before Dean Inge preached his Bampton Lectures on "Christian Mysticism" It was therefore perhaps hardly to be expected that he would include Rolle in these lectures, but we should have welcomed some notice of him in the later volume, *Studies in Mysticism* (1921), more especially as Walter Hilton and Dame Julian, who have each an essay to themselves, were really followers of Rolle, Hilton especially owing a great deal to his master.

[1] Vol ii., pp. 126, 337.

[2] Vol. ii., p. i.

[3] Early English Text Society, Orig. Series, 1879. The three texts are: MS. C.C.C. Oxford 155, *fol.* 250v; MS. Gg. 5.31, *fol.* 1, Camb. Univ. Library; and a MS. at Caius Coll. 84, *fol.* 173.

Horstman attributes it to Rolle because it contains a prayer to be said at the Levation which is identical with a rhymed prayer in *The Form of Living,* "a fact," he says, "which goes far to support R. Rolle's authorship of the Mass poem, the more so as it was designed for the chapels of the great and not for monasteries." But this is very inconclusive evidence; the correct argument to draw is probably that Rolle knew the book and quoted the poem from it. Indeed Horstman is extremely vague about all the poems of MS. Reg. 17. B. xvii., which he prints in vol. ii., as we have seen in the note we have already quoted (pp. 211–12). A careful examination shows that not one of these pieces can be definitely ascribed to Rolle; and if, as seems likely, the poem was written originally in French, it would be unlikely that Rolle had any part in it, for we find no translations by Rolle from the French, and, what is perhaps more remarkable, very few traces of French influence beyond a sprinkling of French words in the lyrics; he uses words of French origin occasionally in his prose writings.

The only difference in these versions is the additional two lines in the Harl. MS., which Rolle probably added when he incorporated the prayer into his own book. There is, however, nothing unusual in finding quotations from one MS. embodied in another, as if a part of the same. As we shall see later, Rolle's verses are frequently incorporated into other MSS. He would have been familiar with this early mass book (which Canon Simmons conjectures in his preface to be almost a century before his time), very probably he knew it by heart and cites it, thinking it suitable to be used as a grace before or after a meal; and swinging into the rhythm adds two more characteristic lines of his own. I give both versions.[1]

From *The Lay Folk's Mass Book*:

[1] In all the poems quoted I have modernised the spelling, retaining the old words whenever possible, and for the sake of the rhyme; giving the meaning in a footnote the first time such a word occurs. A Glossary will also be found on p. 329. I have retained the northern forms still in use in Scottish dialect as a reminder of the origin of the lyrics.

MS. Reg. 17. *B. xvii.*
  fol. 10.

> Loved[1] be thou king
> and thanked be thou king
> and blessed be thou king.
> Ihesu all my joying.
> Of all thy giftes good
> that thou for me spilt thy blood
> and died upon the rood.
> Thou give me grace to sing
> the song of thy loving.[1]

And from *The Form of Living*[2]:

MS. Harl. 1022
  fol. 55.

And when thou art at thy meat, praise thy God in thy thought at ilk a morsel and say thus in thy heart:

> Loved be thou king
> and thanked be thou my king
> and blessed be thou king.
> Ihesu all my joying
> of all thy giftes good
> that for me spilt thy blood
> and died on the rood.
> Thou give me grace to sing
> the song of thy loving
> my lof[1] to thee ay spring
> withouten any feigning.

and think it not anely at thy meat but both before and after.

---

[1] *Loved, loving* and *lof* are used in Middle English for "praised," "praising" and "praise," often making it difficult to distinguish between "praised" and "loved," "praising" and "loving," etc.

[2] There are numerous MSS. of *The Form*; the best-known have been described in the preceding chapter. I give the reading of MS. Harl. 1022 since it contains the two additional lines which are not in the *Mass Book*, nor in the MSS. already mentioned.

CHAPTER III

LYRICS WHICH ARE ALMOST CERTAINLY BY ROLLE

HAVING cleared the path of those poems which scholars are now agreed are not by Rolle, the wisest course will be to examine next the verses of those which are almost certainly genuine; we shall then be better able to come to some conclusion concerning those about which considerable uncertainty still remains, and a further class where the probability of Rolle's authorship seems to be very doubtful.

It is no easy task to authenticate the verse of Rolle, for in those days men wrote, no more than they built, for fame. As occasionally we find in some odd corner of our cathedrals a sculptor's sign or mark, so we may find a name attached to a writing, but more often, as is the case with Rolle, we have only a note made by the copyist. In the fourteenth and fifteenth centuries his name was very familiar, and as the desire to give the author of a book grew, it was associated with many writings which we are now certain are not his. *The Scale of Perfection*, the *Contemplations of the Dread and Love of God*, and *The Remedy against the Troubles of Temptations*, besides *The Prick of Conscience*, were all attributed to him in *The Lay Folk's Mass Book*; as well as the long list of Latin works which is given us by Horstman.[1]

The lyrics concerning which we have little doubt are either (i.) incorporated in his prose works or, (ii.) closely connected with them or with his other poems, and so similar in style and phrase that the evidence lies upon the side of Rolle's authorship.

That they are closely associated with one another is seen by the constant parallels, and actual repetitions of the same line, or very close variants, are common. As the clearest way of distinguishing these I have made the

---

[1] Vol. ii., pp. xxxviii–ix.

following table. The Arabic numbers refer to the number of the lyric as given in the table, and the Roman number following to the stanza of the lyric.

TABLE OF PARALLELS IN LYRICS

1. *The Form of Living.*   "When wilt thou come to comfort me."

2. Lyric i. in *Ego Dormio.*   *Meditatio de Passione.* "My King that water gret."

3. Lyric ii. in *Ego Dormio.*   *Cantus Amoris.* "My song is in sighing."

4. "Ihesu Christ, Saint Mary's Son."

5. "Ihesu, God's Son, Lord of Majesty."

6. "Love is life that lasts ay."

7. "Thy joy be ilk a deal" and "All vanities forsake."

8. "Hail Ihesu, my Creator."

WHEN WILT THOU COME TO COMFORT ME (1)

Let us take first the verses incorporated in the prose works.

The Form of Living

From the roughness of the rhymed lines found in *The Form* we should judge them to be the earliest, nor are they, properly speaking, "incorporated" in, but rather a part of, the prose; like the first attempts of a sculptor to chisel a block of marble into shape. Every now and again the verse fails entirely. The lines in chapter vi. beginning:

Loved be thou king

are, as we have seen, a quotation from *The Lay Folk's Mass Book*, which book was probably as familiar to Rolle as the Prymer or the Breviary.

The other set of verses are to be found in chapter viii., beginning:

When wilt thou come to comfort me.

The choice of MSS. is very large as *The Form* was the most popular of all Rolle's English prose tracts. Dr. Horstman gives a list of twenty MSS., to which others might now be added. Apparently it was known in all parts of England since copies exist in midland and southern dialects as well as in northern. The Simeon MS., which I give as being one of the best readings, contains forms from all three dialects, the northern being retained chiefly for the sake of end rhymes.

MS. Simeon
fol. 149.

And among other affections thou mayest in thy languishing sing this in thine heart to the Lord Ihesu, when thou covetest his coming and thy going:

> When wilt thou come to comfort me
> and bring me out of care,
> And give thee to me, that I may see
> and have for ever mare?
> Thy love is ever sweetest to me
> of all that ever were.

Mine heart for love when shall it burst
that languishing it may no mare.
For all on love mine heart is set
and I am fain to go.
I stood astonied in still morning
of one lovelokes [1] of lore.[2]
My love is long longing,[3]
it draweth me to my day [4]
the bond of love burning,
for it holdeth me ay
from place and from playing [5]
till that I get it may,
the sight of my sweeting
that wendeth never away.
In wealth [6] be our waking
without noy of night.
My love is lasting
and longeth to that sight.[7]

[1] The other MSS. read *loveliest*.
[2] *Lore* can be used for "behaviour."
[3] Yearning; i.e. "my love is yearning for long."
[4] Probably *my day* refers to the day of death.
[5] Pleasure.
[6] i.e. happiness, well-being.
[7] i.e. yearns for the sight of Jesus, "my sweeting."

MY KING THAT WATER GRET (2)

The "Ego Dormio"

There are fewer MSS. by far of the *Ego Dormio* than of *The Form*. Horstman (i., p. 49) only mentions four: MS. Dd. 5.64 (*fol.* 122), MS. Vernon (*fol.* 338ᵛ), MS. Arund. 507 (*fol.* 40; imperf.), and two copies in MS. Rawl. A. 389 (now Bod. 11272) (*fol.* 80, and *ff.* 97 and 98ᵛ), one of which is in the southern, and the other in the northern dialect. But in some MSS. the *Ego Dormio* follows immediately on *The Form*, without break or title, as e.g. in the Simeon MS. (which Horstman does not cite) and in the Cambridge MS. Dd. 5.64. Nor was Horstman aware of the existence of the Pepys MS. 2125 when he wrote.

Lyric i.

ON THE THEME OF THE PASSION

In most MSS. there is a rubric in the margin with the titles: *Meditacio de passione cristi*, and *Cantus Amoris*.

The first line of the *Meditacio* varies. The Vernon and Simeon MSS. read:

How þi kyng he water wepte and he blode swette.

The Pepys MS.:

Haf mynde vpon þi kyng, how he þe water wepte.

and the Cambridge MS. Dd. 5.64:

My keyng þat water grette . . .

I give the text from this latter MS. as being the best and oldest northern version. It is written as prose, but I have divided it into lines varying in length according to the rhyme. It is very irregular in form, the number of stresses in each line being unequal and the stanzas unequal in length; not unlike the old French *lais*, which had been taken over into the folk-songs, and would probably be known to Rolle; just as St. Francis in Italy borrowed from the *stradella* of the Tuscan peasant.

The part of the *Meditacio* which is italicised in the text was attributed to St. Augustine, and was translated into English verse between 1244–58. These lines are also found separately in two MSS., viz. MS. Eccl. Durham, A. III.12, and MS. Bod. 42.[1] The latter is dated in Coxe's catalogue, 1300–20. The translation in the Durham MS. is "written upon a small piece of vellum and inserted, and forms no part of the original volume."

The Latin original of the verse occurs in cap. vi. of the *Meditationes* (formerly attributed to Augustine); but neither the Meditations nor the Soliloquies are to be found among his authenticated works. I have traced the original in an old edition (printed at Genoa MDCCXCI.) of the *Meditationes, Soliloquia et Manuale*, cap. vi., p. 17. It is printed as prose thus:

"Sic debemus cogitare de Christi passione et dicere; O bone Ihesu: Candet nudatum pectus, rubet cruentum latus, tensa arent viscera, decora languent lumina, regia pallent ora, procera rigent brachia, crura pendent marmorea, rigat tere-bratos pedes beati sanguinis unda," and continues, "Specta, gloriose Genitor, gratissimae prolis lacerata membra & memorare benignus, quae ea est substantia," etc., which does not scan as verse.

It is thus translated in MS. Bod. 42 (now MS. 1846) (*fol.* 250, col. 1):

> White was his naked breast
> and red of blood his side,
> Blood was his fair neb,[2]
> his wounden deep and wide.
> Stark [3] were his arms
> i-spredd upon the rood.
> In five steads [4] in his body
> streams urne [5] of blood.

It is interesting to note that although the rest of the lyric is written as prose, when the scribe comes to these lines he copies them as two long couplets, probably recognising them as being a quotation.

---

[1] See E.E.T.S., vol. 15 (re-edited in 1903), *Political, Religious and Love Poems*, p. 243. Cf. also Warton's *History of English Poetry*, vol. i., p 24, note.

[2] Face (O.N. *nef*).   [3] Rigid.   [4] Places.

[5] Ran; MS. reads *hi-spredd* and *hurne*, inorganic *h* being prefixed to the initial vowel.

(Lyric i. from the "Ego Dormio")

Meditatio de Passione Xti.

MS. Dd. 5.64
fol. 126.

I will that thou be never idle, but be ay either speaking of God, or working some notable work, or thinking on Him, and principally that thy thought be ay having Him in mind. And think oft on His passion:

> My king that water gret [1]
> and blood sweat
> sithen [2] full sare bet,[3]
> so that his blood him wet
> when their scourges met.

> Full fast they gan him ding [4]
> and at the pillar swing,[5]
> (and) [6] his fair face defouling
> with spitting.

> The thorn crowns the king;　　　　　　(5. ix.)
> full sare is that pricking.
> Alas, my Joy and my Sweeting,[7]
> so deemed [8] to hing.　　　　　　　　(5. ix.)

> Nailed were his hands,
> nailed were his feet,
> and thirled [9] was his side
> so seemly and so sweet.

[1] Wept; cf. Sc. *greet*.
[2] i.e. after.
[3] Beaten; a weak p.p. of the O.E. strong verb *bēaten*; such weak forms do occur in the fourteenth century.
[4] Strike (O.N. *dengja*).
[5] O.E. *swingan*=vibrate; hence to beat so excessively as to cause vibration.
[6] ( ) brackets denote that the word is in the MS. but destroys the rhythm; [ ] brackets are used when a word is inserted to make the sense clearer, or for the sake of rhythm.
[7] Darling, beloved.
[8] Doomed to hang (O.E. *dēman*=to judge).
[9] Pierced; cf. *nostril*.

Naked is his white breast
and red his bloody side;   (5. x.)
wan [1] *was his fair hue,*
his wounds deep and wide.   (5. x.)

In five steads of his flesh
the blood gan down glide.   (5. ix.)
As streams of the strand,   (5. x.)
his pine [2] is nought to hide.

This to see is great pity   (6. xxii.)
how he is deemed to the dead,[3]   (5. ix.)
and nailed on the rood tree   (6. xxii.)
the bright angels' bread.   (5. ix. and xi.)

Driven he was to dole [4]
that is our ghostly good;   (8. v.)
and (also) in the bliss of heav'n
is all the angels' food.   (5. ix. and xi.)

A wonder it is to see,
who so understood,
how God of Majesty
was dying on the rood.

But sooth then is it said
that "love leads the ring"; [5]
that him so low has laid
but love it was na thing.

Ihesu receive my heart
and to thy love me bring;
all my desire thou art,   (8. iii.)
(but) I covet [6] thy coming.

Thou make me clean of sin   (4. x.; 7. xx.; 5. iv.)
and let me never twin,[7]   (4. x.)

---

[1] Pale.   [2] Suffering, pain.
[3] i.e. to death; the use of the substantive *dead*—death is a northernism.
[4] Sorrow, grief (O.Fr. *doel, dueil;* Lat. *dolum*).
[5] Apparently a reference to some old game or proverb. The meaning is that it was hate not love which nailed Christ upon the Cross.
[6] i.e. desire; no bad sense is implied as in modern usage.
[7] i.e. forsake thee.

kindle me fire within   (7. v.; 5. iii.)
that I thy love may win,   (7. v.; 5. iii.)
and see thy face, Ihesu, in
joy that never shall blin.[1]

Ihesu, my soul thou mend,
thy love in to me send   (4. xii.)
that I may with thee lend [2]
in joy withouten end.

In love thou wound my thought [3]   (4. x. and xix.)
and lift my heart to thee,
my sawl thou dear has bought,   (4. xix.; 6. xx.; 11. ii.)
thy lover make it be.   (8. iv.)
Thee I covet,
this world nought
and fro it I flee.
Thou art that I have sought,
thy face when may I see.

Thou make my sawl dear,   (7. vi.)
for love changes my chere,[4]   (7. vi.)
how long shall I be here [5]
oft to hear sang
that is lasting so lang;
thou be my loving
that I [thy] love may sing.

If thou wilt think this ilk day, thou shall find sweetness
that shall draw thy heart up, that shall gar [6] thee fall in
greeting,[7] and in great longing to Ihesu.

---

[1] Cease.   [2] Abide; O.E. *lendan* (see Glossary).
[3] MS. Pepys reads *wynde*=wind. The phrase occurs elsewhere
(pp. 239). *Wound* may be (1) the O.E. verb *wunden*=to injure, and we
can take it simply as a prayer that Christ should pierce the thought
or heart with love, which is a very common expression with mystic
writers; (2)=hast wound, i.e. the pret. indic. of O.E. *windan*=to
wind: the meaning being: "thou (i.e. Christ) hast wound (i.e. wrapt)
my thought or heart in love and lifted it to thee."
[4] Countenance; i.e. to change countenance as the effect of anger,
joy, etc.: hence "makes me joyous."
[5] Horstman inserts here: "when may I nigh thee near thy melody
to hear," lines which are taken from "Thy joy be ilk a deal" (see
vol. i., p. 56, and cf. vol. i., p. 82).
[6] make; Sc.   [7] i.e. weeping; cf. *gret*.

MY SONG IS IN SIGHING (3)

(Lyric ii. from the "Ego Dormio")

Cantus Amoris.

ON THE THEME OF THE HOLY NAME

MS. Dd. 5.64
  fol. 128.

Now I write a Song of Love that thou shall delight in when thou art loving Ihesu Christ.

My song is in sighing	(5. vi.)
my life is in langing	(5. vi.)
til I see my king	(5. vi.)
so fair in thy shining.	(5. vi.)

So fair in thy fairhead [1];	
intil thy light me lead,	
and in thy love me feed:	(4. xii.)
in love make me to speed	
that thou be ever my meed. [2]	(4. xii.)

When wilt thou come,	(1)
IHESU my joy,	
and cover [3] me of care, [4]	(1)
and give me thee,	(1)
that I may see	(1)
[thee] living, evermare? [5]	(1)

All my coveting [6] were come
if I might til thee fare;
I will na thing but ainly thee,
that all my wille [7] were.

---

[1] Beauty.   [2] Reward.
[3] Recover (aphetic).   [4] i.e. from care.
[5] MS. Pepys reads: *thee having ever mare.*
[6] Desire.   [7] i.e. desire (O.E. *willa*).

IHESU my saviour,   (4. ix.; 8. i.)
IHESU my comforter,   (4. ix.; 8. i.)
of all my fairness flower;
my help and my succour,   (4. ix.; 8. i.)
when may I see thy tower? [1]

When wilt thou me call?   (7. xxiii.)
Me langs to thy hall   (7. xxiii.)
to see thee, then, all.[2]
Thy love let it not fall [3]:
my heart paints the pall
that steads us in stall.[4]

Now were I pale and wan
for love of my Leman,[5]
IHESU baith God and man,
thy love thou lerd me [6] than [7]
when I to thee fast ran,
forthy [8] now I love can.

I sit and sing   (5. viii.)
of love langing
that in my breast is bred.   (5. viii.)
IHESU. IHESU. IHESU.
Where were I to thee led?   (5. viii.)

Full well I wate [9]   (5. viii.)
thou seest my state,   (5. viii.)
in love my thought is stead:
when I thee see
and dwell with thee,
then am I filled and fed.

[1] In M.E. *tower* is often used meaning "heaven."

[2] The meaning is "to see thee, then I have all." MS. Vernon reads: *to see thee and have all.*

[3] i.e. Keep me in Thy love. In desire I paint the canopy which serves us in the place (prepared for us) (cf. St. John xiv. 2).

[4] *Heart* may be used as "mind" or "desire"; and we may take *hall* above as referring to heaven; in which case we may paraphrase the lines thus: "When wilt thou call me who yearns for thy hall (i.e. heaven); to see thee face to face?"

[5] Lover.

[6] Taught me; cf. Sc. *learned me*, pret. of O.E. *lǣran*, to teach.

[7] M.E. form for *then*.   [8] Therefore.

[9] Northern form of *wote*=know.

IHESU, thy love is fest [1]
and me to love thinks best,
my heart when may it brest [2]
to come to thee my rest.

IHESU. IHESU. IHESU.
til thee it is I mourn;
for[thy] my Life and my Living,
when may I hethen [3] turn?

IHESU, my dear and my drury, [4]   (4. xvii.)
delight art thou to sing.   (4. xvii.)
Ihesu, my mirth and melody,   (4. xvii.)
when wilt thou come, my king?

IHESU, my heal [5] and my honey,   (cf. 4. xviii.)
My quart [6] and my comforting,   (cf. 4. xviii.)
IHESU, I covet for to die
when it is thy paying. [7]

Langing in me is lent [8]   (5. vii.)
that my love has me sent,
all woe is from me went [9]
sen [10] that my heart is brent [11]   (5. vii.)

In Christ's love sa sweet,   (5. vii.)
that never I will lete [12]
what ever to love I hete,[13]
for love my bale may bete.[14]

---

[1] i.e. made fast.   [2] Burst; i.e. for love.
[3] Hence; i.e. "to thee my Life and my Living" (i.e. my means of life).
[4] Beloved (O.Fr. *druerie*).   [5] i.e. health.
[6] Health, comfort (O.N. *kvort*).   [7] Pleasure (O.Fr. *paie*).
[8] P.p. of O.E. *lendan* (see Gloss.), alighted upon, come (the phrase is quoted in the Oxford English Dictionary).
[9] i.e. is gone from me, left.
[10] Since.   [11] Burnt (O.E. *brennan*).
[12] i.e. leave undone, cease from.   [13] Promise, vow.
[14] i.e. make better my bale (evil). This is a very common M.E. tag (O.E. *bētan*=to remedy. The meaning is: "I will never leave undone what I have vowed to love (i.e. Christ); for love may abate or assuage my woe."

And til his bliss me bring
and give me my yearning,
IHESU, my love, my sweeting.

Langing in me is light,[1]
that binds me day and night
till I it have in sight
his face sa fair and bright.

IHESU, my hope, my heal,
my joy ever ilk a deal,[2]
thy love let it nought keel[3];
that I thy love may feel,
and wone[4] with thee in weal.

IHESU, with thee I big and bield[5];
liefer me were to die
than all this world to wield[6]
and have (it) in maistry.[7]

When wilt thou rue[8] on me
IHESU, that I might with thee be
to love and look on thee?

My settle[9] ordain for me
and set thou me therein,
for then mun[10] we never twin;

And I thy love shall sing
through sight of thy shining
In heaven withouten ending.   Amen.

[1] i.e. alighted upon me.
[2] i.e. my entire joy; *ilk a deal*, lit.=in every part.
[3] Northern form for *cool*.
[4] Dwell.
[5] I grow big and bold (O.E. *bīeldan*). "Big and bold" is a common doublet.
[6] Possess (O.E. *wīeldan*).
[7] In power, mastery.
[8] i.e. have rue or pity.
[9] i.e. my seat, or place in heaven. This is a favourite word with Rolle which he uses for the Cross, and a throne.
[10] Must, can (see Glossary).

IHESU CHRIST, SAINT MARY'S SON (4)

This lyric is found only in the Thornton MS. It has been printed in the E.E.T.S., *Religious Pieces in Prose and Verse* (Orig. Series, 26, pp. 79–82), edited in 1867 by George G. Perry; but the revised edition of 1913 is the best (by Horstman, vol. i., pp. 304–5), and is also included in *The Middle English Penitential Lyric*, by Dr. Patterson (pp. 131–2). He considers it to be a blending of two lyrics. The first (consisting of the first ten stanzas) "is," he says, "a pure penitential lyric"; the second (that is the remaining ten stanzas) "is a song of love-longing" (p. 190).

There is no suggestion of any such division in the MS. The poem is full of parallels and repetitions from the two *Ego Dormio* lyrics which we have just been considering, and suggest the Charter poems which we shall speak of later [1]; and we might truly say of the *Ego Dormio* lyrics that the first, the Passion lyric, is penitential, and the second—as its name, the *Cantus Amoris*, tells us—is a song of love-longing: but the parallel lines in the first and second half of this lyric (4) are taken alike from the Passion lyric and from the Love lyric; and I should be inclined rather to make this division at stanza 9, where the repetitions begin and the more formal prayer ends. But there is no real division; for we have seen that Rolle's thought is almost entirely devoted to these two subjects: the Passion and the Holy Name; which he seldom keeps distinct. This song, like the last, is written in praise of the Name of Jesus; therefore to emphasise the devotion to the humanity of Christ as expressed by the repetition of the Name Jesus, [2] it is printed in capitals in these two lyrics.

Therefore I have not tried to arrange this group of lyrics under headings. Indeed, it is almost impossible to disentangle the threads of similar lines and phrases by which they are interlaced; like the threads in some piece of tapestry, they cross and recross, are intermingled and blended. Rolle never seems to weary of stringing these love verses together, repeating them again and again, as if to the strings of a lyre. In these songs he appears to be rather the musician than the poet.

Yet in this lyric there is an advance upon those earlier lyrics in *The Form* and the *Ego Dormio*, although stanzas 9–12

---

[1] See infra. pp. 277–8.

[2] In the next two chapters we shall have to deal more particularly with (1) the theme of the Passion, and (2) the Holy Name.

(inclusive), and 17, 18 and 19, are substantially the same, the lines only being in a different order. But whereas there was no regular method in the earlier lyrics provided the rhymes were plentiful, sometimes there being one single rhyme, and sometimes alternate, or very irregular rhymes, here the rhymes alternate *a b, a b*, in four-line stanzas. The earlier lyrics have a closer resemblance to folk-songs, being uneven in form.

MS. Thornton
fol. 211.

(1)

IHESU CHRIST, Saint Mary's sone,
Through whom this world was worthily wrought,
I pray thee come and in me wone,
And of all filths cleanse my thought.

(2)

IHESU CHRIST, my God veray,[1]
That of our dear Lady was born,
Thou help now ever and aye,
And let me never for sin be lorn.

(3)

IHESU CHRIST, God's son of heaven,
That for me died on the rood,
I pray thee hear my simple steven,[2]
Through (the) virtue of thy holy blood.

(4)

IHESU CHRIST, that on the third day
From death to life rose through thy might,
Thou give me grace thee serve to pay,[3]
And thee to worship day and night.

(5)

IHESU of whom all goodness springs,
Whom all men owe to love by right,
Thou make me to geme [4] thy biddings,
And them fulfil with all my might.

[1] i.e. true.   [2] Voice.
[3] i.e. to serve thee to thy satisfaction; a common M.E. phrase.
[4] Heed (O.E. *gēman*).

(6)

IHESU CHRIST, that tholed [1] for me
Pains and angers,[2] bitter and fell,[3]
Let me never be parted fra thee,
Nor thole the bitter pains of hell.

(7)

IHESU CHRIST, well of mercy,
Of pity and of all goodness,
Of all the sins that ever did I
I pray thee give me forgiveness.

(8)

IHESU, to thee I make my mane,[4]
IHESU, to thee I call and cry,
Lat never my sawl with sin be slain,
For the mickleness [5] of thy mercy.

(9)

IHESU that is my saviour,
Thou be my joy and my solace,
My help, my heal, my comforter,
And my succour [6] in ilka [7] place.

(10)

IHESU, that with thy blood me bought,   (5. ii.)
IHESU, thou make me clean of sin,   2; 7. xx.)
And with thy love thou wound my
        thought,[8]   (2; 7. xx. and cf. st. 19.)
And lat me never (mare) fra thee twin.   (2)

(11)

IHESU I covet to love thee
And that is wholly my yearning;
Therefore to love thee thou learn me,
And I thy love shall sing.

[1] Endured; cf. Sc.   [2] Also in M.E.=griefs, hardships.
[3] Cruel.   [4] Moan (northern form).
[5] Greatness; cf. Sc. *mickle*.   [6] Also=protection, shelter, in M.E.
[7] Every (Sc. *ilk*).   [8] See note, p. 230.

(12)

IHESU, thy love in to me send,	(2)
And with thy love thou me feed.	(3)
Ihesu, thy love ay in me lend.	(2)
Thy love ever be my sawl's meed.[1]	(2; 3)

(13)

IHESU, my heart with love thou light.
Thy love me make ever to forsake
All worldly joy, both day and night,
And joy in thee ainly to make.

(14)

IHESU, thy love me chafe [2] within
So that na thing but thee I seek:
In thy love make my sawl to brin,[3]
Thy love me make baith mild and meek.

(15)

IHESU, my joy and my loving,[4]
IHESU, my comfort clear,
IHESU my God, Ihesu my king,
IHESU withouten peer.

(16)

IHESU that all has made of nought,	
IHESU that bought me dear,[5]	(3)
IHESU join thy love in my thought	(3)
So that they never be sere.[6]	(3)

(17)

IHESU, my dear and my drury,	(3)
Delight thou art to sing:	(3)
IHESU, my mirth and my melody,	(3)
Into thy love me bring.	

[1] These lines are very similar to the *Ego Dormio* lyrics, but not exactly parallel nor in the same order.
  [2] i.e. to make warm (O.Fr. *chauffer*).   [3] Burn.
  [4] i.e. "the object of my love, my beloved"; a common use with Richard Rolle.
  [5] Cf. stanza 19, and the Charter poems.
  [6] Separated (O.N. *sĕr*).

(18)

IHESU, IHESU, my honey sweet,   (cf. 3.)
My heart, my comforting;
IHESU, all my bales thou bete,
And to thy bliss me bring.

(19)

IHESU, in thy love wound my thought,   (2)
And lift my heart to thee,
IHESU my sawl, that thou dear bought,   (2; 6. xx.)
Thy lover make it to be.

(20)

Now IHESU, Lord, thou give me grace,
If it be thy will,
That I may come unto that place,
And wone ay with thee still.

EXPLICIT TRACTATUS THORNTON. AMEN.

IHESU, GOD'S SON, LORD OF MAJESTY (5)

There are three copies of this lyric extant: the northern in
MS. Dd. 5.64, and the southern in the Lambeth MS. 853,
fol. 90: and also one in the private collection belonging to the
Marquess of Bath (Longleat MS.). The two first differ little,
save in dialect; the Lambeth MS. being evidently copied from
a northern poem by a southern scribe; and in it this lyric is
inserted in "Love is Life," between stanzas 17 and 18.

Dr. Carleton Brown describes it as "A song of love-longing
to Jesus in twelve 4-line stanzas with occasional medial
rhyme" (vol. ii., p. 159). In the Cambridge MS. it is written
in long lines; but in the Lambeth MS. in short, and though
in the latter MS. the song seems to be wrongly inserted into
the lyric "Love is Life," they are both in the same metre,
which I have followed, writing it as eight short rhyming lines,
instead of four lines with medial rhymes; for it is a ballad
metre, and seems to sing itself better in this form. In "Love is
Life" the rhymes usually run *a b, a b, a b, a b*—sometimes *a b,
a b, c b, c b*—but the rhymes of this lyric (5) are uneven. The
second, fourth, sixth, and eighth lines always rhyme, but
the first and third, and the fifth and seventh only do so
occasionally.

As will be seen, the similarities to the *Ego Dormio* lyrics
are very great, especially in stanzas 4, 6, 7, 8, 9 and 10. We
notice that the first five stanzas are addressed directly to Christ
and we shall have to refer to this poem again when discussing
the *Charters of Christ*. It has been printed by the E.E.T.S.,
Hymns to the Virgin, etc. (Orig. Series, 24), and by Horstman,
vol. i., pp. 75–6.

MS. Dd. 5.64
fol. 37.   (1)

Ihesu, God's son,
  Lord of Majesty,
Send will to my heart
  Ainly to covet thee.
Reave me liking of this land,[1]
  my love that thou may be.
Take my heart intil thy hand;
  set me in stability.

[1] i.e. Take from me delight in this world.

(2)

Ihesu, the maiden's son,
    that with thy blood me bought;
Thirl my sawl with thy spear
    that mickle love in men has wrought.
Me langs: lead me to thy light
    and fasten in thee all my thought.
In thy sweetness fill my heart,
    my woe make wane til nought.

(3)

Ihesu my God, Ihesu my king,
    forsake[1] not my desire,
My thought make it to be meek,
    I hate baith pride and ire.
Thy will is my yearning,
    of love thou kindle the fire,   (2)
That I in sweet loving,
    with angels take my hire.[2]

(4)

Wound my heart within,   (2; cf. 4. xix.)
    and wield it at thy will
In bliss that never shall blin: (2)
    thou gar me fest my skill[3]
That I thy love may win: (2)
    with grace my thought thou fill
And make me clean of sin,
    that I may come thee til.*   (2; cf. 4. x.)

(5)

Root it in my heart,
    the memory of thy pine:
In sickness and in quart
    thy love be ever mine.

[1] Refuse.
[2] i.e. pay, reward.
[3] *Skill* in M.E. always=reason, discernment; "thou make me make fast (strengthen) my will that I may attain, or win, thy love." MS. Vernon reads: *þow fastne me þat y not spill.*

R

My joy is all of thee,
    my sawl take it as thine:
My love ay waxing be
    sa that it never dwine.[1]

(6)

My sang is in sighing,   (cf. 3)
    while I dwell in this way [2];
My life is in langing,
    that binds me night and day.
Till I come til my king,
    that I wone with him may,
And see his fair shining
    in life that lasts ay.*

(7)

Langing in me is lent   (cf. 3)
    for love that I ne [3] can let,
My love, it has me schent,[4]
    that ilk a bale may bete.
Sen that my heart was brent
    in Christ's love sa sweet
All wae fra me is went
    and we [5] shall never meet.†

(8)

I sit and sing of love langing   (3)
    that in my heart is bred:
Ihesu, my king and my joying,
    why ne were I to thee led?
Full well I wate, in all my state,
    in joy I should be fed:
Ihesu me bring til thy woning,[6]
    for blood that thou has shed.†

---

[1] Dwindle.
[2] i.e. while I am in this life.
[3] *Ne* always expresses negation.
[4] Brought to nothing, destroyed.
[5] i.e. I and woe.
[6] Dwelling; cf. *wone*=to dwell.

(9)

Deemed he was to hing,   (cf. 2)
  the fair angels' food;
Full sare they gan him swing,
  when that he bounden stood:
His back was in beating,
  and spilt his blessed blood:
The thorn crowned (the) king,
  that nailed was on the rood.†

(10)

White was his naked breast
  and red his bloody side.
Wan was his fair face,
  his wounds deep and wide.†
The Jews would not wand [1]
  To pine [2] him at in that tide.
As [the] stream does of the strand,
  his blood gan [3] down glide.

(11)

Blinded were his fair e'en,
  his flesh bloody for-bet [4];
His lovesome [5] life was laid full low
  and sorrowful umbeset.[6]
Death and life began to strive
  whether might [7] maistry mare:
When angels' bread was damned to death,
  to save our sawls sare.

(12)

Life was slain and rose again,
  in fairhead may we fare,
And death is brought til little or nought.
  and cast [8] in endless care.[9]

---

[1] Hesitate, fear (O.E. *wandian*).
[2] Hurt, cause to suffer.   [3] Did (O.E. *beginnan*).
[4] Beaten severely, covered with bruises (the phrase is quoted in the Oxford English Dictionary); *for* is an intensive.
[5] Lovely.
[6] i.e. surrounded with sorrow.   [7] *Have* understood.
[8] i.e. cast down, overthrown.   [9] Woe (O.E. *caru*).

On him that thee bought, have all thy thought,
   and lead thee in his lare [1]:
Give all thy heart til Christ thy quart,
   and love him evermore.

[1] i.e. guide thee in his knowledge (*lare*=northern form of *lore*). Lore is used vaguely in alliterative poetry; sometimes it means knowledge, sometimes behaviour.

* The alternate lines of these verses are the same as Lyric 2 (p. 228), only here they are in a different order.
† Verses 7, 8 have a close similarity to Lyric 3 (p. 231) and verses 9, 10 to Lyric 2 (p. 228).

LOVE IS LIFE THAT LASTS AY (6)

This lyric is found only in two MSS. the northern version in MS. Dd. 5.64, and the southern in MS.: Lambeth 853. It is printed in the E.E.T.S. (No. 24), *Hymns to the Virgin and Christ* (p. 23), and in Horstman, vol. i. p. 76; and has been chosen as a type of Rolle's verse in two modern anthologies, viz. *A New Golden Treasury*, edited by E. Rhys,[1] and *The Oxford Book of Mystical Verse*, edited by D. H. S. Nicholson and A. H. E. Lee.[2] Mr. Sisam has also included it in his book of *Fourteenth Century Verse and Prose*.[3]

As we have noted, the lyric "Ihesu, God's Son, Lord of Majesty," in the Lambeth MS. is inserted between stanzas 17 and 18, and there is certainly a very evident break at the end of stanza 17.

The first seventeen stanzas are a close parallel to caps. xl. and xli. of the *Incendium Amoris*[4]; after stanza 17 this parallelism entirely ceases, and the poet breaks out into a love-song which is full of reminiscences of the earlier lyrics in the *Ego Dormio*. Therefore in this poem we may have more lyrics than one; certainly two; for if the scribe of the Lambeth MS. was correct, the lyric "Ihesu, God's Son" comes before stanza 18, and that stanza may have been a continuation of it since it seems to link itself on to something which has gone before but is now missing.

It begins:

(18)

Sigh and sob, baith day and night,
  for ane sa fair of hue;
There is na thing my heart may light
  but love that is ay new. . . .

This and the remainder of the poem is different in style from the stanzas immediately preceding, and has more in

---

[1] Everyman's Library, vol. 695 (Dent & Sons), 1914. Two verses only.

[2] Published by the Clarendon Press (1916), p. 1.

[3] Published by the same (1921), pp. 37–40.

[4] See an article in the *Modern Language Review* for 1919 (vol. xiv., pp. 320 sqq.). Miss Allen says: "It would appear that the relation of the lyric to the *Incendium* somewhat decreases the chance of Rolle's authorship of the former. It must be pointed out, however, that both in his verse and prose he was constantly repeating both sentiments and phrases. A certain amount of repetition is probably bound up in the mystic's habit of concentration on a few subjects of thought, and some of the repetitions found in Rolle's writings are doubtless more the subconscious echoing of past experience."

common with the lyrics we have already read, and is full of the same repetitions.

If we read the poem with an unbiased mind, I think we shall be conscious of a sudden and abrupt change from stanza 17 to 18. Stanza 17 would not be an unsuitable finish to a poem, for it ends thus:

> If thou will love, then may thou sing
> til Christ, in melody.
> The love of Him o'ercomes all thing;
> thereto thou traist truly.

Again, if we take the last stanza (12) of "Ihesu, God's Son, Lord of Majesty," we shall find a natural connection between it and stanza 18 of "Love is Life":

(12)

> Life was slain and raised again,
> in fairhead may we fare,
> And death is brought til little or nought,
> and cast in endless care.
> On him that thee bought have all thy thought,
> and lead thee in his lare:
> Give all thy heart til Christ, thy quart,
> and love him evermare.

And then might follow stanza 18 of "Love is Life":

(18)

> I sigh and sob baith day and night
> for ane sa fair of hue;
> There is na thing my heart may light
> but love that is ay new;
> Whoso had Him in his sight
> or in his heart Him knew,
> His mourning turned til joy full bright,
> his sang intil glew.

The scribe of the Lambeth MS. probably perceived this and copied them as one poem.

It may also be argued that the last line of stanza 12 of "Ihesu, God's Son" is a very usual tag for the ending of a lyric by Rolle; and that it is quite probable that these last two lyrics we have been discussing (5 and 6) consisted originally of three, viz.:

(1) "Love is life that lasts ay," composed of stanzas 1–17 inclusive.

(2) "Ihesu, God's Son, Lord of Majesty."

(3) "I sigh and sob both day and night," being stanzas 17 to the end.

The first seventeen stanzas are an answer to the question put in chapter ix. of *The Form of Living* [1]: What is love? although the answer only occasionally recalls the English tract, as e.g. stanzas 3 and 12. A translation of the Latin parallels is given on the opposite page so as to make this point clearer.

It is open to question whether the first seventeen stanzas are by Rolle or one of his followers and imitators; also, whether the poem was written after or before the prose. Did Rolle first write the chapter on Love, and afterwards paraphrase it? Generally speaking, verse is earlier than prose, but in this case I should judge that the English lyric was made as an aid to memory for the nuns for whom, probably, Rolle wrote the *Incendium*. It has been argued that a nature as impatient as he shows himself to have been would not have paraphrased his own work, but he is now nearing the end of his life, and his natural impetuosity has been controlled and calmed by years, as we can see from *The Commandment*, a tract expressly written for a nun of Hampole, and of which there are many reminders both in this lyric (6) and in the one following (7). But whatever conclusion we may arrive at concerning the first part of the poem, it is clear that the latter part is Rolle's genuine work, unless we deny that these other lyrics we have already considered are genuine.

As we shall see, there has been the same confusion in the next lyric, only in this case the reverse has happened; one lyric having been split into two. Such mistakes were very likely to occur. If the scribe found another set of verses in the same metre as those which he had just copied, and supposedly by the same author, he would not hesitate to write them as one poem; or, on the other hand, as in the lyric "þy joy be ilk a dele to serve thy God to pay," which follows, the scribe growing tired of copying and seeing a break in the subject might cease his work before he reached the end of the poem. We have always to be prepared for such aberrations on the scribe's part in these early MSS.; nor are these divisions a matter of very great importance, save for the confusion of authorship which may sometimes result.

In the present case the original scribe, whom I take to be the copyist of MS. Dd. 5.64, and who may possibly have been one of the nuns in the Cistercian convent at Hampole which Rolle served (and therefore was very familiar with the *Incendium Amoris*, which some critics think was written for their benefit and which Rolle himself had often used as the theme of his lyrics), may have written this rhymed paraphrase of the book she so much loved, copying Rolle's style and metre and annexing it to his own verses. This surmise can only be taken tentatively, pending the work of a scholar with whom I can make no claim to compete [1]; but I think the question is at any rate worth raising.

---

[1] Miss Allen's work on the Canon of Rolle is now, I hear, in the press, and may appear simultaneously with this volume or even before it.

MS. Dd. 5.64
  fol. 38.   (1)

Love is life that lasts ay
  where it in Christ is fest,[1]
For weal ne wae it change may,
  as written have men wisest;
The night it turns intil the day,   (7. xvii.; cf. st. 24)
  thy travail intil rest;
If thou wilt love thus as I say
  thou may be with the best.

(2)

Love is thought, with great desire,
  of a fair Loving [2];
Love I liken til a fire
  that slaken may na thing:
Love us cleanses of our sin,
  love us bote shall bring,
Love the king's heart may win,
  love of joy may sing.

(3)

The settle of love is lift high,
  for in til heaven it ran;
Methink on earth it is sly,[3]
  that makes men pale and wan.
The bed of bliss it goes full nigh,
  I tell thee as I can;
Though us think the way be dregh,[4]
  love couples God and man.[5]

[1] i.e. made fast.   [2] i.e. the object of love, the beloved.
[3] Full of artifice, hence=secret (as here).
[4] Long, tedious (O.E. *dregh*, cf. Sc. *dree*. Rhymed with MS. *nee* =nigh).
[5] The meaning of this verse seems to be: "The settle of love" (which I take to be the Cross) "is lifted high, for it reached to heaven; here it makes men secretly suffer, making them pale and wan, but it draws them nigh to the bed of bliss" (i.e. the espousal bed of Christ and the soul which may be taken as another name for the eternal rest of endless joy; cf. passage in *The Fire*). "Though the way" (i.e. life) "may seem long, yet this love 'is a life' uniting God to man" (and thus time is wiped out) (cf. Psalm lxxxiv. 10). Cf. *The Form*, chap. x.: "*Love is a life coupling together the loving and the loved*," and the first line of this lyric: "*Love is life that lasts ay where it is made fast in Christ.*"

The corresponding passages in *The Fire of Love.*[1]

(1)

Love is life without end, abiding where it is set [and made firm in Christ]. When this love after loving desire is rooted in the heavens, *neither prosperity nor adversity may change it, as the wisest men have written*. Then no marvel *it shall turn the night to day*, darkness to light, heaviness to melody, noy to solace, and *labour to sweet rest*.

This love truly is not of imagination or feigned, but true and perfect, and given to Christ without parting, yielding angel's song with melody to Jesu. And forsooth *if thou love in this manner as I have said*, full glorious *shalt thou be with the best* and worthiest in the Kingdom of God. (p. 179).

(2)

Love is continual thought with great desire for the fair, the good and lovely. . . .

This love I liken to fire unslakened, the which no power of enemies can cast down, no softness of flattery can overcome. *This love cleanses us from our sins*, and burns in unmeasured heat the obstacles that might let to love, and in the hottest flame of God's love makes us clearer than gold and brighter than the sun. *This love brings us ghostly medicine;* . . . Therefore before all things that we can do *it gets the heart of the Everlasting King, and is worthy to be contemplated in joyful song*. (pp. 180–1.)

(3)

The seat of love is lift on high for into the heavens it runs, and on earth also methinks it subtly and craftily makes men, sometime lovely, wan and pale. It makes them to wither that afterward they may wax green, and to fail that they may be strong. *Therefore he draws near to the rest of endless joy*, and dreadless himself, mingles with those singing to his Maker; for the more burningly he loves the sweeter he sings and the more delicious he feels that that he strongly desired. *And if the way seem sharp and long* to them that love not, *love nevertheless couples God and man*, and with short labour fulfils the abiders. (p. 182.)

[1] I quote from my modernised edition published by Methuen, 1913. The words in italics are those which bear the closest resemblance to the lyric.

(4)

Love is hotter than the coal,
 love may none beswike,[1]
The flame of love who might it thole,
 if it were ay alike?
Love us comforts and makes in quart,
 and lifts til heaven's rike,[2]
Love ravishes Christ intil our heart,
 I wate na lust [3] it like.

(5)

Learn to love if thou wilt live
 when thou shalt hethen fare;
All thy thought til him thou give,
 that may thee keep fra care;
Look thy heart fra him nought twin,
 if thou in wandreth [4] were;
So thou may him wield and win,
 and love him evermare.

(6)

Ihesu that me life has lent,[5]
 intil thy love me bring;
Take til thee all mine intent
 that thou be my yearning.
Wae fra me away were went,
 and come were my coveting,
If (that) my sawl had heard and hent [6]
 the sang of thy loving.[7]

[1] Deceive.
[2] Kingdom (O.N. *riki*).
[3] Pleasure, delight.
[4] Trouble, poverty (O.N. *vandræi*).
[5] Given (from O.E. *lǣnan*=to give. Not to be confused with O.E. *lendan*=to abide. See Glossary).
[6] Caught, apprehended.
[7] Praise (see note, p. 221).

(4)

The love to which we ascend in this work *is quicker than a burning coal,* and shall produce its effect in us, for it shall make our souls both burning and shining. *This is the love that can not be beguiled* by a creature or scorned in heaven nor put from meed. *Who could long suffer the flame of this fire if it should ay last in one measure;* but ofttimes it is tempered, lest it waste nature that through the body corrupts and grieves the soul; . . .

. . . *It comes again* to us truly whiles we turn again to God, and *makes us mend from sickness of mind and gives sweetness.* It delivers the body also from many sicknesses, and whiles it keeps us in temperance and soberness it *raises our souls to heavenly desires* so that we have no delight in low things.

This is the love that ravishes Christ into our hearts and makes our minds sweet, so that within we burst out in songs of praise, and as it were in chanting we sing. *I suppose no delight be like to this,* for it moistens with clear sweetness and gladdens with holy liking. (pp. 183–4.)

(5)

Learn to love thy Maker if thou desire to live when thou passest hence; so do that thou mayest love God [in thy life] if thou wilt live after thy death. *Give all thy mind to Him that He may keep it from temporal and eternal sorrows. Beware that thy heart be not sundered from Him though thou be set in adversity or wretchedness; for so shalt thou* be worthy to *have Him with joy, and to love Him withouten end.* (p. 184.)

(6)

O good Ihesu, thou gavest me life, lead me desiring into Thy love. Take unto Thee all mine intent so that Thou mayest be all my desire, nor nothing beyond Thee shall my heart desire. *Sorrow* and all heaviness *would pass from me, and that I desire come to me, if my soul had received or heard the song of Thy praise.* (p. 185.)

(7)

Thy love ay is lasting
    fra that we may it feel,[1]
Therein make me burning,
    that na thing gar it keel;
My thought take into thy hand,
    and stable it ilk a deal,
That I be nought heldand [2]
    to love this world's weal.

(8)

If I love any earthly thing
    that pays to my will,[3]
And set [there] my joy and my liking,
    when it may come me til,
I may dread of parting
    that will be hate [4] and ill;
For all my wealth is but weeping
    when pine my sawl shall spill.[5]

(9)

The joy that men have seen
    is likened til the hay,
That now is fair and green,
    and now wites [6] away;
Swilk [7] is this world, I ween,
    and beës til domes day,
All in travail and teen [8];
    flee that na man may.

(7. i.)

(10)

If thou love in all thy thought,
    and hate the filth of sin,
And give him thy sawl, that it bought,
    that he thee dwell within,
As Christ thy sawl has sought,
    and thereof would nought blin,
Sa thou shall to bliss be brought,
    and heaven wone within.

[1] i.e. from the time that we experience or perceive it.
[2] Inclining (*and* is the northern form for the pres. part.).
[3] That pleases me.
[4] Hot, burning=attended with violent or raging suffering.
Cf. the prose reading.
[5] Destroy. [6] Passes, withers. [7] Such; cf. Sc. [8] i.e. toil and trouble.

(7)

Thy love would ever [unweariedly] *bide in us, so that we can perceive it. Take my mind into Thy power and make it stable* that it come not to nought with vain and unprofitable fantasies, nor be scorned by errors, *nor be bowed to earthly felicity* or love or praise, *but my mind being so settled in Thee may in Thy love so burn that by no* sudden nor avised *chance it may be cooled.* (p. 185.)

(8)

If I love any creature of this world that shall in all kinds please my list and set my joy and the end of my solace in it, when it should come to me I well might have dread of the burning and bitter parting. For all felicity that I have in such love *is but greeting* and sorrow in the end, *and that pain,* when it draws near, *most bitterly will punish the soul.* (p. 185.)

(9)

All pleasure also that men have beholden in this exile *is likened to hay that now flourishes and waxes green, but suddenly vanishes* as if it had not been.

No marvel that to them that behold rightly, *the joy of this world thus seems*; and to them following the solace of those bound in sin; *it never abides in one estate but passes until it come to nought. Nevertheless all stand in labour and grief, and no man can eschew that.* (p. 185.)

(10)

If thou love Christ with all thy will, thou hatest all filth of wickedness, and thou givest thy heart to Him that bought it so that He may be thy Lord by grace, and not the fiend by sin. *As Christ has truly* and unfeared *sought thy soul, and would not cease in seeking* until the time thou foundest Him, *so to endless joy thou shalt be led, and be near to God in a blessed seat.* (p. 186.)

(11)

The kind [1] of love is this,
    where it is traist [2] and true,
To stand still [3] in stableness,
    and change it for nought new.
The life,[4] that love might find
    and ever in heart it know,
From care it turns—that kind—
    and lends in [5] mirth and glew.[6] *

(12)

For now love thou, I rede,[7]
    Christ, as I thee tell,
And with angels take thy stead;
    that joy thou nought sell.
In earth thou hate, I rede,
    all that thy love may fell [8];
For love is stalwart as the dead,
    love is hard as hell.

(13)

Love is a light burden,
    love gladdens young and old;
Love is withouten pine,
    as lovers have me told;
Love is a ghostly wine
    that makes men big and bold,[9]
Of love shall he na thing tine [10]
    that it in heart will hold.

(14)

Love is the sweetest thing
    that man in earth has ta'en,
Love is God's darling,
    love binds blood and bane:

[1] Nature.   [2] Faithful.
[3] To remain.   [4] i.e. the living one, the man.
[5] Alights upon (cf. Glossary); brings.
[6] Glee, happiness.   [7] Counsel.   [8] Destroy, abate.
[9] Cf. p. 234; a doublet.   [10] Lose.

(11)

The nature of true love and not feigned is this, that it stands ay stable and is changed by no new thing.

Therefore *the life that can find love and truly know it in mind, shall be turned from sorrow to joy unspoken, and is conversant in the service of melody.* (pp. 185–6.)

(12)

Therefore I counsel thee to love as I have expounded, and take thy place with the angels. Beware thou sellest not this joy and honour for foul vanity of fleshly lust. . . . *Hate thou no wretchedness on earth except that that thy pure love can cast over and disturb, for perfect love is strong as death, true love is hard as hell.*[1] (p. 186.)

(13)

Love is a light burden, not charging but lightening the bearer; *the which makes glad the young with the old*; . . .

Love without pain bides in the soul of a lover, *as lovers have shown,* for love makes perfect and pain destroys. . . .

Love is ghostly wine moistening the minds of the chosen and *making them bold and manly. . . .*

Therefore *by holy love no lover can lose* but needs win mickle *if he keep it truly in his heart.* (p. 187.)

(14)

Love is the sweetest and most profitable *thing that ever reasonable creature received. Love is most acceptable and liking to God*; it not only binds the mind with bands of sweetness and wisdom and joins to God, but also *it constrains*

---

[1] See *The Form of Living* (Horstman, vol. i., pp. 39–40) : "For love is stalwart as death, that slays all living thing in earth; and hard as hell, that spares nought til them that are dead." And cf. *The Commandment of Love to God* (Horstman, i. 63), where Rolle expounds thus: "In this (singular) degree is love stalwart as death and hard as hell. For as death slays all living things in this world, so perfect love slays in a man's soul all fleshly desires and earthly covetousness. And as hell spares nought til dead men, but torments all that come thertil, thus a man that is in this degree of love not only forsakes the wretched solace of this life, but also he desires to suffer pains for love of God."

In love be our liking,
    I ne wate na better wane [1]
For me and my Loving [2] ;
    love makes baith be ane.

(15)

But fleshly love shall fare
    as does the flower in May,
And lasting be na mare
    than ane hour of a day.
And sithen sigh [3] full sare
    their lust, their pride, their play;
When they are cast in[to] care,
    til pine that lasts ay.

(16)

When their bodies lie in sin
    their sawls may quake and dread,
For up shall rise all men
    and answer for their deed.
If they be found in sin,
    as now their life they lead,
They shall sit hell within
    and mirkness have as meed.

(17)

Rich men their hands shall wring,
    and wicked works shall buy [4]
In flame of fire, baith knight and king,
    with sorrow, shamefully.
If thou will love, then may thou sing
    til Christ, in melody.
The love of Him o'ercomes all thing,
    thereto thou traist truly. [5]

---

[1] i.e. dwelling.   [2] i.e. Beloved (cf. p. 248).
[3] i.e. sigh for, regret.
[4] i.e. abye=pay the penalty for, expiate.
[5] In the Lambeth MS., "Ihesu, God's Son, Lord of Majesty," is inserted here, and stanza 18 begins with "I," which verse follows after stanza 12 of this latter lyric. Here the paraphrase of *The Fire of Love* ceases.

flesh and blood that man slip not into beguiling sweetness and into divers desires of errors. *In this love our life should stand* and wax mighty and strong. *A better dwelling-place* nor sweeter *found I never, for it has made me and my love one, [and made] one out of two.* (p. 187.)

(15)

Yet worldly love shall grow and perish as the flower of the field in summer, and shall be joying no more but as it were one day, so sickerly shall it last a short while, *but after that end in sorrow.* And so doubtless it shall be bitter to fond lovers. *Their pride and play in false beauty shall be cast into filth, that shall be with them endlessly when they are downcast into torments.* (pp. 187–8.)

(16)

(There is nothing corresponding to this stanza in *The Fire of Love*, nor to the first four lines of stanza 17.)

(17)

. . . for if we *love we shall sing in heavenly mirth to Christ with melody, whose love overcomes all things.* Therefore let us live and also die in love. (p. 188.)

S

(18)

Sigh and sob, baith day and night,
  for ane sa fair of hue;
There is na thing my heart may light
  but love that is ay new.
Whoso had him in his sight
  or in his heart him knew,
His mourning turned til joy full bright,
  his sang intil glew.

(19)

In mirth he lives, night and day,
  that loves that sweet Child;
It is Ihesu, forsooth I say,
  of all meekest and mild:
Wroth fra him would all away,
  though he were never so wild[1];
He that in heart loved him that day
  fra evil he will him shild.[2]

(20)

Of Ihesu most list I speak,
  that all my bale may bete:
Methink my heart may all to-break[3]
  when I think on that sweet:
In love laced[4] he has my thought
  that I shall never forget;
Full dear methink he has me bought (2; 4. x.–xix.)
  with bloody hands and feet.

(21)

For love my heart is boun[5] to brest
  when I that Fair [One] behold;
Love is fair, where it is fest,
  that never will be cold;
Love us reaves the night's rest,
  in grace it makes us bold;
Of all works love is the best,
  as holy men me told.

[1] i.e. however sinful or unruly he were.
[2] Shield.   [3] Completely break.
[4] Ensnared (O.Fr. *lacier*).   [5] Ready (O.N. *búinn*.)

(22)

Na wonder if I sighing be
  and sithen in sorrow be set,
Ihesu was nailed upon the tree   (cf. 2)
  and all bloody for-bet;   (5. xi.)
To think on him is great pity,   (2)
  how tenderly he gret:
This has he suffered, man, for thee,
  if that thou sin will let.

(23)

There is na tongue in earth may tell
  of love the sweetness;
That steadfastly in love can dwell
  his joy is endless;
God shild [1] that he should til hell
  that loves, and longing is,
Or ever his enemies should him quell,
  or make his love be less.

(24)

Ihesu is Love that lasts ay,
  til him is our longing;
Ihesu the night turns to the day,   (cf. st. I)
  the dawning in til spring.[2]
Ihesu think on us now and ay,
  for thee we hold our King;
Ihesu give us grace, as thou well may,
  to love thee withouten ending.

[1] i.e. God forbid.
[2] i.e. the first appearing of the morning. Cf. "Whereby the day-spring from on high hath visited us."

* The meaning of these last four lines is: The man that can find this love (i.e. true and faithful love) and experience it, it drives away sorrow, and brings mirth and joy.

THY JOY BE ILK A DEAL TO SERVE THY GOD, TO PAY (7)

(a) "THY JOY BE ILK A DEAL": and
(b) "ALL VANITIES FORSAKE"

These are really one lyric although in the Camb. MS. Dd. 5.64 they are divided; (a) being written on *fol.* 140ᵛ and (b) on *fol.* 142. There is, however, a rubric at the end of stanza 12 of (a) which reads: *Al vanites forsake if þou hys luf wil fele &c. ut supra*, as if to show that the copyist had made a mistake; and in the Thornton MS. we find them written as one poem.[1]

Except for the private collection of the Longleat MSS., which contains (a), they are only found in the two well-known northern MSS. we have cited, where they are evidently considered as one poem, and hence they are so treated here. In MS. Dd. 5.64 (a) is imperfect, having only nine stanzas in place of twelve; and in the Thornton MS. the poem ends at stanza 22, the last page being torn off. It seems best, therefore, to give the Thornton version, and add the last five stanzas of (b) from MS. Dd. 5.64. I have noted the important differences in the two MSS. In many places the Camb. MS. (which I call simply Dd.) gives the better reading; in these cases I have followed it. Both (a) and (b) are written in the same metre, and we can either treat them as Horstman does, viz. as stanzas of four long lines, with medial and end rhymes; or as eight short lines, rhyming *a b, a b, a b, a b*, as is done here. They have been printed by Horstman, vol. i., pp. 79–82, and pp. 370–2; and by the E.E.T.S., Orig. Series, 26, pp. 107–13 (1914).

We shall find many parallels to the *Ego Dormio* lyrics and to the others which we have cited, and the whole tone and style and wording of the poem bears Rolle's mark. It has much in common with his tract, *The Commandment*, which he wrote late in life for a nun of Hampole. It is written in the same metre as the last lyric, "Love is Life," only whereas that poem has alternate lines of three and four stresses, here there are only three stresses in each line.

[1] Dr. Carleton Brown treats them as two. In his *Register* he describes (a) as "An exhortation to love Jesus, twelve 4-line stanzas with medial rimes" (vol. ii., p. 358); and (b) as "A warning against worldly vanities, fifteen 4-line stanzas" (ii., p. 36); and he catalogues them as separate poems.

MS. *Thornton*
fol. 222.

(1)

[1] Thy joy be ilk a deal
   to serve thy God, to pay [2];
For all this world's weal
   thou seest it wites away.   (6. ix.)
Thou fand [3] his love to feel,
   that last will with thee ay,
And then thy care shall keel,
   and pine turn thee to play.[4]   (cf. st. 25)

(2)

In Christ thou cast thy thought,
   hate [thou] all wroth and pride;
And think how he thee bought
   with wounds deep and wide.   (3; 5. x.)
When thou himself has sought
   full well thee shall betide [5];
Of riches reck thou nought,
   fra hell but [6] he thee hide.

(3)

They turn their day to night   (cf. st. 17)
   that love this earthly sin;
And slain are in that fight
   where we our life shall win;
For that they love unright,
   and thereof can nought blin;
They lose the land of light
   and hell sit within.*

(4)

Thou do as I thee rede,
   lifting up thy heart;
And say til him [that] was dead,
   Christ, my heal thou art.

---

[1] In the Camb. MS. Dd. this rubric heads the page: *Iterum secundum eundem Ricardum*.

[2] i.e. to the satisfaction of thy God.

[3] Make trial of (O.E. *fandian*, experience).

[4] i.e. pleasure.   [5] i.e. it shall betide thee.   [6] If only.

Sin sinks ay as lead,
  and far falls fra quart,
Forthy stable thy stead [1]
  where smiting may nought smart.

(5)

Learn to love thy king,
  whose love evermore will last;
Have him in thy thinking,
  and fest his love sa fast
That for nane earthly thing,
  nor quaintness,[2] may be cast.[3]
Thy sang [be his, for] thy [4] sweeting
  he will be at the last.*

(6)

In Christ knit thy solace,
  his love change thy chere [5];   (2)
With joy thou take his grace,[6]
  and sigh to sit him near,
Ever seeking his face
  make thou thy sawl clear [7];   (2)
He ordains high thy place
  If thou his love will lere.[8]

(7)

Thou keep his biddings ten,
  Hold thee fra deadly sin,
Forsake the joy of men
  that thou his love may win.   (2)
Thy heart [for] him shall bren [9]
  with love that never shall twin,[10]
Langing he will thee len [11]
  to wone heaven within.

---

[1] Therefore make thy place secure.
[2] Cunning, skill.   [3] Cast down, overthrown.
[4] These words are rubbed in the MS. Horstman emends: *This
sang (and thy) swetynge*. Cf. *Religious Pieces*, E.E.T.S., Orig. Series,
26, p. 108, (revised ed., 1914).
[5] Change thy countenance; i.e. to joy.
[6] MS. Dd. reads *trace*; i.e. follow his footsteps.
[7] Pure.   [8] Learn.   [9] Burn.
[10] This is the reading of MS. Dd. Thornton reads: *Your lufe sall
neuer twyn*.   [11] i.e. give.

(8)

Thou think of his meekness,
    how pure that he was born;
Behold his bloody flesh,
    his head pricked with thorn;
Thy love let it nought less,[1]
    he saved thee, forlorn,
To serve him in sweetness;
    for all that have we sworn.

(9)

Fasten [2] thy heart to flee
    all this world's care,
That thou in rest may be
    thou salve thy sawl's sare;
His love, take it to thee,
    and love him mare and mare;
His face that thou may see
    when thou shall hethen fare.*

(10)

If thou be in fanding [3]
    of love thou hast great need.
To stead thee in stabling,[4]
    and give thee grace to speed;
Thou dwell ay with thy king,
    and in his love thee feed:
For little have I cunning
    to tell of his fairhead.

(11)

But love him at thy might,
    whiles thou art living here,
And look up to that sight
    that nane be thee so dear;
Say til him day and night,
    "when may I nigh thee near? (2)
Raise me up to thy light
    thy melody to hear." (2)

[1] Grow less, lessen.   [2] i.e. make fast.   [3] i.e. temptation.
[4] To place thee in security. MS. Dd. reads: *to stedde in stallyng.*

(12)

In that life thee stead
   that thou be ay loving,
And give him love to wed [1]
   that thou with him will stand.[2]
Joy in thy breast is bred
   when thou art him loving,
Thy sawl then has he fed
   in sweet love ay burning.

"ALL VANITIES FORSAKE"

(13)

1.   All vanities forsake
   if thou his love will feel [3];
Thy heart til him thou take,[4]
   he can it keep full well;
Thy mirth na man may make,
   of God [it] is, ilk a deal;
Thy thought let it nought quake,[5]
   thy love let it nought keel.

(14)

2.   Of sin, the bitterness
   thou flee ay fast there fra,
This world's wickedness
   let it nought with thee ga [6];
This earthly business
   that has men workëd wae,
Thy love it will make less
   if thou it to thee tae.

(15)

3.   All we love some thing,
   that knowing have of skill,[7]

---

[1] As a pledge.   [2] Remain.
[3] Rolle uses *feel* for all the senses; and also, as here, of the mind;
=*to experience.*
[4] i.e. entrust.   [5] i.e. tremble.   [6] go; cf. Sc.
[7] i.e. that have knowledge or sense of what is right; *skill*=what
is reasonable or right. Cf. Glossary.

And have therein liking
　　when it may come us til;
Forthy do Christ's bidding
　　and love him as he will,
And with joy that has no ending
　　thy heart he will full fill.[1]

(16)

4.

They that love fleshly [2]
　　are likened to the swine,
In filth then will they lie,
　　their fairhead will they tine;
Their love [de]parts purely [3]
　　and is put in pine;
Sweeter is love ghostly
　　that nevermare will dwine.

(17)

5.

If thou love, whiles that thou may,
　　the king of majesty,
Thy wae wends away,
　　thy heal hies to thee,
Thy night turns into day,　(6. i. xxiv.; cf. st. 3)
　　thy bliss must ever be:
When thou art as I say,
　　I pray thee think on me.

(18)

6.

Our thoughts shall we set
　　together in heaven to dwell;
For there the good are met,
　　that Christ holds fra hell.
When we our sins have gret
　　then tidings may we tell,
That we from far have fet,[4]
　　the love that nane shall fell.

---

[1] MS. Thornton: *Whas lufe hase nane endynge, and ioye withowten ill*. Here also I have followed the reading of MS. Dd.
[2] i.e. carnally.　　　　[3] Entirely.　　　　[4] Fetched (O.E. *fetian*).

(19)

7.

The world cast it behind
　　and say, "Ihesu my sweet,
Fast in thy love me bind,
　　,and give me grace to greet[1];　　　(8. ii.)
To love thee turn my kind,[2]
　　for ay to love thee I hete,
That I thy love may find,
　　that will my bales well bete."[3]

(20)

8.

With love wound me within,　　(2; 4. x. xix.)
　　and to thy light me lead;　　　(8. vii.)
Thou make me clean of sin　　(2; 4. x.)
　　that I there nought thee dread[4];
As thou to save mankin'
　　suffered thy sides to bleed,
Give me wit to win,[5]
　　the sight of thee to meed.

(21)

9.

His love is traist and true,
　　whoso him loving were,
Sen first that I it knew
　　it keepëd me fra care;
I find it ever new
　　to learn me God's lare,
And now (there) [6] I nought rue
　　that I have suffered sare.

(22)

10.

In love thy heart thou high [7]
　　and fight to fell the fiend;

[1] i.e. for my sins; but the line is merely a tag, as are many in this lyric.

[2] Nature: i.e. "incline me to love thee." MS. Dd. reads: *To lufe þe ouer al thyng*, which does not rhyme.

[3] Well remedy my sins.

[4] MS. Dd.: *þat I þe ded noght drede*.

[5] Grant me to gain wisdom.

[6] MS. Dd. *thar*; MS. Thornton. *thaie*; but the word is only inserted for the sake of the metre; the meaning is: "now I do not repent that I," etc.

[7] Adverb used for a verb.

Thy days shall be undregh,[1]
    that thee na sorrow schend [2]
When thy death nighs nigh
    and thou shall hethen wend,
Thou shall him see with eye,
    and come to Christ thy friend.

(23)

11.   [3] Aforce thee for to fest
    in Christ thy coveting;
And choose him for the best;
    he is thy wedded king.
For joy thy heart burd [4] brest
    to have swilk a sweeting;
Of all I hold it worst
    to love another thing.

(24)

12.   His love is [the] life of all
    that well living may be;
Thou stead him in thy stall [5]   (cf. 3)
    let him nought fra thee flee;
Full soon he will thee call,   (3)
    thy settle is made for thee,
And have thee in his hall,   (3)
    ever his face to see.

(25)

13.   This [to] meed,[6] forthy, I say,
    that thou kindle thy thought,   (2)
And make the love verray [7]
    in him that thee has wrought;

---

[1] Untedious, i.e. happy; cf. *dregh*.

[2] Confound, shame. This line is not found in MS. Thornton. I supply it from MS. Dd.

[3] The rest of MS. Thornton is torn off, and the remainder of the poem is taken from MS. Dd. 5.64, *fol.* 41.

[4] i.e. must burst; pret. of O.E. *gebyrian*=to behove.

[5] *Stall* may here be translated "heart." "Make a home (for Christ) in thy heart."

[6] To deserve, win; referring to the former verse.

[7] True, real.

For all that love him may
and they thereof will nought,[1]
Till pine turns their play;   (cf. st. 1)
themselves have it sought.

(26)

14.
Sin that is sa sour,
give it in thee na girth,[2]
Of love take the flower
that thou may lake [3] thee with;
Sweeter is that savour
than any field or firth.[4]
Set him in thy succour [5]
that lends thee limb and lith.[6]

(27)

15.
Take Ihesu in thy thinking,
his love he will thee send;
Thy love and thy liking
in him thou let it lend.[7]
And use thee in praying;
therein thou may be mend,[8]
Swa that thou has thy king
in joy without ending.

[1] i.e. all who may love him and will not.
[2] Sanctuary, home; cf. O.N. *griδ*=a home.
[3] Sport, play.
[4] For *frith*=a small wood; "field or firth" is a poetic tag=field or coppice.
[5] Shelter.
[6] Limb and life; a phrase meaning all the bodily faculties.
[7] Here=tarry, dwell; i.e. "let thy love and delight dwell in Him (Jesu)."
[8] i.e. restored, healed.

* Denotes that the verse is omitted in MS. Dd.

HAIL IHESU MY CREATOR (8)

There is little doubt of Rolle's authorship of this lyric, for in it we find many echoes of the *Ego Dormio* lyrics; and the familiar expressions which are so marked a feature of his style, e.g. "my bale may bete," "chaunges my mode," "langing to þi sight." Also it is found only in the Cambridge MS. Dd. 5.64, which tells in favour of its genuineness.

There is great affinity in this lyric to the *Charters of Christ*, especially in stanza 6. It might have been placed in chapter iv., or from its theme in chapter v.; but indeed all these lyrics we have been considering have played around these two themes of the Passion and the Holy Name; they can never be divided the one from the other, but are interchangeable.

These last four lyrics have shown an increasing mastery of expression and a freer handling of rhymes and metre compared with *The Form* and *Ego Dormio* lyrics; and in this, the last of the group, we can trace a still farther advance and freedom, especially in the first stanza. Like "Love is Life" it is written in alternate lines of four and three stresses each, but they fall differently. There is difficulty in marking all the parallels, as it is the similarity of thought, rather than the actual words, that is noticeable. There is hardly a line in it that could not be referred back to some other lyric, and more especially to the two lyrics of the *Ego Dormio*, which really should be read side by side with this lyric. It is printed only by Horstman (vol. i., p. 78).

MS. Dd. 5.64
fol. 40.

(1)

Hail Ihesu, my creator,
  of [the] sorrowing, medicine!
Hail Ihesu, my saviour,   (3)
  that for me suffered pine!
Hail Ihesu, [my] help and succour,
  my love be ay thine!
Hail Ihesu, the blessed flower
  of thy mother, virgin!

(2)

Hail Ihesu, leader to light,
  in sawl thou art full sweet!
Thy love shines day and night,
  that strongs me in this street [1];
Lene me langing for thy sight,   (cf. 2)
  and give me grace til greet,   (7. xix.)
For thou, Ihesu, has that might
  that all my bale may bete.

(3)

Ihesu, thy grace my heart inspire, (cf. 2 for the whole verse)
  that me til bliss may bring;
On thee I set all my desire,
  thou art my love langing.
Thy love is burning as the fire
  that ever on high will spring;
Far fro me put pride and ire,
  for them I love na thing.

(4)

Hail Ihesu, price of my prayer,
  Lord of majesty!
Thou art joy that lasts ay,
  all delight thou art to see;
Give me grace, as thou well may,
  thy lover for to be.   (2)
My langing wends never away
  til that I come til thee.

(5)

Ihesu to love ay be me lief [2]   (cf. 2 for the whole verse)
  that is my ghostly good.
Alas, my God is as a thief
  nailed til the rood!
His tender veins begin to brest,[3]
  all runs of blood;
Hands and feet with nails art fest,
  that changes my mood.[4]

[1] Way; i.e. strengthens me in this life.
[2] i.e. be my delight ever to love Jesu.
[3] Burst.   [4] i.e. makes me sad.

(6)

Ihesu my king is me full dear, (2; 4. x. xix.; 6. xx.)
    that with his blood me bought;
With spitting spread is all that chere,[1]
    to death with beating brought.
For me he tholed these pains sere,[2]
    the which, wretch,[3] he wrought,
Forthy they sit my heart full near
    that I forget them nought.

(7)

Ihesu, [by] fortune of ilk a sight
    thou grant me grace to speed,
that I may love thee right,
    and have thee to my meed.
Thy love is fast in ilk a fanding, (cf. 7. x.)
    and ever at all our need;
[Thou] through thy grace art my yearning,
    in til thy light me lead. (7. xx.)

---

[1] Face.   [2] Several, different.
[3] *Wretch* refers to Christ; i.e the wretched or afflicted One.

CHAPTER IV

LYRICS ON THE THEME OF THE PASSION

THUS far the lyrics we have considered have been echoes from other writings of Rolle's; and we have found that they are so closely blended and intermingled that if one is genuine, all must be so. And we have seen that there is only a part of one whose authenticity is doubtful.

In none of them has the theme of the Passion been absent. We might indeed liken Rolle's lyrics to a rosary, the thread on which the beads are strung being the Passion and suffering of Christ. He seems to think of Christ only in terms of suffering love.

It has been said with truth that "the mediaeval Christian is a man of one event." The passage is worth quoting in full:

Except by the preachers of the Evangelical Revival the message of Calvary has never been so powerfully set forth. Contemplation on the Crucified had been for centuries the supreme exercise of devotion, and the fourteenth century had inherited a spiritual experience the depth of which we can scarcely appreciate. . . . As the early Protestants were men of one book—their language borrowed from the Bible, their thought coloured by it—so the mediaeval Christian was a man of one event. The Passion of Christ was his daily meditation. It was not for nothing that he crossed himself so often. Over the whole mediaeval world lay the broad shadow of the cross. With the fifteenth century new interests broke in to disturb the contemplation, but for men living in the fourteenth century the old experience was still valid and unchallenged.[1]

But we must not forget that in England long before the fourteenth century men had seen the beauty of the Cross. *The Dream of the Rood* may be called the gem of Old English poetry; yet it is as far remote in thought as it is in beauty from the crude mediaeval conception of the Cross.

[1] *The People's Faith in the Time of Wyclif,* by B. L. Manning, p. 25 (Camb. Univ. Press, 1919).

We could as well compare the Greek type of perfect beauty in Adonis—interpreted by some Italian Renaissance painter into a St. Sebastian dying pierced by arrows—to the bleeding figure of the crucified Christ painted on the walls of a thirteenth- or fourteenth-century English church. The one did not evolve from the other; they are different conceptions.

But yet this tortured Christ has been the constant theme of the greatest art. Birth and death—the two enduring realities of this world—are topics which can never be exhausted; and round the birth and death of Christ all religious painters, poets, and sculptors have exercised their greatest gifts. Italy, the land of the sun and of colour, has ever been the land of birth, of fecundity; the cradle of the Renaissance. Children are cherished there as the gardener cherishes his plants. Was it surprising that the Italian artists of the Quattro- and Cinque-cento never grew tired of painting and carving the Madonna with her Child? All their tenderest art was shed upon the Nativity, and the crib was often laid amid a bower of roses, or under a lemon-tree. The purple iris, the red anemone, the pure white lily, all these find place in the old Italian pictures.

But in the England of the fourteenth century how different it was! There the labourer toiled to produce crops which were blighted by a long-enduring winter or an early frost. The children grew up under gloomy skies, amid a sombre colouring of green and grey. Before their life had properly come to maturity they grew old, and death seemed to them ever nearer than birth. Old English poetry is impregnated with the haunting dread of Wyrd, of some fate which steps in and puts an end to all. Life is only an interlude, as the bird who flies from out the darkness through the lighted hall, and back again into the unknown. The Day of Doom is a constant theme, and sin is feared less as an offence against Love—as with Francis and Jacopone da Todi—than for the terrible penalty which it was believed to entail.

Yet generalisations can never be entirely true, and there was a tendency in every country at that age to materialism; and in Italy also we meet with much the same crude conception of judgment and purgatory, although perhaps a less grim delight in this topic is shown than by the authors

T

of *The Prick of Conscience* and of *Cursor Mundi*. Moreover, in Italy it was the *pietà* rather than the Cross which most attracted the early painters; the sleep of death rather than the agony of dying.

It is only by contrasting Rolle with his immediate predecessors and contemporaries that we realise how far he rises above them; just as we can never grasp the greatness of Shakespeare until we have read deeply in the Elizabethan playwrights. To Rolle the Cross is the measure of sin. Love has been crucified. It is that which irradiates his Passion poems, and makes of the saddest thing on earth the most beautiful. We can never so truly judge them and give them the praise which is their meed as when we turn the leaves of some fifteenth-century MS.[1] with its crudely drawn and roughly coloured pictures; or trace the dim frescoes, on the walls of some early church, of the grotesque and tortured figure of Christ, punctured by wounds, with streams of blood pouring from hands and feet and side. Such crude materialism may revolt us, but we cannot do justice to these Passion poems of Rolle's unless we remember that these rude pictures were made familiar to him every time he entered a monastery or church by the frescoes on the walls, and out of such images he could fashion the lyric we must next consider.

[1] For a description of such a MS. see appendix ii.

MY TRUEST TREASURE SA TRAITORLY WAS
TAKEN (9)

Dr. Brown describes it well when he calls it "A song of the Passion," for song indeed it is. Professor Saintsbury compares it to Swinburne's *Itylus*:

> Swallow my sister, O sister swallow,
> How can thy heart be full of the spring,

and to the great stanza of *The Triumph of Time*.[1]

It is truly haunting in its melody and in everything most modern except the subject. But we know there was no subject dearer to the heart of the hermit than this of the Passion, and nowhere has he risen to a higher level than here. In its strange beauty it is worthy of being placed beside that other masterpiece, *The Dream of the Rood*, which it naturally recalls because of the alliteration. Unlike his prose, there seems here nothing forced or strained in the alliteration, and it adds to, rather than detracts from, the lilt of the verse.

We possess only a single copy of this lyric in the northern MS., MS. Dd. 5.64, *fol.* 134ᵛ. It has been printed only by Horstman (vol. i., p. 72). I can see no reason to doubt its authenticity. The alliteration and the diction are both similar to his other lyrics, and the use of such phrases as " þi bak burd breke"; " þi ryg on þe rode"; " þow bete al my bales," are all suggestive of Rolle's authorship. It is the only unmistakably genuine lyric in which Rolle seems to have taken some of the colouring from the songs of the trouvères, e.g. " þi moder and hir menȝhe vnlaced þi scheld"; and the expression "My pereles prynce" is, as far as I know, not found elsewhere in his lyrics.

MS. Dd. 5.64
fol. 134ᵛ.   (1)

> My truest treasure sa traitorly was taken;
> Sa bitterly bounden, with biting bands;
> How soon of thy servants was thou forsaken,
> And loathly for my love hurled [2] with their hands.

[1] *A Short History of English Literature*, by Professor Saintsbury, p. 76.
[2] For love of me struck; cf. Sc. *harl.*

275

(2)

My well of my weal, sa wrongously writhed,[1]
Sa pulled out of prison to Pilate at prime.
Their dules [2] and their dints full drearly thou dree'd,[3]
When they shot in thy sight [4] baith slaver and slime.

(3)

My hope of my heal, sa hied to be hanged,
Sa charged with thy cross and coroned with thorn;
Full sare to thy heart thy steps they stanged [5]
Methink thy back burd break, it bends for-born.[6]

(4)

My salve of my sare, sa sorrowful in sight,
Sa naked and nailed, thy rig [7] on the rood
Full hideously hanging, they heaved thee on height,
They let thee stab [8] in the stane; all steeked [9] that there
    stood.

(5)

My dearworthy darling, sa dolefully dight,
Sa straitly up-right, strained on the rood;
For thy mickle meekness, thy mercy, thy might,
Thou bete all my bales with bote [10] of thy blood.

(6)

My [de]fender of my foes, sa fond [11] in the field,
Sa lovely lighting,[12] at the evensang tide.
Thy mother and her mengey [13] unlaced thy shield,
All wept that there were, thy wounds were sa wide.

[1] Unfairly twisted; probably refers to the judgment of Christ,
meaning His words were twisted.
[2] Cognate with *dole*; here probably used of physical pain.
[3] Suffered (O.E. *drēogan*); cf. Sc. *dree one's weird*.
[4] i.e. face.
[5] Goaded (O.N. *stanga*).
[6] Submissively; cf. forbear (O.E. *forboren*).
[7] Back (O.N. *hryggr*).
[8] Be thrust (passive); the idea being that there was a stone socket
into which the Cross was dropped.
[9] i.e. placed ready (cf. Sc. *stooks* of corn, and *Stooky* Sunday).
[10] Remedy.
[11] Possibly = tested (O.E. *fandian*).
[12] Lovingly alighting; i.e. from the Cross.
[13] Her companions (O.Fr. *mesniec*).

(7)

My peerless prince so pure, I thee pray
Thy mind of this mirror [1] thou let me nought miss;
But wind up my will to wone with thee ay,
That thou be buried in my breast and bring me to bliss.

                              Amen.

The next two lyrics have some similarity to the *Charters of Christ*. These poems were written in imitation of the mediaeval charters and legacies, and purport to represent a grant made to man by Christ of the bliss of heaven, on condition that man gives his love in return, to God and to his neighbour. We find the expression "Christ's last will" in St. Ambrose. In his commentary on St. Luke, speaking of the words which Christ addressed to St. John from the Cross, he says:

"Testabatur de cruce Christus, et Testamentum eius signabat Joannes, dignus tanto testatore testis. Bonum Testamentum non pecuniae, sed vitae: quod non atramento scribitur sed spiritu Dei vivi." (Lib. x.)

Testamentum translates a Greek word which has the meaning of both "covenant" and "testament"; so that the figure is twofold, meaning:

(i.) The last will and testament made by Christ at His death.
(ii.) The covenant or charter which Christ bought by His blood when He died for man upon the Cross, and by which man receives the promise of eternal happiness; the condition being that he gives in exchange his love, to God and to his neighbour.

There are five forms of these *Charters* extant: two in Latin prose and verse, and three in English verse. We also find references to them in many English prose pieces, and translations. For example, there is an addition by an English translator to *The Privity of the Passion* which runs: "And when He was thus spread abroad on the cross, more strait than any parchment skin is spread on the harrow, so that men might tell all the blessed bones of His body." And the same motive is taken over into the later mystery plays, where we find prayers to Christ in which the sufferings of the Passion are recounted in detail as a cause for lamentation and penitence. "No single motive," writes an American critic, "in the devotional poetry of the day seems to have been turned to literary uses so frequently, and no motive enables

---

[1] Used in sense of Lat. *speculum*; i.e. "let me not miss the meaning or intention of this example."

the writers of the time to rise to more fervid and more moving heights of lyric poetry." [1]

Save for the common theme of the redemption of man by Christ's death upon the Cross, the *Charters* seem to have less influence upon the lyrics than upon some of the prose tracts of Rolle. There is affinity rather than likeness between them and the lyrics. In the last chapter we noted in passing that two of the lyrics: "Ihesu Christ, Saint Mary's Son" (4), stanzas xvi. and xix., and "Ihesu, God's Son, Lord of Majesty" (5), stanzas ii., iv., v., etc., are reminiscent of the *Charters*. In thought and theme they constantly recall them; for example, the simile of Christ buying the soul with His blood, and the request that He should wound the heart and thought and lift it up to Him who has bought it so dearly. Both are addressed by man to Christ, as are the two lyrics which follow: "Ihesu, als thou me made and bought," and "Lo, Leman sweet, now may thou see."

IHESU, ALS THOU ME MADE AND BOUGHT (10)

Only in *MS. Dd.* 5.64

fol. 135.

Ihesu, als thou me made and bought,
Thou be my love and all my thought,
And help that I were to Thee brought;
Withouten thee I may do nought.

Ihesu, als thou may do thy will
And naething is that thee may let;
With thy grace my heart fulfill,
My love and my liking in thee set.

Ihesu, at thy will
I pray that I might be;
All my heart fulfill
With perfect love to thee.

That I have done ill
Ihesu, forgive thou me;
And suffer me never to spill
Ihesu, for pity.

Amen.

[1] See an article on "The Middle English Religious Lyric in Relation to Corpus Christi Plays," by G. C. Taylor of Colorado (*Mod. Phil.*, vol. v., 1907–8), and compare MS. Add. 37049 (see appendix ii.).

There follow six lines of prose in the MS., every capital letter being in red:

"On four manners may a man know if he be out of deadly sin. One is: If he hear devoutly the word of God. The second: If he find him ready to good works. The third: If he be in purpose to abstain him from sin. The fourth: If he have sorrow for his sins that he has done."

LO, LEMAN SWEET, NOW MAY THOU SEE (11)

Only in *MS. Dd.* 5.64
fol. 134.

(1)

Lo, Leman sweet, now may thou see
That I have lost my life for thee,
What might I do thee mare?
Forthy I pray thee specially
That thou forsake ill company
That woundës me so sare.

(2)

And take mine arms privily
And do them in thy treasury,
In what stead so thou dwellst.
And sweet Leman forget thou nought
That I thy love sa dear have bought,   (2)
And I ask thee nought else.

In the MS. "My truest Treasure" runs straight on with no break.

This last lyric must not be confused with the two following short lyrics, also addressed directly to Christ. They have been attributed to Rolle but their origin is uncertain. Sometimes they have been printed as if two stanzas of the same lyric,[1] but they are in different metres and Dr. Carleton Brown catalogues them as two. They are:

(*a*)   Ihesu Christ, my Leman sweet
                That diedest on the rood tree;

and

(*b*)   Ihesu that diedest on the rood
                For the love of me.

---

[1] See Patterson, p. 137.

(*a*) occurs in four MSS., viz.: MS. Simeon, *fol.* 90ᵛ, col. 2 (where it forms the last verse of *A Mourning Song of God's Love*, which begins: "To love I will begin"). In MS. Vernon there are two versions: on *fol.* 114, col. 2, and *fol.* 300, col. 2; the latter being also appended to the *Mourning Song*. MS. Harl. 2316, *fol.* 25; and MS. Lambeth 559, *fol.* 35ᵛ.

These have been printed by Mr. Patterson in *Penitential Lyrics*, p. 137; in the *Minor Poems of Vernon MS.*, E.E.T.S., pp. 22 and 476; and in *Reliquiae Antiquae*, vol. ii., p. 119, edited by Thomas Wright and J. O. Halliwell, 1841.

It is unlikely that lyric (*a*) is by Rolle, since it is found in no northern MS. Many versions exist, and it is a curious fact that the more versions there are of a poem which is imputed to Rolle, the less seems the likelihood of his authorship. It is probably by some follower of his who may have heard or read the lyric (11) in the northern MS. and tried to re-produce it, but only remembered the two first lines.

However, I give both, since they are very short.

IHESU CHRIST, MY LEMAN SWEET (12) *

MS. Vernon   (*a*)
fol. 114.

> Ihesu Christ, my Leman sweet
> that diedest on the rood tree,
> With all my might I thee beseech,
> for thy wounds two and three,
> That all so fast might thy love
> in my heart fixëd be
> As was the spear into thine heart
> when thou suffredst death for me.

And then follows: "Ihesu that diedest on the rood," which is not in the Simeon MS. in spite of the close similarity of this MS. to the Vernon MS. In the latter (*fol.* 114, col. 2) it has been copied by a southern scribe from the northern version in the Thornton MS. Only these two copies of it are known, and it reads like a verse by Rolle; the rhymes, wording and manner are his, and it is found in close companionship with others about which there seems little doubt, so that there is every reason to think that this second lyric (*b*) is genuine; though the authorship of the first remains open to doubt.

---

* Doubtful.

It has been printed by Patterson, *Penitential Lyrics* (p. 137);
Horstman (vol. i., p. 364); E.E.T.S., *Minor Poems of Vernon
MS.* (pp. 22 and 476).

IHESU THAT DÏED ON THE ROOD FOR THE LOVE OF ME (12)

MS. Thornton   *(b)*
 fol. 192.
  Ihesu that dïed on the rood for the love of me,
  And bought me with thy precious blood, thou have mercy
      of me.
  What me lets of any thing for to love thee,
  Be it me lief, be it me loth, do it away from me.[1]

The next lyric, "Ihesu of whom all true love springs," is
also a prayer to Christ. It is found only in the Thornton MS.,
no southern copy being known. The evidence therefore lies in
favour of Rolle's authorship. "In thy love be my liking" is
a most characteristic line, and it is in a metre which he often
uses. The opening line recalls "Ihesu of whom all goodness
springs" (4, v.). It has been printed in *Religious Pieces* in
E.E.T.S. (p. 78) and by Horstman (vol. i., p. 364).
  This lyric has no very direct connection with the *Charters*,
but seems to fall naturally here among these short lyrics on
the Passion. In many respects Rolle's verses bear a closer
resemblance to the *Respice* poems, which we shall now consider, than to the *Charters*, though, as we have seen, the theme
of the *Charters* was a very favourite one of Rolle's.

IHESU OF WHOM ALL TRUE LOVE SPRINGS (13)

MS. Thornton
 fol. 192.
      Ihesu of whom all true love springs
        That for my love tholëd pain,
      Til lusty love of earthly things
        Thou thole me never turn again;

  [1] This lyric again must not be confused with a longer poem of
eight stanzas beginning:
        "Ihesu that diedest upon the tree
          And tholest death for love of me . . ."
which is commonly known as "An Orison to the Five Wounds."

In thy love be my liking,
   And thereto make me glad and fain;
And for thy love to make mourning
   That for my love would be slain.

Amen. amen. Amen. amen. pur charity.

There are a number of Middle English poems which are paraphrases of the same lines of a passage taken from a *Meditation on the Passion* which was attributed to St. Augustine, and which is cited on p. 227. These are generally called the *Respice in faciem Christi* lyrics. The earliest is to be found in the Kildare MS. (Harl. 913), which belongs to the first quarter of the fourteenth century; and there is another version in the Vernon MS. The following lyric is based upon these, and is found also in the English translation of the *Meditatio de Passione Jesu Christi* by St. Bonaventura, called *A Meditation on the Passion and Three Arrows on Doomsday*, which is referred to on p. 148. It was a very popular poem and is found in numbers of MSS., and is also embodied in another Middle English treatise called *The Book of Penance* in MS. Dd. 5.64. in the Cambridge University Library.[1] It was evidently ascribed to Rolle as we find a variant of this poem, twice repeated in slightly different versions, in a most interesting MS. in the British Museum which contains extracts in rough English verse from the *Incendium*, and many other paraphrases of Rolle's lyrics.[2] But this only evidences to the popularity of the lyric and not to its authenticity. In no sense can it be said to be original, but is merely an adaptation of an earlier poem. Very similar lines are found also in the *Cursor Mundi*.

UNKIND MAN GIVE KEEP TIL ME (14) *

MS. Dd. 5.64
  fol. 134.
       [3] Unkind man give keep til me
       and look what pain I suffer for thee.
       Sinful man on thee I cry,
       alanely for thy love I die.

[1] This MS. appears to be unique.
[2] See appendix ii. where I give a fuller account of this MS. Add. 37049.
* Doubtful.
[3] In the MS. it is written as if prose, the verse only being marked by colons, and every second line is initialled with red.

Behold the blood fra me down rins,
not for my guilt but for thy sins.
My hands, my feet, with nails are fest,
sinews and veins all to-brest.
The blood out of my heart's root,
look, it falls down to my foot!
Of all the pain that I suffer sare
within my heart, it grieves me mare,
the unkindness that I find in thee,
that for thy love thus hanged on tree.
Alas, why lovest thou me nought
and I thy love sa dear have bought?
But thou me love, thou dost me wrang,
sen I have loved thee [so] lang.
Twa and thirty year and mare
I was for thee in travail sare;
With hunger, thirst, heat and cald,
for thy love baith bought and sald,
Pined, nailed, and done on tree
all, man, for the love of thee.
Love thou me as thee well awe,[1]
and fra sin thou thee draw.[2]
I give thee my body, with wounds sare,
and thereto shall I give thee mare.
Over all this I-wis [3]
in earth my grace, in heaven my bliss.

                              Ihesu. Amen.

[1] Ought.   [2] i.e. withstand.   [3] Surely, certainly.

CHAPTER V

ON THE THEME OF THE HOLY NAME

WE cannot, properly speaking, dissociate the lyrics on the theme of the Holy Name from those on the Passion, or from the other Love lyrics, since, as we have already shown, these subjects are inextricably blended. Almost every lyric in chapter iii. bears some reference to the Name of Jesus. If we take "Ihesu Christ, Saint Mary's Son," we shall find that nearly every line of stanzas 15 and 16 is an invocation to the Holy Name; and "Ihesu, God's Son, Lord of Majesty," as well as "Hail, Ihesu, my Creator," are in praise of the Name of Jesus. Indeed, we have only to except the first half of "Love is Life," "Thy joy be ilk a deal," and the short lyric in *The Form of Living*. All the others are devotions to the Person of Christ, typified by the Name of Jesus.

The great song of the Holy Name was the *Jesu dulcis Memoria*—which for long has mistakenly been said to be by St. Bernard of Clairvaux, and to which reference has already been made.[1] Many English hymns were modelled upon this *cursus*, but none can with certainty be attributed to Rolle. Most are of earlier date. Those best known are:

(a)   Sweet Ihesu, now will I sing
         To thee a song of love longing;

which is a combination of the two lyrics: (i.) "Sweet Ihesu King of bliss," and (ii.) "Ihesu, sweet is the love of thee"; and

(b)   Ihesu thy sweetness who might it see.

The earliest version of (a) is found in MS. Harl. (2253). It is partly a translation of *Jesu dulcis Memoria*, and partly an imitation of it. The date of the MS. is *c.* 1325, which in itself precludes Rolle's authorship, at any rate of this version. It was written at Leominster Abbey, in Herefordshire, and is in a southern dialect. The poem is copied in

---

[1] Cf. p. 142 supra.

double columns, and with no divisions into stanzas. French
poems upon Our Lady precede and follow the first poem,
which begins on *fol. 75*, and the second on *fol. 77*ᵛ has the title
Dulcis Ihesu Memoria. The first has no heading, but begins:

fol. 75

> Suete ihesu king of blysse,
> myn huerte loue min huerte' lisse;
> þou art suete myd-ywisse
> wo is him þat þe shal misse.

and the second:

*fol. 77*ᵛ.

> *Dulcis Ihesu Memoria*
>
> Iesu suete is þe loue of þe
> no þing so suete may be,
> al þat may wiþ eȝen se
> haueþ no suetnesse aȝeynes þe.

The first poem has fifteen stanzas, and the second fifty
(if we supply four lines which are missing). The Latin hymn
also contains fifty stanzas. From this we should judge the
second poem was meant to be used as a rosary, being arranged
in five decades answering to the fifty *Ave Marias* of the
rosary.[1]

The Latin hymn [2] was originally a fragment of a very
extensive *jubilus* or *cursus de aeterna sapientia.* There are
an immense number of translations of this hymn, which are
divided into varying centos; the best known being:

(1) "Jesu dulcis memoria."
(2) "Jesu Rex admirabilis."
(3) "Amor Jesus dulcissimus."
(4) "Jesu decus Angelicum."

Suso (1300–63) arranged the poem into centos of three
stanzas each, with a Gloria, to suit the canonical hours; and
this was translated into English, probably sometime in the
sixteenth century.

There are twenty-four stanzas, not counting the Glorias,
since it includes the office of matins. It is quite a beautiful

---

[1] We must remember that praying with stones, and later with
beads (which of course is derived from O.E. *bidden*, to pray), was
older than Christianity, but was adopted by Christians at a very early
stage; though the divisions into decades came later, yet they are
considerably earlier than St. Dominic to whom the devotion of
the rosary is often wrongly ascribed.

[2] Two very beautiful MSS. of the original are in the Bodleian
Library, viz. MS. Laud. Misc. 668, *fol.* 101 (with musical
notation), and MS. Rawl. C. 510, *fol.* 3ᵛ, beginning *"Dulcis Jesu
memoria."* They both date from late twelfth or early thirteenth
centuries.

translation and may have influenced the almost innumerable modern translations; but it bears no resemblance to the earlier English versions.[1]

We also find an interesting shortened form of the poem among the prayers written in another much later hand at the end of the *Processional of the Nuns of Chester* [2] with the title: *Carmen xpo Ihesum*. This is later in date and contains only thirty-one verses, all the insertions relating to the Passion being omitted. It exactly corresponds to the Vernon MS. in the verses it contains, although it is only a third of the length of that poem and appears to be a copy of a southern MS. by a later scribe. Although so short a version there are three invocations to Mary, which points to its having also been used as a rosary.

These many different versions testify to the extreme popularity of this hymn, and of the devotion to the Sacred Name; yet the Feast of the Holy Name was not authorised until 1530, nearly two centuries after Rolle's death; and it did not find its way into the Roman Calendar until the eighteenth century.

When we extract all the stanzas of which we find equivalents in the Har. MS. 2253, little remains that bears much trace of Rolle's authorship. His poems have been marked by all absence of any direct invocations to Our Lady, nor is the long-sustained account of the sayings from the Cross suggestive of him in either method or manner. I do not therefore include it. It is very long and the Vernon version is easily accessible in the E.E.T.S. No northern MS. of the original poem exists, which is in itself a strong argument against Rolle's authorship; and indeed if he did write a part of one of the versions of the poem, it would have been only an adaptation, and not, properly speaking, original.

Being based upon the Latin *cursus* of the *Jesu dulcis Memoria* it naturally follows, or rather attempts to follow, the Latin iambic metre of that hymn. None of Rolle's genuine verses are in this metre, although this fact taken alone could hardly be said to be evidence against his authorship: since if he had worked upon this poem and make additions to it, he would in all likelihood have copied the original metre. Whoever was the composer it will be found to be not altogether a successful attempt. Dr. Horstman (vol. ii., pp. 9 ff.) has printed the versions from the Vernon and Royal MSS. side by

---

[1] Cf. *A Dictionary of Hymnology*, by John Julian, D.D., revised edition, p. 568 (Murray, 1907).

[2] Printed by the Henry Bradshaw Society, vol. xviii., 1899, pp. 30 sqq. Edited by Dr. Wickham Legg. "Mr. Warner of the British Museum assigns the writing of the greater part of the book to a date near 1425—but not much before that date—while the writing of the end of the book is much later than this." See p. x of introduction.

side; and also the Harl. MS. 2253. MS. Harl. 2253 has been edited and printed by C. H. Böddeker in *Altenglische Dichtungen des MS. Harl.* 2253 (1878), pp. 191 and 198; MS. Vernon by Dr. Furnivall in *Minor Poems of the Vernon MS.*, E.E.T.S., vol. ii., p. 449.

(b) "Ihesu thy sweetness who might it see" also shows the influence of the *Jesu dulcis Memoria*, but not to the same extent. No less than fifteen MSS. of it are listed by Dr. Carleton Brown, and it has been printed in many collections. It is not in the Cambridge MS. Dd. 5.64; but there is a copy of it in MS. Thornton. Even Dr. Horstman allows that "The authorship of this piece is doubtful, as the o-forms sore, lore, wore, are frequent; but perhaps allowance must be made for the metre"; and he adds: "The same poet wrote the poems on Hell, Purgatory, etc., in MS. Reg. 17. B. xvii." (vol. i., p. 368). But this latter poem is an abridgment of *The Prick of Conscience*, and therefore not by Rolle. If therefore Dr. Horstman is right in his conclusion that the writer of this lyric is the same as the writer of "Hell, Purgatory, etc.," Rolle cannot be the author; but I cannot myself trace much resemblance between this latter poem and the hymn or poem we are considering. The lyric shows traces of the influence of such writings as the *Meditatio de Passione Christi*, then attributed to St. Augustine; St. Bernard's *Tractatus de Passione Christi*; and *The Privity of the Passion* which was a free rendering of St. Bonaventura's *De Mysteriis Passionis Jesu Christi*. It was a subject so common to Rolle and beloved by him, that it is not surprising he should be credited with this poem. It can hardly be classed as a lyric, for it is an attempt to copy the iambic Latin hymn metre, and is based upon the *cursus* of hymns on the Name of Jesus which we have been discussing. It seems also in places to recall the *Ancren Riwle*, more especially chapter vii., where Christ is likened to a knight, and the Passion is described under the terms of a tournament.

There are many stanzas in this poem which suggest that the writer knew the *Riwle*. The poem is also threaded together by the motive of the *Charters of Christ*; compare especially stanzas 13, 15, 18, 19, 27.

There are so many existing MSS. of "Ihesu thy sweetness" that it is difficult to know which to choose to transcribe. I have examined the following:

MS. Thornton (*fol.* 219); MS. Vernon; MS. Lamb. 853 (*fol.* 14); MSS. Harl. 1706 (*fol.* 9), 2339 (*fol.* 78); MS. Add. 37787 (*fol.* 8ᵛ); MS. Sloan 963 (*fol.* 19), which is a later MS.; MS. Douce 322 (*fol.* 8); and MS. Rawl. A. 389 (*fol.* 104ᵛ).

The Thornton MS. has been printed by Horstman (i., p. 368), and the Vernon and Lambeth MSS. by the E.E.T.S., viz. *Minor Poems of the Vernon MS.*, p. 45, and in *Hymns to the Virgin*, p. 8, and are therefore easy of access. Thus it has seemed well to choose a version not yet printed, and which gives one of the best readings, i.e. MS. Harl. 2339, *fol.* 78.

In the MS. the poem is divided into stanzas of four lines, separated by blue paragraph marks. The date is about the fifteenth century. There is a rubric which reads: "Here sueth [followeth] the sweetness of the Love of Ihesu."

THE SWEETNESS OF THE LOVE OF IHESU (15)

MS. Harl. 2339
fol. 78.   (1)

Ihesu, thy sweetness who might it see
And thereof have to have a clear knowing.
All earthly love bitter should be
But thine alone without leasing.

(2)

I pray thee Lord that lore learn me
After thy love to have longing;
And sadly [1] (to) set my heart on thee,
And in thy love to have liking.[2]

(3)

So liking [3] love in earth none is
In soul, who could him soothly see,
Him to love were mickel bliss
For King of Love callëd is he.

(4)

With true love I would i-wis
So fast to him bounden be
That mine heart were wholly his,
That no thing liked me but he.

(5)

If I for kindness [4] should love my King
Then, me thinketh in my thought,
By kindly skill [5] I should begin
At him, that hath me made of nought.

[1] Firmly.　　　[2] Delight.　　　[3] i.e. a love so delighting.
[4] (1) the natural affection arising from kinship; (2) near relationship.
[5] i.e. by natural reason; i.e. naturally, in accordance with nature.

(6)

His semblant [1] he set my soul within,
And all this world for me he wrought;
As father he fondeth [2] my love to win
For to heaven [3] he hath me bought.

(7)

As mother, of him I make mind
That before my birth to me took heed,
And sith [4] with baptism washed my kind [5]
That foulëd was with Adam's deed.

(8)

With noble meat he nourished my kind,
For with his flesh he doth me feed:
A better food may no man find,
To lasting life it will me lead.

(9)

My brother and sister he is by skill, [6]
For he said and learnt [7] that lore:
Whoso wrought his Father's will
Mother and sister to him were.

(10)

My kind also he took theretil,
Full truly trust I him therefore;
He will never let me spill [8]
But with his mercy salve my sore.

(11)

The love of him passeth i-wis
All earthly love that may be here,
God and man, my spouse he is,
Well ought I wretch to love him dear.*

---

[1] i.e. likeness.   [2] Tries.
[3] MS. Thornton reads: *Heritage in heaven.*
[4] Afterwards.   [5] Nature.
[6] i.e. by right.   [7] Taught.   [8] Perish.

U

(12)

Both heaven and earth wholly is his,
He is a Lord of great power,
And called he is the King of bliss.
His love me longeth for to lere.[1]*

(13)

After his love behoves me long
For he hath me full dear bought,
When I went fro him with wrong,
From heaven to earth he me sought.

(14)

My wretched kind for me he fong [2]
And all his noblay [3] set at nought,
Povert(y) he suffered, and pains strong
Agen to bliss ere he me brought.[4]

(15)

When I was thrall he made me free,
My love from heaven to earth him led,
My love alone have would he,
Therefore he laid his life in wed.[5]

(16)

With my foe he fought for me,
Wounded he was and bitterly bled,
His precious blood—full great plenty,
Full piteously for me was shed.

(17)

His sides blue and bloody were,
That sometime were so bright of ble [6] ;
His heart was piercëd with a spear,
His ruddy wounds were ruth to see.

[1] Learn.   [2] Took.
[3] i.e. nobility of rank or nature.
[4] i.e. before he brought me back to bliss.
[5] Pledge.   [6] Hue, colour.

(18)

My ransom, i-wis, he paid there,
And gave his life for guilt of me;
His death should be to me full dear
And pierce mine heart for pure pity.

(19)

For pity mine heart must break in two
To his kindness, if I took heed,
Encheson [1] I was of all his woe,
He suffered full hard for my misdeed.

(20)

To lasting life that I should go
He suffered death in his manhead;
When his will was to live, also
He rose agen through his godhead.

(21)

To heaven he went with mickle bliss
When he had vanquished his battle,
His banner full broad displayed is
Whenso my foe will me assail.

(22)

Well ought mine heart to then [be] his,
For he is (the) friend that never will fail;
Nothing he will have of me, i-wis
But true love for his travail.

(23)

Thus would my spouse for me fight,
And for me was he wounded sore;
For my love he [to] death was dight,
What kindness might he do more?

(24)

To yield [2] his love have I no might
But love him truly I should therefore;
And work well, with works right,
That he hath me learnt with lovely lore. [3]

[1] Cause, fault.   [2] Requite, repay.
          [3] i.e. lore of love.

(25)

His lovely lore with work fulfilled,
Well ought I, wretch—if I were kind—
Night and day to work his will,
And evermore have that Lord in mind.

(26)

But ghostly foes grieve me ill,
And my frail flesh maketh me blind;
Therefore his mercy I take me til,
For better bote can I none find.

(27)

Better bote is none to me
Than to his mercy truly me take,[1]
That with his blood hath made me free,
And me, wretch, his child would make.

(28)

I pray that Lord, for his pity,
That he for sin me never forsake;
And give me grace fro sin to flee,
And him to love let me never slake.

(29)

Ihesu, for the sweetness that in thee is
Have mind on me when I hence wend;
With steadfast truth my wits thou wis,[2]
And Lord, thou shield me from the fiend.

(30)

For thy mercy forgive me my miss,[3]
That wicked work my soul not schend;
And lead me, Lord, into thy bliss,
To wone with thee withouten end.

A. M. D.

[1] i.e. commit myself; refl. as *betake*.
[2] Guide (O.E. *wissian*).   [3] i.e. misdeeds.
* Denotes that the stanza is not found in the Thornton MS.

CHAPTER VI

PARAPHRASES AND DOUBTFUL POEMS

To these two paraphrases, based upon prayers in the *Speculum Ecclesiae* of St. Edmund Rich, afterwards Archbishop of Canterbury, reference has already been made.[1] Translations and paraphrases of the *Speculum* were abundant. There is an English prose translation in MS. Thornton (*fol.* 197) which seems to be a copy of a southern translation; and a southern translation is found in MS. Vernon (*fol.* 355) about fifteen years earlier in date than that in MS. Thornton. Horstman prints the Thornton version, ascribing it to Rolle (vol. i., p. 219).

The paraphrases are more likely to be genuinely Rolle's, since only this northern version exists, and a copy in a private collection, which is noted in Dr. Carleton Brown's *Register* (vol. i., p. 469), who dates it as belonging to the end of the fourteenth century. It is now in the possession of J. H. Gurney, Esq., Keswick Hall, Norfolk.

The first (16) follows the Latin prayer very closely, which runs: "Gracias ago tibi, domine ihesu criste, qui me in hac nocte custodisti, protexisti, visitasti, sanum, salvum & incolimem ad hanc horam peruenire fecisti, et pro aliis uniuoisi beneficiis que mihi de tua sola bonitate contulisti. Qui vivis et regnas deus . . ."

This verse, as we see, is separated from those following by "Amen." The two following verses are not really a part of it. They paraphrase the prayer *In manus tuas* of the *Speculum*.[1] They are all three printed by Horstman (vol. i., pp. 363–4), and in Perry's *Religious Pieces*, E.E.T.S., Orig. Series, 26, revised 1914, p. 77.

ALMIGHTY GOD IN TRINITY (16)

MS. Thornton
   fol. 191[v].

> Almighty God in Trinity
> Inwardly I thank thee
> For thy good deed that thou me wrought,
> And with thy precious blood me bought,

[1] See supra, pp. 157–58.

And of all good that thou lenes [1] me,
Lord, blessed may thou be.
Honour, joy and loving
Be til thy name, without ending.

Amen.

LORD GOD ALLWELDAND [2] (17)

(1)

Lord God allweldand,
I betake [3] to-day into thy hand
My sawl and my body,
And all my friends specially,
Baith the quick and the dead;
Grant them part in my bede.[4]
Keep us all in earth here,
For the prayers of thy mother dear
And all thy hallows that are in heaven,
Fra the deadly sins seven,
And fra fanding of the evil wight
And fra sudden death; baith day and night.

(2)

Shield us fra the pains of hell
That bitter are to thole, and fell;
And with thy grace fulfill us all
That ready we may be to thy call;
And let us never part fra thee
As thou for us died on a tree;
Grant us, Lord, that [it] sa be.
Amen. Amen. pur charity.

The next two lyrics deal with mercy; the first being a prayer for mercy, while the second is written in praise of mercy. Prayers for mercy were much commoner than poems extolling mercy. Dr. Patterson gives us about ten examples in his collection of *Penitential Lyrics*. One of these is a long poem of twenty-two stanzas, beginning: "Ihesu mercy, mercy I cry" (p. 75), and has a refrain: "Ihesu mercy for my mysdede." Another notable poem based upon the *Miserere* begins

---

[1] givest (see Glossary).   [2] i.e. all-possessing.
[3] Yield, commit.   [4] i.e. prayer.

"Mercy God of my mysdede." This is not quoted by Patterson, but it has been printed by Dr. Furnivall.[1] There is also the well-known poem in the form of a dialogue between the Sinner and Mercy, beginning: "Bi a forest as y gan walke," with the refrain: "His merci passiþ his riȝtwisnes," in the Lambeth MS. 853, *fol.* 66.[2]

But all these are long poems of many stanzas, whereas this verse attributed to Rolle is simply a prayer translated into English in three rhymed couplets. It hardly merits the name of lyric, being little more than doggerel rhyme which any scribe might easily improvise after copying religious prayers, verses, and sermons, as a diversion. It is only found in the Thornton MS.

It seems to me of very slight importance in our estimate of Rolle's verse, being a mere stringing together of favourite rhymes and tags. More likely than not it is by some imitator of Rolle, such as the anonymous author of the patchwork of rhymed verses in MS. Add. 37049, which is quoted in appendix ii.

It has been printed by Horstman (vol. i., p. 368) and by R. H. Benson (p. 37).

IHESU CHRIST HAVE MERCY ON ME (18)*

MS. Thornton
  fol. 213ᵛ.

> Ihesu Christ have mercy on me
> Als thou art King of magesty,
>
> And forgive me my sins all
> That I have done, baith great and small,
>
> And bring me, if it be thy will,
> Til heaven, to wone ay with thee still.
>
> > Amen.

The following lyric in praise of mercy is only found in the northern MS. Dd. 5.64, fol. 136, and has been printed only by Horstman (vol. i., p. 74). It is written in the same ballad metre as "Love is Life"; the stresses are uneven, but the rhymes are perfect, and those in stanzas (1) and (4) are very uncommon with Rolle—indeed I know of no other example of these rhymes: "prayse," "rayse"; "suppryse," "lyse"; or "aloynt," "anoynt," in Rolle's verse. It is also unusual to find a subject so well sustained as here, for, as we have

---

[1] *Political and Religious and Love Poetry*, E.E.T.S., pp. 279–85.
[2] Printed in *Hymns to Virgin*, E.E.T.S., p. 95; and in several modern anthologies. It is dated *c.* 1430.

often noted, Rolle is generally more discursive; one thought
brings another to his mind, and he passes from theme to theme
as if playing idly upon an instrument. This lyric is, however,
upon the one note of mercy. If it is by Rolle I should be
inclined to place it as one of his latest lyrics, written towards
the end of his life after he had gained greater mastery of
rhyme. If so the lines:

> Til the Judge shall I come,
>   but I wate nought my day;

have a curious significance, for it is more likely than not
that the plague swept him off suddenly.

This expression "my day," meaning death, occurs also in
the lyric from *The Form of Living*. This is the only hint there
is of any memories of the early lyrics; but the poem constantly
recalls the first portion of "Love is Life." It may be that they
are both written by the same author, or it is also possible
that the paraphraser of "Love is Life" knew this later lyric
by Rolle and imitated it in his paraphrase. It is one of those
difficult points about which we may generalise but can come
to no definite conclusion. In favour of its authenticity is the
fact of only this one northern copy being known. There are
more French words here than in any other of the lyrics we
know to be genuine, and all we can say is that Rolle's authorship of this lyric is not certain. It reads like his, and may
have been written when, all unconsciously, death was over-
shadowing him. In mercy Christ is personified; it is a confident
appeal to the mercy he is extolling:

> Mercy likës me sa weel,
>   for through mercy was I bought;
> I ne wate what I may do or say
>   til mercy, that is ay sa good.
> Thou grant mercy, that mercy may
>   that is my solace and my food.

It is a fitting lyric with which to close. The three other sets
of verse which Horstman prints as Rolle's (vol. i., pp. 73-4
and pp. 365, 367), viz.:

> All synnes sal þou hate, thorow castyng of skylle,

> When Adam delf and Eve span, spir, if þou wil spede,
> Where was þan þe pride of man, þat now merres his mede,

and

> Fadir and sone and haly gaste,
> Lorde to þe I make my mone,

are not given here; for I can find no likelihood of their being
genuine. Neither in matter, style nor diction do they resemble
any of the lyrics we know to be by Rolle.

MERCY IS MAIST IN MY MIND (19)

MS. Dd. 5.64
fol. 136.

(1)

Mercy is maist in my mind
    for mercy is that I maist praise.
Mercy is courteous and kind,
    fra all mischieves he may me raise;
Alas, so lang have I been blind
    and walkëd wil[fully] always.
Mercy would I fain find
    to lead me in my last days;
Mercy lead me at the last
    when I out of this world shall wend;
To thee crying, I traist fast
    that thou save me fra the fend.[1]

(2)

Mercy is true as any steel,
    when it is right up-sought;
Whoso will mercy feel,[2]
    seek it, for it fails nought.
Mercy is sight of all my heal,
    therefore I have it maist in thought;
Mercy likës me sa weel,
    for through mercy was I bought;
I ne wate what I may do or say
    til mercy, that is ay sa good.
Thou grant mercy, that mercy may,[3]
    that is my solace and my food.

(3)

Mercy would I fain honour,
    it is sa sweet unto my sight;
It lies in my Creatour
    that made us of his own might.

---

[1] Enemy.   [2] i.e. experience (cf. Glossary).
[3] i.e. "that may have mercy"; he is here addressing Christ his solace and food.

Mercy is all my succour
   til lead me to the land of light,
And bring me til the royal tour
   where I may see my God sa bright.
God of all, Lord and King,
   I pray thee, Ihesu, be my friend,
Sa that I may thy mercy sing
   in thy bliss withouten end.

(4)

Mercy is sa high a point
   there may na sin it surprise;
To thy mercy is my heart noynt [1]
   for therein all my liking lies;
Lord, let it nought be aloynt [2]
   when thou shall set thy great assize,
With thy mercy my sawl anoynt
   when I shall come to thy Jugise.[3]
Til the Judge shall I come,
   but I wate nought my day;
Mercy is baith all and sum;
   wherein I traist, and after pray.

[1] Aphetic form of "anoynt."   [2] Far off (O.Fr. *aloynir*).
[3] Judging, Judgment (O.Fr. *jugise*).

APPENDICES

APPENDIX I

A TRANSLATION OF THE LEGENDA IN THE OFFICE PREPARED FOR THE BLESSED HERMIT RICHARD [1]

The office of Saint Richard, hermit, after he shall be canonised by the Church, because in the meantime it is not allowed to sing the canonical hours for him in public, nor to solemnise his feast. Nevertheless, having evidence of the extreme sanctity of his life, we may venerate him and in our private devotions seek his intercessions, and commend ourselves to his prayers.

Lesson I. The saint of God, the hermit Richard, was born in the village of Thornton, near Pickering, in the diocese of York, and in due time, by the efforts of his parents, he was sent to be educated. When he was of adult age Master Thomas Neville, at one time Archdeacon of Durham, honourably maintained him in the University of Oxford, where he made great progress in study. He desired rather to be more fully and perfectly instructed in the theological doctrine of Holy Scripture than in physics or the study of secular knowledge. At length, in his nineteenth year, considering that the time of mortal life is uncertain and its end greatly to be dreaded (especially by those who either give themselves to fleshly lusts or only labour that they may acquire riches, and who, for these things, devote themselves to guile and deceit, yet they deceive themselves most of all), by God's inspiration he took thought betimes for himself, being mindful of his latter end, lest he should be caught in the snares of sinners.

Hence, after he had returned from Oxford to his father's house, he said one day to his sister, who loved him with tender affection: "My beloved sister, thou hast two tunics which I greatly covet, one white and the other grey. Therefore I ask thee if thou wilt kindly give them to me, and bring them me to-morrow to the wood near by, together with my father's rain-hood." She agreed willingly, and the next day, according to her promise, carried them to the said wood, being quite ignorant of what was in her brother's mind. And when he had received them he straightway cut off the sleeves from the

---

[1] From the *York Breviary*, vol. ii., appendix v. Pub. by Surtees Soc. (1882).

grey tunic and the buttons from the white, and as best he could he fitted the sleeves to the white tunic, so that they might in some manner be suited to his purpose. Then he took off his own clothes with which he was clad and put on his sister's white tunic next his skin, but the grey, with the sleeves cut out, he put on over it, and put his arms through the holes which had been cut; and he covered his head with the rain-hood aforesaid, so that thus in some measure, as far as was then in his power, he might present a certain likeness to a hermit.[1] But when his sister saw this she was astounded and cried: "My brother is mad! My brother is mad!" Whereupon he drove her from him with threats, and fled himself at once without delay, lest he should be seized by his friends and acquaintances.

Lesson II. After having thus put on the habit of a hermit and left his parents, he went to a certain church on the vigil of the Assumption of the most Blessed Virgin, Mother of God, and therein he set himself to pray, in the place where the wife of a certain worthy squire, named John de Dalton, was wont to pray. And when she entered the church to hear vespers, the servants of the squire's house wished to remove him from their lady's place. But she from humility would not permit them, lest he should be disturbed in his devotions. But when vespers were over, the sons of the said squire, who were scholars and had studied in the University of Oxford, noticed him as he rose from prayer, and said that he was the son of William Rolle, whom they had known at Oxford.

Then, on the day of the aforesaid feast of the Assumption he again entered the same church; and without bidding from any one, he put on a surplice and sang matins and the office of mass with the others. And when the gospel had been read in the mass, having first besought the blessing of the priest, he went into the preacher's pulpit and gave the people a sermon of wonderful edification, insomuch that the multitude which heard it was so moved by his preaching that they could not refrain from tears; and they all said that they had never before heard a sermon of such virtue and power. And small wonder, since he was a special instrument of the Holy Spirit, and spoke with the very breath of Him whose it is, as saith the apostle to the Romans, to divide to every man severally as He will,[2] and to make intercession for us with groanings which cannot be uttered.[3]

Lesson III. Therefore, after mass, the aforesaid squire invited him to dinner, but when he entered his manor he

---

[1] *Confusam similitudinem heremite.*
[2] I Cor. xii. II.   [3] Rom. viii. 26.

betook himself to a certain mean and old room; for he would
not enter the hall, but sought rather to fulfil the teaching of
the gospel, which says, "When thou art invited to a wedding,
sit down in the lowest room; that when he that bade thee
cometh, he may say unto thee, Friend, go up higher," [1] and
this too was fulfilled in him. For when the squire had sought
for him diligently, and at last found him in the aforesaid room,
he set him above his own sons at the table. But he kept such
perfect silence at dinner that not a word proceeded from his
mouth. And when he had eaten enough he rose, before the
table was removed, and prepared to depart. But the squire
who had invited him said that this was not customary, and
so prevailed upon him to sit down again. When the meal was
over he again wished to depart, but the squire, seeking to
have some private talk with him, detained him until all who
were in the room had gone, when he asked him if he were the
son of William Rolle. Then he rather unwillingly and with
reluctance answered: "Perchance I am"; since he feared that
if he were recognised the plan on which his mind was set would
be hindered. For this squire loved his father as a friend with
warm affection. But Richard—newly made a hermit without
his father's knowledge and against his wish—had taken this
estate upon him because he loved God more than his earthly
father.

Lesson IV. And when the aforesaid squire had examined
him in private, and convinced himself by perfect evidence of
the sanctity of his purpose, he, at his own expense, clad him
according to his wish, with clothing suitable for a hermit; and
kept him for a long time in his own house, giving him a place
for his solitary abode and providing him with food and all
the necessaries of life. Then he began with all diligence, by
day and night, to seek how to perfect his life, and to take every
opportunity he could to advance in contemplative life and to
be fervent in divine love. And to what excellent perfection
he at length attained in this art of fervent love for God he
himself records, not for boastfulness nor to seek vainglory,
but rather after the example of the glorious and humble
apostle Paul, who, narrating his rapture to the third heaven,
where he heard secrets which are not lawful for a man to utter,
also avows the greatness of the revelations made to him by
God, and openly exalts his own labours above the labours of
all the other apostles.[2] All which things he wrote in his epistles
for the profit and edification of others, and left them for others
to read. So too this holy hermit, Richard, in chapter one of
his first book of *The Fire of Love*, tells to what high and sweet
delights he attained by contemplation, so that others may

---

[1] Luke xiv. 10.   [2] 2 Cor. xii. 4–8; 1 Cor. xv. 10.

obtain hope of advancing likewise in acts of contemplation and of love for God, if only watchfully, constantly, and perseveringly they persist in those works which are ordained for the attainment of this most desirable state of perfection, and hate and cut off as poison all impediments to contemplation.

Lesson V. For in the aforesaid book he thus speaks: "I marvelled more than I can say when I first felt my heart grow warm and burn, truly, not in imagination but as it were with sensible fire. I was indeed amazed at that flame which burst forth within me; and at this unwonted comfort—because of my inexperience of this abundance—I have often felt [1] my breast to see if perchance this heat was due to some outward cause. But when I knew that this fire of love had blazed forth only from within, and was not of the flesh but a gift of my Maker, I was full of joy and dissolved in a desire for yet greater love; and chiefly because of the inflowing of this most sweet delight and internal sweetness which, with this spiritual burning, bedewed my mind to the core. For I had not thought before that such sweet heat and comfort might come to pass in this exile." [2]

See then by these words how far he had advanced in attaining the most sweet love of God; but, because there are many steps preparatory to the kindling of this love—as, for example, those things which diminish and remove the loves opposed to it—therefore this saint wore down the lusts of the flesh; to the love of which many are borne off by a mad and bestial impulse. He spurned the world too with its riches, being content with only the bare necessaries of life, that he might more freely enjoy the delights of true love. For these reasons, therefore, he mortified his flesh with many fasts, with frequent vigils, and repeated sobs and sighings, quitting all soft bedding, and having a hard bench for a bed, and for a house a small cell; fixing his mind always on heaven, and desiring to depart and be with Christ,[3] his most sweet Beloved.

Lesson VI. Yet wonderful and beyond measure useful was the work of this saintly man in holy exhortations, whereby he converted many to God, and in his sweet writings, both treatises and little books composed for the edification of his neighbours, which all sound like sweetest music in the hearts of the devout. And amongst other things it seems worthy of great wonder that once, when he was seated in his cell (one day, after dinner), the lady of the house came to him, and many other persons with her, and found him writing very quickly. And they besought him to leave off writing and speak a word of edification to them, which he immediately did, exhorting

---

[1] *Palpavi*=lit. stroked.   [2] *The Fire*, p. 11.   [3] Phil. i. 23.

them most eloquently to virtue and to renounce worldly vanities and stablish the love of God in their hearts. Yet in no way on account of this did he cease from writing for two hours without interruption, but continued to write as quickly as before, which could in no wise have been possible unless the Holy Spirit had at that time directed both his hand and tongue; especially as the occupations were discrepant one from another, and the spoken words differed utterly in meaning from those which he wrote. The saint also was sometimes so absorbed in spirit while he prayed that once, when his cloak with which he was clad was taken from him, he did not feel it; and when, after patching and stitching it, they replaced it on him he did not notice it.

Lesson VII. But the more laboriously and effectively this blessed hermit, Richard, studied to acquire perfect holiness of life, so much the more cunningly the devil—the enemy of the human race—sought to entangle him by deceitful snares. So, as appears from a writing in the saint's own hand found after his death in a small volume of his works, the devil, in the form of a certain woman, tried to subvert him with the cords of illicit desire. Thus in the aforesaid book he says [1]: "When I had perceived my especial vocation, and laying aside my worldly dress had determined to serve God rather than man, it befell that on a certain night in the beginning of my conversion there appeared to me, while resting on my bed, a very beautiful young woman, whom I had seen before and who loved me –in honourable love—not a little. And when I looked on her and was marvelling why she had come to me in solitude and at night, suddenly, without delay or speech, she placed herself beside me. When I felt this, fearing lest she should entice me to evil, I said I would arise and, with the sign of the cross, invoke the blessing of the Holy Trinity upon us. But she held me so strongly that I could neither speak nor move my hand. Whereupon I perceived that not a woman, but the devil in the form of a woman, was tempting me. So I turned me to God, and when I had said in my mind: 'O Jesu, how precious is Thy blood!' and made the sign of the cross on my breast with my finger, which had now begun in some measure to be capable of movement, behold, suddenly all disappeared, and I gave thanks to God who had delivered me. From that time therefore I sought to love Jesus, and the more I advanced in His love the sweeter and more pleasant did the Name of Jesus savour to me; and even to this day It has not left me. Therefore blessed be the Name of Jesus for ever and ever. Amen."

---

[1] This tale is printed in *English Prose Treatises of Richard Rolle de Hampole*, edited by G. G. Perry. E.E.T.S., Orig. Series, 20, 1866.

X

Lesson VIII. Also this holy hermit, Richard, out of the abundance of his charity used to show himself very friendly to recluses and to those who were in need of spiritual consolation, and who suffered disquiet and vexation in soul or body through the malignant work of evil spirits. God granted him singular grace in helping those who were troubled in that way. And thus it once happened that when a certain lady was drawing nigh to death—in whose manor Richard had a cell (but a long way off from the family), where he was wont to live alone, and give himself to contemplation—a great multitude of horrible demons came to the room where the lady lay. It was little wonder, therefore, that when she saw them visibly she fell into great fear and trembling. Her attendants sprinkled holy water in the room and made devout prayers; nevertheless, the demons departed not, but still continued to vex her greatly. At length, by the wise and discreet advice of her friends, the blessed Richard was called to the room, so that, if possible, he might bring the said lady the aid of comfort and peace. And when he had come to her consolation, and had admonished her holily, and had urged her to place all her hope in the superabundant mercy of God and in His overflowing grace, he then set himself to pray God with a fervent heart that He would take from her the fearsome sight of the demons. And the Lord heard him instantly, and at the prayer of His beloved Richard was pleased to put all that terrible troop to flight. Yet as they fled they left behind them astounding traces of their passage; for all the bystanders saw that in the rush-strewn floor of the room where the demons had passed the rushes seemed to be burned and reduced to black ashes, and in these ashes there were marks impressed like the hoof-prints of oxen.

But when the demons had lost the prey which they had sought in that place, they tried to take vengeance on Richard, who had put them to flight. Accordingly, they went forthwith to his cell and disturbed him so much that for the time they made the place unfitted for his contemplation. But the saint of God, being stedfast in his faith, fled repeatedly for refuge to the sanctuary of prayer, and by his entreaties once more prevailed with the Lord to put them to flight. And, to the comfort of the aforesaid lady's friends, he told them that she was saved, and that after quitting this life she would be a joint-heir in the kingdom of heaven.

After this the saint of God, Richard, betook himself to other parts, doubtless through the providence of God so that dwelling in many places he might benefit many unto salvation, and sometimes also that he might escape impediment to contemplation, as we read in the book of the *Lives of the Fathers* that many of the most holy fathers in the desert used to do. For frequent change of place does not always come from inconstancy; as is the accusation of certain who are given to quick and perverse judgment of their neighbours, but whose crooked interpretations and habits of detraction ought not to make a sensible person neglect those things which he has found by experience to be good and conducive to virtue. For in the canon and decrees of the Church many causes sometimes are assigned for which change of place may be made; of which the first is when pressure of persecution makes a place dangerous; secondly, when some local difficulties exist [1]; and thirdly, when the saints are harassed by the society of evil men.

When, therefore, this holy man, for urgent and most practical reasons had betaken himself to dwell in Richmondshire, it befell that the Lady Margaret, who had once been a recluse at Anderby in the diocese of York, on the very day of the Lord's Supper [2] was so overcome by a grave attack of illness that for thirteen days continuously she was utterly deprived of the power of speech. Moreover, it caused her such pains and prickings in her body that she could not rest in any position. Now a certain goodman of that town, knowing that the holy hermit Richard loved her with a perfect affection of charity—since he was wont to instruct her in the art of loving God, and to direct her, by his holy teaching, how to order her life—quickly hastened on horseback to the hermit, who was then living twelve miles from the dwelling of the recluse, and besought him to come to her with all speed and bring her consolation in her great need. And when he came to the recluse he found her unable to speak and troubled with very grievous pains. And as he sat by the window of her dwelling and they were eating together, it befell at the end of the meal that the recluse desired to sleep; and so, oppressed by sleep, she drooped her head at the window where Richard, the saint of God, reclined; and after she had slept thus for a short time, leaning slightly upon Richard, suddenly a violent convulsion seized her in her sleep with fearful vehemence, so that it seemed as if she wished to break the window of her house. And being still in this most terrible convulsion, she awoke from sleep, and the power of speech being granted her, with great devotion she burst forth with these words: *"Gloria tibi Domine,"* and blessed Richard finished the verse which she had begun, saying: *"Qui natus es de Virgine,"* with the rest which follows in the compline hymn. Then he said to her: "Now thy speech is restored to thee, use it as a woman whose speech is for good."

A little while after, when she was again eating at the

---

[1] *Cum difficultas locorum fuerit:* doubtless meaning natural difficulties, such as lack of water and the like, making the place uninhabitable.

[2] *Ipsa die Cene Domini*—i.e. Thursday in Holy Week.

aforesaid window, in exactly the same way as before, after
dinner she fell asleep, and leaning upon the saint aforesaid, the
same convulsions returned, and she became, as it were, mad,
and was shaken by extraordinary and violent movements. But
when the holy Richard was trying to hold her with his hands,
lest she should rend herself or strive in any way to injure
the house, she suddenly slipped from them, and in her fall
was shaken out of sleep and thoroughly wakened. Then
Richard said to her: "Truly I thought that even if thou hadst
been the devil I should still have held thee; nevertheless, I
give thee this word of comfort, that as long as I shall remain
in this mortal life thou shalt never again suffer the torment
of this illness."

None the less, when the courses of several years had passed,
the same illness—except that she had her tongue free for
speech—returned to her. Therefore the recluse sent for the
goodman aforesaid, and asked him to hasten quickly on horseback to the house of the nuns at Hampole—which place was
far distant from her own dwelling—where the said Richard
at that time led a solitary life, and to see what had befallen
him. For she doubted not that he had passed from this world,
because she knew that he was faithful to his promise; and he
had promised her that as long as he lived in the flesh she
should never again suffer such torment. So the said man came
to Hampole, and he learnt that the saint was dead to this
world; and after diligently inquiring the hour of his passing,
he found that the aforesaid illness had returned to the recluse
shortly after the hour of Richard's departure. But afterwards
the recluse betook herself to Hampole where the holy body
of the said hermit was given burial; and never afterwards was
she afflicted with the suffering of this horrible illness.

Lesson IX. But yet, lest it should lie hidden from men—
especially from those who by devout and diligent study are
instant towards the attainment of the perfect life—how and
by what means that blessed zealot of God, the hermit Richard,
reached the stage of perfect love and charity, as far as is
allowed in mortal life, so that all other love became mean and
worthless for him and begat a dreadful horror: be it known,
therefore, that he himself, in his first book concerning the Fire
of Love, chapter thirteen,[1] speaks thus: "In process of time,"
he says, "great increase of spiritual joys was given me. For
there passed three years—all but three or four months—from
the beginning of the change of my life and mind to the opening
of the heavenly door, so that, with unveiled face,[2] through
the eyes of the heart,[3] the soul might contemplate the heavenly

---

[1] Chap. xv. of my edition, pp. 70–2.
[2] Cf. 2 Cor. iii. 18 (R.V.).   [3] Eph. i. 18 (R.V.).

beings, and see by what way to seek her Beloved and pant after Him. Then, the door remaining open, nearly a year passed before the heat of eternal love was verily felt in my heart. I was sitting, forsooth, in a certain chapel, and, while I was finding great delight in the sweetness of prayer or meditation, suddenly I felt within me an unwonted and pleasant heat. And though at first I wavered, doubting for a long time whence it might be, I became convinced that it was not from the creature but from the Creator, because I found it grow more warm and pleasant. But when half a year, three months and some weeks had passed by—during which that warmth of surpassing sweetness continued with me—there was borne in on my perception a heavenly spiritual sound, which pertains to the song of everlasting praise and the sweetness of the invisible melody. Invisible I call it because it can be neither known nor heard except by him to whom it is vouchsafed; and he must first be purified and separated from the world. For while I was sitting in the same chapel, and chanting psalms at night before supper, as I could, I heard as it were the tinkling music of stringed instruments, or rather of singers, over my head. And while my whole heart and all my desires were engrossed in prayer and heavenly things, suddenly, I know not how, I felt within a symphony of song, and I overheard a most delightful heavenly harmony, which remained in my mind. For straightway, while I meditated, my thought was turned into melody of song, and for meditation I, as it were, sang songs. And that music voiced itself even in my prayers and psalmody; and by reason of the interior sweetness which was outpoured upon me, I was impelled to sing what before I had only said. Not publicly, forsooth, for I did it only before God the Creator. Those who saw me knew it not, lest if they had known they might have honoured me above measure; and thus I might have lost part of that most fair flower, and might have fallen into desolation.

"Meanwhile wonder seized me that I had been chosen for such great joy while I was in exile, because God had then given me gifts which I knew not to ask, nor thought that even the most holy could receive such in this life. Therefore I trow that these are not given for merit, but freely, to whomsoever Christ will. Nevertheless I think no man shall receive them, unless he especially love the Name of Jesus and honour It so greatly that he never lets It from his mind except in sleep. He to whom it is given to do this may, I think, attain that also.

"Whence, from the beginning of my conversion even to the highest degree of the love of Christ to which, by the gift of God, I was able to reach—and in which state I proclaimed the praise of God with joyous songs—I remained for four years and about three months. For this state, when once the previous states are conformed to it, remains unto the end; nay, it will be more perfect after death, because here the joy of love and charity begins and in the heavenly kingdom shall receive its glorious consummation."

The following prayers are from the Mass for the Saint

Secret. O Lord, we beseech Thee that these our oblations may, through the holy intercession of the blessed hermit, Richard, be accepted by Thee; that by their virtue we may be protected from all dangers, and may be strengthened in the love of Thy Name ever more and more. Through our Lord.

Postcommunion. We beseech Thee, Almighty God, that by the prayers of the blessed hermit, Richard, we, Thy servants, refreshed by the sacrifice of the Body and Blood of Thy Son Jesu Christ, may ever receive that most precious food to our salvation; and so be inwardly nourished by the most sweet charity and peace which that sacrifice represents. Through the same our Lord.

HERE BEGIN THE MIRACLES OF THE BLESSED HERMIT RICHARD

TO BE READ DURING THE OCTAVE OF HIS FEAST

(The following extracts are from the Sunday Lessons)

Lesson I. But after the passing of this saint, Richard, so dearly beloved by God, God did not desist from showing forth to men his sanctity and glory by wonderful miracles. For example, in a town near to the dwelling of the nuns of Hampole there was a certain householder called Roger, who on the night of the Feast of the Assumption of the Virgin Mary, Mother of God, and on the two following nights, in his dreams saw the blessed hermit Richard come to him, and he conversed with him about many things. Afterwards, for six nights together, he appeared to him when he was wide awake, and taught him plainly about many secret things, and inflamed him with the love of God and with a spirit of holy devotion. Therefore he made up his mind that he would at once honour the saint with grateful acts of reverence; and he believed that he could please him especially by bringing stones, with his own labour and that of his beasts, to build his tomb in the church of the nuns of Hampole, where now his body is buried.

Lesson II. One day, therefore, while he was occupied with the aforesaid work of piety, and had got ready twelve oxen for drawing, it happened that when he had reached the gate of the churchyard at Hampole carrying great stones, his poor beasts by an unhappy accident turned aside from the path, and the cart collided with the side-post of the gate and cast the said stones with great force upon Roger himself. Yet he was in no wise hurt by this, nor felt any shaking or pain of body; and though his foot was very tightly jammed by the stones, he was able to get it out without injury to foot or leg. And, indeed, that this miracle should not be forgotten, one of these stones was set up at the gate of the churchyard, so that those coming that way might see it; and another is placed on the tomb of the saint.

Thus, as long as he lived, this saintly man was wholly on fire with divine love, seeking nothing except that he might please Jesus Christ, his most sweet Beloved; and any who would offer him faithful service, and by devout prayers make him his mediator and intercessor with the same Jesus Christ, has a most powerful argument from this history. And if he be not in himself an obstacle, he will obtain his wholesome purpose.

Lesson IV. A certain woman called Joan being vexed with demons lost the use of speech, and her bodily strength was so reduced and exhausted that everyone that saw her thought she must die. But one day the blessed Virgin Mary, Mother of God, appeared to her in most beautiful white garments, drawing near to her and leading the blessed hermit Richard by the hand. And he, seeing the demons cruelly vexing the woman, placed himself between them and her and made them depart. Then the blessed Richard put a ring on the woman's finger as a token of the miracle and his saving help. When he had done this, at once the woman ceased to feel the vexation of the demons; and recovered the use of her speech and was healed of all her infirmities.

A table is here appended of all the miracles; since it would take up too much space to give them in full.

	To be read on:	Name.	Place.	Date. (Where given)	Nature of Miracle and Conditions.
1.	*Sunday* Lect. i., ii.	Roger.	Hampole.	Vigil of the Assumption.	Preserved from accident while engaged in building the saint's tomb.
2.	Lect. iii.	John.	—	F. of the Epiphany, 1381.	Wounded by an enemy, John is raised from apparent death by prayer and the placing of money on his body, as an offering to the saint.

	To be read on:	Name.	Place.	Date. (Where given)	Nature of Miracle and Conditions.
3.	*Sunday* Lect. iv.	Joan.	—	—	Demoniac: cured by intervention of B.V.M. and the saint, who places a ring on her finger.
4.	Lect. v.	Woman.	Wrang-broke, near Hampole.	—	Saint appears to a paralysed woman and restores her, bidding her tell her neighbours.
5.	Lect. vi.	Thomas Bell.	Morehow, near Doncaster.	—	Bedridden: hearing in the night a voice bidding him to send a candle of 1½ lb. to be burnt before the image of the B.V.M. at Hampole, Thomas does so by his wife and family; and being alone in the house the saint appears to him and, asking where the pain is, touches the spot and heals him.
6.	Lect. vii.	Son of Isabella (aged 4).	Leicester.	F. of the Assumption, 1383.	Boy drowned by falling into a well. A passing pilgrim tells them to visit the hermit's tomb at Hampole. They do so, and pay a denarius [1] at the tomb and the child is restored to life.
7.	Lect. viii.	Hugh (aged 3).	Fishlake, near Thorne.	Cured on the F. of St. John Baptist.	Falls into a well: is revived by his mother's vow to offer a candle of the length of her dead son at the saint's tomb.
8.	Lect. ix.	William son of Ralph (aged 10).	—	Pilgrimage made on the third *feria* of Whitsun week.	Bitten by snake and thought to be dead: but restored by a vow to make a pilgrimage to the saint's tomb. This miracle is confirmed on oath.
9.	*Feria* 2. Lect. i.	John son of Wm. Spynke (aged 8).	—	F. of SS. Philip and James.	Crippled in arms and legs: restored by promise of yearly pilgrimage to the saint's tomb.

[1] "*Plicabant igitur amici pueri, prout moris est, denarium offerendum pro ipso ad sancti sepulchrum.*"

	To be read on:	Name.	Place.	Date. (Where given)	Nature of **Miracle** and Conditions.
10.	*Feria* 2 Lect. i.	Isabella.	—	—	Deaf for seven years: cured by praying at the saint's tomb.
11.	Lect. ii.	Beatrice.	York.	F. of the Holy Trinity	Dumb for six days: cured by praying at the tomb.
12.	Lect. iii.	Julia.	York.	Vigil of St. John the Baptist.	Demoniac, and dumb for twelve days: falls asleep at the saint's tomb, and Richard and the B.V.M. appear in a vision and tell her to ask the priest to whom she will confess her sins, and she will be healed in mind and body. She narrates that the brightness of the vision nearly blinded her.
13.	*Feria* 3. Lect. i.	John.	Sutton, near Doncaster.	—	Deaf for ten years: cured by praying at the saint's tomb.
14.	,,	Woman.	York.	—	Also deaf: cured at the saint's tomb.
15.	,,	Alice.	—	Easter.	Dumb from St. Katherine's Day to Easter: cured by praying at the saint's tomb.
16.	Lect. ii.	John.	—	Easter.	Insane: led to the tomb by his friends and there cured.
17.	,,	Agnes.	York.	—	Insane for three months. Her friends offer a wax candle, measured to her height,[1] at the saint's tomb, and she is immediately restored to her senses.
18.	Lect. iii.	Isabella.	—	—	Blind of one eye for twenty years: makes a pilgrimage to the tomb and is cured.

[1] Compare *St. Thomas of Canterbury: his Death and Miracles.* "They measured the boy for a candle to S. Thomas" (495). "They measured a baby's head for a candle" (527), etc. "Measure me for S. Thomas" (778), etc. By Edwin Abbott (Black, 1898).

	To be read on:	Name.	Place.	Date. (Where given)	Nature of Miracle and Conditions.
19.	*Feria* 3. Lect. iii.	Agnes.	Auston, near Worksop.	—	Deaf for three years: restored at the tomb.
20.	*Feria* 4. Lect. i.	Robert.	—	F. of St. Mary Magdalene.	Totally blind for three years: hears a voice bidding him go to the hermit's tomb and obeying, is cured.
21.	Lect. ii.	Boy of 5.	—	—	Choked by an apple for three days and thought to be dead: revived by a denarius placed on his head as an offering to the saint.
22.	Lect. iii.	Boy of 4.	—	—	Bad ulcer in the child's mouth prevented his feeding. By wise counsel a denarius is laid upon his head, and the ulcer vanishes and the child can suck.
23.	*Feria* 5. Lect. i.	Joan.	Sprotborough, near Doncaster.	F. of St. Peter in chains.	Fell into a mill-pool: rescued after an hour, and revived by prayer and being "measured for a candle."
24.	Lect. ii.	Woman.	Durham.	—	Deaf for two years: makes a pilgrimage to the saint's tomb and is cured on the spot.
25.	,,	John.	—	Purification of B.V.M.	Deaf for a long time: is cured by the merits and prayers of the saint.
26.	Lect. iii.	Woman.	—	—	Her child is still-born and she is thought to be dead: restored by being "measured for a candle" to the saint.
27.	Lect. iii.	Isabella (four-year-old daughter of John).	Near the nunnery of Hampole.	—	The child falls asleep upon a heap of straw and is smothered by it. When found is thought to be dead, but restored to life on being "measured for a candle."

APPENDIX II

MS. Add. 37049 in the British Museum.[1] The Catalogue describes it as "a Northern manuscript belonging to the first half of the fifteenth century, with coloured drawings in the crudest style." It is carelessly written, on paper, and is full of abridgments and imitations of Rolle's writings.

On *fol.* 31ᵛ is a summary in prose, in one paragraph, of the *Ego Dormio*; with a drawing on the opposite page representing a hermit lying asleep on the ground, while above is the image of Our Lady, with the Divine Child in her arms: and on the scroll in the hand of the sleeping hermit is written: "*Ego dormio et cor meum vigilat.*"

> I slepe & my hert wakes to þe
> swete Ihesu þe son of Mary fre.

On *ff.* 36ᵛ and 37 are two slightly different versions of the same poem (?) which is really a composite of Rolle's verse, beginning with a paraphrase of chapter xv. of the *Incendium*. Both these versions are headed by a crude drawing of Christ upon the Cross, and a pierced heart below, with the legend: "*Ihesu est Amor meus*"; and a figure of a hermit seated beneath the Cross. That on *fol.* 37 is not dissimilar to the well-known picture, supposed to be of Rolle, in the Faustina MS. B. VI. 2 of the *Desert of Religion*—a northern poem which is also contained in this MS. on *fol.* 46.

I give here the second version of these curious patchwork verses (on *fol.* 37), which begin with a few lines translated from chapter xv. of the *Incendium* in rough rhymed metre.

fol. 37.

> Whils I satt in a chapel in my prayere
> A heuenly sounde to me drewe nere,
> For þe sange of sanges I fest in me
> And my þoght turned into luf dyte—
> Of þe houenly & swoete armony,
> þe whilk I toke in mynde delitabylly.

---

[1] The contents of this MS. are given in Dr. Carleton Brown's *Register* (vol. i., pp. 44, 414–18). There are only ninety-six folios, yet seventy-one different pieces are listed in the Catalogue of the British Museum; which shows their fragmentary nature. I quote from the MS. without modernising the spelling since, by aid of the poems in the text, they will be found, I think, quite easy to read, and are more interesting in their original form.

þerfore I sytt & syng
Of luf longyng,
þat in my brest is bred.
Ihesu. Ihesu. Ihesu.
My kynge & my ioyinge,
When wer I to þe ledde,
Ihesu receyfe my hert,
& to þi luf me brynge.
Al my desyre þou ert
I couet þi cumynge.
In luf þou wounde my þoght,
& lyft my hert to þe,
þe saule þou has dere boght,
þi lufer make me bee,
Bot þe I couet noght,
þis warld for þe I flee,
When wil þou cum to comfort me,
& brynge me oute of care,
And gyf me þat I may se,
Hafyng þe euermare.
þi luf is ay swettist
Of al þat euer ware.
My hert when sal it bryst,
þan langwys I na mare.
Ihesu my saule þou mende.
þi luf in to me sende
þat I may with þe lende
In ioy withouten ende.
A wonder it is to se,
Who so understode,
How god of mageste
Was dyinge on þe rode.
Bot sothe þan is it sayd
þat luf ledes þe rynge,
þat hym sa lawe has layde,
Bot luf it was no þinge.
In fyfe stedes of his flesche
His blode gan downe glyde;
As streme dos of þe strande,
þis payne is noght to hyde,
To þink it is gret pyte,
How demyd he is to dede—
And nayled on þe tre,
þe bright angels brede.

We also have a variant of the verses "Unkind man give keep till me,"[1] which is twice repeated, under the title: *Querela Diuina, fol.* 20, as follows.

The close connection with the *Charters of Christ* is here very evident.

---

[1] Cf. p. 282 supra.

Querela Diuina.

O man unkynde
Hafe in mynde
My paynes smert.
Beholde & see
þat is for þe
Percyd my hert.
And ȝitt I wolde,
Or þan þou schuld
þi saule forsake,
On cross with payne
Scharpe deth agayne
For þi luf take;
For whilke I aske
None oþer taske
Bot luf agayne.
þe þan to luf
Althyng abofe
þow aght be fayne.

And in this MS. the response is given.

Responsio humana.

O lord right dere
þi wordes I here
With hert ful sore;
perfore fro synne
I hope to blynne
And grefe no more.
Bot in þis case
Now helpe þi grace
My freilnes,
þat I may euer
Do þi pleser
With lastyngnes
þis grace to gytt;
þi moder eke
Euer be prone
þat we may alle
In to þi halle
With ioy cum sone.
                    Amen.

This is written in short lines, as given here, on the left-hand side of the page; on the other side is a very rude drawing of Christ bespattered with blood and with blood streaming also from hands and feet. With one hand He points to His wounded side, while beneath the other hand is a large heart with a gaping wound, round which is written: "þis is þe mesure of þe wounde þat our Ihesu crist sufferd for oure redempcioun." Below this heart a man kneels in prayer. He is unshaven and has long hair, and may represent a hermit.

Above the drawing of the heart is a scroll with this verse, written as two lines:

> þies woundes smert
> þere in þi hert
> & luf god aye.
> If þow do þis
> þe sal haf blys
> withowten delay.

On *fol.* 24 we have another, even cruder, illustration of the same kind. Christ is here represented as showing a heart three times as large as the painter has depicted Him, on which the wounds are numbered, to a monk kneeling at His feet. Above are six lines of verse written as two:

> O man kynde,
> hafe in þi mynde,
> my passion smert.
> And þou sal fynde
> me ful kynde;
> lo here, my hert.

and then follows:

> þe nowmer of ihesu cristes wowndes ar fyve þowsande foure hondreth sexty & fyftene þi whilk in his body war felt & sene.

Then below is written:

> Ihesu my luf my ioy my reste,
> þi perfite luf close in my brest
> þat I þe luf & neuer reste
> and make me luf þe of al þinge best,
> and wounde my hert in þi luf fre
> þat I may regne in ioy euer more with þe.

And then the number of the *drops* of blood which Christ shed is given:

> Fyve hundreth thowsande for to say
> And fower & fowrty þowsande withouten delay
> Fyve hondreth also gret & smalle
> þis is þe nowmer of þame alle.

The same conceit of numbering the wounds of Christ is found in the *Charters*, but as far as I know the drops of blood are not counted in them.

APPENDIX III

MS. Vesp. E. 1. Formerly belonging to Henry Savile. Written on parchment, in black letter. It contains 254 leaves. Quarto.

Contents (From the Brit. Mus. Catalogue of 1802)

(1) Liber Bonaventurae. *Stimulus amoris* or *Meditationes super Passionem Domini. fol.* 3.

(2) *Meditationes Bonaventurae,* fratris minoris. *fol.* 69.

(3) *Tractatus secundum Ricardum Heremitam,* super primum et secundum versiculum canticorum. *fol.* 78.

(4) Nova oratione (sic) *de nomine Jesu.* Valde devota, secundum B. Bernardum. *fol.* 95ᵛ. (This is the *cursus Jesu dulcis Memoria.*)

(5) Liber fratris Amandi: scil.: *Speculum humanae salvationis* (in rhyme). *fol.* 100.

(6) Tractatus B. Bernardi, abbatis de Clarevalle, super *Contemplationem Dominicae Passionis. fol.* 176.

(7) *Evangelium Nicodemi. fol.* 182ᵛ.

(8) Meditatio B. Bernardi: De lamentatione B. Virginis. *fol.* 196ᵛ.

(9) Meditatio B. Bernardi: De compassione Christi. *fol.* 202.

(10) Tractatus contemplativus de cruce Christi quem frater de Bona fortuna composuit. *fol.* 204ᵛ. (A commentary on the Latin hymn "O crux.")

(11) Narratio quaedam motiva de *spiritu Guidonis* de civitate Alestiae, qui obiit 1323. *fol.* 219ᵛ.

(12) *Speculum peccatoris* per b. Bernardum. *fol.* 231.

(13) Sedecim *orationes de passione Christi. fol.* 236.

(14) *Liber meditationum* b. Bernardi. *fol.* 239. Beginning: "Multi multa sciunt et semetipsis nesciunt." (In a later and small cursive hand.)

(15) Epistola Augustini ad Cyrillum de apparitione Hieronymi. *fol.* 253.

LIST OF BOOKS CONSULTED

ALLEN, HOPE EMILY.

The Authorship of the Prick of Conscience. Radcliffe College Monographs, No. 15. (Ginn & Co., 1910.)

The Mystical Lyrics of the Manuel des Péchiez. "Romanic Review," vol. ix., pp. 154 sqq. (Columbia Univ. Press, 1918.)

Lyrics of Richard Rolle. "Modern Language Review," vol. xiv., p. 320. (1919.)

Writings Ascribed to Richard Rolle, Hermit of Hampole; and Materials for his Biography.[1] (Oxford Univ. Press.)

ANSELM, ST.

For text, Migne, vols. 158–9. *The Devotions of St. Anselm* (translated). Edit. by Prof. Clement Webb, with Introduction. (Methuen, 1903.)

BENSON, R. H.

A Book of the Love of Jesus. (Pitman.)

BERNARD OF CLAIRVAUX, ST.

Cantica Canticorum. Trans. by S. J. Eales. (Elliot Stock, 1895.)

De Diligendo Deo (Select Treatises). Edit. by W. W. Williams. (Camb. Univ. Press. 1926.)

Des Poèmes Latins attribués à Saint Bernard, par B. Hauréau. (Paris, 1890.)

BISHOP, EDMUND.

Origin of the Prymer. (Early English Text Society, Orig. Series, 105. 1895.)

BOASE, C. W.

Oxford. Historic Towns Series. (Longmans, Green & Co., 1903.)

BONAVENTURA, ST.

Opera Omnia. (Ad Claras Aquas. Published by the College of St. Bonaventura, 1882–1902.)

The Privity of the Passion. A translation and abridgment from M.E. of *Meditationes vitae Christi* (Horstman, vol. i., pp. 198 sqq.). A modernisation of this is included in *Some Minor Works of Rolle*, by Dr. Geraldine Hodgson. (J. M. Watkins, 1923.)

[1] Published during the preparation of this volume.

BRAMLEY, H. R. *See under* ROLLE.

BROWN, DR. CARLETON.
A Register of Middle English Religious and Didactic Verse.
(Bibliographical Soc., Oxford, 1916– .)

BUTLER, ABBOT CUTHBERT, O.S.B.
Western Mysticism : the Teaching of SS. Augustine, Gregory and Bernard on Contemplation ; with "Afterthoughts." (Constable. 2nd edition, 1926.)

CLAY, ROSA M.
The Hermits and Anchorites of England. Antiquary Series. (Methuen, 1914.)

COOK, PROF.
The Christ of Cynewulf. (Ginn & Co., 1900.)

DAWSON, REV. C. B.
The Mirror of Oxford. (Sands, 1912.)

DEANESLEY, MARGARET.
The Incendium Amoris. Edit. by M. Deanesley. (Manchester Univ. Press, 1915.)
The Lollard Bible. (Camb. Univ. Press.)

DENIS, PÈRE LÉOPOLD, S.J. *See under* ROLLE.
Du Péché à l'Amour Divin, ou l'Amendement du Pécheur. Translated into French from La Bigne, 1677. (Desclée, Paris, 1927.)

DUGDALE, SIR WILLIAM.
Monasticon Anglicanum. (London, 1846.)

EALES, S. J.
St. Bernard, Abbot of Clairvaux. (London, 1890.)
Cantica Canticorum. Translated by S. J. Eales. (Elliot Stock, 1895.)

EDMUND, ST. (Archbishop of Canterbury).
A Middle English translation of *The Speculum Ecclesiae* is printed by Horstmann (vol. i., pp. 219 sqq.), and in E.E.T.S. by Perry, and is modernised by Miss Hodgson in *Some Minor Works of Richard Rolle.*

FARGES, MGR. A.
Mystical Phenomena : compared with their Human and Diabolical Counterfeits. Translated from second edition. (Burns, Oates & Washbourne, 1926.)
Ordinary Ways of the Spiritual Life. Translated 1927. (Burns, Oates & Washbourne.)
Fasciculus Joanni Willis Clark dicatus. (Camb. Univ. Press, 1909.)

FURNIVALL, F. J. *See under* ROLLE.
Y

GALLARATI-SCOTTI.
Life of Fogazzaro. Translated by Mary Prichard Agnetti. (Hodder & Stoughton.)

GARDNER, EDMUND G.
The Cell of Self-knowledge. (Chatto & Windus, 1910.)

GREEN, J. R.
History of the English People. (Macmillan, 1892.)

HASTINGS, J.
Encyclopædia of Religion and Ethics. Edit. by J. Hastings. (Art. on "Scholasticism," vol. ix., p. 247.)

HAURÉAU, J. B.
Des Poèmes Latins attribués à Saint Bernard. (Paris, 1890.)

HEILER, DR.
The Gospel of Sadhù Sundar Singh. Abridged translation by Olive Wyon. (Allen & Unwin, 1927.)

HÉLYOT.
Histoire des Ordres Monastiques, etc. (8 vols. Paris. 1792.)

HODGSON, GERALDINE, LITT.D.
The Sanity of Mysticism : a Study of Richard Rolle. (The Faith Press, 1926.)
(*And see under* ROLLE.)

HOME, GORDON.
The Evolution of an English Town. (Dent, 1905.)

HORSTMANN, DR. CARL. *See under* ROLLE.

HÜGEL, BARON FRIEDRICH VON.
The Mystical Element in Religion. (Dent, 1908.)

HUTTON, EDWARD.
The Franciscans in England, 1224–1538. (Constable, 1926.)

INGE, DEAN.
Outspoken Essays. Second Series. (Methuen, 1922.)

JESSOPP, REV. AUGUSTUS, D.D.
The Coming of the Friars. (Fisher Unwin, 1888.)

JOHN OF THE CROSS, ST.
The Living Flame. Edit. by Lewis and Zimmerman. (Parker, 1912.)

JULIAN OF NORWICH, DAME.
Revelations of Divine Love. Edit. by G. Warrack. (Methuen, 1901.)

JULIAN, JOHN, D.D.
Dictionary of Hymnology. Revised edition. (Murray, 1907.)

LECLEF, M. L'ABBÉ. *See under* ST. VICTOR, RICHARD OF.

LITTLE, A. J.
The Grey Friars in Oxford. Oxford Historical Society.
(Clar. Press, 1892.)

LYTE, H. C. MAXWELL.
*History of the University of Oxford from the earliest times to
the year* 1530. (Macmillan, 1886.)

MADAN, FALCONER.
Oxford outside the Guide-books. (Blackwell, 1923.)

MALLET, SIR CHARLES.
History of the University of Oxford. (Methuen, 1924.)

MANNING, B. L.
The People's Faith in the Time of Wyclif. Thirlwall Essay.
(Camb. Univ. Press, 1919.)

MIGNE, J. P.
Patrologia Latina. (Paris, 1667–90.)

PATTERSON, FRANK ALLEN, PH.D.
The Middle English Penitential Lyric. (Columbia Univ.
Press, 1911.)

PERRY, G. G. *See under* ROLLE.

POULAIN, PÈRE, S.J.
The Graces of Interior Prayer. English translation. (Kegan
Paul, London, 1910.)

PRINGLE-PATTISON, PROFESSOR A. S.
Articles on *Mysticism* and *Scholasticism* in the *Encyc. Brit.*

RAGEY, PÈRE.
Histoire de Saint Anselme. (Paris, 1890.)

ROLLE, RICHARD.

TEXT

Prose

Richard Rolle of Hampole and his Followers. Edit. by Carl
Horstmann. ("Yorkshire Writers": Library of Early
English Writers.) (Swan Sonnenschein & Co., 1895–6.
2 vols.)
The Fire of Love and Mending of Life. Translated by R.
Misyn. Edit. by R. Harvey. (E.E.T.S., Orig. Series,
106. 1896.)
The same modernised, by F. M. M. Comper. Introduction
by Evelyn Underhill. (Methuen, 1913.)
Incendium Amoris. Edit. by M. Deanesley. (Manchester
Univ. Press, 1915.)
French Translation of *The Mending of Life*, under title:
Du Péché à l'Amour Divin, par Père Léopold Denis, S.J.,
with Introductory Essay. (Éditions de la Vie Spirituelle.)
(Desclée, Paris, 1927.)

ROLLE, RICHARD—*continued*
Prose—continued

English Prose Treatises of Richard Rolle. Edit. by G. Perry.
(E.E.T.S., Orig. Series, 20. 1896.)

The Psalter translated by Rolle of Hampole. Edit. by Rev.
R. H. Bramley. (Clar. Press, 1884.)

The Form of Perfect Living. Edit. by Geraldine Hodgson,
D.Litt. (It contains two other writings probably not
by Rolle, on *Daily Work*, and *Grace*.) (Baker, 1910.)

Some Minor Works of Richard Rolle. Also edit. by Miss
Hodgson. (Containing Rolle's *Ego Dormio, The Commandment of Love*, and a good many other tracts
not authenticated, with some of St. Bonaventura's.)
(J. M. Watkins, 1923.)

Verse

Horstmann. Vol. i. (See above.)
Patterson. *Penitential Lyrics*.
Benson. *A Book of the Love of Jesus*.
Furnivall. *Hymns to the Virgin*.
          Political, Religious and Love Poetry.
Perry, G. G. *Religious Pieces*, in E.E.T.S.

OFFICIUM

York Breviary. (Surtees Soc., vol. ii. app. v., 1882.)
The Officium and Miracula of Richard Rolle. Edit. by Dr.
Woolley. (S.P.C.K., 1919.)
Also an imperfect copy in Perry. (E.E.T.S., 1896.)

ST. VICTOR, RICHARD OF

De quatuor gradibus violentae caritatis; translated into French
as *Les Quatre Degrés de l'Amour Ardent* par M. l'Abbé
Ed. Leclef. (Desclée, Paris, 1926.)

The Benjamin Minor. An English translation printed by
Pepwell in 1521 is given in *The Cell of Self-knowledge*.
(*See* GARDNER, EDMUND G.)

SAINTSBURY, PROFESSOR G.

A Short History of English Literature. (Macmillan, 1898.)

SAUDREAU, L'ABBÉ AUGUSTE.

Degrees of the Spiritual Life. (1907.)
The Mystical State. Translated by D. M. B. (1924.)
The Life of Union with God. Translated from third edition
by E. J. Strickland. (1927.) (All published by Burns,
Oates & Washbourne.)

SCHOFIELD, PROFESSOR W. H.
English Literature from the Norman Conquest to Chaucer.
(Macmillan, 1906.)

STEVENS, J.
Continuation of Dugdale's Monasticon Anglicanum.

TAYLOR, G. C.
*The Middle English Lyrics in Relation to the Corpus Christi
Plays.* ("Mod. Philology," vol. v., 1907–8.)

THOMPSON, REV. H. L.
The Church of St. Mary the Virgin. (Constable, 1903.)

WARRACK, GRACE. *See* JULIAN OF NORWICH, DAME.

WELLS, J. E.
A Manual of the Writings in Middle English, 1050–1500.
With Supplements. (1916–   .)

WEST, G. H.
Gothic Architecture in England and France. (Bell & Sons,
1911.)

LIST OF THE WRITINGS ASCRIBED TO RICHARD ROLLE [1]

LATIN

The more important Latin works:

Melum contemplativorum ardentium in amore Dei : or *De gloria et perfectione sanctorum praecellentium. Incipit :* "Amor utique audacem efficit animum."
(It is characterised by the Old English tendency to balance and love of alliteration, being written partly in alliterative verse and partly in alliterative prose, and consisting of a series of postils in fifty-seven chapters in praise of contemplative life.)

Regula Heremitarum. Incipit : "Heremita dicitur ab hereo."
(It is based upon the so-called Augustinian Rule. This is "probably identical with (or part of) his *Libellus de vita eremitarum,* mentioned in *Job.*" See Horstman, vol. i., p. xxxvii.)

Liber de amore Dei contra amatores mundi. Incipit : "Quoniam mundanorum insania."
(Chapters xi. and xii. of the *De Emendatione Vite* are also found in this book. See Miss Allen, *Mod. Lang. Rev.,* vol. xiv., 1919.)

Postillae super novem Lectiones mortuorum (Job). *Incipit :* "*Parce mihi Domine:* Exprimuntur autem in his verbis."

Postillae super Cantica (on Cant. i. 1–3); viz.: *Osculetur me osculo oris sui. Incipit :* "Suspirantis animae deliciis." *Quia meliora sunt ubera tua vino. Incipit :* "Fidelis et delicate depasta." *Fragrantia unguentis optimis. Incipit :* "Cum laudasset sponsa." *Oleum effusum nomen tuum. Incipit :* "Expulsus de Paradiso." *Ideo adolescentulae dilexerunt te nimis. Incipit :* "Et quia tale est nomen tuum." *Trahe me post te. Incipit :* "Radix cordis nostri sit caritas." *Curremus in odore unguentorum tuorum. Incipit :* "Ecce fratres mira amatoris."

Postilla super Threnos, sive Lamentationes Jeremiae. Incipit : "Et factum est postquam."

---

[1] This list can only be tentative, pending the publication of Miss Allen's work upon the Canon of Rolle.

Expositio Psalterii. Incipit : "Magna spiritualis iocunditatis suavitas."

Tractatus super Psalmum xx. Incipit : "Cum Christus qui est veritas."

Judica me Deus. Incipit : "A Deo qui scrutatur."
(An epistle addressed to a priest and treating of God's judgment as against man's.)

Cupienti mihi.
(An epistle to a parish priest inculcating charity and contemplation.)

Istis iam dictis.
(An instruction to parish priests for hearing confessions.)

Incendium Amoris. Incipit : "Admirabar amplius quam enuncio."

De Emendatione Peccatoris : or *Emendatio Vitae. Incipit :* "Ne tardes converti."

Super "Mulierem fortem quis invenit." Incipit: "Quantum aurum argento est pretiosius."
(A short piece on Contemplation, possibly by Rolle.)

Many other short tracts and fragments are listed by Horstman, as well as miscellanies and prayers; but they are doubtful. The *Moralia in Job*, and *Consilia Isidori*, if by him, are merely extracts and not in any sense original.

ENGLISH

The Form of Perfect Living.
(In two parts of six chapters each; viz. *Forma vivendi* and *Amore langueo*. It is an epistle to Margaret Kirkby; and was also made to do duty for "Cecil." In some MSS. it is called *The Prick of Love*.)
Beginning : "In each sinful man and woman."

The Ego Dormio et cor meum vigilat.
(In several MSS. it is written as a continuation of *The Form*. It is addressed to a nun of the priory at Yedingham.)
Beginning : "Thou that list love, hearken and hear of love."

The Commandment of Love to God.
(An epistle to a nun at Hampole. It describes the degrees of love as in *The Form*.)
Beginning : "The commandment of God is that we love our Lord."

Meditatio de Passione Domini.

(Based on *The Privity of the Passion*, which was a translation from Bonaventura's *De Mysteriis Passionis*. It is the most poetical of all Rolle's prose works, and links up with *A Talking of the Love of God.*

Beginning : "Sweet Lord Ihesu Christ, I thank Thee."

Commentary on the Psalter.

(Also written for Margaret Kirkby. Mr. Wells thinks it is a close translation of Peter Lombard's Commentary. The Canticles and Magnificat are appended to it.)

A Tract on Prayer.

(This is found in the Thornton MS. and some leaves are missing. Cf. Horstmann, vol. i., pp. 295 sqq. Contains about three thousand words of rhythmical prose.)

Beginning : "Prayer is a gracious gift."

A Tract.

(A fragment of 120 words. In MS. Dd. 5.64. Mr. Wells thinks it is possibly by Rolle. See *Manual*, p. 452.)

Beginning : "A great clerk that men call Richard of Saynt Victor."

GLOSSARY

M.E.=Middle English. O.E.=Old English. O.F.=Old French.
O.N.=Old Norse. Sc.=Scotch.

Ainly: only (north.; cf. Sc.)

alanely: alone (north.)

allweldand: all-wielding, i.e. all-possessing (*-and*=north. ending of pres. part; see *wield*)

aloynt: far off (O.Fr. *aloynir*)

anger: hardship; pain, grief

awe: owe, ought (north.)

bale: evil, woe (cf. *my bale may bete*)

bede: prayer (O.E. *gebed*)

beswike: deceive (O.E. *beswīcan*)

bet: beaten (pt.) (O.E. *bēaten*)

betake: commit, entrust (refl. of *take*)

bote: amend, assuage (O.E. *bētan*)

bield: grow bold (O.E. *bīeldan*); cf. *big and bold*, a common doublet

ble: colour, hue (O.E. *bléo*); variant of *blee*

blin: cease from, stop (O.E. *blinnan*)

bote: remedy (O.E. *bōt*)

boun: ready (O.N *būinn*)

brent: burnt (O.N. *brendr*)

brest: burst (O.N. *bresta*)

brin: to burn (O.N. *brenna*)

burd: must (O.E. *gebyrian*=to befit, behove)

but: except, if only

buy: abye=expiate, atone for

care: woe (O.E. *caru*)

cast: cast down, overthrow

chafe: make warm (O.Fr. *chauffer*)

chere: (i.) countenance; hence (ii.) disposition (cf. *change my chere*=make me glad)

clear: (i.) bright, unsullied; hence (ii.) pure

cover: recover (aphetic)

covet, coveting: desire, desiring (with no bad intention)

dead (sb.) [*the*]: death (northernism)

dearworthy: precious, costly; formed from *dear-worth* (O.E. *dēorweorþ*)

deemed: doomed, judged (O.E. *dēman*)

dight: array with, make ready (O.E. *dihtan*)

ding: strike (O.N. *dengja*)

dole: grief (O.Fr. *doel, dueil*; cf. Lat. *dolum*)

dreed: suffered (O.E. *drēogan*)

dregh: long, tedious (cf. Sc. *dree one's weird*)

drury: beloved (O.Fr. *druerie*)

dule: doublet of *dole*, used sometimes for physical pain

dwine: dwindle, grow less, wane

encheson: cause, fault (O.Fr. *encheson*)

fairhead: beauty

fand (vb.): to try, experience (O.E. *fandian*)

fanding (sb.): temptation

fang: northerly form of *fong*

feel: used of all the senses, hence (i.) = to perceive by smell, taste or touch; (ii.) to experience mentally, believe, think

feld: field, in the expression *frith and feld*

fell (adj.): cruel (O.Fr. *fel*)

fell (vb.): to destroy, abate (O.E. *fiellan, fellan*=to fell)

fest: made fast

329

fet : fetched (O.E. *fetian*)

fong (part.) *:* embraced, grasped (O.E. *fōn*)

forbet : beaten severely, covered with bruises

forborn : submitted to, endured (O.E. *forboren*)

forlet : intensive form of *let*

forsake : refuse

forthy : therefore, hence

frith (or *firth*) *:* (i.) a small wood; (ii.) unused pasture ground (O.E. *(ge)fyrhðe*) (*feld or firth* is a poetic tag=field or coppice)

gan : did, began (O.E. *onginnan*= to begin)

gar : make (cf. Sc. *gar*)

geme : take heed (O.E. *gēman, gȳman*)

girth: peace, protection, sanctuary (O.N. *griþ*)

glew : melody, joy, glee (O.E. *glēow*)

greeting, gret : weeping, wept (O.E. *grētan*; cf. Sc.)

hate : bitter, violent (north. form of *hot*)

heal (sb.) *:* health (O.E. *hǣlu*)

heldand (adj.) *:* inclining, leaning (-*and* is north. form of pres. part. O.E. (vb.) *hieldan, hieldende*)

hent : caught, grasped (O.E. *hentan*)

hete, het : vowed, promised (O.E. *hāten*)

hethen : hence

hire : pay, hence=reward

hurled : struck; dragged; driven (cf. Sc. *hurl*=to drag; and *harl*=to rough-cast)

ilk a : each, every (cf. *ilk a bale*= every ill; *ilk a deal*=in every part, completely)

i-wis : certainly, truly (O.E. *gewiss*)

jugise : judgment (O.Fr. *juise*)

keel : to cool (north.; cf. Sc.)

keep : (i.) to lie in wait, catch; (ii.) watch for, greet; (iii.) desire, care for, heed (O.E. (late), *cēpan*)

kind : nature

kindly : in accordance with nature; naturally

kindness : kinship; natural affection arising from kinship

laced : ensnared (O.Fr. *lacier*)

lake : play, sport (O.E. *lācan*= to play)

langing : longing, yearning (north.)

langs : longs, yearns (north.)

lare : (i.) rule of behaviour; (ii.) knowledge (north. form of *lore*)

learn : to teach; cf. Sc. usage, *learn you*=teach you (O.E. *leornian*, in form with the meaning of O.E. *lǣran*)

len, lene : give (pres.) (O.E. *lænan*=to lend)

lend : (i.) arrive, come; (ii.) tarry, abide; (iii.) (with *in*), alight upon (O.E. *lendan*= to arrive)

lent : past part. of (i.) *lendan*= arrived, came; alighted on; (ii.) *lǣnan*=given

lerd : (i.) taught (past tense of *lǣran*); (ii.) learned, learnt

lere : learn (pres. tense)

let, lete : (i.) cease from, forsake; (ii.) hinder, prevent

lief : dear (O.E. *lēof*)

light in : alight upon (O.E. *lihtan*)

lighting : alighting

liking : (sb.) delight, pleasure; (adj.) that which delights

lith : lit.=joint; in the phrase *limb and lith*=all the bodily faculties (O.E. *liþ*)

lore : behaviour; knowledge (see *lare*)

love: often used meaning "praise"

lovely : lovingly (p. 291=of love)

lovesome : beautiful; worthy of praise

loving: (i.) praising; (ii.) the object of love, the beloved (cf. p. 248)

lust: desire, happiness (generally used in a good sense)

maistry: mastery
mane: moan (north.)
mase: makes (north.)
mengey: company (O.Fr. *mesniee*)
mickle: great (cf. Sc.)
mickleness: greatness
miss: misdeed, offence
mun: must, can; used generally for the future tense (cf. Yks. *mun*; O.N. *man, mun*)

na: no (cf. Sc.)
nane: none (Sc.)
ne: used for negation; not, never, etc.
neb: face (O.E. *nebb*=nose, face)
noblay: nobility, of rank or nature; variant of *nobley*
noynt: anoint (aphetic)

of: generally=from

pay: to please (O.Fr. *paie*)
paying: pleasing
pine: (sb.) suffering, pain; (vb.) to hurt, torture
play, playing: pleasure, joy
purely: fully, entirely

quaintness: cunning, skill
quart, quert: health, comfort (O.N. *kvirt*)

reave: to bereave, take away (O.E. *rēafian*=to plunder)
rede: counsel (O.E. *rǣdan*=to give advice)
rig: back (north. form of *ridge*; O.N. *hryggr*)
rike: kingdom; cf. bishopric (O.N. *riki*)
rue (on): to have pity (upon)
ruly: pitiful, woeful (O.E. *hrēŏwlic*)

sadly: firmly; closely, constantly
schend: to shame, confound (O.E. *scendan*)
schent: brought to nothing, destroyed (part. of *scendan*)
sen: since
sere: (i.) different, varied; (ii.) severally (O.N. *sēr*)
settle: seat; used for (i.) the cross; (ii.) a throne, seat in heaven
shild: shield; cf. *God shild* (O.E. *scildan*=to protect)
sight: often=face
sith, sithen: since, after
skill: in M.E.=that which is reasonable or right; hence= reason, discernment
slake: diminish, quench (O.E. *slacian*)
sly: secret
spill: to destroy; (intrans.) to be destroyed; perish
spred: past part. *i-spred*=spread out, stretched
stab: (i.) to thrust into, make a hole through; (ii.) jolt. (Before 1530 only found in north. writings)
stabling: security, stability
stand: stand still, remain (Lat.)
stanged: goaded; pierced (O.N. *stanga*=to prick) (north.)
stark: rigid, incapable of action
stead: (vb.) to place; (sb.) a place, home
steeked: placed, made ready (cf. Sc. *stooks* of corn, and *Stooky* Sunday)
steven: voice (O.E. *stefn*)
street: a way, a path (is used figuratively) (O.E. *strǣt*)
succour: shelter, protection
sweeting: lover, darling
swilk: such (north.)
swing: (i.) to vibrate; hence (ii.) to beat to excess (thus causing vibration) (O.E. *swingan*)

take: (refl.) to commit; entrust; give oneself (cf. *betake*) *teen* (sb.) *:* suffering, sorrow (cf. *travail and teen,* a common doublet)

than : north. form for *then*

thirled : pierced (O.E. *þyrlian*)

thole : suffer, endure; cf. Sc. (O.E. *þolian*)

tine : lose (O.N. *tyna,* cog. with O.E. *tēon*=injury)

to-break : break to pieces, entirely break (*to* is intensive)

to-brest : entirely burst

tour : tower; often used in M.E. for "heaven"

traist (adj.) *:* trusty, true; strong (O.N. *traustr* (adj.) = firm, trusty

travail : toil; cf. *teen* (O.Fr. (vb.) *travailler*)

twin : (i.) to put asunder, separate; (ii.) part, renounce; hence (iii.) escape, forsake (M.E. *twinnen*)

umbeset : surround (O.N. *umb* (prep.), = round about; O.E. *ymbsettan*)

undregh : not be weary, impatient —opposite of *dregh*=tedious (cf. Sc. *shortsome* for meaning)

urne : ran (O.E. *eornan*)

verray : true, real

wan : (i.) dark; (ii.) sad; (iii.) of an unwholesome colour; hence (iv.) pallid, pale (O.E. *wann*)

wand : hesitate; fear (O.E. *wandian*)

wandreth : trouble, poverty (O.N. *vandrǣði*)

wane : dwelling

wate : north. form of *wot*=know

wealth : well-being, happiness

wed (sb.) *:* pledge (O.E. *wedd*)

went (past part.) *:* gone away from, left

whether : (i.) whither (O.E. *hwiðer*); (ii.) however, nevertheless (O.E. *hwæðer*)

wield : possess (O.E. *wieldan*)

wille : desire (O.E. *willa*)

wis (vb.) *:* to guide, point out the way; govern (O.E. *wissian*)

wites : passes, withers (O.E. *witan*)

wone : (vb.) to dwell; (sb.) a dwelling (cf. O.E. *wunian*= to dwell)

woning : dwelling

writhed : twisted, contorted; used both of body and mind (O.E. *wríþan*=to hoist)

wrongously : in an evil manner, unfairly

yield : (refl.) to hand over, repay, requite (O.E. ȝ*ieldan*)

INDEX

333